By Quentin Reynolds

Books by Quentin Reynolds

The Wounded Don't Cry

London Diary

Convoy

Only the Stars Are
  Neutral

Dress Rehearsal

The Curtain Rises

Officially Dead

70,000 to One

Leave It to the People

Courtroom

I, Willie Sutton

The Amazing Mr. Doolittle

The Man Who Wouldn't Talk

Headquarters

The Fiction Factory

They Fought for the Sky

Minister of Death,
  the Eichmann Story

Known but to God

By Quentin Reynolds

For Children

The Wright Brothers

Custer's Last Stand

The Battle of Britain

The F.B.I.

The Life of St. Patrick

BY QUENTIN REYNOLDS

London
Toronto
New York

McGraw-Hill Book Company, Inc.

Contents

1 Why don't you write a book about it?   1

2 You can take the boy out of Brooklyn but – – –   8

3 My life at sea—all 30 days of it   28

4 Just a touch of larceny   40

5 In quest of a trade   60

6 On the road   76

7 Thanks to Damon Runyon   87

8 The midget on Morgan's lap   101

9 The easy years   127

10 The wounded don't cry   151

11 London could take it   187

12 Yours faithfully, Winston Churchill   212

13 Potluck at the Kremlin   229

14 Only the stars were neutral   253

15 In the valley of the shadow   273

16 They called it bloody Salerno   291

17 You, too, can capture a Jap   306

18 Libel comes on horseback   319

19 Epilogue   352

1

"Why don't you write a book about it?"

Blame Dorothy Parker for the next three hundred and some pages. Dorothy is a neighbor of mine in a New York apartment house that is only a few blocks from Frank Campbell's funeral parlor, an establishment that she and I find ourselves visiting with increasing frequency as the years creep up on us and our tired friends surrender their ghosts. We have now been there so often that the doormen, the elevator men, and the attendants greet us by name. They seem politely disappointed that we are once more able to walk in as mourners instead of being carried in as paying clients.

The public image of Dorothy Parker is that of a master of satire and cynicism, but Dorothy herself is a complete contradiction of this image. I have known this poet and short-story writer for a long time, not as the woman who once terrorized pseudo intellectual New Yorkers with the corruscating wit that has made her a legend in her own time, but as a generous, gentle, humble, rather shy person—and the only one I ever met, incidentally, who knows all the words to the second stanza of "The Star-Spangled Banner," to say nothing of the third and fourth.

One evening after we finished paying respects to a late friend at Mr. Campbell's, I invited Dorothy to gather up her poodle, Cliché,

1

and come to my place for a drink. While Cliché had some peanuts, Dorothy and I lifted our glasses to the memory of the departed. Not unnaturally, we talked of mortality.

Unlike so many writers, Dorothy is an intensely practical person. She can even change the ribbon on her typewriter in a matter of an hour or two with virtually no outside help. Now her quite unpredictable mind turned to a problem that would one day concern us both.

"I live on the ninth floor, you on the sixth," she said, her brow lined with worry. "When we die, how are they going to get us out of here? The elevator isn't large enough to hold a coffin unless they stand it on end, and that would be quite undignified."

"The service elevator," I suggested.

Dorothy shook her head. "It would really not be chic to be lugged out that way. There is, as I see it, one solution. We've both lived here quite a while, so the management might listen if we presented a constructive idea. Let's suggest that they build a chute from here to 'New York's Most Respected Funeral Institution.' We'd arrive in good condition and the trip would take only a minute."

"This is a rather morbid subject, Dottie," I protested. "Let's see what's on TV."

"I find television much more morbid than death," she said firmly. "Death really isn't a morbid subject. Do you remember the story Heywood wrote about it? In it he pictured Death as a jolly man."

Dorothy did not mention the author's last name, but for both of us there was only one writer, one friend, who bore the name Heywood. After Dorothy and Cliché went home I took from my shelf a collection of Heywood Broun's stories and reread the one called "Death Says It Isn't So." In it, a Sick Man lies in a hospital. He knows he is dying but perversely refuses to accept his fate. One afternoon he finds a fat, friendly little man sitting by his bed. "I'm Death," says the visitor. The Sick Man is at first unconvinced. "Where's your sickle? Why don't you rattle when you walk?"

Death brushes this aside and tells the Sick Man that if he will come along without making trouble, he will see plays by George Bernard Shaw that Shaw never wrote on earth, a Christmas play that Ibsen has just completed, and a review starring Nell Gwyn. He will play golf on a seven-thousand-yard course and go around in fifty-four. He will see the baseball greats of another day in action, and he will sit in the press box any time there is an important game. As a final inducement

2

Death whispers a secret joke to the Sick Man. The Sick Man roars with laughter, and then quite happily goes away with the Jolly Fat Man. . . .

I had been at Heywood's house in Connecticut when a priest whom Heywood had met in St. Louis came to dinner. He related that he had used "Death Says It Isn't So" as the basis of his Easter sermon, because it conveyed in a vivid colloquial way the Catholic viewpoint. Then he asked Heywood what the secret joke was that Death used to convince the Sick Man.

Heywood seemed a bit embarrassed. "As I recall," he replied, "Death just whispered 'It isn't so.' "

The priest said he had gathered that, but what did Death mean by it?

"I never quite figured it out," Heywood confessed. "Maybe he was telling the Sick Man that death was nothing to be afraid of, and that, as your religion teaches, he would be a lot happier in the hereafter than he ever was in life." And then Heywood defended himself, the way any author would, by pointing out that his story was fiction. "Sometimes when I write a story like that, I can't explain it even to myself," he concluded.

The priest's rejoinder was that Heywood had explained the point quite well. "And I'm sure that one day you will be able to explain it to yourself, too," he added.

For the moment, that was the end of it. But when Heywood died, several years later, a few months after his conversion to Catholicism, it was with a smile on his lips, as though he had shared a secret and comforting joke with the Jolly Fat Man who had come to take him home. . . .

Thoughts of death and a good night's sleep are things that cannot, in my experience, be accommodated at the same time. Finishing my rereading of Heywood's story, I found that I was not sleepy, even though the story's ending was as reassuring as the ending of the catechism I had learned as an eight-year-old at Sunday School. While I am not a deeply religious man, I was born a Roman Catholic and expect to die one. This thought was a good companion, but against the nameless fears of that midnight it seemed not enough. Then I recalled reading how even the ancient Egyptians had never thought of death as a fearsome figure. Their religion had been based on the conviction that life hereafter was infinitely better than life here could possibly be. They had had great feasts, with wine flowing and music playing, and at the height of it a huge, smiling image of death would be brought into the hall, and the host would cry out, "Eat, drink, and be merry, for such shalt thou be when thou art dead." Four thousand years ago, the Egyptians had thought of death as a gay, merry person, and I knew of nothing in the Scriptures that invalidated this concept.

Giving up trying to sleep normally, I went to my medicine chest and took two sleeping pills. They were mild ones, and while they made me drowsy, they did not immediately send me off. As I lay in bed waiting, I thought of all those I had loved who were now dead. I thought of my mother and my father, and of my brother Don, cut down by illness at age forty-seven. I thought of such old friends as Mark Hellinger and Bill Corum, and Joe Connolly, who had given me my first real break in the newspaper game, and of men I had gone to college with—Nathaniel West was one—and the disturbing realization came to me that all these friends had been younger than I when they died. For the first time, I began to consider the possibility that I might die. No one who is in good health, I suppose, ever really admits to himself that his days are numbered. A few years before this I had had a slight heart attack. After my recovery, the doctors had read the electrocardiographs and assured me that my heart was as good as new. But did they really know? Wondering, I fell asleep. Not surprisingly, I had a fantastic dream. It was almost as though Heywood's short story came to life.

My dreams usually neither frighten nor amuse me, and I seldom remember them long enough to think about them. This time it was different. I awakened shaking. How much of the dream, I wondered, had been a mischievous trick of my subconscious? Fully awake, I went to my kitchen, poured myself a glass of milk, and sat down to consider what I had just been through. My typewriter was handy, and I put down the conversation I had had with a character very much like Heywood's Fat Man.

He walked into my dream, perched on the windowsill, and said pleasantly enough, "I suppose you know who I am?"

It was dark, and I could see only his outline. "I'm not sure. Are you the *Malach Hamoves?*"

"How do you know Hebrew?" he asked suspiciously.

"I don't, except for a few words. And anyway, that's not Hebrew but Yiddish. In Hebrew it would be *Malach Hamoveth*. Either way,

4

though, it means Angel of Death. But if you are the Angel of Death, where in hell are your wings?"

My visitor winced at the word "hell." He said contemptuously, "We gave up wings about the same time you were acquiring them at some sand dune in North Carolina a few minutes ago."

"A few minutes ago? If you're talking about the Wright Brothers, they made that flight sixty years ago."

"Years, minutes," he said. "Where you're going, it won't matter. You ready?"

"Of course not! I thought I had lots of time left."

"Oh, come now!" he said reprovingly. "I can answer every one of your clichés with another. 'The time you think you have left doesn't belong to you.' I've been handing that one to people for more centuries than I care to remember. Everywhere I go I get the same old excuses from people who want to stay a few more years on this absurd planet. Practically all of them say, 'Let me live my life over again and everything will be different. I won't make the same mistakes. I'll obey every rule in the book.' "

"You won't get that kind of nonsense from me, Big Brother."

"Don't call me that," he said irritably. "I've read Orwell. But why do you say I won't get this kind of nonsense from you?"

"Because I'm a man with more than the usual weaknesses, and because if I had my life to live over, I know I'd make the same thousand mistakes again. Even if you gave me a few more years I'd keep on making them, because I just don't happen to have much will power."

"That's curious," he said, shifting his seat a little closer to me. "Suppose you had a chance to be reborn. Who would you like to be?"

"Myself. And I'd want to be born to the same parents and have the same brothers and sisters. And have the same jobs and write the same things, even though I'm not very proud of a couple of the books I wrote. Matter of fact, I've done plenty of things I was ashamed of afterward. I've broken or bent several of the Commandments, and I can almost guarantee it would happen again. By the way, will you have a drink?"

"Not while I'm on duty," he said. "Now hear this. I report directly to the Committee on Admissions. They don't give me much discretion in selecting my—well, you might call them candidates. They just hand me a list of names and say 'Bring 'em home.' But we messengers

5

are told that if we ever find a party who doesn't try to bribe us with frantic promises of the pure life he would lead if given an extension, we can pass him up for the time being. I say *he* and *him* because I'm in the Men's Division. Now, about nine hundred and ninety-three thousand out of every million give me the same old nonsense about how they would practically qualify for sainthood if granted just a few more years. You haven't done that, so I can cross your name off my list. That is, for the time being."

"Well, I don't care much one way or another," I said with a show of bravado.

"That's another point in your favor," he said gloomily. "You're what we call an optional case. You can either come now or stay a while. Weigh it seriously."

"Could you tell me," I asked politely, "approximately how long I have left if I choose to stay?"

"Well, now, that really isn't up to me. I have a suggestion, though. I've looked through your records. I won't say you've led a good life, but it has been an interesting one. Why don't you write a book about it? A Hemingway, a Faulkner, an O'Hara you are not, but you could tell the customers about the famous and not so famous people you've met and all the places you've been. Start that book and I can promise you we won't call you in until it's finished."

"It's a thought," I said. "Anyhow, you don't leave me much choice."

My visitor sighed. "I've wasted a lot of time here. I'll be seeing you."

"I bet," I said—and even as the words crossed my lips, I woke. Though it was a windless night, it seemed to me the curtains at the open window were swaying. . . .

So, drinking my milk, I made notes of my conversation with the genial *Malach Hamoves*. Of course I no more believe in the significance of dreams than I do in palm reading or in the hoary superstition that the poker player who wins the first hand is sure to end up a loser. Regardless, the troublesome dream stayed with me, and when next I saw Dorothy Parker, I told her about it.

Her unexpected comment was: "Rather than write my life story I would cut my throat with a dull knife." Then she reflected. "But let's face it, friend; this is something you could pull off. At least your autobiography would be different. For once we wouldn't have a man blaming his failures on an unhappy childhood. You had a wonderful

6

childhood and lots of friends. Good Lord—do you realize you've never been to a psychiatrist? You're a horribly normal man. I doubt if many horribly normal men write their autobiographies."

"Well, I might try it," I said doubtfully, "but one thing troubles me. A man who writes his autobiography ought to have a few lessons to teach. I have none. His experiences should have given him some deep-rooted philosophy worthy of consideration. I have none. The hard fact, Dottie, is that I'm no smarter today than I was when I graduated from college a hundred years ago."

"Skip the lessons and just write about what happened to you," she snapped.

And that is what I've done. As I said earlier, if you don't like the result, you can thank Dorothy Parker.

2

You can take the boy out
of Brooklyn but—

I have always taken a beating from direct sunlight. I don't just get sunburned. I develop a fever and then lie in bed wishing I were dead until the poison has run its course. This low broiling point has kept me from playing golf, tennis, or baseball in any substantial amount. When I was at Brown University I boxed and swam, both indoor pursuits, and while I played a lot of football, the season for that is when the sun is benign, especially in Providence, Rhode Island, the home of Brown.

As a young man, I went to a succession of dermatologists, most of whom gave me interesting and expensive tests and then announced that my trouble was a lack of pigmentation in my skin. They had no explanation for the fact, and no treatment—beyond the suggestion that I keep out of the sun.

It was not until November, 1941, that I was finally given the reason for my affliction. Then on the staff of *Collier's* magazine as a war correspondent, and facing a visit to the British army in the Libyan Desert, I went to the shop of Cairo's leading military tailor to buy my uniform. The tailor looked unbelieving when I insisted that the

8

sleeves of the tunic touch my knuckles. When I also ordered woolen gloves and a heavy scarf, he held his head.

Suitably clad, I went to the front. In that miserable desert northwest of Cairo the sun was merciless. I extended my defenses by not shaving and by wearing sunglasses. As far as my undependable epidermis was concerned, everything was fine until I found myself with a beleaguered regiment, the 1st Royal Sussex, at a bit of nowhere called Sidi Omar. Surrounded by German tanks and Italian artillery, we had several bad days and nights. But while the Axis wasted a lot of ammunition on me, another enemy stealthily worked its havoc. The morning I got away from Sidi Omar I fell asleep for half an hour on the desert sand. That was all it took. My gloves treacherously slid off, my sleeves—as sleeves will—crept up, and heaven knows what became of my scarf. When I woke, the fever already on me, I saw my friend Colonel Desmond Young shaking his head as he regarded me pityingly. "This won't do, old boy," I heard him saying. "You have had it."

A few hours later we drove into Meddalena, the advance British air base. Here Air Vice-Marshal "Maori" Coningham, the RAF commander, took one look at me and said to Desmond Young, "Get this boy to Cairo at once. Send him in my plane."

Vaguely I recall arriving in Cairo and Desmond's keeping me going through a BBC broadcast to London as well as the hasty writing of my desert experiences for *Collier's*. My next clear memory is of waking in a cool hospital bed. A doctor, Colonel Ian Miller, was studying me. Afterward I learned that he was one of England's leading dermatologists.

"Where were you born, Mr. Reynolds?" he asked.

To me, this seemed somewhat irrelevant. "New York," I told him. "Borough of Brooklyn."

He looked surprised. "And your parents?"

"New York City."

"Your grandparents?"

When I told him they were born in New York too, he shook his head in disbelief. "Your great-grandparents, then?"

"Ireland," said I.

"That's better! What county, please?"

"Donegal."

He nodded. "I thought so. They're the ones you can blame for this.

9

In Donegal it rains about three hundred and twenty days a year. For centuries your ancestors plodded around in the peat bogs, very seldom being exposed to the sun. Therefore, the absence of pigmentation in your skin. Today, when we discover the condition in children we can often treat it effectively."

"My brothers and sisters can wallow in the sun without getting knocked out," I protested.

"That's how it works," Colonel Miller said. "It skips generations and then finds its victims. When you were a lad, I dare say you had red hair and freckles."

"Right," I said. "But the rest of the family had black or auburn hair and none had a fair skin."

"Well, that's how the cookie crumbles." He smiled. "At your age there's really only one prescription, and no doubt you've heard it before: Stay in the shade."

The next time I was in New York, early in 1942, I went over to Brooklyn to see the assistant superintendent of public schools, Dr. James Reynolds, feeling sure that he would be interested in Colonel Miller's diagnosis. My father listened thoughtfully while I reproached him for his poor judgment in having Donegal bogtrotters in his line. Unexpectedly, he took me up on a side issue. "What made you tell that doctor you were born in Brooklyn?" he asked. "Surely you know you were born in the Bronx? I don't remember the street, but it was two blocks from Ebling's Brewery."

For one who had lived forty years in the conviction that he was as true a specimen as the Borough of Brooklyn ever produced, this was quite a blow.

"Your mother and I were married just after I got my law degree from NYU," Pop said, "and my first teaching job was in the Bronx. We lived there a little over a year."

This part of the story, at least, I knew. Pop's first choice had been the law, and his hope had been to open an office with his boyhood pals, Bob Wagner, later to become a United States senator, and Jerry Mahoney, later to become a judge of the New York Supreme Court and after that one of New York's leading corporation lawyers. Since none of them, after getting their law degrees, could even have furnished a waiting room for their prospective clients, all three decided to teach school for a year and work up some savings. But Pop began that year by falling in love with Jerry's sister Katharine, and when

10

they were married and I was on the way, he decided to stay with teaching. Now it appeared I had been born before, not after, Pop was made principal of P.S. 122 in Brooklyn, at twenty-eight the youngest principal in the New York public school system.

Having thus made me a Brooklynite by adoption, so to speak, Pop went on to tell me something else I had never known—the origin of my unusual first name. It had been the bane of my youthful years. My brothers and sisters had names that never raised an issue—Don, James, Marjorie, Constance—but in our predominantly Irish neighborhood in Brooklyn, where boys were simply Mike or Terry or John, my foreign-sounding moniker more than once got me into fights, none of which I remember winning.

"Your mother's sister was the cause of it," Pop told me, astonished that I was still in the dark about this. "Your mother was very ill when you were born, so the doctor handed you to your Aunt Mary. When you started to turn blue, she hustled you across the street to our church to have you baptized before you died.

"The priest took one look at you and hurried Aunt Mary to the font. 'What shall I name the child?' he asked. Aunt Mary was at a loss, for your mother had never expressed a preference. 'Let's not be slow about this,' said the priest. 'He doesn't look as though he would last long.' Because Aunt Mary's favorite book was *Quentin Durward,* the worst happened. But the priest said he could only baptize a child in the name of a saint. 'I think Quentin Durward was named for a saint,' said Aunt Mary, ransacking her memory of the novel. 'I can settle it,' said the priest, 'for there's a *Lives of the Saints* in the rectory.' In a few minutes he was back with the news that Saint Quentin had lived in Rome in the third century.

"So you see, Quent," Pop concluded, "you can't blame your mother or me for that one."

Thus it was, after belatedly learning the reason for—as Pop once put it—my light pelt, I learned where I was born and how I was named. Other phases of my family history I heard from Pop when I was a boy and he and I and my brother Jim were fugitives from church. This sounds worse than it was. We all went to mass, naturally, but unlike Mom and the girls, and Don, we older boys and Pop usually left right after communion. Pop had a firm faith in God, but he also loved and respected the English language. The usual parish priest is not a scholar, after all, and most Sundays the sermons at Our

Lady of Refuge Church were an ordeal. Sunday after Sunday, when the weather was good, Pop and Jim and I would slip out and finish the morning in Prospect Park. It was during these sessions that I heard our family stories. Many of them starred our mother's father, the elder Jerry Mahoney. Pop had known him better than his own father, who had died when Pop was very young. One story Jim and I loved had to do with Grandpa Jerry's glasses. Strolling through Central Park one day, he spotted a pair on a bench. Putting them on and finding that they gave him a certain distinction, he never took them off again. He was laid out wearing those spectacles.

Grandpa had run a saloon on Cherry Street, on Manhattan's Lower East Side, and it seemed he had both a literary flair—his friends called him the Poet Laureate of the Bowery—and a sense of civic duty. A quack doctor practiced a few doors from Grandpa's saloon, and Grandpa settled his hash with these lines—which incidentally were some of the first I ever learned by memory:

> At the corner of Cherry
> Where Roosevelt comes in,
> There lived a bad doctor;
> His name was McGinn.
>
> Three bogus diplomas
> Hung up on the wall,
> And whene'er a poor devil
> Got sick and caved in—
> " 'Tis a sure case of cholera!"
> Said Dr. McGinn.
>
> One day the bad doctor
> Got in a great heat,
> With a loaded revolver
> He ran through the street;
> But the man with the shield
> On his breast took him in—
> And knocked all the fight
> Out of Dr. McGinn!

The habitués of Grandpa's bar used to sing this masterpiece for all the neighborhood to hear, and one day, as foretold, the police came

12

and took McGinn away. Pop said that Jerry never got over the fact that he, a mere tavern keeper, had helped to send an allegedly superior citizen to the clink.

One Sunday Pop told us of Grandpa's less than admirable Civil War record. Besides being on in years when his draft number was called, Grandpa, like many New Yorkers, had been a Southern sympathizer. For five hundred dollars he had hired a substitute—one of his bartenders, a man without a family—and the poor fellow had been killed at Gettysburg. "Your grandpa always thought this was quite a joke," Pop told us. "So you see, perhaps you ought not to inquire too closely about your ancestors."

Pop also told us of his own boyhood life. As he grew up within sight of the Fulton Fish Market, his playmates were the sons of Russian, German, Polish, Italian, and Irish immigrants. The East River was their swimming hole, the Bowery and Chinatown their playgrounds. As a twelve-year-old, Pop had had a thrilling moment running across the Brooklyn Bridge the day it was opened.

A class or two behind Al Smith, Bob Wagner, and Bernard Baruch, Pop had attended P.S. 1. Two classes behind him, in turn, was dark-haired Katharine Mahoney, but Pop wasn't even aware of her until some years later when she was preparing to become a teaching nun in the Order of the Sacred Heart. The founder of the order, Madeleine Sophie Barat, though dead for eighty years, proved a tough opponent for Pop to overcome. Katharine was fascinated by her brother Jerry's handsome, witty friend, but she had long since made up her mind to be a bride of Christ. However, she saw nothing wrong in going on boat rides in Central Park with the handsome, witty Jim Reynolds, or in gazing at the city with him from a seat in a horsecar. After all, he was her brother's best friend.

One day, Katharine realized she was thinking more about Jim than about the Order of the Sacred Heart. Panic-stricken, she ran to her convent to make a retreat and resolve her doubts. For a long time she prayed and struggled. The mother superior said reassuringly, "God will show you the way." Eventually, seeing what the way was for her, Katharine Mahoney became Mrs. Reynolds and my mother.

Barring that initial stretch in the Bronx, I lived in Brooklyn for the first twenty-eight years of my life, and there never was a better place, in my opinion, for growing up. Having said this, I must add that there is no such place as Brooklyn. There is Flatbush and Greenpoint and

Park Slope and Williamsburg and Brownsville and Bushwick and Red Hook, each a community as large as many a state capital, each having a definite personality of its own. The Flatbusher has difficulty following the speech of the Greenpointer, the native of Brownsville has about as much in common with the Park Sloper as he would have with someone from Fort Worth, Texas. Only an outsider would make the mistake of lumping all these individual communities together and calling the result Brooklyn.

To the world at large, of course, Brooklyn often still means the Dodgers, always suggests an accent that is a hard and unpleasing deviation from the norm, and calls up vistas of churches. The Dodgers, of course, are now only a sad memory; the so-called Brooklyn accent is employed by not more than 10 per cent of the population; and there are, by reliable count, only 551 churches to serve the needs of Brooklyn's 2,881,000 inhabitants. Those of us who grew up in Brooklyn are always puzzled by the laughter of audiences at the slightest reference to our native heath. What in the world is so funny about Brooklyn? Danny Kay, a fellow Brooklynite from whom I once sought enlightenment on the subject, considers it inexplicable. "All I know," he told me gloomily, "is that if I make a crack about Dallas or Chicago, and it dies, all I have to do is substitute Brooklyn— even if I'm playing in London—and it's good for a roar."

The Brooklyn I grew up in was the world. It had everything. When we wanted to go fishing, we had the whole Atlantic to try. We'd go to Sheepshead Bay and for a dollar get a place on a fishing boat, and within an hour we'd have our haul of flounder. We had the Navy Yard, and whenever one of the battlewagons was tied up there, our schools arranged for us to visit it. We had the theater. When plays finished their Broadway runs, they crossed the East River to Fulton Street, their first stop on the road. Mom took me to the Orpheum or Majestic to see William Gillette playing Sherlock Holmes and Walter Hampden playing Cyrano, and like everybody else I knew, I fell in love with Maude Adams as Peter Pan. Later, when we studied art at Manual Training High, our teacher took us to the Brooklyn Art Museum, and there we learned to appreciate what made a great painting great. The zoo at Prospect Park was our lab when we studied natural history, and we learned about plants and flowers not only from books but from the live exhibits at the Botanical Gardens.

14

Still later, we learned that there were great law and medical schools in Brooklyn, that forty per cent of New York City's population lived in our borough, that Brooklyn's forty-five hundred industrial plants made it one of the largest manufacturing centers in the world. All this we took in without surprise, for to us Brooklyn was *it*. When I entered high school, I started earning my first pay as a reporter, doing night assignments for the Brooklyn *Eagle* (which, of course, was *the* newspaper; only foreigners read *The New York Times* or the *Evening World*). Covering Bar Mitzvah celebrations, Polish weddings, and Burton Holmes' travel lectures at the Academy of Music, and raking in the heady sum of a dollar a story (some nights I turned in three items), I was carrying out the precept of the *Eagle*'s editor, H. V. Kaltenborn, over whose desk appeared the slogan: A DOG FIGHT IN BROOKLYN IS BIGGER THAN A REVOLUTION IN CHINA. That pretty well summed up our provincialism, but another name for it was pride in our community.

There was wealth in Brooklyn, and there was poverty, but I myself had little experience with either. Pop's salary as a school principal during our childhood was five thousand a year—if it sometimes left him short, it was at least adequate for a family of seven, and he had an additional source of income as a writer of textbooks in math, English, and American history. His publishers, Noble & Noble, sent Pop his royalty check in December, and the value and number of our Christmas gifts depended on the size of that check. Mom, like all the mothers we knew, was a good manager. She baked her own bread and cakes, of course, and even in France I've never eaten better homemade bread than hers. She raised us on meat and potatoes, with roast beef or chicken and apple pie every Sunday. On holidays and birthdays we churned ice cream in the back yard. I've heard Southerners wax nostalgic about the fried chicken they ate in their youth; Mom and the rest of the Bushwick section would have said the flavor was fried out of it. In Brooklyn a chicken was fricasseed or boiled.

Over the years we lived in two homes. Our first, at 732A Jefferson Avenue, Bushwick, was a comfortable three-story brownstone bounded on the north by the Stuyvesant section, mysterious and forbidding; to the south by Highland Park; to the east, Brownsville; to the west, Williamsburg. Only rarely did we children venture from our neighborhood into these strange territories, and then only in the

15

security of numbers. When the first snow fell, I remember, those of us who were altar boys at Our Lady of Good Counsel on Putnam Avenue would stage a quick foray to Gates Avenue, five blocks distant. There we would joyously pelt the boys and even the girls entering or leaving P.S. 26. The cops drove us off only when we loaded our snowballs with lumps of coal.

Along Jefferson Avenue, season by season, all life seemed to pass. We would know it was spring when we heard the call "Flowers—flowers!" and saw the approaching wagon laden with geraniums, daffodils, daisies, hyacinths, and roses. For Mom to splurge twenty cents for daffodils was the official sign that it was time to take off our long drawers and put away the sleds and get out our roller skates. Mom's potted plant, bought from the usually potted flowerman, had an importance for us that went beyond the advent of spring. Presently it would be planted in the back yard, where our stretched lace curtains were drying from their spring laundering. There it would fight a losing battle in the barren earth, but while it lived it was Mom's secret weapon against the pain of a baby tooth or a cut finger or a splinter. As each loose tooth was pulled by Mom's firm fingers, there was the comforting promise that the "bunny" would replace it with something good if we left it under the magic plant before we went to bed. Sure enough, next morning the tooth (or the bandage or the splinter) would be gone and in its place we would find a banana or an orange or maybe, for a really big splinter, a nickel.

When it wasn't the flowerman coming along Jefferson, it would be the knife sharpener swinging his big brass bell as he carried his portable grindstone; or it would be the leather-lunged woman who shouted "Horseradissh, horseradissh!" like a Wagnerian Valkyrie. We never bought from her, but she and her knuckles of white root and her dangerous-looking tin grater always held a fascination for us.

Then would come the waffleman with his marvelous-smelling wagon, and the old-clothesman, shouting "Any ol' close?" Each had a sound all his own, and they made the music of our street. The iceman, the ashman, and the garbageman—all of them with their faithful horses clopping along from house to house or standing quietly at noon, munching their bags of oats while the boss ate his salami sandwich and drank his bottle of beer. In the summer the horses wore straw hats with holes cut through for their ears.

16

Of all the sounds that came down our street none beat the breathtaking excitement of the clanging fire engine. Drawn by three pounding Percherons, the shining silver pump with sparks and flames belching out the top was like all hell on wheels. Surely Ben Hur and his chariot dashing into the Colosseum could not have presented a more thrilling sight. If you were lucky enough to be outside the firehouse on nearby Quincy Street when the alarm sounded, as I was one day, you really lived! Down the brass pole came the driver and the firetender, and out of their stalls, without command, came the great horses to their positions under the harness. The harness dropped into place by the pull of a rope as the driver sprang into his seat. Fire burning, harness fastened, bell clanging, the engine was on its way in less than a minute, and as it shot into the street the boy who didn't quake with excitement must have been the cold-blooded son of a Republican from Flatbush.

I remember the day my brother Jim and I chanced to be passing the firehouse at just the right moment. "Where is it?" we asked one of the firemen. "The church on Greene Avenue!" he shouted back. That was only two blocks away. I grabbed Jim's hand and we ran there as fast as we could and climbed the front steps of the house opposite the high-domed Episcopalian church. Soon the cops arrived to chase the crowd away, and one of them told us to move on. Displaying a quick intelligence I never showed at school, I called back, "We live in this house." The cop went on, and Jim looked his admiration at me.

The firemen were playing their hoses on the church, but it was a losing battle. The building rose so high above the neighboring houses that the men could do no effective work from the rooftops. More fire companies arrived but they were helpless as the flames continued to blossom from the windows and shoot high in the air before dying in clouds of smoke. Finally came the spectacular climax: the roof, completely aflame, crashed with a roar. The showering sparks fell all about us, but had they landed on us I doubt if we would have felt them. We stayed, watching, until the last fire company disappeared. I was not to see a fire to surpass that one for many years, and then it included the burning of another church. It was the night in 1941 when London burned and I saw St. Paul's almost destroyed.

As a boy's playground, Jefferson Avenue had every advantage.

17

There were patches of earth for marbles, fire hydrants and trees and fences for follow-the-leader, and the whole long street for stickball. If our rubber ball rolled down a sewer, we would pry the metal cover off and the bravest of us would go down for it. The sky over Jefferson Avenue was there for our kites if a breeze came up, and once we got them above the housetops, all the magic of space was ours. If the string broke, as it did sometimes, there would be a race to the corner, and then block after block to retrieve the stricken kite and the long tail we had made from Mom's dust cloths.

On Halloween, we stuffed black stockings with flour and went looking for victims. Thanksgiving meant more than Mom cooking a turkey dinner. We dressed in funny clothes, put on masks, and went begging. Not quite sure what the holiday was all about, we'd cluster outside the saloons. Infected by the jollity of the men within, we'd sometimes sneak in, grab a piece of bologna, the standard free-lunch item, and run. We had another great desire on Thanksgiving—to get a turkey bladder. This we'd blow up, dry, tie to a stick, and have a perfect weapon to belt an unsuspecting character on the head. Come mid-November, the butcher on the corner was plagued with our "Please, mister, can I have a bladder?" When he had one, we'd get it, and once in a while a slice of bologna to boot!

The butcher, the grocer, the ice-cream man—we loved them all. They were not impersonal figures; they were friends and neighbors to whom we would give Mom's order for a "lean steak and please trim off most of the fat," usually adding, "and Mom wonders if you happen to have a nice soup bone." We never asked Mr. Schumacher for a head of lettuce without requesting that it be "firm," and Mom's occasional order for a quart of mixed chocolate and vanilla always went to Mr. Weinecke with "and please pack it tight." In this friendly relationship many a bill went unpaid for months without a complaint when other demands had accounted for Pop's cash.

The Chinese laundryman did Pop's collars, but Mom did all the rest of our laundry, and she did it humming a tune, the way she did most of her heavy work. I can see her now, bending over the wash-tub with the scrubbing board—up and down, up and down in the billowing suds.

I have no memory of her ever complaining that she was overworked.

Mom, who loved good singing, must have been greatly disappointed in her children. My brother Jim had the makings of a very bad

18

Irish tenor, but as singers the rest of us were either as mute as penguins or fortunately soon learned to be. Mom used to love to sit at the piano and have Jim stand beside her rendering "Danny Boy" or "Kathleen Mavoureen." To her, he was the John McCormack of the future, but as poor Jim reached for the high notes his face would get red, his head would quiver, and you had to love him to stay in the room.

At age seven, my sister Marge was Mom's choice for the instrumentalist in the family. She took piano lessons until she and the rest of us could hardly stand it. I can still see her, practicing scales by the hour with tears occasionally trickling down her cheeks, Mom standing by hoping that by some miracle the spark would catch fire.

While our cultural progress left much to be desired in the musical line, we all became great readers. Pop didn't really care what we read so long as we read—though he made certain there were plenty of good books around—and if I spent many hours with the *American Boy* and Tom Swift and Horatio Alger and the works of Jules Verne, I certainly spent as many reading *Huckleberry Finn* and *Tom Sawyer* and Kipling's *Jungle Books,* and *Plain Tales from the Hills.* "Gunga Din" and "Danny Deever" are poems I can still recite, and because our dinner table presented Pop and Mom with a captive audience, there was a time when most of us were also walking anthologies of Shakespeare, not to mention Tennyson and Keats. Pop and Mom had it all by heart—"The quality of mercy is not strained," "All the world's a stage," "There is a tide in the affairs of men"—and if we wanted our corned beef and cabbage, we had to listen. I'm grateful, now, that so much of it rubbed off on me.

When I was in the eighth grade I discovered the delights of vaudeville at the Bushwick, a two-a-day house of the Keith Circuit. Every Friday night, thanks to Bernie Goldstein, a schoolmate, I saw the first half of the show for nothing. I saw the two black-faced comics, Moran and Mack. I heard Harry Lauder sing "It's Nice to Get Up in the Morning, Ah, But It's Nicer to Lie in Your Bed." I heard the beautiful Nora Bayes sing and I joined in with everyone else when the incomparable soft-shoe dancer, Pat Rooney, urged the audience to sing "Sweet Rosie O'Grady." But of all the stars the one I awaited most eagerly was the great Houdini, and showman that he was, he had the whole house in awe even before he got down to the business of being handcuffed, laden with ballast, and dropped into a pool of water—from which, of course, he magically escaped. As if that were not enough, I then watched him make a live elephant vanish from the stage!

What went on in the second half of these bills I never knew. The reason for this was that Bernie Goldstein, the boy who got me into the Bushwick as a candy butcher, was, as I was, something of a swindler. Every Friday night we would arrive a half hour before the asbestos went up, don white jackets, and be in place in the second balcony with our taffy bars and peanuts when the customers began arriving, breathless and hungry after their climb up hundreds of stairs. Before the show started we moved a lot of merchandise for our boss, a local muscleman we avoided as much as possible, but our big moment came at the intermission

Just before the house lights went up, Bernie and I would go down our aisles to the front of the balcony. In the first balcony and in the orchestra other white-jacketed lads likewise hurried to their stations. As the lights blazed, the drummer would give a roll and crash, and then our boss, down in front of the orchestra pit, would shout: "Ladeez and genelmen, may I have your attention, please." All eyes would be on him as he held up one of the boxes that each of us had in good supply in our wicker baskets. "I hold here in my hand a box of delicious candy kisses. In each and every such box that our boys have for sale, in addition to the finest candy ever imported from Switzerland, you will find a beautiful and valuable prize." And to prove it, the box would be opened and a watch would be pulled out. "Worth at least five dollars, ladeez and genelmen . . . and in each and every box another valuable prize . . . the candy and the prize selling tonight not for a dollar, not for fifty cents, but for just twenty-five cents!"

This was our cue to start hollering "Who'll have one?" and go quickly up the aisles grabbing the quarters and tossing the boxes of candy to the suckers. Then—down the stairs, off with the jackets, and out of the theater before the customers found the tin whistles, McKinley buttons and miniature American flags made in Japan. It was an awful first exposure to the free enterprise system, but I saw a lot of good vaudeville while it lasted, and that run downstairs every Friday night was good exercise for a twelve-year-old boy.

Once a year Mom would announce that the time had come for our visit to the Hippodrome. Going to the Hippodrome involved a journey into a foreign country—Manhattan—and that was part of our

20

excitement. We started on the Brooklyn-Lexington Avenue Elevated, and Mom and Pop always let us ride in the front car, next to the motorman's cab, so that we could have the best view of all the exotic sights. The trip across the Brooklyn Bridge was an adventure in itself, for here we would seem to be as high as heaven itself, while way below us we could glimpse ships and tugs.

At Park Row we would change to the Third Avenue El, and now came new thrills: Chinatown and the Bowery, where our parents had lived as children and then Cooper Union, where Mom's brother Dan had gone to school. Then at last we would be at the Hippodrome, nothing of it really forgotten from the previous visit but all of it new again in its incredible vastness, with the statues of naked ladies that timid boys didn't look at except maybe a peep or two, and then the lights and music. Mom and Pop were as full of wonder about it all as we were, and we all knew still another emotion that we didn't think much about at the time: shared love, deep and warm and secure, each one of us for the other.

The Hippodrome had ice skaters, Toto the Clown, elephants, and at the end of the show a great swimming pool into which the lithe Annette Kellerman would dive and into which, down a long stairway, would parade a line of beautiful girls, slowly walking deeper into the water until they disappeared. My heart would nearly stop with the suspense of it, and all the way home we would be wondering where they went. Come to think of it, I'm still wondering.

For a long time our universe in Brooklyn extended only as far as our roller skates could whirl us. It was the bicycle that broadened us. When I was twelve, my pals and I would pack our lunches and head for Prospect Park on our bikes. Prospect makes Central Park look like a shabby back lot. We would pedal to the top of Lookout Mountain and stand awed at the magnificence of the Park's five hundred and thirty acres spread below us. A year later we were big enough to pedal clear to Coney Island. By now I was selling *Saturday Evening Post*s and taking in a smart $1.50 a week, and my pals, who had newspaper routes, were equally flush. At Coney, we could really spread ourselves. The swimming didn't interest us; we were all YMCA kids, and our pool in the Bedford Y was a lot more attractive than the crowded Coney beach. It was the roller coaster we spent our riches on, and we tried to brazen out our terror as we were hurled down the track at sickening speeds. And then, bone weary, we'd bike over to

21

Brighton Beach and take in the Rocking Chair movies. They were free, but of course you had to buy something. Usually it was sass (sarsaparilla) and a hot dog, costing all of ten cents, and then we could occupy the rocking chairs and watch Douglas Fairbanks or William S. Hart for three delirious hours.

I had another source of income around this time, and I remember it with special affection. Two doors away from our house was a synagogue, and the job of lighting the gas lamps and stove on the Sabbath had to be performed by someone not of the faith. Somehow, I got the job. Perhaps it was the money—an easy fifteen cents a week —but I prefer to think it was the gentle dignity of the old orthodox rabbi that inspired me with a deep respect for the Hebrew faith that I retain to this day.

I never heard Pop or Mom use the word *tolerance*; they just lived the ideal and somehow this rubbed off on the five of us. By now, Pop was district superintendent of schools, and part of his domain was Brownsville, which was about 98 per cent Jewish. Pop spoke German so it was easy for him to make the transition to serviceable Yiddish. When a new *Schule* was opened the rabbi in charge and the president of the synagogue or temple usually needed advice from a professional. There were fire laws to be observed in the school, and there were sanitary problems, and such questions as whether or not a smoking room should be provided for its teachers.

I remember the rabbis and presidents coming to dinner at our house when they sought Pop's advice. When they were orthodox, Mom, warned by Pop, would get in kosher food from a restaurant on Ralph Avenue. None of us saw anything incongruous about this— after all, we had our own dietary observance in fish every Friday. Furthermore, we all took a liking to gefülte fish, chopped chicken liver and kreplach. When the reformed rabbis came to dinner, we ate less exotically—whatever Mom had on hand, and the guests might have a cocktail with Pop before the meal or a glass of beer with it, and afterward smoke one of Pop's cigars.

Sprawling on the floor of our living room with my homework after dinner, I overheard some of Pop's discussions with the visitors. I recall his exploding one night after he had gone over some building plans and then looked at the proposed cost: "Damn it all, Rabbi, I've supervised the construction of six public schools this year, and I can tell you this contractor is at least ten thousand dollars out of line. He's cheating you, and I'd say that if he was your own brother."

"Dr. Reynolds," replied the rabbi sadly, "he is my brother."

All the more reason, Pop said, to ask a dozen more contractors for new estimates. "Your people are poor, and it's taken them five years to raise the money for this school. Don't let the graspers get their hands on a penny of it." And before he finished, he swore again.

Both the rabbi and Mom were shocked, and Mom said firmly to us, "Kiddies, get to bed!" My sisters and little Don were too young to know what it was all about, but Jim and I felt a new respect for Pop. It was good to know that your old man could be tough if he had to. To us, as I look back on it, he often seemed more of an idealist than a practical man. It was at such moments as this that we began to understand his ability and dedication. If he was not a saint like Mom, he was one hell of a guy. The late Joe Palmer, racing writer for the New York *Herald Tribune,* once said of a certain trainer: "You couldn't catch a finer man if you planted a bear trap in the aisle of a cathedral." That's my feeling about Pop, whom I loved even to the smell of his after-shave lotion when he kissed us good-by in the morning and the smell of his inevitable after-dinner cigar.

Pop, who worried no more about the color of a man's skin than the color of his socks, had a couple of young Negro teachers in his schools whom he thought a great deal of, and as a result they often came to our house to dinner. One of them later went out west to teach, but the other, John King, stayed on and is today Deputy Superintendent of New York's public schools. The last time I saw him, he told me with some feeling that he wouldn't be where he is now if Pop hadn't been color-blind.

Pop, it sometimes seemed, knew everyone in Brooklyn. How he and Andy Neiderretier, the promoter at the Broadway Sporting Club, became friends I do not know, but every week passes came for the Tuesday night fights. Usually Pop attended with Charley Springmeyer, the principal of P.S. 85, but there came a Tuesday when I filled in. Mom, unlike me, was dead set against my seeing anything so brutal as a prize fight, so Pop struck a bargain. "Katharine," he said, "I'll take the boy to the fights this once. The chances are, when he sees the blood it will cure him for all time."

Our seats were ringside, on the aisle. The semifinal was between someone whose name I have forgotten and a supposedly deaf and dumb battler billed as Dummy Martin. When Dummy came down the aisle with his seconds, he caught sight of Pop, and it was then that I and the rest of the customers for several rows around learned that Dummy's affliction was for publicity purposes only. He not only talked but at some length recalled the days when Pop, as principal of P.S. 122, had saved him from being expelled after he had beaten up several of his classmates. It seemed that Pop, by persuading Dummy to join the Y and learn to box, had been the making of him, and Dummy would never forget it. His gratitude taking a practical form, he urged Pop to get a little bet down that he would knock out his opponent in three rounds.

Pop, who so far as I know never made a bet in his life, assured Dummy that he would try to make one before the bell rang, and we then watched Dummy floor his opponent on schedule. I felt excited but also a little sad that Pop had done nothing to profit by his tip.

The main bout was between two middleweights, "Soldier" Bartfield and "Sailor" Toland. It went ten furious rounds to a draw.

I do not remember the walk home. I was transported. Mom was waiting up for us.

"Wasn't the blood awful?" she asked me anxiously.

I had to tell her I hadn't noticed any. "It was just wonderful," I said. "One more round and Bartfield, who gets away with a backhand punch, even though Pop says it's illegal, would have stiffened the Sailor."

Mom looked sharply at Pop. "You and your brilliant ideas," she said.

From then on I went regularly to the fights, seeing Freddie Welsh and Benny Leonard and Jack Britton and Ted "Kid" Lewis and other great battlers of the day.

We were a happy, close-knit family, and only rarely during those early years did we know a crisis. Unwittingly, at my twelfth or thirteenth Christmas, I was the instrument that might have destroyed our happiness.

Yielding to my importunities, Pop saw that a BB gun appeared under our tree. My brother Jim and I immediately rigged up a target in the cellar and banged away at it until we thought all the pellets were gone. I then suggested that we play cowboys and Indians, and we had fun with the supposedly empty gun making loud pops—until

24

suddenly it made a different sound. I looked at Jim. He was pressing one of his eyes, and I was horrified to see blood appearing from under his fingers.

Wordlessly, we ran up the stairs. Mom took one look and telephoned Victor Zimmerman, our family doctor, who hurried over from his home on nearby Stuyvesant Avenue. While we waited for him, Mom held Jim in her arms. I stood by, feeling that I was under a death sentence.

Dr. Zimmerman, who had brought Jim and the younger children into the world, and knew all of us almost as well as he knew his own family, examined the wound and then said soothingly: "It's all right, Quent. It struck above his eye."

But all I heard, before fainting, was the "all right." When I came to, the smell of ammonia in my nose, my first question was, "How is Jim?"

"Better than you are," Dr. Zimmerman said gently.

I have never pointed a gun at anyone since that morning, and barring a few rare instances, I have never even had one in my hand.

When I was fifteen, Pop became assistant superintendent of schools and this necessitated our moving from Bushwick to Flatbush—specifically, to a large house in Wellington Court. For us children it was a wrench comparable to moving a family of Eskimos from Hudson's Bay to, say, Trinidad. The people in Flatbush looked different, dressed differently, talked a different language, and had different attitudes. In Flatbush the boys had dates with girls, a custom we had ridiculed in Bushwick. In Flatbush I don't recall that any boy ever put coal in a snowball. And Prospect Park, which had once seemed remote and infinitely mysterious, was practically in our back yard, with much of its allure gone.

Not long ago I went back to Bushwick to see how much it had changed. It hadn't changed. The subway ride cost me fifteen cents instead of a nickel, and there were buses on Halsey Street instead of trolleys, and they had taken away the El that used to roar over Fulton Street, but these, after all, were details. The kids were still delivering papers and magazines, still making the same adventurous trips to Coney Island that we made, and I learned that the altar boys at Our Lady of Good Counsel still think of the boys at P.S. 26 as their natural enemies.

I walked around my old neighborhood. Although it seemed a little shabbier, time really hadn't done much to it. At Jefferson and Reid, a block from my old home, I dropped into the bar where I had once snatched slices of bologna. I asked for a beer, and for a moment half expected the elderly bartender to yell, "Get outta here, kid!" Instead, he slid the glass across the bar, looked at me closely, and said, "You useta live in the neighborhood, usen't you?"

"I uset," I told him happily.

3

My life at sea—all 30 days of it

Just before our move to Flatbush, hoping to find a teacher who could make me into a speller, Pop transferred me from P.S. 70 to Charley Springmeyer's P.S. 85. My lifelong ineptitude in spelling must never have been easy for Pop to take, especially since his own book, called *The Reynolds Speller,* was the standard text during my elementary years. Faced with my record, there was a period when Pop theorized that memorization was no more important in spelling than it was in music. Consequently, when our piano teacher finally gave me up in disgust, Pop appeared delighted. "You have to have an ear for it," he told Mom, "and Quent has no more ear for music than he has for spelling." Needless to say, I adopted this excuse as soon as it was available, but Mom remained unconvinced and nearly cried each time a report card reaffirmed my supposed tin ear for the written word.

But if Charley Springmeyer could not help to make me a speller, he assigned me a teacher who, as much as anyone, was responsible for the fact that I eventually became a writer. Young and wrapped in dark beauty, Miss Inez Wallace both deflated and inspired me. I had been turning in ambitious compositions that owed much to the exploits of Tom Swift and Captain Nemo. One afternoon, keeping me

27

after class, Miss Wallace asked, "Quentin, what did you do when you left school yesterday?"

Her question took me off guard. "I went to the Y," I said. "I've been practicing on the parallel bars and trying to do the giant swing on the vertical bars. I'm no good at either," I added miserably.

"Why don't you write about that for me?" She gave me one of her dazzling smiles as she handed me back my latest opus. "I don't think you really know much about travel in airships or conditions in Tibet. I'd like to see you write about something you know well, no matter what it is."

"Maybe about what happened day before yesterday?" I volunteered. "My bike broke on the way home from school, and a cop fixed it for me."

"Was he a nice cop?"

"He certainly was. After he fixed it, he gave me a nickel and told me to go have a soda."

She nodded. "These are the things you should be writing about— things that have happened to you, things that have impressed you or moved you. Try it."

I promised I would, not yet really convinced that her approach was right. But for Miss Wallace, had she suggested it, I would have written compositions about the multiplication tables. As I turned in stories about life as I knew it on Jefferson Avenue, my marks went up, and by the end of the year I was getting A over E every time. The E, which never improved, was for spelling, punctuation, and grammar.

The only time I strayed from subjects close to home was after we had learned Longfellow's poem commemorating the midnight ride of Paul Revere. I made that the subject of a composition, a protest that although everyone knew the name of the silversmith, no one knew the name of the horse which had carried him the twenty-odd miles from Charlestown to Lexington. In those days a child could have ridden that distance; it really took one hell of a horse to make a fast, nonstop gallop. Yet the horse had received no recognition for his historic ride. Why not? Why wasn't there a statue of this memorable horse in the Smithsonian Institution or somewhere else? And what was his name? For some reason or other, this lack of recognition compelled me to protest. I expected of course that Miss Wallace would tell me the name of the horse when she corrected our compositions and discussed them a day or two later in class, but she confessed she didn't know.

28

She went further and told me that she had not only checked the *Encyclopaedia Britannica* but had found a book in the library called *The True Life of Paul Revere* by Charles F. Gettemy, and that neither mentioned the name of the horse.

"Why does it seem important to you, Quentin?" she asked curiously.

"Well, Miss Wallace," I was a bit embarrassed to be thus singled out of the class. "The other day I saw in the Brooklyn *Eagle* that a horse named Old Rosebud had won a race called the Kentucky Derby. It was on the front page. The man who wrote the story said that Old Rosebud had run faster than any horse since the one who carried Paul Revere back in 1775. So, I would like to know the name of Paul Revere's horse."

"Perhaps your father might know," Miss Wallace said gently.

I asked Pop but he didn't know—I was shocked. Pop had never let me down before. I made up my mind that some day I'd find out the name of that horse.

In 1942, when I returned home after my war coverage in Europe, Pop gave a big party for me over in Brooklyn, and invited people to it I had known all my life. Charley Springmeyer was there, representing P.S. 85, but, disappointingly, not Miss Wallace. Pop had not forgotten her, I learned, but she had declined his invitation, saying, "When Quentin was in my class he thought I was somebody quite special, and I would like to have him remember me as I was then." And so I do remember her—not only as the first beautiful woman I fell in love with, but as the first one to give me some practical advice on writing.

After our move to Flatbush, I entered Manual Training High School, not, I think, because Pop considered that the compulsory courses in blacksmithing and carpentry (relics of the days when Brooklyn's transportation system consisted of horsecars) would be of use to me in later life, but because the principal, Horace Snyder, was one of his close friends and would keep an eye on me.

About the time I had mastered the arts of forging a horseshoe and turning out a wooden coat-rack, I faced the dual problem of electing and learning a foreign language. Some senior whose judgment I instinctively trusted assured me that German was easier than Spanish or Latin, and for this reason alone I chose it. Otis Mageworth earned his salary the hard way with me in his class, but years later I was to remember his efforts with gratitude, because it was the wisps of German that still clung to me—*Im Winter solltest du den schweren Mantel tragen* (In winter you ought to wear your heavy coat), and *In diesem Leben ist nichts ideal* (In this life nothing is ideal)—that resulted in my being sent to Berlin on my first assignment as a foreign correspondent.

The highest academic distinction one could achieve at Manual was to be selected for Arista, the honorary society. In my senior year, quite incredibly, I made the grade. I was so elated at the news that, with Ulrich Calvosa, a classmate who had been nominated on more solid grounds, I cut the rest of the day's classes. Unfortunately, a school official noticed us in Prospect Park, and almost as soon as the little blue and gold button was within our grasp, our names were struck from the list.

Cal and I promptly ran to Ira Bloom, our fiery little football coach. Ira had recently made himself a hero in our eyes by interceding successfully on behalf of two players who had been caught stealing from the school's commissary. His defense of the culprits was based on the pleas that both were seniors, both had been accepted by good colleges, and both faced blasted futures if the ax should fall. After getting our stories, Ira marched off to the principal's office to see how well he could do for us. He, and we, got nowhere.

Of course I had to break the sad news to Pop and Mom. And even worse, the reason for it. It really hurt them. I put a little extra agony into the story, hoping that it would move Pop to telephone his friend Horace Snyder and obtain a reversal. And he did call, but only to assure Snyder that he had made the right decision.

From this academic record, of which I am certainly not proud, it is a relief to turn to the football field, where I managed to do slightly better, especially after learning to loathe our arch rival, Erasmus. The feeling between the schools was something like that between the Hatfields and the McCoys, and every Manual player dreamed of making a touchdown against the enemy. Life, it was felt, could not hold many sweeter prospects. Our annual game at Ebbets Field was always a sellout, and my big chance came the year I made the line-up.

When we tramped wearily off the shadowed field and the board read Erasmus—3, Manual—0, I felt I could know no greater defeat. Compensation came later when we read what was always about the biggest news story of the year: *Eagle* columnist Jimmy Murphy's naming of his annual all-scholastic team. The proudest moment of my young life came when I found my name on Murphy's roster as third-team fullback.

After the events of World War II began to become significant in my adult life, I sometimes wondered why the first war had made so little impression on any of us at Manual. True, we hated the Hun, but it was in a half-hearted way, and while we bought war savings stamps out of our lunch money, the European battlefields were hard to imagine as we sauntered along the streets of Brooklyn. One day a famous Manual alumnus, Arthur Guy Empey, returned to tell us of his experiences as a combat infantryman with the British in France. The author of the best-selling *Over the Top,* Empey, in highly emotional terms, convinced us of the gallantry and courage of the Allied soldiers, and the barbarism of the enemy. His address had a profound effect on all of us for about twenty-four hours, but our annual game with Erasmus was coming up, and it was much easier to hate our known rivals than it was an unknown enemy across an ocean. Our lack of interest in the war, due in part to our provincialism, was probably heightened by the fact that very few of us had older brothers or other relatives in the armed forces. Whatever the explanation, Brooklyn, for me and most of my contemporaries, was then still the world.

During our senior year at Manual, in spite of our failure to make Arista, Cal Calvosa and I were accepted by Brown University, Cal on the basis of his marks and I on the recommendation of one Dave Fultz, a Brown alumnus now practicing law in Brooklyn and looking for good football material to send up. Brown would not directly subsidize an athlete, but it would grant an academic scholarship on a suitable recommendation. When I learned from my sponsor that the scholarship was for one year only but might be renewed year to year if my marks warranted, I had a sensation of going to Rhode Island under a handicap.

Finishing high school in February, 1919, I had the summer ahead of me. What to do with my time? Because I had just read *Captains Courageous,* the answer seemed to be, Go to sea. For some reason connected with the end of the war there existed a helpful manpower shortage on the deep, and Pop, through one of his friends, soon found me a job on the freighter *K. I. Luckenbach.* It took some persuading to convince Mom that the experience might be broadening, and that it at least could not hurt me.

For a week I crammed on such matters as S wrenches, monkey wrenches, Stillson wrenches, alligator wrenches, and socket wrenches, so that when a man from the engine room came to me, the store-keeper, and asked for a particular tool, I could issue it. The pay for checking the tools in and out was a hundred dollars a month. For that kind of money, had I been asked to, I would have pushed that 15,000-ton freighter across the Atlantic singlehanded.

We sailed for Europe on April 11, which happened to be my seven-teenth birthday. For the first few shifts all was easy, and between busy moments I managed to read several of the detective stories I had brought along in quantity. Then the ship stuck her bow into a gale. The seas piled up, and even the oldest salts admitted the weather was dirty enough to make a gull walk. In the groaning, pitching storeroom a green-gilled boy lost his hankering for adventure in the fabled ports of Europe and longed for the solid pavement of Flatbush. Oddly enough, it was the one time in my life I have ever been seasick. But I was thoroughly, completely seasick, the condition continuing even after the storm died down, and to this day *mal de mer* strikes me as an impossible theme for jokes.

Though my place of work was almost on the waterline, I was able much of the time to keep a porthole open, neutralizing the engine room's stench of hot oil with a blast of fresh air. One night when I went off duty I forgot to screw down the porthole cover. While I slept the heavy sea returned. About midnight I was rudely sum-moned from my bunk. The first engineer, it seemed, wished to see me below.

I staggered to the engine room to be confronted by the red-faced, ill-humored man we called the Chief. With a few witheringly foul words, he led me to the storeroom. I blanched. A foot of greasy sea water was sloshing to and fro. Hundreds of tools had been knocked from their racks. Two men from the engine room, giving me dirty looks but saying nothing, were reducing the flood with pails, since there was neither drain nor pump handy.

"Get in there and help them," the Chief snarled. "Then wipe every tool dry, grease them, and return them to their racks."

"Yes, sir," I said meekly.

"And when you're finished with that," he added, "get to the shaft well. You'll be wiper for the rest of the trip."

Without fully realizing what this change of job meant, I recognized

32

that I was being downgraded. Ten hours later, finished with my work in the storeroom, I was hating the Chief. The responsibility for the havoc was mine. That I recognized. However, it seemed to me some allowance ought to be made. After all, this was my first time at sea. More in chagrin than anger, I said to the Greek wiper who had been helping me, "I'm going to kill that man."

The Greek said immediately, "Do nothing, kid. We know how to take care of his kind. He's rotten to all of us, not just you." There was a tone to this that suggested something definite might be in the wind. I also gathered that I should ask no questions.

My new assignment left me no time for detective stories. The shaft well was the hundred-foot-long tunnel through which two massive steel shafts connected the engines with the propellers. The place smelled horribly of oil. As wiper, my job was to see that not a bit of rust clung to the gleaming, spinning shafts, or to the steel platform beneath them. There was headroom in the well of about four feet. Sometimes the stern of the ship lifted the propellers clear of the water. At such moments the well trembled as though it would collapse. I had to work there eight hours a day, and my pay for this agony was half what it had been in the storeroom.

Now and then the Chief would crawl into the well to see how I was doing, and needle me with some vituperative remark. Feeling I could take no more of it, I sought out the man who had spoken to me in the storeroom about the Chief. "Don't touch him while we're aboard," he warned. "That would be mutiny."

One morning another of the engine-room men, a good-looking, hard-bodied Greek of about twenty-five named Demetrios, came to my bunk and shook me awake. "You've been praying for land," he said. "Come on deck and see it."

I brushed the sleep out of my eyes and followed him. Off the port bow, a long line of cliffs was gleaming in the morning sun.

"Dover," Demetrios told me. "Those cliffs are all chalk. They look good, eh?"

Indeed they looked good, although any land would have looked good after my fourteen days of seasickness and tour of duty in the shaft well. Staring at the Dover cliffs as if they were about to deliver me miraculously from the Chief, I formed a lasting impression of their wonder. Twenty-one years later I would stand on those very cliffs and watch a handful of RAF pilots beat off Hermann Göring's *Luft-*

waffe, and I would get to know the English Channel the way I knew Prospect Park.

A day after we entered the Channel, we arrived at Antwerp. As a seventeen-year-old in Europe for the first time, I was naturally excited. Since we were to be in port seven days while a shore gang overhauled our engines, Demetrios suggested we go sightseeing to Louvain, some fifty miles off.

"There you will see the German way of doing things," he said bitterly. "It is a sight everyone should see."

In 1914 the Germans had just about destroyed Louvain. Walking through the city, gazing at the ruins that still lay open to the sky—including the charred wreckage of the university that had been founded in 1425—I became aware for the first time of what the war must have meant to the people who were actually in it. The tragedy in Europe had once seemed to me almost as small and far away as the Battle of Gettysburg as it was summed up in Pop's story about Grandpa Mahoney and his hired substitute. The picture of Louvain brought it home in a form I was never to forget.

When we returned to Antwerp, Demetrios took me out on the town, insisting that I was to be his guest. As one of the *K. I. Luckenbach*'s top crapshooters he had plenty of money to spend while I had little. We went from bar to bar, drinking nothing worse than beer, and came at last to a place called the House of All Nations, which Demetrios knew from previous visits. We were welcomed and given a table near a small but loud orchestra. A dozen scantily clad young ladies sang and danced—not very well. Most of them knew Demetrios, and two, Renée and Monique, soon sat down with us. Neither would have gotten far in an American beauty contest, but both were amiable.

After he had paid for a round or two of beer, Demetrios whispered something to Renée, then announced that he would return in a little while. I was somewhat mystified when he made a point of pressing money into my hand as he left the table. After all, I had just seen him settle our bill for the drinks. Monique, on the other hand, noticed his sporty transfer of operating capital and soon asked, "Do you not wish to go upstairs with me?"

With complete innocence in my Brooklyn heart I replied, "The music is nice down here. Why go upstairs?"

On the way back to the ship, having had his laugh at me, Demetrios reviewed some of the simpler facts of life that I seemed not to know.

34

I replied, perhaps too primly, that the thought of paying for love made me sick.

"When you spend your life at sea," he said, "That is the only kind of love you can have."

Though his reasoning seemed irrefutable, I mentally chalked up one more point against a sea career.

A few days later we sailed for New York, delaying twenty-four hours because the first engineer did not appear. We left without him. At the first opportunity, I asked Demetrios what had become of the Chief.

He fixed me with a look. "You and I know nothing about it, Kid. We were in Louvain, remember?" From his tone I gathered that he knew perfectly well why the Chief had not shown up, but all I could get him to add was the comment that "We Greeks do not like to be pushed around."

To my knowledge, the missing man was never referred to again. Under the new first engineer, a thoughtful-looking quiet chap, I found myself once again in the storeroom, keeping track of the wrenches.

When I rolled into Flatbush with the air of a man who has been far places and lived life to the hilt, I secretly knew that, Kipling or no Kipling, the sea and I were incompatible. With most of the summer still before me, I decided to take the first step toward the profession I would eventually enter. Which would it be—law or medicine? I had a genuine interest, I thought, in both. Pop, even as a lawyer who had never practiced, had always been something of an inspiration to me, and then there was the shining example of Mom's brother, who was now a judge of the New York Supreme Court. In the early 1900s Uncle Jerry had been the national decathlon champion and holder of the world's record for the high jump. Since I shared Uncle Jerry's love for sports, it dimly occurred to me that I might, by analogy, make a lawyer.

As for the scalpel, I had been a convert ever since the day Dr. Zimmerman placed me on our kitchen table in Bushwick and removed my tonsils. At the sight of his ether can I had been for calling the whole thing off, but Dr. Zimmerman, smiling his irresistible smile, had assured me that when I woke up I would be allowed to eat all the ice cream I wanted. When the stuff was there as promised—all I could eat and more—my faith in doctors and interest in medicine soared.

35

Pop, when I went over my career plans with him, characteristically did not try to influence me. Either trade, he said, would be a fine one. As for the months directly ahead, he could either find me a job as office boy for some lawyer he knew or get me into the Hospital for the Ruptured and Crippled, over in Manhattan. I chose the hospital—why, I no longer remember—and after a spell of tending the telephone switchboard on the night shift, felt that I had made another mistake.

However, I soon became friendly with some of the younger doctors, and before long one of them asked me if I would like to watch an operation. Would I! Donning a gown and cap, I went into the gallery of the operating room with my guide, intern Jim Bradley, who explained what was going on. The operator, Armitage Whitman, a handsome white-haired man I had often seen in the corridors, was the acknowledged god of orthopedic surgery. I found that neither the sight of blood nor the sound of his saw cutting through bone bothered me—from the first I could rationalize it—and with Dr. Bradley's permission, I became a frequent spectator.

The hospital's superintendent, Pop's friend, heard of my interest and made me a surgical orderly, adding room and board to my compensation. My new duties, though much more interesting than helping people get wrong numbers, called more for physical than mental ability. With another orderly, Harry Lear, I would move a stretcher up to a patient's bed, lift him aboard, and wheel him off to the anesthesia room. Here, while a doctor administered ether, Harry and I stood by. Often the patient would resist, and it was our job to maintain the peace till the ether took effect. Next, with one of the surgical assistants directing, I would expose the operative site and paint it with iodine and alcohol. At first I was puzzled by the fact that all patients, male or female, seemed to be as hairless as babes, at least in the areas I worked on. Then I discovered that the hospital's barber shaved more than faces.

Once the painting was done, Harry and I would wheel the patient into the operating room and transfer him or her to the table. We then stood by till the operation was over. There was no air conditioning in the operating room, and at times the heat was withering. Whenever a surgeon stood back from the table and cried "Lemonade!" a nurse would slip his mask off while Harry or I would rush up with a glass of it, hastily drawn from an icy pitcher.

Our other principal concern was flies. I was told that one fly might

36

carry on its feet as many as a million lethal germs, and that the patient's life might well depend on my marksmanship with the swatter. One morning while the eminent Dr. Whitman was operating, we all heard an ominous buzzing. Dr. Whitman hurriedly covered the wound with sterile towels, then stood motionless while I stalked the invader. Where it lit was of no matter; I was to kill it with the first swing.

The dear little monster settled on Dr. Whitman's forehead. I disposed of it perfectly and almost disposed of Dr. Whitman. "You have a strong right arm, son," the great man said when he was again able to speak, "but I agree it's better to maim a doctor than kill a patient."

During my three months in the hospital, only one operation ever troubled me, and it was the aftermath, not the actual surgery, that did it. One night I was routed out of bed to handle the lemonade and the fly swatter while a man's leg was removed. In those days it was the law that amputated limbs had to be checked into the city morgue at Bellevue Hospital, and after the operation I was instructed to make the delivery. Without thinking much about it, I changed into my street clothes and collected the leg, now neatly encased in a long narrow cardboard box. Then, as I walked through the dark streets, realizing I had part of a man under my arm, I began to have an eerie feeling and a great wish to be done with the job. At the Third Avenue El I paid my nickel and boarded a nearly empty car. It had been a long day, and as the train rolled downtown, I dozed. The train lurched, and I woke to see the box, which had been stretched across my lap, slithering across the floor. While I watched in horror, it stopped in front of a little old lady.

"You're taking your girl some flowers!" she said coyly as I retrieved the box from under her feet.

It was hardly the hour to be taking flowers to anybody, being well after midnight, but I grabbed at the suggestion. "That's right, ma'am— she likes the long-stemmed kind."

I returned to my seat with the box, and the little old lady beamed at me all the rest of the way.

Three weeks before I was due at Brown, I turned in my gown and mask and went for a vacation to Greenwood Lake, New Jersey, where Pop, several years before, had bought a summer bungalow. The big man at the lake was Young Bob Fitzsimmons, son of the great heavyweight, and when I had checked in with my family, I went over to Bob's training camp, near the Sterling Forest Hotel. The past two sum-

37

mers my brother Jim and I had run with Bob on his daily jaunts and even sparred a little with him. As soon as Bob saw me this time he invited me to put on tights and gloves, saying he wanted to see if I had improved any since last we'd sparred.

Actually, though Bob was one of the cleverest defensive boxers I ever watched, he completely lacked the killer instinct. His approach was cerebral, not emotional, and since he could never quite manage to hate a nice guy like Jack Dempsey, he never made it to the top. He was simply a kind, gentle, thoughtful man completely miscast in his role of professional fighter. But all this is hindsight. Those summers at the lake I thought he was one of the greatest boxers ever.

As we sparred, Bob made me look good. If I so much as tapped his chin he grimaced as though really hurt. And when he suggested that I ought to go out for boxing at Brown, I had a sudden vision of life in the ring, rather than in court or the operating room. Fortunately, the vision did not last.

It was during this same visit to Greenwood Lake that I made my personal discovery that even married girls like boys. Saturday nights there was always a fairly steep crap game at the Sterling Forest Hotel, and while the men played, their wives went untended. One night one of them, a little the worse for gin, suggested that I take her for a canoe ride. After four summers at the lake I considered myself an expert paddler, and I was quite happy to show off my skill.

The night was beautiful, the water like glass. I had paddled out about a hundred yards when the little doll said lazily, "Don't sit up there. Come down here with me. I'm chilly."

Innocently, I complied. What happened next so startled me that I recoiled—and the canoe went over. "Stupid brat!" sputtered the lady when she surfaced. And with that she swam off, leaving me to push the capsized canoe to shore. She was waiting for me there. "I'm going to tell my husband I fell off the dock," she said angrily, "and if you know what's good for you, you won't say anything to anyone."

When I went home, Pop was still up. He noticed my wet clothes. "Fall in the lake?" he asked.

"Don't ask," I said. "I had a tough night." Then it occurred to me that Pop or someone else in the house might hear talk about one of the hotel's female guests going for an accidental swim. Still, I didn't feel like discussing it. "Whatever you hear," I warned Pop, "it was an accident, it wasn't my fault, and nobody got hurt."

38

"Sure, Quent," Pop said, laughing.

Somehow I had the feeling he was reading my mind. No one fooled Pop. I guess I was still pretty naïve when I was seventeen, but maybe our parents brought us up right—if a bit slowly. Sophistication comes to the adolescent soon enough. Two years after dumping that girl from the canoe I was back at Greenwood Lake looking for her. I found her and asked her to go for a canoe ride with me.

She laughed. "Little boy, run along. You don't even know what a canoe is for."

"I do now," I assured her.

"It's too late, boy," she said. "I have another paddler tonight."

4

Just a touch of larceny

A realistic account of my four years at Brown sees the material falling neatly into two large divisions: the serious academic side and what might be called the other side. I'll deal with the other side first, then take up the serious academic side—that is, if I can remember any.

Soon after my arrival, faced with a basic problem in freshman economics, I applied for a job with the college placement service. They found me a berth—literally—with an outfit that answered burglar alarms. The pay was eight dollars a week, which was not bad, considering I had to sleep at the company's headquarters and had no rent to pay. A senior, Lou Nichols, and I worked as a team. Practically every important business concern in Providence subscribed to our service and had its alarm wires running into our combination office and dormitory. Whenever a buzzer sounded, the dispatcher would consult his panel and call out the address of the place that presumably was being burgled. Shoving guns in our pockets, Lou and I would race to the scene, by taxi if it was at a distance, on foot if it was near.

During my first week it sometimes seemed to me that Providence must be the nation's crime center. We didn't get through the night without being routed out at least once. However, all the alarms proved to be false. Sometimes an employee had neglected to close a window,

40

or the wind had shorted the wires on a roof, or rain was fouling things. Lou and I would explore empty stores and offices, find nothing, and hurry back to headquarters just in time to find another alarm ringing.

Actually, it wasn't a bad life for the pay, and though I consider it a doubtful asset, the experience gave me a knowledge of Providence's streets and alleys that endures to this day. It was my constantly interrupted sleep that hurt. After a couple of weeks of it Coach Ed Robinson, watching my performance on the football field, shook his head sadly and told me I was just not fast enough to be a back. That I was doing my best running at 3 A.M. was no excuse. From then on I was a tackle of sorts.

I held my job for two months without once seeing a thief or a cracked safe, and then one night the dispatcher, who chanced on that occasion to be our boss, told us that The Outlet, the city's largest department store, had just been entered. Since the store did a big business in furs and jewelry, Lou and I, hurrying there, had the feeling that this would be it.

Stealthily searching the place floor by floor, we eventually closed in on a startled night watchman who sheepishly confessed that he had tripped over the alarm wires. It was near dawn when we returned to the office and I handed over my gun. The boss did something he had never done before. He broke it and spun the cylinder. "Where in hell are your bullets?" he snapped.

"In the drawer there," I murmured.

"Why aren't they in your gun?"

"I never put them in the gun," I said.

"Why not?"

I gulped. This was going to be hard to explain. "Well," I said, "I figured if Lou and I ever do find a hoodlum, which seems unlikely, we're big enough to take care of him. Anyhow, I don't like guns."

The poor man looked more and more bewildered. Then he began to foam. Lou stayed on, but my career as a gumshoe ended then and there.

After that promising start on the side of law and order, I regret to say that some of my next money-making ventures had a different complexion. But at the outset, let's absolve the college placement service. Following that first venture, I operated on my own.

One of my little rackets involved one of my two best friends at Brown—not gentle, upright Cal Calvosa, but tough little Roy Clay-

41

field, who had been an outstanding quarterback at DeWitt Clinton High in New York. Throughout the four years, Cal and Roy and I were very close. Most of Brown's students were conservative New Englanders, and the rushing season, which began soon after our arrival on the campus, was a hectic time for those freshmen who were impeccably Nordic and of distinguished ancestry, who had money, or who were athletes. Those of us who were deficient in one or more of these assets were not so eagerly courted, and with this in mind, Cal and Roy and I agreed we would not join a fraternity unless the three of us were accepted together.

Delta Tau Delta was the doubtful winner, and together we began the sadistic and absurd week of hazing. At all times we had to address the upper classmen as "sir." As soon as we entered the fraternity house we had to pick up a wooden paddle and have it available at all times. Whenever the mood moved one of our brothers-to-be he would ask for our paddle, snap, "Bend over," and then take several healthy wallops at the exposure. For this we had to say, in a tone of unmistakable pleasure, "Thank you, sir." Several times during the week we were paraded in downtown Providence with our faces painted, and made to amuse the bystanders. Once in a while a junior or senior might be human enough to say, "It'll be over soon and you can take it out on the pledges next year." That was small comfort, just as it was small comfort to know that two or three hundred other freshmen were going through the same ordeal to enter other fraternities. I still don't know what this week of torture was supposed to teach us. Humility perhaps, but as freshmen we were humble to begin with. What still puzzles me is that the president of the university, the dean, and the whole faculty gave the tradition tacit support by their silence.

Looking back, I can think of no American stratification more debasing than the fraternity system of those years, though when I was involved in it perhaps I was not fully conscious of all its nastiness. Once I remember, I asked an older fraternity brother why we had no Jewish members. I had in mind Pep Weinstein, who will shortly appear in these pages and who was then living in a dormitory. The answer was that we were a national fraternity and that the national charter prohibited the acceptance of Jews. Besides, the brother said, the Jews had a fraternity of their own on the campus.

I pointed out that while there was also a Catholic fraternity, I had been rushed by Delta Tau Delta. At that, the brother seemed a bit embarrassed. "It's true we don't take in many Catholics," he said. "To begin with, Brown is a Baptist college, and not many Jews or Catholics come here. In your case, frankly, we like to have a certain number of athletes in the house, so we overlooked the fact that you're a Catholic."

I told him I thought that was damn big of him.

"Look, Red," he said earnestly, "we didn't invent this system. We inherited it, and there's nothing we can do to change it."

This reasoning, which God knows is still to be heard in the world of human relations, even then seemed out of place in an institution of learning, but I suppose the Delt pin and the solemn and nonsensical pledge we took at the end of the hazing hypnotized me out of any lasting thought about it.

But I have drifted from the point—my relationship with Roy Clayfield. During our sophomore year Roy and I shared a room in the fraternity house. We made our own beds, and if mine wasn't perfectly cornered, Roy would give me hell. During the football season, I would occasionally sneak a cigarette; if Roy caught me, it was the end. Roy wasn't a Catholic, but he'd always get me out of bed to make ten o'clock mass on Sunday. I think he's the only man I ever knew who scared me. Even though I outweighed him by forty pounds and later when I was heavyweight boxing champion, whenever this dark-haired, snub-nosed little 137-pound terror would snarl "Hit those books!" I would answer meekly, "OK, Roy." It has been years, now, since I have seen Roy (because geographical distances have parted us), but if he were to phone me at six tomorrow morning and bark "Out of bed, Red, and to your typewriter!" I'm sure I would say, "OK, Roy."

Pop could rarely send me pocket money, and there were times when I had in my pocket only twenty cents. No matter, I would go into the Brown Cafeteria and confidently heap my tray with a steak, soup, pie, milk, and an array of health-inducing vegetables. Presenting this load to the cashier, I would glance unconcernedly about the premises while the imposing tally was ticked up on the register, hoping that the check, dropped face down on my tray, would later prove to be for fifteen cents. The cashier was a fraternity brother.

Early in my sophomore year I took a job in town that required the wearing of a tuxedo. The purchase price, twenty-five dollars, looked like a hopeless overextension. Cal Calvosa and Roy came to my res-

43

cue with unsecured loans, and as a matter of fact I was soon able to pay them back. My place of business was a dance hall that was frequented by both Brown and Providence College students. The owner, troubled by liquor-sparked fights that gave his place—not to mention the two student bodies—a bad name, hit on the idea of hiring me, a boxer, and Art Connor, the captain of the Providence football team, as peacemakers. Our method was direct and effective. If a Brown boy overstepped, we would converge on him and I would do the punching. If the offender was a Providence lad, Connor would settle him down. Between us we soon made the dance hall a place the mayor would not have been afraid to take his grandmother. When the place closed at midnight, Art and I often went on to Atwells Avenue, the speakeasy district, and finished the evening drinking ten-cent beer, a product of the time that no self-respecting brewer would have recognized though it certainly contained alcohol. Occasionally we even did a little bartending in one or another of the bistros, adding to our incomes and getting further mileage out of our costly dinner coats.

During my junior year I prospered for a while as assistant hat checker at the Providence Masonic Temple. Since all the Masons wore hats and were good tippers, and since as many as a hundred turned out for meetings, there was a period when I was one of the richest kids at Brown. Then religious prejudice reared its ugly head. It was learned that I was a Roman Catholic. Even though I, in my innocence, assured everyone that I had no feeling whatsoever against the men whose hats I looked after, I was dismissed.

The same year, in another setting, I became something of a tycoon. We had at Brown an odious duty called chapel, indirectly the work of John D. Rockefeller, Jr., one of Brown's most illustrious graduates. John D. had made Dr. William Herbert Perry Faunce president of the university, elevating him from the Baptist ministry in New York, but this wasn't enough for Dr. Faunce, who had the look of a small walrus, a wonderfully mellifluous voice, and hardly a memorable thought in his head. Three times a week, at the barbaric hour of 8:30 A.M., all undergraduates were expected to be in place to hear Dr. Faunce spin out his platitudes, and in order that this expectation should be regularly fulfilled, student monitors were assigned to take attendance. I was lucky enough to snag one of these precious assignments. The pay for certifying the presence of twenty of my class was hardly princely—thirty dollars a semester—but an old hand at the monitoring game soon showed me how to parlay this. "A lot of the guys would like to cut chapel, but they've already used up their cuts," this lad explained. (Eight misses had been set as the limit; absenteeism beyond that point might well lead to dismissal.) "Charge 'em a dime every time you mark them present when they're not, and you'll make some smart money."

There was some grumbling when I put this system in operation—I'd already been faking the record for my fraternity brothers out of the simple goodness of my heart—but the message was clear: pay or die. I had one client, the wealthy son of a New York State Supreme Court justice, who was good for thirty cents a week *ad infinitum;* with my help he set the all-time record for chapel-skipping, a year and a half.

Carrying on this sordid record of chasing the illegal buck, I come now to the business venture of my senior year that almost led to my expulsion. Had it not been for the literary talent of Nat Weinstein, who was belatedly to be recognized as one of America's finest satiric novelists under the name of Nat West, I would have gone home in disgrace. So it is that my memory of sleepy-eyed, slow-talking Nat— inappropriately known as Pep—is bound up with my graduation.

There was, in the depths of Providence, a quite repulsive hangout called the Green Lantern Tea Room. You could buy dreadful food there, and you could bring your girl and your flask of gin and dance there, but you would have gotten nowhere by asking for a cup of orange pekoe—it wasn't that kind of place. Three of my fraternity brothers played piano, sax, and fiddle at the Green Lantern, and the owner, a woman of uncertain age, had for one of these musicians feelings hardly to be confused with those of a mother for a child. At his behest she signed me on as bouncer.

I broke up a few arguments for the lady, but it remained a second-rate job until, with the help of a pal at the Delt house, I started a sideline. My ingenious friend was a chemistry major and had a mind like a cash register. After field work along Atwells Avenue, he advised me that he could safely and almost instantly produce virtually any alcoholic beverage for four dollars and eighty cents a gallon, including the bottles and attractively printed labels. All he needed, it seemed, was water, ethyl alcohol, certain elementary flavoring agents, and a quiet place in which to combine them. Since the going rate for the stuff was three dollars a pint, it was obvious that this could be a splendid operation.

45

We went to work in the cellar of the fraternity house, and the good news quickly spread through the Green Lantern's clientele. Only the proprietor seemed to be unaware of what was going on. From her far from platonic friend on the bandstand I had learned that she was a secret drinker, and the very first night I arrived with ten assorted pints neatly packed in a suitcase, I passed a sample of our gin along. It was a favor that became a custom.

My partner never appeared at the Green Lantern. I quite understood why. He came from a respected New England banking family and naturally wished that no hint of scandal should ever touch him. (To mention his name even at this late date might be to shake— quite needlessly—the confidence of depositors.) This gifted youth, I might also make clear, did not really need the money. Though he doubtless had an instinct to acquire money for the sheer pleasure of it, he was actually bottling his elixirs as an exercise in chemistry and to do me a favor.

At the Green Lantern, in the pockets of what we then called a "tuxedo," I routinely carried four pints: one each of our Scotch, rye, bourbon, and gin. When a guest would stroll up and say casually, "Can I see you for a minute, Red?" I would suggest a retreat to the men's room. Once there, my client would state his preference, produce his cash, and a moment later be back with the crowd. One night my friend Cal witnessed one of these transactions. "If your distinguished father," he said thoughtfully, "ever knew you were peddling rotgut in the gents' room of a fleabag, he would drop dead."

My unconcerned reply was, "Why should he ever know?"

For two months my partner and I cleared a gratifying sixty dollars a week. Then the blow fell. Through a fraternity brother who clerked in the dean's office we heard that a self-righteous Brown alumnus had tattled. We were to be summoned, he told us, the following day. There followed a dreadful hour during which the chemist and the salesman tried, without success, to figure out a reasonable defense. "You'll have to make one hell of a speech," my partner said gloomily, putting the onus on me.

With the thin-lipped face of Dean Otis Randall already seeming to loom before me, I thought of Pep Weinstein, the idea man, the quick thinker. He might see a way out for us. Hurrying to his dormitory, I told him what had happened. As one of our good customers who bought at a discount, Pep got the picture at once.

"The dean has ice water in his veins," I said miserably. "We'll never be able to soften him."

"I'm not so sure," Pep said. "Here—take some notes." Handing me a pad and pencil, he began pacing. "You will start by telling Randall of the stroke your father had which has kept him from working for two years. Your sister is still in the hospital recovering from her serious operation—"

"It'll never work," I said.

"Just take the notes," Pep said coldly, continuing to pace.

An hour later I had filled the pad. It was such a heart-rending tale as I read it back to Pep that tears almost came to my eyes. The author, listening critically to his work, seemed pleased.

"Take it home and rehearse it till you've got it cold," he ordered. "And keep this in mind—you want a degree from Brown so badly that you'd lie, steal, even sell bootleg liquor to get it. It has always been your dream. Things finally got so bad at home that you had to send something to your parents every week, and that's why you risked everything by engaging in this despicable activity. And wait—here's a nice touch. Tell him that only yesterday you went to confession and told the priest all about this. He made you promise to give it up, and you agreed. Now, get the hell home and study it!"

Next morning came the expected summons. I went through my speech for the benefit of my panic-stricken partner. He was properly impressed, but also perplexed. "What's *my* excuse? Randall knows there's no privation at my house."

"If I can save myself, you'll be saved," I said, echoing what Pep had told me. "You, out of the kindness of your Baptist heart, simply lent me the money to get started."

The two most nervous college boys in Rhode Island entered the dean's office. We found him alone. Although mature judgment suggests that he was a good man doing a difficult job in a difficult time, he then impressed me as an authentic type from the works of Horatio Alger—the banker who takes delight in evicting a family on Christmas Eve.

He waved us to seats and began the ceremony with a recital of the indictment. His voice seemed to drip satisfaction, as though he relished the dual role of prosecutor and judge. It was quite a speech, covering not only our disgrace of the university and two fine families, but also, rather obscurely, the American flag. But the dean's lines, unlike mine,

47

had not been written by the man who would, within a few years, adorn American literature with *The Dream Life of Balso Snell, Miss Lonely-hearts, The Day of the Locust,* and *A Cool Million.* Closing with the expected announcement that he had no alternative but to expel us, he asked almost perfunctorily, "Have either of you anything to say for yourselves?"

My partner sadly said he had not.

"Yes, Dean, I have," I said shakily, rising to my feet. "Of course we had no idea you were going to call us in today, so naturally we are not prepared with any defense worth your attention, but if you would give me just a few minutes I would like to say—" And I launched into my tale of woe. After five minutes I knew that I had the dean hooked. Within ten I myself was almost believing the lies I was uttering, and my partner was sobbing.

On the deliberately lame note written into the script, I finished and groped for my seat. The dean looked searchingly at me but could find no guile in my well-controlled eyes. Then he took out a handkerchief and mopped his forehead. I noticed that his hands were shaking. Leaning back in his chair, he said in a strangely hollow tone, "I don't want to ruin your lives. You both have good marks and are due to graduate. I have also noticed that you have perfect chapel-attendance records. I'm going to give you one more chance."

"God bless you, Dean!" my associate murmured.

For the moment I was too overcome to speak—the first honest emotion I'd had since entering the room. When we went out of the building, feeling as convicted murderers must when reprieved at the last moment, we were too dazed to show our happiness. Our savior, who had been waiting for us, asked in some anxiety for the verdict.

"It went well," I answered humbly, "thanks to you, Pep."

That evening we solemnly closed out the operation in the Delt house cellar, with Pep as guest of honor. "Gentlemen," he said, raising a beaker of our rye, "to graduation."

We drank to that one, and I offered the next toast. "Here's to the greatest literary talent I know—Pep Weinstein."

I meant it that night as a saved twenty-two-year-old. Thinking back on all the writers I have known since then, I'm not sure that I wouldn't offer the same toast to Pep were he alive today.

In this generally sorry recital, I come once more to a legitimate job: reporting our intramural sports for the Providence *Journal*. Charlie

48

Coppen, the sports editor, liked the trial story I did for him, which dealt with an inter-fraternity contest in which my friend Calvosa made basketball history. With ten seconds to go and the score 20–20, Cal picked up a loose ball, dribbled it beautifully down the floor amid screams from the crowd and dropped it in the basket. The screams continued—Cal had used the wrong basket and won the game for our rivals. A mass expedition to Atwells Avenue, with Cal paying for the beer, was the only way he could make amends.

The story of that game, minus the sequel, earned me $2.50, and I reported for the *Journal* from then on.

During my senior year, thanks to Charlie Coppen, I secretly played professional football. Our season ended the Saturday before Thanksgiving. After our last game, Charlie phoned me at the Delt house with news that the New York Giants had had some serious injuries and were looking for a tackle and a center for their Thanksgiving Day game with the Philadelphia Yellow Jackets. "They'll pay you fifty dollars and expenses," he said, "and it'll give you the chance to go home for Thanksgiving."

I protested that I didn't want to disqualify myself from the swimming team by playing pro. "Just don't give them your right name and no one will ever know," Charlie said. "Now, who can you get to play center? Actually, he probably won't have to play. They just want a reserve in case their man gets hurt."

I thought of Bill Stevens, a mild-mannered, soft-spoken fellow Brooklynite who, like me, had been depressed about not having the price of a holiday ticket home. During his sophomore year Bill had suffered a broken shoulder, and thereafter most of his football playing had been done from the sidelines. When I proposed that he go incognito to Philadelphia with me, he was not only delighted but assured me his shoulder had mended perfectly.

The game was scheduled for 11 A.M. We arrived at the Giants' dressing room in Philadelphia an hour earlier, and the coach gave us a few terse instructions. His team used the single-wing offense we used at Brown so the signals presented no problem.

In 1923 pro football was not the highly organized game it is today. The Yellow Jackets were the exceptional team, regarded as the best in the country. In their starting lineup were eight all-American players. When the game began, Stevens and I were sitting happily on the bench, thinking of all the money we were going to collect and hoping we would remain where we were. Unfortunately, the Giants' center was injured on the kickoff, and Stevens had to go right in. This didn't bother him at all. He was a fighter at heart and once he had removed his glasses he would gladly have taken on the whole Philadelphia team himself. But it bothered me. One bad crash, I knew, and his shoulder would be a mess. Stevens hadn't played all year because of it and he was not in condition. He played the entire game on sheer guts.

I did much better. The injured tackle I was supposed to replace had regained his health and was playing brilliantly. I didn't get into the game until two minutes before the finish. Then the Giants' right end was hurt and the coach asked if I could fill in. I answered a confident yes, although once when I had played end for Brown, Yale had beaten us 45–0, with most of the scores coming around my end. As I went into the game the referee asked me my name. I grabbed at random and came up with "Eddie Burke." The referee didn't hear me. "Damn it, man," he snapped, "are you so ignorant you don't know your own name?" For some reason this annoyed me, and I snapped back "Ignorant Eddie Burke, replacing Joe Sweeney!"

The Yellow Jackets were leading by a touchdown. The Giants had the ball. Our quarterback called an off-tackle play on my side of the line, meaning I had to block out the opposing tackle. I examined him. He looked about twice my size. When Bill Stevens snapped the ball I hurled myself forward with all the energy of my 175 pounds—and bounced. The tackle then took a step to his left and casually brought down the ball-carrier right on the line of scrimmage.

I was still lying on the ground, dazed, when the tackle came over, helped me to my feet, and said mildly, "Take it easy, son, it's only a game."

That was my first meeting with all-American tackle Lou Little. As we left the field after the game he slapped me on the back and said amiably, "Nice going, boy. What's your name?"

"Please don't ask," I said. "I'm still in college and I'm here under-cover."

Lou grinned understandingly. Years later, when I was working for *Collier's* magazine and Lou was coaching at Columbia University, I helped him write a series of newspaper articles. When I reminded him of the incident, I found he had not forgotten it.

As soon as Bill Stevens and I were paid off, we headed for Brooklyn to be with our families. On the train, the battered, weary Stevens

50

looked at me out of one half-closed eye and said, "I certainly am indebted to you, Red. That was the easiest money I ever made. Think of it—fifty bucks for fifty-nine minutes' work!"

Since my hair hadn't even been mussed, barring that one collision with Little, I prudently said nothing.

At our Thanksgiving dinner table that night, after I told my story, Pop said he didn't see how I could play in a pro game without losing my intercollegiate standing.

"But I didn't really play," I said. "The fellow who played right end was some bum named Ignorant Eddie Burke."

"I don't know where you ever picked it up," Pop said, shaking his head. "Somewhere in you, I'm afraid, there is just a touch of larceny."

"Don't talk like that, Father," Mom said reproachfully. "Quentin, have some more turkey."

There were, of course, the classes. If you gave Brown half a chance, the old university could provide you with an education. The trouble was, I consistently gave Brown less than the required half. Except for my English courses, I merely went through the motions, and when, in my freshman year, I failed a horror called Integral Calculus, the scholarship I had obtained via the good Mr. Fultz was not renewed. From then on I had to work my way through. In my first year, also, I was completely disabused of the idea that I could ever become a doctor. I had about as much capacity for biology and anatomy as an ape for card tricks—perhaps less, the way apes seem to be developing these days.

On the credit side, English and I soon discovered we could get on together. Part of this I owe to our instructors, for nearly all of them were agreeable and stimulating men. One of them, Percy Marks, became during my senior year a national celebrity with the publication of his novel, *The Plastic Age*. By the standards of the day it was a hair-curler, and it immediately achieved the distinction of being banned in Boston. Marks had made it obvious that his "Sanford College," where so much drinking and wild living went on, was modeled after Brown, and one of his more startling disclosures was that girls attending Sanford dances checked their corsets in the cloak room. Since none of us barbarians knew any girls who wore corsets, there was a good deal of speculation about where and how the bachelor author had gathered his data.

Had the good-looking, well-dressed, witty Marks been a doctor, it would have been said of him, no doubt, that he had the bedside manner. As an English instructor who wanted very much to be liked by his students, he rarely flunked anyone. A case in point was Jim Kerry, a distant cousin of mine, who operated on the theory, fairly widely held in the 1920s, that you could get through college without opening a book. Better men than he had come a cropper playing that game at Brown, but for a long time he got away with it. In our final exam in poetry, one of the questions was, "What is the story of *The Rape of the Lock?*"

Sitting next to me and breathing hard, Jim Kerry whispered out the side of his mouth, "Who in hell raped the lark?"

Since Percy Marks had thoroughly dissected the poem for us only the day before, I assumed Jim was kidding. Only later did I recall that, with his eyes wide open, he usually slept through the class. In the spirit of the thing—so I thought—I whispered back, "You dope, the lark was raped by an eagle."

Jim proceeded to write a no doubt quite colorful paragraph about the big bad eagle and his evil passions. After the exam, when he thanked me warmly for the dozen answers I had given him, especially the one on the Rape, I was horrified. Coming upon that lapse, Marks would just have to fail Jim, in spite of his principles.

Percy Marks was only about ten years older than we were, and liked to think of himself as one of us. Knowing this, I waylaid him as he came out of the exam room, our papers bundled under his arm, and suggested that he join me and perhaps Roy Clayfield, Cal Calvosa, Pep Weinstein, and Sid Perelman in an end-of-term celebration on Atwells Avenue. Marks' eyes lit up at this tangible evidence of our regard for him. The boys I named were all legitimate A students in his courses. Sid Perelman, who today signs his stuff S. J. Perelman and makes an appreciable part of his living roasting such vintage chestnuts as *The Plastic Age,* was unfortunately not available for our rescue effort, but I had no trouble enlisting the others.

We led Marks to one of our hangouts, plied him with needled beer, and steered the conversation to the subject of football, knowing that Marks was quite a fan. When he asked us about the prospects for our team, he was told that everything depended on Jim Kerry as center. Understandably, Marks had no memory of Kerry as a football player.

"He hasn't played this year because of scholastic difficulties," I said, "but he's been studying hard and we're sure he'll be on the team next year."

"Except that he has his problems," Roy Clayfield interposed.

"That's right, Percy," I said. "Jim's the damnedest practical joker you ever saw. Wait till you see the one he pulled on you today."

"Pulled on me?" Marks was puzzled.

That indicated that he had not yet looked at our exams. "Let me tell you what Jim said," I went on. "He was laughing his head off. 'I'd love to see Percy's face when he reads what I wrote on *The Rape of the Lock*,' he told me. 'He'll pass out. I know that poem as well as I know "Our Father," so for the hell of it I made up an answer about an eagle raping a lark.' Now, that worried me. I told Jim you wouldn't realize he was being funny. 'Sure he'll know,' Jim insisted. 'Percy's got the keenest sense of humor of any prof at Brown.' "

Having done my best for my irresponsible cousin, I sat back to await the results. Marks thought a moment, then said, "I couldn't be responsible for our having a poor team. Probably I'll kill that answer and mark him on the rest."

At this triumphant moment it was time for another round of beer, and it was my turn. I had to confess that I was out of funds. Marks, with a great show of generosity, handed me a dollar from a roll of bills that made us all blink.

"Sure you can spare it?" I asked.

"Of course, Red," Marks said grandly. "Pay me back whenever it's convenient."

It took will power to keep my mouth shut. Although Marks' novel had not yet begun its wildfire sale, it was general knowledge that the motion picture makers were fighting for it, and that his coffers were rapidly filling. We all took a dimmer view of Marks after that episode, though it was tempered by his giving my cousin a passing grade. As for Jim himself, though he graduated with the rest of us the following year, he squeaked through without ever being able to play football. That would have been too much of a good thing.

Among my English instructors, Benjamin Crocker Clough was something else. Unlike Marks, he didn't have to court popularity, and in Clough's classes, unlike Marks', no one ever wanted to sleep. I had been taking courses in Shakespeare and nineteenth-century literature, neither of which had stirred me beyond apathy. After this it was a revelation to start with Clough and learn that there were living writers just as worthy of attention as Dickens and Thackeray; G. B. Shaw, Theodore Dreiser, Max Beerbohm, Hilaire Belloc and G. K. Chesterton among others. If there was anything that could be called a revelation during my college years it was learning that one did not have to be a snob about taste, and that Chesterton's Father Brown detective stories, for example, could be judged by the same canons one applied to supposedly more serious literature. Clough even started me reading the literary page of the New York *World,* where I first encountered the columns of Franklin P. Adams, Alexander Woollcott, and Heywood Broun.

When I took an advanced writing course with Ben Clough, my marks continued much as they had with Miss Wallace at P.S. 85. That is, Ben could do something about my way of telling a story but almost nothing about my spelling, split infinitives, and dangling participles.

One theme I wrote for Ben Clough was a spirited attack on New England, which honored such early heroes as William Bradford, Roger Williams, Cotton Mather, John Winthrop and others, but which never honored the horse Paul Revere had ridden on that historic night in 1775. Why not? What was his name?

A few days later Ben Clough told me unhappily (just as Miss Wallace had told me so many years before) that he didn't know and had been unable to find out.

"I'm sorry, Quent," Ben Clough said apologetically.

"I'll find out someday," I said determinedly.

My enduring weakness in the spelling and grammar departments led to an unhappy incident after my graduation. I had an affluent fraternity brother, a junior who was on the swimming team and who, like my cousin Jim Kerry, was barely able to hold his franchise as a student. Hearing about my A's in English, he came around at the end of the year when we were given back our themes and talked me into selling him thirty of my themes at twenty-five cents apiece—which took no great amount of talking. I assumed that he was acquiring them mainly for their ideas. Not so. A year later I ran into this cretin and learned that he had copied them word for word. Ben Clough might not have remembered the subjects, but he could never forget the spelling. He flunked the boy halfway through the course, which meant he did no more swimming.

I have been back to Brown only three times since I graduated— twice for reunions and once to receive an honorary degree. (The old joke is true: this degree plus fifteen cents will entitle me to ride on the subway.) The truth is, I went back each time to see Ben Clough. It isn't often that the years allow you to keep the same heroes you had as a youth, but I feel for Clough today the same total admiration as when I was his student.

Aside from my English courses, what I remember of my Brown experiences is my undistinguished football career. The game we played, to be sure, resembles the game seen today about as much as the horse and buggy resembles the jet airplane. Even today's Ivy League teams, hampered as they are by scholastic requirements unheard of in my time, could, I feel certain, have made the best teams of my time look silly. We were all committed to a standard offense, usually a single or double wing. The razzle-dazzle offense based on the T-formation, the gentle art of mouse-trapping (letting an opposing lineman come through unhindered so that he can be sideswiped) and the screen pass—all standard now—were unknown. We played the traditional 7-2-2 defense or occasionally, when we felt that a forward pass was inevitable, the six-man line, and we crouched inflexibly in our positions. Today, the jitterbug defense, with linemen shifting to confuse the defense, and other strategies are commonplace.

Today, too, the game is big business, calling for a tremendous organization and budget. At Brown we had three coaches, and the head man, gentle old Ed Robinson, had been on the job for twenty years. Only age finally retired him. These days, if a coach has two losing seasons, he is handed his walking papers.

But if the football we played was sometimes unimaginative, it was always exciting, and it had one great virtue that has almost been lost: on the whole it was an amateur sport. Only someone wearing blinkers could say as much of today's game—except for the Ivy League where decency is a handicap.

As a player, I was neither best nor worst, but I was accident prone. In my senior year, despite an impressive record of physical mishaps in practice, I was picked to kick off in our first game. In practice, I had booted the ball an average of forty yards. I did it again—but this time the damn ball went straight up. It was perhaps the worst kick-off in Brown's history. In addition, I put so much strength into it that a Charley horse forced me out of the game and kept me limping for two weeks.

But I had my moments later in the season—or perhaps I should

55

say that not all my accidents were unlucky. When we played Rhode Island State, a game supposed to be a breather, the field was un-adulterated mud. None of our backs could do any running, and to pass the soggy ball was out of the question. With about five minutes to go we were faced with the humiliating prospect of a scoreless tie. The ball was at mid-field—Roy Clayfield kicked. It landed on our opponent's five-yard line and dropped dead. They tried unsuccessfully to move out of the shadow of the goal post and then were forced to kick from behind the goal line. Beside me at guard, Jim Barrett, a really great player, somehow managed to keep his footing and rush into the Rhode Island backfield, where he blocked the kick. Me? I managed to lumber as far as the goal line before slipping and falling. I heard the thud of the ball as it hit Barrett's chest. Then it bounced into my arms. I was just over the line, so it counted: the first touchdown I had ever scored.

I wasn't so lucky in our game against Harvard. It was a tradition for Brown to beat Harvard—for the reason that when we played them, the week before they played Yale, they kept most of their first-string players in reserve. Two of our ends were injured early in this game that meant nothing to Harvard, and in desperation Coach Robinson put me in at end. We were then ahead by two touchdowns. We had the ball at mid-field and in the huddle Roy Clayfield asked doubtfully, "If I throw a pass, Red, do you think you can catch it?"

"If you can hit me in the belly with it, I can," I told him. And I caught it on the twenty-five-yard line. There was only one man be-tween me and the goal—the umpire. I took one step, crashed into him, and we both went to the ground—taking care of my dream of making a touchdown against Harvard.

I had a happier experience the following week when we played Dartmouth at Fenway Park in Boston. To us, this was the traditional big game, and this time we began it very much the underdogs. Coach Robinson gave us a brief pep talk before the game. A man who de-plored violence, he never resorted to the go-out-and-die-for-dear-old-Brown technique. Now, without referring to our recent bad defeat by Yale, he simply said quietly, "Boys, go out there and do the best you can. Don't forget those Dartmouth boys are just boys your own age. They are not supermen. Get out there now, and don't any of you get hurt."

When I went into the game in the third quarter we had the ball on our goal line and it was the fourth down. Roy, of course, called for

56

a punt. It went to mid-field. The Dartmouth quarterback was a good friend of mine from St. John's in Brooklyn, Eddie Dooley, all-American that year. He signaled for a fair catch. While he had never dropped a punt return before, this was his day to do it. Actually he was blinded by the sun. The ball hit his chest and bounced right into my arms. I started running and kept on running. Though I was probably the slowest man on the field, Brown players seemed to spring up around me to form a protective phalanx. At the five-yard line Dooley slipped through and tackled me so hard I bounced across the goal line to score the second and final touchdown of my life.

Dartmouth beat us 16–14, which was better than we had hoped for. The next day the Providence *Journal* ran a picture of me with the caption: RHODE ISLAND RED MAKES TOUCHDOWN AGAINST DARTMOUTH ON 50-YARD RUN. I borrowed a dollar from Calvosa and sent ten copies of the paper home.

The first two summers away from Brown I spent with my family at Greenwood Lake, where I worked at various part-time jobs. Behind the counter of Creighton's Ice Cream Shop, next to the railroad station, I was a hero to my brothers and sisters, and I'm sure that kindly Mrs. Creighton, though she never said anything about it, knew that I did not always charge them for the cones I filled.

Then for several weeks I worked as delivery boy for Mr. Miller, the baker, which meant being up before dawn in order to take a boatload of bread, pies, and cakes across the lake to one of the hotels. The stuff was still warm from the oven, and inevitably I would get into the peach tarts on the way over. After a month of this I developed a loathing for peach tarts that endures to this day.

The third summer I decided to strike out for myself again in New York. It wasn't the independence that attracted me, it was the big pay —at least big by Greenwood Lake standards. I did not land in the city cold. Pep Weinstein's father, a contractor, was building an apartment house, and had a job waiting for me as hod carrier.

Climbing a shaky ladder with a load of bricks or mortar was fun the first few times. After that it was drudgery even though the forty dollars a week seemed like riches. Theoretically, I hodded from eight to four, but I could never seem to make it from my boardinghouse on time. Pep, working as timekeeper, took care of that by always checking me in. And if I disappeared at three-thirty in the afternoon, looking for some of the finer things in life, Pep checked me out at four.

57

The foreman was a good-natured Irishman who had the proper respect for the boss's son.

Most evenings would find me, not at my boardinghouse, but at Pep's home in the Bronx, where his parents were always happy to feed and entertain their son's friends. Another regular visitor to the Weinstein household was Brown's other gift to American satiric letters, the Brooklyn-born Sid Perelman. I won't say that he was the dour type, like a lot of humorists, but he possessed a certain reserve. Quite a while passed before Pep and I realized that Sid was not coming up to the Bronx to see us. The attraction was Laura, Pep's beautiful sister. They were married soon after Sid graduated from Brown.

Six weeks of hod-carrying and I'd had it—another profession tried and found wanting. There was also the fact that the apartment house had now risen practically to the cloud zone, causing me a good deal of anxiety every time I went aloft on the dripping, wind-swept planks. Some years ago, while doing a crossword puzzle, I was delighted to learn that *acrophobia* is the term for such feelings as mine. The term somehow dignified the weakness. It causes me no trouble when I board an airplane, but I still avoid looking out of house windows when they are much above the first floor.

Of my senior year at Brown, 1924, there is little to say except that it was the easiest. My fraternity elected me Head of the House, which gave me a free room. In return for this I had to preside at our weekly meetings—solemn affairs at which I had to recite our silly century-old ritual, now mercifully forgotten. The meeting always ended with our song of brotherhood. It began "Delta Tau Delta, you are my greatest shelter," which only a New Englander could make rhyme. Such goings-on seem pretty ludicrous in retrospect, but we took them with marvelous seriousness. Our world was young.

Class Day, one of the high points of the year, occurred in the spring, and to me, quite unexpectedly, was given the honor of being the speaker. Traditionally, the speech had to be both learned and humorous—if possible, even ribald. After a dozen fruitless attempts to hit on a theme, I gave up and went once again to my friend Pep for help. For no consideration at all except our friendship—and possibly the chance to try some of his stuff on an audience—he agreed to write me a speech. He worked hard on it. In fact, when the preparation time ran out he was still reworking it, aware that he had concocted a minor masterpiece. Being then a devotee of James Joyce,

58

Pep made the speech something that the author of *Ulysses* might have sprung on a select gathering of like-minded wits over a bottle of veritable *uisgebeatha*. Obscurely off-color anecdotes succeeded one another, and a barrage of cockeyed classical allusions and educated puns clothed the central theme—if there was any.

Reading the final draft and laughing helplessly, I confessed that I couldn't understand the point, and couldn't even understand why I was laughing.

"No one else will understand it," Pep assured me, "but they'll laugh."

Class Day was big stuff—the first time we seniors wore cap and gown. I was as nervous as an elephant in a tree as I stepped to the rostrum and launched into my address. My ghostwriter had prophesied perfectly. No one really fathomed what I was saying but they hung on every word, bleating like happy sheep and frequently applauding. Only one man didn't laugh—Pep—but I noticed that he looked quite pleased at the way his stuff was going over.

Afterward, everyone congratulated me to the point of embarrassment, and Ben Clough, meeting me later in the day, said, "I didn't realize you were such a Greek and Latin man."

"I'm not," I admitted, determined that at least Ben should know the truth. Of all our professors, it seemed to me he would be the one most appreciative of the fraud and of Pep's talent. "If you stop to think of it," I said, "there's only one man on this campus who could have written that speech. You know who." Ben grinned and nodded.

When Ben next saw Pep, he offered his congratulations.

"If Red Reynolds told you I helped him with that crazy tripe," Pep said innocently, "he was kidding you. I had nothing to do with it."

That was Pep, a man I'll never stop missing.

5

In quest of a trade

The Bachelor of Philosophy degree I carried away from Brown, though I flashed it hopefully around Manhattan, opened no promising doors, nor did my Uncle Jerry when he wrote letters of introduction to the heads of several advertising agencies. These men—polite, patronizing, and formidable—all told me to come back when I'd had a couple of years' experience. They talked as if they had been reading each other's scripts.

I then ran into Ed Conklin, whom I'd known when he was a sparring partner of Young Bob Fitzsimmons. Ed was now head lifeguard at the Dreamland Swimming Pool in Newark, and when he offered me forty dollars a week to join his crew, I jumped at it. What better prospect than to swim the hot summer away and get paid for it?

The pool was huge, the swimmers legion, and a dozen times an afternoon there would come screams for help. We handled these cases on a rotation basis: whenever I plucked a waterlogged novice from the depths and carried him or her ashore to recover, I took it easy until Conklin and the other two guards had matched me. This was a pleasant routine until the manager of the pool noticed that I stayed in the shade whenever possible, clad in a long-sleeved robe and straw hat. When he finally learned why I was not constantly parading

60

around the rim of the pool looking for clients, he let me go, despite the string of rescues to my credit.

Thirty summers later, incredibly enough, this brief tour at the Dreamland Pool was to figure as evidence in my libel suit against Westbrook Pegler.

I next took on two jobs: playing with the Newark professional football team and working on the Newark *Press,* a paper into which Cornelius Vanderbilt, Jr., was sinking his money with a lavish hand. I signed on as a rewrite man, assuring the managing editor that I had done quite a bit of this work for the Providence *Journal* while I was at Brown. For three days I got away with it. Then the boss called me in.

"Don't tell me you ever were on rewrite," he said icily. "To begin with, you can't spell. Second, on the tabloid, you condense. A fight in a speakeasy on Market Street isn't worth a hundred words. You've given it a thousand."

I had to confess that I had done more reporting than rewriting, though even that was giving myself the best of it. The boss said I could stay on as a reporter if I wanted to, at a suitable reduction in salary. I wanted to very much—at least until the football season began—and so found myself attending Rotary, Kiwanis, and Lions Club luncheons where I listened to interminable speeches that had to be fine-combed for anything worth reporting.

Virtually every luncheon began with a rendition of "The Star-Spangled Banner." It soon struck me that the club men were advertising their loyalty to the nation as much as they advertised themselves by means of the name cards they flaunted on their lapels. When a man saw a stranger approaching, he would thrust out his hand with a cheerful, clipped, "Jones, Newark Bag and Twine." Grinning earnestly as he grasped the hand, the stranger would reply, "Smith, East New Jersey Slumber Suit." All the spirit seemed just that deep. During the meal the hearty song leader who had held everyone together for the National Anthem would inspire participations in such numbers as "Down by the Old Mill Stream" and "Sweet Adeline." When the tired chicken and cold peas had been bolted, and the singing finished, a man would rise and tell the toastmaster that he had a guest to introduce. "Let him introduce himself, Clarence," the toastmaster would counter happily. The guest, rising, might say, "I'm Elmer Trowbridge from Trenton. I'm with the New Jersey Telephone Company."

61

At this the toastmaster would cry out in feigned fright, "Don't tell me, Elmer, they've sent you here to collect some overdue bills! Ha Ha, Elmer, I'm only kidding. Enjoy yourself, and if there's anything any of us can do for you in Newark, you just shout." I'd look around listening to the laughter that greeted this and similar examples of wit, and wonder how such men had ever become the successes in business that most of them so obviously were. Even more depressing was the fact that every man in the room, including the waiters, was making at least three times as much money as I was.

These painful affairs had to be covered on the remote chance that some office holder might let go with a blast at the opposition party, or some reformer might take off against the men who quite openly ran Newark's well-patronized speakeasies, gambling places, and brothels. The few times something like this happened the *Press* had a story; never was it anything Gutzon Borglum might have found worth engraving on Mount Rushmore, but it was enough to justify my regular attendance.

About two months after I began my free-lunching, Mr. Vanderbilt wisely closed his dreary little paper. Happily, my severance coincided with the start of the football season. As a team, we were no better, no worse than our opponents, and since by unspoken agreement none of us played hard enough to hurt anybody, and the pay was fifty dollars a game, I passed a relatively pleasant and profitable autumn.

When the season ended and I went home, Pop, by speaking to another of his many friends, found me a job as editor at the Brooklyn *Times*. It sounds impressive even now, unless you notice the "at." All I edited, however, was the six-page contest weekly that the circulation department issued for the paper's five hundred newsboys. The only thing good about the job was that it took me into the composing room at midnight when the work was slack. Here I not only learned to like the clatter of the Linotype machines and the not unpleasant smell of fresh black ink, but began to distinguish between the various type faces and see how a newspaper column came alive on the page. When I'd leave to return to my desk in the circulation department, I used to hope that someone would notice my hands were stained with ink.

It was in the composing room that I became acquainted with one of the staff's real newspapermen. Nearly every night Jimmy Woods, a snub-nosed, dark-haired Irishman who wrote a sports column, would come up to get the proof of the page on which it would appear. One

62

night Jimmy, who came from Williamsburg, mentioned that he had gone to school at P.S. 122. He then asked if I happened to be related to the Jim Reynolds who had been the principal. From that moment I was Jimmy's friend and protégé.

A sports writer was given two tickets to the events he covered and the only restriction was No Women in the Press Box. Going along with Jimmy, I not only got to know most of the leading sports writers of the day, but fell hard for Madison Square Garden. It was then what is now called the "old" Garden—actually on Madison Square at Twenty-third Street, as it no longer is. Walking into the place from the fresh air and greenery of the square, you entered a many-scented haze of smoke that never thinned. Every event ever held there seemed to have left its trace: the sweat smell from a thousand fighters, the pungent odors of rubbing alcohol, of the ammonia used to rouse the fallen gladiators, of the astringents that closed their cuts. The circus played the Garden: its bouquet lingered on. The odors of tanbark and horses revived memories of the Buffalo Bill Show. And dominating it all were the immediate, hunger-stirring smells of peanuts roasting and frankfurters frying.

With Jimmy I saw fights, wrestling matches, and it was he who introduced me to a wacky event I had hardly been aware of before— the six-day bicycle race. Especially during the early morning hours this could become exciting, when wealthy theatrical producers, publicity-seeking actors and actresses, esteemed figures in the worlds of finance and crime, and that nebulous group identifiable merely as "well-known sportsmen" crowded in to stir the racers to action. Someone would yell "A hundred dollars for a one-mile sprint!" His money would be collected, his name taken, and the public-address system would announce the event. A gun would blast, and the nodding somnambulists would wake to career madly around the sharply banked wooden saucer. As the mile approached its climax, every spectator would be on his or her feet shouting encouragement—and every pickpocket east of Chicago would be collecting the wallets bulging in hip pockets or in coats forgotten on seats. A good light-fingered dip could average ten wallets a night, and if he got lucky, make enough during the six days to tide him through the winter till the horse tracks opened in the spring. Wallets were not the only game. There were specialists in snatching overcoats, either for what might be in the pockets, or for the garment's resale value. A Garden cop told me that he had once nabbed a thief leaving the place with eight overcoats on his skinny frame, one inside the other.

Having made me a Garden fan, Jimmy Woods badgered Len Wooster, the *Times* sports editor, into giving me an occasional assignment. For these I was paid space rates—seven dollars a column. Even though I seldom wrote anything worth more than a third of a column, I began to feel that I at last had my toe in the door. The Rotary luncheons seemed far in the past. I was now writing about what I loved.

On our way to the Garden, Jimmy and I would often eat in some restaurant where the steak could be accompanied by a glass of beer or the *osso bucco* by a glass of chianti. While the papers frequently carried grim stories about the gang wars led by Legs Diamond and Hymie Cohen, his partner in the Hotsy Totsy Club, or Dutch Schultz, Vannie Higgins, Arnold Rothstein and others, it was difficult for me to connect these practitioners of violence with the pleasant atmosphere I found in the eating places and speakeasies they supplied and controlled. Rarely did I have any personal awareness of danger, and like hundreds of thousands of others in the Prohibition era, I accepted things as they were, paid my money, and enjoyed myself.

The hangout Jimmy introduced me to that I liked the best was Joe Madden's. Not only was the food and drink good—you saw and met celebrities: fighters, managers, detectives, mob guys. Regardless of any crosscurrents among these characters, the atmosphere in the place was always strictly neutral. Joe Madden saw to that. Raised on the West Side when it was the toughest section in New York, Joe had been a prize fighter himself, and he still had the air of a man who could, if need be, back up his wishes.

One night Joe introduced me to a customer at his bar, a small, affable gentleman named Mitchell. Just who he was or what he did, Joe did not reveal, and the little man himself did not enlighten us as he and Jimmy Woods and I had a pleasant drink together. "I'll see you boys again," he said as he took his leave. Next morning the newspaper headlines told us we would not see Linkey Mitchell again. He had been found dead in a snow drift on Tenth Avenue with five bullets in him. His reward for highjacking a truckload of whisky from a competitor had overtaken him not ten minutes after he had left Madden's.

"He shouldna oughta of done that," Joe commented the next time I saw him. He was referring, of course, not to the assassin but to Linkey's poor judgment in heisting another man's booze. That wasn't done. Joe seemed to regard the action as a breach of taste, perhaps like smoking in church.

While I was having a good time in all this, my job at the *Times* did not develop. When Pop told me one day that an associate of his was looking for a night-school English teacher, I suggested myself. Mom beamed, hoping in her heart that I might yet wind up in the teaching profession. Pop, I am afraid, knew that it was only my desire to make a quick buck that led me to volunteer for the one semester.

When I went over to the Knights of Columbus Evening High School in Manhattan, the principal, Edward Bream, told me that my class would be mostly city employees who had quit high school and now needed to make up the work so they could qualify for civil service exams. I would find them, he told me, the most eager students I ever faced.

Leaving unspoken the news that I had never faced any, I told Bream I was sure I could handle the assignment as long as I did not have to teach "spelling."

"Spelling?" He looked at me in surprise. "You're teaching algebra and geometry."

Though my heart sank, I determined to give the job a try. Without even bothering to tell Bream that he and Pop had gotten their signals crossed, I took home the books he handed me and began cramming.

Then for the first time I stood in front of a class—forty-five men who had worked at their jobs all day and now wanted to work for the diplomas that would give them the chance to better themselves. The realization that they were all looking to me was frightening: I had as much right to be teaching them the relationship of the squares on the sides of a triangle as I would have had to give violin lessons to Mischa Elman. Perhaps it was the eight dollars a night that kept me from quitting after the first session, but I like to think that the challenge had something to do with it.

Mr. Bream had suggested that a good way to begin a class was to ask review questions. I quickly noticed that one man, by day the driver of a garbage truck, always raised his hand and that his answers were always correct. Now I could encourage the others to interrupt me any time they didn't get my drift. They did it frequently, and whenever I couldn't field the ball, I would say, "Suppose we ask Mr. Cross to answer that one?" Bless him, he never missed, and no one ever tumbled to the fact that I was doing as much homework as anyone.

A few days before the final exams, Phillip Stewart, the head of the department, asked if I would like to look over the tests he had prepared. Would I! I took them home and memorized them. The next evening I faced my men, determined that they were not going to suffer from my incompetence, and said, in a wild understatement, "I think I know the type of question that will be asked. Tonight and tomorrow I'm going to throw questions at you on the supposition that some quite like them may come up."

Embedded in the fifty I asked in each subject were Phil Stewart's ten. If the citizens of Athens heard a whirring sound those nights, it was doubtless caused by Pythagoras and Euclid turning in their graves.

All my men passed. Phil Stewart congratulated me, noting that he had been forced to fail nearly 10 per cent of his classes, and Mr. Bream said he would be happy to have me continue. However, I'd had it. Teaching, at least the only way I could do it, was not for me.

Next, at the goading of Sid Perelman, I became a writer of sorts. Sid, now living in Greenwich Village, had become a regular contributor to *Judge,* selling that weekly not only humorous articles but cartoons. Under his tutelage I concocted a sketch about a shopgirl named Mamie who described her adventures of the day to her roommate in pure Bronxese. The editors at *Judge* liked it and asked for more. I ground out another dozen stories about Mamie, then Sid decided it was time we made our mark on the literary scene with a novel. Convinced that it would be an easy matter, we fashioned a kind of plot about a rich young man who lived in the Village and had limited interests: speakeasies and girls. My part was to type out the rough chapters; Sid's was to clothe them with his mad humor and decorate them with this sort of introduction:

The storm at sea—In which our heroine breasts the waves and vice versa——Bertha writes Goethe a letter—Goethe writes Bertha a letter —They tear up each other's letters—Futility.

The longer haired critics, had any of them been interested, might have classified our effort as a surrealistic satire, but to us it was just good not so clean fun—something to howl with laughter at as we turned it out. Thinking back, it was I who did most of the laughing. Sid, the perfect humorist, liked his stuff, but faced it calmly.

66

A respectable publisher, Horace Liveright, astonished us both by deciding to take a chance with our little monstrosity. His one suggestion—and it was a command—was that we produce a less alarming title than the one we had selected, which was *Through the Fallopian Tubes on a Bicycle.* Under the somewhat calmer *Parlor, Bedlam, and Bath,* the book was serialized in *College Humor* before it was offered in hard covers to the discriminating readers of America, who treated it to a good deal of inattention. Some years later when Sid was in Hollywood writing scripts at Paramount, he looked up the studio's original report on our effort. It was terse: "More bedlam than parlor or bath." So far as I know, the only man who ever thought the book was funny besides us and Mr. Liveright was Groucho Marx, who once proposed to make a Marx Brothers' film of it. Cooler heads prevailed.

Sid Perelman wasn't the only literary influence at work on me during these years. His brother-in-law, whom all of us now called Nat West, had taken on what was for me a highly convenient job as night manager of a hotel his father owned. If I found myself in Manhattan late at night, instead of the long subway ride to Flatbush, I would go to the Sutton, on East Fifty-sixth Street, and be given a room and no nonsense about signing the register or paying. Besides this attractive feature, the Sutton had a swimming pool, and many a midnight when the hotel was quiet, Nat would turn over his duties to the head bellboy and we'd go swimming. After that, sitting around with something to drink, we would talk, usually about writing—Nat's and other men's. By lending me his copies of *Men Without Women* and *The Sun Also Rises,* Nat made me a Hemingway fan. And it was through Nat that I discovered Arthur Machen, a writer whose *The Hill of Dreams,* with its permeating solitude and separation from mankind, struck me as the work of a heavyweight when I first read it.

Over the months that I visited Nat he was finishing the first of his four novels, writing it during the lonely night hours. He often read me passages from the manuscript—those introducing the Trojan Horse that turned up in Balso Snell's back yard, and St. Puce, the flea who was born in the armpit of the Saviour in the manger. As the Saviour grew, so did little Puce, and when he was strong enough he went roaming, which in his old age enabled him to write a definitive work called *The Geography of Our Lord.* When Christ was crucified, Puce had long since retired to his birthplace, but a strong wind blew against the upraised arm, and Puce died of pneumonia at the same moment Christ died.

Some of this material seemed familiar to me. The night Nat read to me about Maloney, the man who, in an attempt to emulate the agony of our Lord, was crucifying himself with thumbtacks, I had it. A lot of *The Dream Life of Balso Snell* had been forecast in the Class Day speech Nat wrote for me.

When I had been out of college about four years and still had no permanent employment in sight, Pop suggested with some force that a law degree might be a handy anchor against the day when I was no longer fast enough to play professional football. Conceding his wisdom, I enrolled in night courses at Brooklyn Law School in the winter of 1928. Others in my class were my old friend Ulrich Calvosa and Irving Paul Lazar, who eventually parlayed his degree into a million dollars as a writer's agent in Hollywood. Criminal Law, I found, was my meat, but the course was considered so unimportant that only six months were devoted to it of the three years. Real Property and Corporation Law, on the other hand, had about the same attraction for me as Integral Calculus had had at Brown. By the accident of alphabetical seating, Freddie Rohlfs, another Brown classmate, was at my elbow. More than once when a professor shot a question at me, Freddie had to rattle off the answer in a low voice as I was getting to my feet. Before exams, Calvosa and Rohlfs would come to my house and spend half the night trying to make me understand that obstacle in Real Property, the Rule in Shelley's Case, or the complexities of Mc-Naughton's Rule, designed to clarify the responsibility of an insane defendant. Although my Uncle Jerry promised me that a place would be waiting for me in his firm, I often wondered if I would ever get there.

The *Times* finally gave up its newsboys' tabloid and me with it. Some months later, after a season of playing on Brooklyn's first professional football team and grinding along with my law courses, I became a reporter for the New York *Evening World*. As usual, it was because Pop knew somebody. Pop always knew somebody. In this case the city editor, Jack Rainey, was the brother of one of his principals. Equipped with a police card, I was assigned to the press room of the Municipal Building, across the street from the paper. Men from the *American,* the *Telegram,* and the *Post* were also there, and we each had a desk with typewriter and phone direct to our paper. Occa-

68

sionally some actor or mobster would apply for a marriage license, which was good for a story on page one. Such developments we would telephone to our rewrite men. The only thing we used our press room typewriters for was personal letters.

After several months of this, Rainey promoted me to swing man, which meant that I covered for other reporters when they were on vacation. This got me to City Hall, Police Headquarters, and the waterfront for ship news, but I was still nothing but a leg man, carrying a pocketful of nickels and phoning the bare facts in to the city desk and then to a rewrite man.

It is an axiom—or cliché—of the newspaper business that an aspiring reporter needs a break. Mine was handed to me—literally—by William Thomas Cosgrave, the president of the Irish Republic, and at that I had so little feeling for what made a story that I almost muffed it.

The visit of the Irish leader to New York in the spring of 1930 was an event to bring out all the city's top reporters. Even Martin Green, our senior rewrite man, left his desk to go out to Cosgrave's ship on the official welcoming boat, *Macon*. My assignment was only to pick up Cosgrave at the Battery and keep near his open car until it moved into Broadway, three blocks away. For his alleged playing of England's game, there was bitter feeling against Cosgrave among many Irish-Americans, and there was always the chance that some fanatic might lob a bomb at him. If nothing of interest happened in my three blocks, I was to return to the city room for another assignment.

With a dozen other insignificant leg men and photographers, I waited at Pier A while the *Macon* pulled in. Grover Whalen, the city's official greeter, his superb teeth gleaming in harmony with his lapel carnation, led the party off the boat. After him came the white-haired little president and his entourage. At the entrance to the pier where the limousines were waiting, we crowded close, purely out of curiosity. None of us had any intention of asking Cosgrave anything. He had already been interviewed by the real reporters. But the Irishman noticed the police cards stuck in our hats, nodded cordially, and said, "Anything you wish to ask me, gentlemen?"

We were all at a bit of a loss, standing there in the sunshine, and Grover the Magnificent was giving signs of wishing to be off for the ceremonies at City Hall. Then I noticed that the little Irishman was carrying an umbrella.

69

"This is a dry country, Mr. President," I blurted out. "You won't need that umbrella here."

He laughed much more than the stale Prohibition joke was worth and said, "Right you are, my lad. Let me present it to you."

The procession moved on, leaving me feeling rather a fool, for I certainly didn't want to throw the umbrella away and neither did I want to carry it. No one tried to assassinate Cosgrave in my assigned territory, which lack of news I dutifully telephoned in and then began walking up Broadway. Paper was still fluttering down from the office building windows. Now that Cosgrave had passed, the crowd was pushing police lines to follow him. A few blocks ahead, where the procession was nearing City Hall, the Sanitation Department Band was playing "When Irish Eyes Are Smiling." The crowd around me took it up, and everyone became, in spirit, an Irishman. I realized for the first time that Broadway could be just as provincial as Flatbush Avenue. Very few in this mob of perhaps two hundred thousand were Irish, and probably even fewer knew or cared about William Cosgrave. Further, half of the people who were cheering so wildly probably had little to cheer about, being unemployed in the wake of the Crash of 1929. "Two things only the people want—bread and circuses," Juvenal wrote long ago. Hadrian was emperor then, and he saw to it that the Roman people received some bread and many circuses. In 1930, the handsome, debonair Jimmy Walker was giving out no bread, but as mayor he could make New Yorkers forget their troubles with the modern equivalent of Roman circus: a ticker-tape parade.

When I walked into the city room, Jack Rainey was in an excellent mood. Martin Green had telephoned in a brilliant story of Cosgrave's arrival, and at the moment George Fife, another of his rewrite men, was on the phone dictating the story of how Jimmy Walker had received the Irishman on the City Hall steps. Spotting the umbrella under my arm, Rainey asked jovially if I was expecting a storm.

"Mr. Cosgrave gave it to me," I replied innocently.

Rainey's expression changed abruptly. "Mind telling me the details?" he asked gently but with unmistakable sarcasm. When he'd heard the story, he told me to write him three hundred words about it, telling it in the first person.

I sat down in front of George Fife's typewriter. It would have taken George all of five minutes. It took me twenty minutes to write three

70

or four leads—the brief summary introducing the story—none of which were good. Then I got the right one.

I handed the story to Rainey. He read it quickly, nodded, and flipped it to one of the copy readers, saying, "Put a two-column head on this and mark it for page one."

Noting my astonishment, he said, "We're a little short on page one, Quent."

I waited in a daze, and then Rainey handed me the edited story and told me to take it up to the composing room. I started for the circular iron staircase that led to the floor above. Rainey called after me, "I've put a by-line on it."

I looked at the story. Sure enough, under the two-column head I read, "By Quentin J. Reynolds." Rainey was grinning at me, as were the men at the copy desk.

I hurried up the stairs and handed the story to John Calvo, who was making up the paper. He read it, congratulated me, then said, "Why not leave off the 'J'? It makes the line too long."

Nodding, I watched John delete the initial that stood for the James I had received at confirmation but never used. I have never used it since.

From there on I began to learn how to become a real newspaperman. There came a week when Martin Green went to Albany on some political story, and another of the rewrite men, Lindsay Denison, was in Chicago interviewing Al Capone. This left the rewrite desk shorthanded, and Rainey asked me to fill in.

At first I wondered how anyone could concentrate in the steady noise of the city room, made up of the clattering teletype machines, bringing us the news from the Associated Press and United Press wires, the metallic barking of the Linotype machines in the composing room overhead, and the rumble of the presses in the basement, seven floors below us. When a boy was needed to run copy over to the city desk, twenty feet away, you had to yell for him. Once I asked George Witte if he found the noise a trial. "What noise?" he countered. It was there, and he knew it, but what was the sense of listening to it? When Rainey called "Reynolds, take it!" this meant that some leg man outside—not long ago it might have been Quentin Reynolds—was on the phone with a story. I'd put on my earphones, take notes, and then slide some paper into my typewriter. Trying to think of a lead, I learned, was the best way of forgetting not only the noise but the

71

tobacco smoke that filled the room even when the windows were open.

After my beginning stint on rewrite Rainey assigned me to cover some criminal trials. These stories I wrote in longhand on yellow sheets, and after each development the copy boy who accompanied me would hurry off with the sheets and phone the story in. When I was through for the day, I'd go to the office and look for my story, which had been put together, really, by Denison or Green or Witte. Nevertheless, the sight of my by-line never failed to thrill me.

Some nights, after an approximately eight-hour day on the job, I'd go to my law classes. Other nights I would go out to dinner with another newspaperman, John McClain, whom I'd known at Brown and who was now the *Sun*'s ship news columnist. Beginning in the Greenwich Village speaks where the drinks were cheap and credit was reasonably elastic, John and I eventually discovered that the proprietors of the gilded saloons further north—the Stork Club, Jack and Charlie's, the Park Avenue, Belle Livingston's, Texas Guinan's, and others—were often disposed to give newspapermen free drinks. Although they seemed to think they were thus buying insurance, I do not recall that any homicide or other regrettable incident occurring in their establishments was ever kept out of the papers. Regardless, John and I appreciated the deferential treatment we received from such outwardly circumspect men as Owney Madden, Bill Dwyer, and Big Frenchie de Mange.

We met the last soon after he had been kidnaped and held for ransom by Vincent Coll, known as "Mad Dog." Owney Madden had within an hour raised the $100,000 cash demanded by Coll, but the incident turned several powerful men sour on Coll. Not long afterward, he was foolish enough to make a phone call from a booth in a drug store—a confining place. A man carrying a violin case walked into the store, put the case on the soda counter, and took a submachine gun out of it. Having cut short Coll's phone conversation, he repacked his instrument, nodded to the terrified man behind the counter, and left.

Whether there was any connection between this event and the unethical kidnaping of Big Frenchie de Mange, I never learned, and so far as I could determine, the police made no effort to find Coll's executioner. Whoever did the job had granted them, and the people of New York, a favor. Some time later I interviewed Chief Medical Examiner Gonzales, who had performed the autopsy on Coll. "There wasn't enough bone left in his right arm to make a toothpick," he said thoughtfully.

With this sort of thing taking up my working and leisure time, I wonder now that I did as well as I did in my law exams. In the spring of 1930 I failed in Constitutional Law and the Law of Agency, the two easiest subjects. Poor Mom felt sick about it but gamely hid her disappointment. Determined not to disappoint her, I took the courses again in the fall, passed them easily, and entered Harold Medina's five-week night course at Columbia that was supposed to prepare me for taking my bar examination.

But while I was plugging along with law, I was also becoming a sports writer. I had already covered a few football games when Vincent Treanor, the *Evening World*'s daily sports columnist, fell ill and retired. To my amazement, I was picked to fill his place. Not only did my salary soar from forty-five to seventy-five dollars a week—suddenly, I was writing about what was most congenial to me. It didn't seem a bit incongruous to leave Professor Medina's lecture hall and hurry to Madison Square Garden for a dressing-room interview with some pug. On the contrary, I could hardly wait to get my degree so I could kiss the law good-by in style and concentrate on writing what I was already calling "my column."

One of the attractive things about sports writing was that you had elbow room. For city stories the space was always tight, and it had to be a first-class divorce scandal or murder to warrant more than 750 words. There was none of this cramping on the sports page. Because the *Evening World* was an afternoon paper, our readers already knew the scores of yesterday's games and last night's fights. I had to find the angle that would catch their interest. It was usually an interview or an analysis of why a team or fighter had won or lost. Whatever the approach, my stories assumed the facts were known and went for the human interest and color behind the scores.

As I worked along at my new assignment, discovering I had a certain knack for humanizing people in print, I again met the writers that Jimmy Woods had introduced me to: Bill Corum of the *Journal,* Westbrook Pegler of the *Post,* Tom Meany of the *Telegram,* John Kiernan of *The New York Times,* among others, all of them craftsmen to emulate as well as real sports lovers. While they were highly individualistic men, on the job they flocked together without jealousy or envy of one another, and all of them were helpful to me, the beginner in their league. In addition to the company, I liked my new hours. Writing a column, my time was my own, so long as I tossed my four typewritten pages on the sports desk before the deadline.

I at last began to feel that I was practicing a profession, not just floundering from job to job. The good feeling lasted just three weeks. One morning I walked into the city room to discover that, quite literally, my *World* had come to an end. Without warning, both the *Evening World* and *Morning World* had been sold to the Scripps-Howard chain, represented in New York by the *Telegram*. Like the other men, I was handed two weeks' pay and that was it. I found it frightening to stand in the city room without hearing the Linotype machines and presses and the cries of "Boy!" from the rewrite desk. Men were sitting around numbed. Lindsay Denison and Martin Green suddenly looked old. Jack Rainey was nowhere in sight. Feeling I couldn't take it there. I hurried to Dondero's, the *World*'s drinking oasis. Several of the sports staff were already there. Bill Abbott, the sports editor, tried to buck me up by reminding me that I had been a columnist, even if briefly. I could only nod, convinced I would never see my name on another column.

Later, that funereal day, I went to a gymnasium with John McClain and played handball till I was exhausted. After that, somehow, life didn't seem quite so hopeless. In the evening I attended Medina's lecture. Then I went home. Mom and Pop were waiting up for me. Once again I appreciated what a safe refuge my home was. Mom made me a sandwich and poured me a glass of milk.

"I'll bet I'm the only ex-*World* man who is sober right now," I told Mom. Then I said, "You've been right all along. I was meant to be a lawyer. This proves it."

"Quentin, don't you become a lawyer because of me," Mother said emphatically. "I only want you to be happy. You do what you want to do most."

"I want to be a lawyer, Mom," I said, and hurried to bed before she could see the tears in my eyes.

Several days later I had a phone call from Joe Williams, the sports editor and columnist of what was now the *World-Telegram*. He told me that the paper was taking on a handful of the men who had been thrown out of work. When I went in to see him, I found that he had read my columns and knew all about me. What he had in mind was that I should go to Florida at once and cover the Brooklyn Dodgers through their spring training, then follow them through the season.

"I'm no baseball expert," I protested, not too emphatically. Within me was a sense of excitement.

Williams replied that he had all the experts he needed. "What I want from you," he said, "is feature stuff about the players. There's a good story in every rookie who comes up. If you do this right, you'll get to know those players and their manager as if they were your brothers."

I told Williams about the crucial decision he was making me face. If I went to Florida, I would miss my bar examination. He was sympathetic but practical. "What do you want to be, a lawyer or a sports writer?" he asked. "You can't be both."

It took me all of ten seconds, then, to decide that the *World-Telegram*'s gain would be the law's loss, or vice versa. The next day I was on the train heading for Florida—having never seen a major-league baseball game, and come no nearer playing the game than playing stick ball on Jefferson Avenue.

6

On the road

Probably one of the pleasantest assignments anyone could hand a young sports writer in the depression spring of 1931 was that of covering a baseball team for a metropolitan newspaper. For one thing it meant spending the cold months in Florida. And it meant good room and board, both during the training period and when the team went traveling. It meant easy hours, since in those days games usually started at three and ended at five. Also, it meant an expense account. In most cases, this was taken care of by the ball clubs. Although outsiders sometimes argued that this arrangement corrupted the writers' integrity, I know of no club owner or manager who ever succeeded in deflecting criticism from himself or his players when the criticism was justified. Finally, the company was congenial.

Westbrook Pegler, who was then widely regarded as one of the best sports writers, had hung a label on my team that seemed to include even the president and manager, Wilbert Robinson. Across the land, thanks to Peg, the Dodgers were known as the "Daffyness Boys." When I got to Clearwater, a sleepy little town with one hotel, one movie house, and one traffic light, I found the description apt. Uncle Robbie, as he was called by many of the players, was an amiable three-hundred-pounder who seldom lost his temper and seldom imposed discipline. If his men were sober enough to deliver on the field, he didn't care much what they did after hours. The players, many of them farm boys to whom even Clearwater seemed a pretty big place, took full advantage of Robbie's tolerance.

Besides me, there were eight writers from New York papers with the team. When I confessed that I knew three strikes was out, but not much more, one of the veterans, Max Kase of the *Journal*, took me in hand. Sitting with him in the press box during practice and exhibition games, I learned the difference between a spit ball and a screw ball, the difference between a pitcher like Dazzy Vance, then perhaps the fastest right-hander in the business, and a canny hurler like Hollis Thurston, who could move the ball around and keep the batter guessing. Max explained to me how a distance hitter like Babe Herman could be made to fan or pop up. The pitcher would keep the ball low and inside, and it was then a matter of leverage; a free-swinging hitter could seldom apply his full power, and more often than not, the ball would hit the handle of his bat. Then there was Robbie's thoughtful batter, Frank "Lefty" O'Doul, who had an IQ that would have qualified him to enter M.I.T. O'Doul's vision was so phenomenal, Max told me, that he could outguess any pitcher.

Skipping the sun-drenched pastimes of the other writers—swimming, fishing, golf—I made it a point to hang around the bull pen while the coaches advised the rookies, and to listen to the athletes in the locker room. Before long I had the confidence of the players, and as the weeks passed, I did everything but hear the confessions of some of the first-year men.

Lafayette "Fresco" Thompson, as much of a brain as Lefty O'Doul, was a master of the gentle art of needling, and for a time his favorite target was Uncle Robbie. I watched him in action during an exhibition game. Hank DeBerry, not much of a runner, had hit a single. Robbie looked down the bench to where Fresco was sitting the game out.

"Thompson," he called, "go in and run for DeBerry, and try to steal second on the first pitch."

"Aw, come on, Robbie," Fresco said plaintively. "Please find someone else. I just had my shoes shined."

"Okay," Robbie said amiably, and started another man in to relieve Hank. Then the full weight of Fresco's excuse hit him. "Get in there!" he roared. "I don't give a damn if you just had your uniform pressed."

77

Fresco shook his head sadly and trotted down to first base. He stole second, stole third, and came on home when O'Doul laid down a perfect bunt to win the game. Robbie's anger was always ephemeral. As Fresco returned to the dugout Robbie yelled to the other players, "Why don't you lead-assed runners take some lessons from Tommy?" He beamed at Fresco. "That was nice work, boy."

"Yeah," Fresco drawled, "but look at my shoes. All covered with dust."

The season was half over before Robbie realized that Fresco was one of the smartest players in baseball. By then, Fresco had given up Robbie as too easy. Henceforth, he directed his verbal barbs at opposing pitchers, and became one of the best bench jockeys in the National League.

Off the field, the Daffyness Boys often provided fairly unpredictable behavior. One afternoon all the writers and seven or eight of the players went to a cocktail party given by a big real-estate owner who was convinced that our daily dispatches, datelined Clearwater, were helping his business. We were having a merry time in this citizen's large and luxurious home when one of the rookies floored me by announcing that he had loaded his pockets with four of the host's silver ash trays, two cigarette lighters, and a couple of ivory figurines. He appeared shocked that neither I nor Max Kase intended to follow his example.

When Max was unable to talk the glassy-eyed youth out of his idea of sending the trinkets home to his wife, he passed the word along to Sid Mercer of the New York *American*. Charming, white-haired Sid, who had been covering baseball for thirty years and was greatly respected by all the players, listened to the facts, then suavely drew the offender outside for a chat. Moments later, Max and I watched him return to the crowded living room and make his way around it, surreptitiously replacing his loot. Sid Mercer told us afterward that it had taken only one warning to change the lad's mind: "I told him that if he kept the stuff, I'd see that every baseball writer heard about it, and he'd end up in the Sally league where he started."

As a matter of fact, the light-fingered outfielder couldn't hit curve balls and was back in the Sally league before the season started anyway, but at least Sid Mercer had saved him from disgracing himself and the rest of us.

When I myself turned to crime, it was of a more genteel sort, done

78

to teach a golf bore a lesson. The Fort Harrison Hotel, our headquarters, also housed a lot of vacationing businessmen, and it seemed to several of us that they had far too little interest in the Dodgers. In the dining room, which was their nineteenth hole, all they could talk about was the fantastic rounds they had played. One afternoon I approached a group of these characters as they were working themselves into a state of shock with their flasks of gin. I told them that while they talked a beautiful game, I thought the hotel was full of dumb ball players, any one of whom could beat them. I was even willing to make a small bet on it.

Gleefully, a squad of the golfers followed me into the lobby. Ball players in training and on the road are notorious lobby sitters. A dozen Dodgers, tired after their day's work, were sprawled out waiting for the dinner bell. I pointed out my accomplice, Lefty O'Doul. He appeared to be asleep.

"There's a great natural athlete," I said. "I don't know if he's ever played golf, but I'll bet you a dollar a hole he can beat any of you left-handed."

One of the golfers grabbed my hand. "It's a bet, Reynolds. If he's got the time, I'll play him tomorrow morning."

At this, I shook O'Doul awake and told him the proposition. He feigned dismay, protesting that he was a ball player, not a golfer.

We met our man on the first tee at nine the next morning. The club pro had found O'Doul a set of left-handed clubs. Acknowledging that he stood little chance of winning, O'Doul told my divot destroyer that he didn't want me to take the whole burden of the wager. He, too, would bet a dollar a hole.

O'Doul's first shot landed somewhere in the Gulf Stream, and on the hole he made a horrendous nine. The mark got himself a par five, perhaps the first honest par he'd ever made, then gallantly suggested we double the bets.

On the second hole he made a six. O'Doul got himself a lucky five. On the third hole the golfer got into trouble and made a nine. O'Doul scrambled to make a pretty bad eight. From there on O'Doul managed to win each hole by a stroke. We collected quite a bit of money from the bewildered loser, and I was all for lining up another sucker to play one of the best left-handed golfers in the country. O'Doul, however, disappointed me by having an attack of conscience. I pointed out that he could afford to be moral when he was making twenty thousand a year, whereas I had simply conned a boaster out of what amounted to my week's salary. O'Doul persisted and a few days later, when we were on our way to Havana to begin the season, he informed me that he had dropped his share of the money into the sucker's mail box. I was shocked by what I regarded as a tasteless display of honesty.

Our Cuban appearances were financed by the biggest brewery in Havana, La Tropical, and since it also owned the ball field, we always had something good in the press box: four or five bottles of chilled beer beside each typewriter. There was even beer in the dugout, and Robbie, falling into the Latin swing of things, did not mind if his athletes occasionally refreshed themselves with it. We had a battery that could outdraw every jai alai game and cockfight in town—the Cuban pitcher Adolfo Luque and the catcher Al Lopez—and for the eight days we played there we had sell-out crowds.

One morning, skipping the usual breakfast of the players and writers, a double daiquiri at the Café Florida, I went into the dining room of our hotel, the Plaza, and found Uncle Robbie brooding over the Cuban team's victory of the day before. "I betta shuffle my line-up," he growled. Then he looked at me. "You been livin' with these guys, Reynolds. You give me a line-up."

It hardly seemed sporting to shake Robbie's confidence in me, so I thoughtfully put down the names. Fred Heimach, a retread from the American League, and slow as a three-toed sloth, was going to pitch, and since for a pitcher he was a pretty good hitter, I put him in the lead-off spot. Second I put Babe Herman, who was not much interested in catching balls as an outfielder but could hit a country mile. Next I put Lefty O'Doul, and in the clean-up spot Fresco Thompson, not because he was a great hitter but because I liked him so much. The rest of Robbie's undistinguished warriors I added in no special order. That afternoon the Dodgers beat the Cubans 10–1.

Robbie was most appreciative of my wisdom and for a moment had me believing I knew what I was doing. The next day he used the same line-up except that pitcher Joe Shute, whose lyric tenor I liked, was lead-off man in place of Heimach. The Dodgers lost that one 15–2 —and Robbie never again asked my advice about anything.

Our second night in Havana, the Bacardi Company, not to be outdone by the beer brewers, threw a party for us at the Hotel Soreno. Very few arms had to be twisted to get a large turnout of Dodgers and attending writers. Our hosts, serving their product well-disguised with lime juice, were both gracious and persistent, and before long several of the traveling scribes, not to mention the players, were pretty well in the bag.

The fun was interrupted when a terrific explosion echoed outside the hotel. Those of us who could still move rushed to the windows—we were on the second floor—to find out who or what had been blown to pieces. Across the street people were fleeing out of Sloppy Joe's Café, the city's best-known tourist trap. After a few minutes someone told us that a bomb had gone off in the place. Then I saw Dan Comerford, the turkey-necked ancient who took care of the Dodgers' baggage, come bounding out of the café. He waved up at us from the middle of the street, yelling: "Nobody got hoited! It exploded in the terlit!"

Though one or two nervous types wondered aloud if a similar surprise might not be ticking away in the hotel, most of our group simply reached for the next cocktail. Sid Mercer, by general agreement the cruise director of the writing contingent, presently called my attention to the fact that at least three of the men were in no condition to file stories for their papers. Since I was the youngest member and still in reasonably good shape, he suggested that I retire to my typewriter and do the noble thing.

I went back to the Plaza and turned out three articles, slugged each with the by-line of the writer I was impersonating, and hustled them off to Western Union. When this night's work was done, I suddenly realized I had to write a story of my own. Although I was weary, I knocked out something and filed it.

Next morning I received a cable from Joe Williams:

WHERE WERE YOU YESTERDAY? IN HAVANA? ALL THE OPPOSITION HAD LIVELY STORIES ABOUT BOMBING OF SLOPPY JOE'S AND BACARDI PARTY. YOUR STORY LOOKED BAD BY COMPARISON. KEEP ON THE BALL. SEND US THE LIVELY FEATURES WE WANT.

Of course there's been a great change in baseball since the year I made its acquaintance. The rookie of today, who has perhaps been paid a bonus and kept in the minor league for a couple of years, can often represent a $200,000 investment, which means he is going to lead a model life. As a result, the game now attracts men of the caliber of Vernon Law of the Pittsburgh team, a church deacon in the off

81

season, and Bobby Richardson of the Yankees, who spends his spare time talking to youngsters at Boys Clubs, YMCAs, and church gatherings. Granted, they play better baseball than we saw during the 1930s, but they aren't the colorful characters we knew.

As we left Havana on the long trip that would eventually end at Ebbets Field, I began filing stories on our special cases. One was grizzled Jack Quinn, who despite his name was a Pole. The record book said he was forty-six. Jack cannily claimed to have been born in a Pennsylvania county where the courthouse and all its records had burned. He belonged to the vanishing race of spit-ball pitchers, and he could get the low-breaking pitch across the plate with rare consistency for two or three innings. When I did a story about him in Macon, Georgia, I asked him to level with me and tell me how old he was.

"I honestly don't know," he assured me. "Besides, it isn't how old you are; it's how you can control that spit ball." I couldn't argue with Jack on that.

Another pitcher I wrote a story on was Clyde "Pea Ridge" Day, who came from Georgia. He told me that in his home town he'd been the champion hog caller. "Do me a favor," I said. "You're pitching tomorrow. When you strike a man out, give out with your hog call. It'll make a good story, and if you keep it up, you'll arrive in Brooklyn a very colorful character." And I reminded him that a colorful character was apt to make more money than a dull one.

It wasn't until the fifth inning, the next day, that Pea Ridge could sound his shrill, piercing call. My confreres in the press box all being city boys or Northerners, I was the only one who knew what it was all about. The story I sent made Joe Williams very happy. The trouble was, my hog caller didn't strike out many men, and lasted only about half the season.

Robbie himself was good copy. When we opened in Boston, I was with him in the dugout when he wrote out his line-up for the umpire. Growling that Babe Herman was getting so he couldn't hit an elephant on the ass with a banjo, he told me he was going to have to start Oscar Roettger in right field. But when it came to writing Oscar's name, he scowled and said "The hell with it. Maybe Babe will start hitting today." He couldn't spell "Roettger."

Alta "Schoolboy" Cohen was a hustling young rookie. He made his debut in Chicago when Robbie sent him in to pinch-hit in the eighth inning. The Dodgers were three runs behind. The single the kid hit seemed to spark our players, and they batted right around. It was two out with a man on first when Schoolboy got up again. To everyone's surprise, he doubled to score the man on first and win the game.

When I interviewed him in the dressing room afterward, I found him a nice, modest kid who could only say, "My mother lives in Newark. I hope she'll know what I did today."

So I wrote my overnight story in the form of a letter to Mrs. Arnold Cohen of So-and-So Orange Street, Newark, New Jersey. I told her just how well her boy had done, and what high hopes his Uncle Robbie had for him. In imagination I could already hear Joe Williams congratulating me on the homey touches. After filing it, I went to bed. At three in the morning the phone rang. It was Joe Val, the night sports editor, wanting to know where the hell my story was. He had already checked with the Western Union office in New York, and suggested I see what was wrong with the service in Chicago. I soon found out. Despite the fact that I had slugged the piece *"World Telegram,"* some helpful operator had dispatched my nine hundred words to Schoolboy's mother. Shuddering at the thought of Mrs. Cohen being awakened in the middle of the night to accept two hundred dollars worth of collect message, I put a recall on it and sent a duplicate to the right address.

That summer was one of the best I ever spent. The writing was easier than I thought it would be, and the whole experience was fun. When the team finally reached Brooklyn and I checked in at the paper, I found a basket of fan letters—the first I had ever received— waiting for me. The one that impressed me most was signed by a *World-Telegram* columnist whom I had not yet met. It read:

I am playing with the idea of writing a novel on ball players but it's been many years since I was a baseball writer. I have read your stories and the Dodgers seem a colorful group. Could you bring a couple of them up to my place for a drink (if they drink), so I can get to learn about modern-day players? I would appreciate it very much if you'd phone me.

It was signed: HEYWOOD BROUN.

The following evening, with Lefty O'Doul and center fielder Johnny Frederick in tow, I called on Heywood at his penthouse apartment on West Fifty-eighth Street. No baseball novel came out of that meeting, or out of Heywood's later meetings with other Dodgers, but for me it was the beginning of a memorable friendship.

Fourteen years older than I was, Heywood was a big, slow-moving man with a shock of unruly curly hair, a slightly crooked nose, and a disarming smile. He stood six feet three, but for all his bulk, he had narrow shoulders, and his expensive custom-tailored suits usually appeared to have been put together by an inexperienced tent maker. He may have looked untidy, with a button or two missing, and his tie off-center (Alexander Woollcott, ever ready to sacrifice a friend for a quip, once likened his appearance to that of an unmade bed), but when Heywood started talking, you forgot sartorial defects.

At the time I met him, he was probably the most admired daily columnist in the country. Having come up as a reporter, rewrite man, baseball writer, drama and literary critic, and novelist, he was writing "It Seems To Me," a title that gave him a limitless range of subject and perfectly expressed his approach. Heywood wrote as he pleased, and if his opinions on social or political or ethical issues didn't agree with those of his publishers, he couldn't have cared less.

That night in Heywood's apartment, and later when he took us to dinner at the Stork Club downstairs, we talked of little but baseball. When Johnny Frederick called Dazzy Vance the fastest right-hand pitcher he had ever seen, and added, "Dazzy could throw a cream puff through a battleship," Heywood glanced at me and nodded. This was the kind of talk he had wanted to hear. For every story Frederick or O'Doul told, Heywood came up with something from the days when he had traveled with the Giants, being paid forty dollars a week and piecing it out by playing bridge on the long train rides. His partner had usually been Christy Mathewson, whom Heywood considered the greatest pitcher he ever saw. It was out of these experiences that Heywood's novel *The Sunfield* had come.

At one point O'Doul recalled the lead of the story Heywood had written the day Babe Ruth, in a series game, had beaten the Chicago Cubs with two home runs. " 'The Ruth is mighty and must prevail,' " O'Doul quoted. Heywood was touched to find that a player had remembered his line.

A few days after our meeting, Heywood invited me to spend the week end at the home he and his wife Ruth had at North Stamford, Connecticut, and not long afterward they lent me the small guest house that was on the place. I took to living there and commuting to

Ebbets Field and my office. Mom and Pop, meeting the Brouns, were as smitten with them as I was, and one or both of them often came to North Stamford to spend week ends with me.

Saturday nights at the Brouns' were traditionally poker nights. Among the regular players were Heywood's neighbors Westbrook Pegler and Deems Taylor. Peg could be counted on to lose forty dollars. All of us were so fond of him that we made no bones about calling him the worst poker player east of the Hudson. Deems Taylor, by contrast, played with a musician's skill, as if there was some correlation between the cards and the notes he knew so well. He was apt to go home a winner. Heywood won or lost and it was all the same to him—the game was simply the excuse for stimulating comradeship.

Heywood was a contradictory personality, as I suppose we all are if one looks far enough. Tough-minded about social justice and conditions for the working man, for example, he was indifferent to his own wages and hours and was even a markedly easy touch. A slashing writer in his column, he appeared to many of his readers an agnostic; yet during the years I knew him he was groping toward his belief in God. And a man of moral courage, he might go to pieces at the thought of an airplane ride. I remember a trip I once made with him and some writers to see the 500-mile auto race at the Indianapolis Speedway. Our host was Eddie Rickenbacker, one of the Speedway's owners, and we flew out with him from New York.

Although the weather was perfect, it was soon apparent that Heywood thought he was living his last hour. "There are twelve of us on this damn thing," he grumbled at one point. "Suppose we crash and we're all killed. You know how the story will read in tomorrow's papers?—'War Hero Eddie Rickenbacker Killed in Plane Crash.' Way down at the end of the story it will say, 'Among the other victims was Heywood Broun, a newspaperman.' And ten to one they'll spell it 'Brown.' "

During that summer of 1931 I had a chance to see what a good ball team looked like. Dan Daniel, who covered the Giants, fell ill, and since the Dodgers were already out of the series race, Joe Williams sent me along on the Giants' western road trip. I was with them when they played in Pittsburgh and in Cincinnati, and I was a guest at the yearly party that manager John McGraw gave at a roadhouse in Covington, Kentucky. Traditionally, the bill of fare was bourbon and fried chicken, and traditionally this was the one night that Mc-

Graw was not a cantankerous, difficult man, but an agreeable host reminiscing about his early days with the Giants, whom he had been managing since 1902. People may have called John McGraw the Little Napoleon and things even less flattering behind his back, but it would never have occurred to anyone to call him "Uncle John." I noticed that even at his party very few called him anything but Mr. McGraw, and if his third baseman, Freddy Lindstrom, was bold enough to address him as "Mack," it was only because he was so good on the field that he could get away with it. Although the fierce-tempered John McGraw died in 1934, many baseball writers still call him the greatest of all managers. My opinion, based on this brief experience with him, is probably not worth much, but it can be put this way: Going from the Dodgers to the Giants was like going from the minor leagues to the big league.

When Dan Daniel recovered, I went back to the Dodgers. It was a hot summer at Ebbets Field, but mercifully there was a cool speakeasy two blocks away. Came the afternoon that the Chicago Cubs gave pitcher Hollis Thurston a terrible clobbering. When he left the game in the fourth inning, eight runs had been scored off him. After the game Thurston, Babe Herman, O'Doul and I retired to the speakeasy and ordered beer. The bartender shook his head. It developed that Uncle Robbie, disgusted by the long losing streak, had finally decided to invoke a bit of discipline. "He told me he'd have me closed," said the bartender, "if I ever served his players another drink."

"What players?" I demanded. "These three aren't players. The Cubs hit Thurston as if they owned him. Herman struck out twice and popped up twice. As for Lefty, the way he's been going lately, he couldn't hit the side of a barn."

"You gotta pernt there," said the bartender, reaching for some tall glasses. "But for God's sake, don't dare leave Robbie know."

All in all, it was a great year and it made me a writer. Then, early in 1932, Joe Williams called me in and gave me the bad news. The *World-Telegram* was embarking on an economy drive. I had been doing a good job, he said, and he personally felt unhappy about the arbitrary order from upstairs, which was that the last men to be hired —those who had come from the *Evening World*—were to be the first to go.

Covering baseball I had been having the time of my life. Overnight I was a bum out of a job.

86

7

Thanks to Damon Runyon

As a two-time victim of the Depression—cast adrift by the *Evening World* and now by the *World-Telegram*—I spent a miserable couple of weeks at home, blaming myself for not having taken my bar examination. Until now I had thought of the Depression as some phenomenon in the distance that caused stock brokers and margin investors to leap from high places. Suddenly, it was close around me.

Bill Corum, whom I had met a couple of years earlier at Madison Square Garden, heard of my plight and tacked this hint to the end of his column in the *Journal-American:* "A young up-and-coming newspaperman is at liberty. Some smart city editor would do well to grab him. His name is Quentin Reynolds." It was nice to read, but the phone did not ring.

Mom had her saints that she prayed to for this and that—St. Anthony if she lost something, St. Scholastica when there was a bad electrical storm, St. Clement when Pop crossed the Atlantic one vacation. I asked her if she wouldn't pray to St. Jude for me, knowing that he was the patron saint of desperate causes. Mom smiled. "You're young, you're healthy, and you've got us," she told me. "Your case isn't all that bad."

An evening or two later, as we were eating dinner, the telephone rang. I answered it. The caller announced himself as Damon Runyon. "I think I have a job for you," he began.

"Very funny!" I yelled into the phone, and hung up.

Then the beau ideal of a sports writer, a man to whom stories and legends clung, Damon Runyon was hardly likely to be phoning me. We had never even met. I naturally assumed it was some pal of mine getting off a tasteless joke.

Mom was not so sure. Telling me that none of my friends would be so cruel, she suggested that I telephone King Features, the Hearst Syndicate, and find out if Runyon had just called me.

At that moment the phone rang again. "Listen," said the voice, sounding amused, "this really *is* Damon Runyon. If you doubt it, call me back at my office and ask for me." Then Runyon told me he had heard from Heywood Broun that I was on the street. On the strength of it had recommended me to Joe Connolly, the head of the Hearst Organization's International News Service, because Connolly was looking for a rewrite man. I was to go in and talk with Connolly—and, what was more, I was to ask him for $125 a week.

When I told Runyon I had been making only $75 on the *World-Telegram,* he laughed. "Don't tell Connolly that," he said, "or you'll make a liar out of me."

I went back to the dinner table in a daze. Mom was smiling complacently, as though she'd known all along that I was to be called. "You must have prayed to St. Jude after all," I said.

"No," she said, "but I did ask St. Francis de Sales to help you." When I needed elucidation on that one, she told me that St. Francis de Sales was the patron saint of writers.

Joe Connolly, a tall, good-looking, gray-haired Irishman, afterward became one of my best friends, but the morning I met him in the Mirror Building on East Forty-fifth Street, all he symbolized was top power in the powerful Hearst organization. He told me that he needed a rewrite man who could also go out and cover city or national stories, and sports too, on occasion. "Damon thinks you can fill this job," he said. "What do you think, Reynolds?"

I passed up the chance to contradict Damon Runyon. My biggest problem, it turned out, was bluffing Connolly into paying me the salary Runyon had decided I was worth, but I managed it, and next morning I was sitting at the INS rewrite desk. With the typewriters

88

and teletypes clattering, the writers crying "Boy!," and coffee served in soggy cardboard containers, it was almost like being back on the rewrite desk at the *Evening World*.

My associates were George McGurk, Jim Kilgallen, and David Sentner, and though I had known none of them before, they all welcomed me cordially. Connolly had bragged to me about all of them, telling me there was nothing in the newspaper business they could not do—which was chiefly write a better story and get it on the wires faster than their opposite numbers in the bigger and more powerful Associated Press and United Press. My immediate boss, editor Barry Faris, a stocky, forbidding-looking man, stressed the need for me to be both fast and factually accurate. So far as INS was concerned, he said, one ability without the other would be worthless. As for the speed part of it, our stories went to twenty-seven Hearst and many non-Hearst papers. Since most of these papers also subscribed to the AP and UP, any time an INS story went on the wires even a minute later than those of our rivals, Joe Connolly would be sure to hear about it.

I soon found that I could keep up with the other men on the desk, but my old nemesis—spelling—still haunted me. One morning I saw Joe Connolly walk into Barry Faris' glass-walled cubicle adjoining the rewrite desk. The place, for the moment, was quiet, and I heard him ask Faris how I was doing.

We wrote all our stories with carbons. The original went to the copy desk to be edited and immediately put on the teletype to our papers; a carbon copy went to Barry Faris. I saw Faris hand Connolly the Bonus Marchers' story I had just written under Jim Kilgallen's byline. Jim was in Washington covering the marchers and phoning in his spot news stories. "He's fast, and he can write," I heard Faris say, "but dammit, he can't spell!"

Connolly finished reading the story and dropped it back on Faris' desk. "Maybe you can hire one of these Ph.D.s to spell for him," he said. "They come cheap."

Hearing that, I breathed easier.

The Chief, as William Randolph Hearst was always called, apparently took pride in the objectivity of INS. Although he aired his personal opinions freely in his newspapers, he left us strictly alone. "We have only two sacred cows here," slow-talking George McGurk told me the morning I took my place at the desk. "God and Marion

Davies. Never rap either one of them." But since neither one appeared in our stories, this could hardly be called slanting the news.

I wrote news and features, and sport stories, and rewrite, and then came a big story—one of the biggest—taxing the facilities and manpower of INS. The night of March 1, 1932, I was home in bed with grippe when Pop shook me awake to answer the phone. "It's your boss and he says it's very important," Pop told me. "He's calling from the office."

Since it was the first time Barry had ever called me at home, I hurried to the phone wondering what I had done wrong.

"The Lindberghs' baby has been kidnaped," Barry told me. "Get down to Hopewell, New Jersey. George McGurk will meet you at Penn Station. Your train goes at eleven. When you get there, tie up a phone, whatever it costs."

With my portable typewriter, a bag of clothes, and a supply of aspirin, I made it to the station just in time. George met me at the gate with a ticket and expense money. Going with us was Dorothy Ducas, an INS reporter. Dorothy was versatile. She could write a sob story about the wife and children of a murdered gangster so that it produced the well-known lump in the throat, but she could also write a hard, fast news story devoid of sentiment. She was an attractive girl, but no one around INS ever patronized her by referring to her as a "woman" reporter.

The three of us left the train at Trenton and went the next twenty-five miles by cab. Normally, Hopewell would have been a sleepy little town, with one hotel, a modest telephone building, and a hole-in-the-wall Western Union office. The main street, when we got there at 1 A.M., was ablaze with lights, and at least a hundred reporters and photographers were milling around in the chilly night. Within a few hours, there would be another hundred. Everyone spoke in hushed tones, as if sensing that this would be no ordinary crime story. While the press had often in the past been antagonized by Lindbergh's rudeness to it, the feeling was now all one of shock and sympathy.

By the time we arrived, the AP and UP representatives permanently assigned to the state capitol at Trenton had tied up the hotel's switchboard and the two public phones at the telephone office. Although the company was already setting extra lines for us, and Western Union was setting up emergency equipment, it would be hours before additional facilities were available. Leslie Randall, the New York representative of the London *Daily Express,* showed us something in the way of initiative by persuading one of the girls at the phone office to let him call London on her office phone. Once he got his paper, he insisted that the phone connection be maintained, claiming that he had not finished dictating his story. Somehow, he talked the phone company into believing that this was one of its own rules, and so for the cost of some $300 an hour, he had an indefinite call to his paper.

In her own way, Dorothy Ducas did as well for INS. While George McGurk and I were finding out the little that was known about the crime, Dorothy went fluttering her eyelashes at various Hopewell citizens. Presently, she drew me out of Paul Gebhardt's general store, which had become headquarters for the press, and took me a block away to meet Mr. and Mrs. Stanley Smith. The Smiths looked upon us as if we were creatures from another world. "This girl gave me fifty dollars so she and you could use our telephone," Mr. Smith said in awe. "That's more than I make in a week."

A few minutes later, having received an additional twenty-five, he handed me a key to his front door so that I could get to the phone at any hour. I then called Barry Faris, and told him what little was known, which was enough to give our early editions a story. Jim Kilgallen, on the rewrite desk, took down what I told him, which was that the kidnaper's ladder had been sent to the state police laboratory for analysis, that the nursery was being examined for fingerprints, and that the police were questioning the Lindberghs' servants as well as looking up all the cooks, butlers, and nurses who had previously worked for the family.

Jim had a suspicious nature. "Where'd you get all this stuff?" he demanded. "You've only been down there half an hour."

"It's routine," I told him. "What else would the cops be doing?"

"Right you are," Jim conceded. "I'll use it for my lead."

Along with the telephones, our competitors had tied up the two taxis in town, but the obliging Mr. Smith owned an automobile, and he and I were soon on the road. A hundred yards from the Lindberghs' secluded home we were stopped by state troopers, and I joined a group of thirty other balked reporters. Ahead of us we could see the large house ablaze with lights. Someone told me that Colonel Schwarzkopf, of the state police, had just sent the ladder to Trenton for investigation and was now questioning the servants. I felt relieved that the story I had given Jim was not fiction after all. When I learned, further,

91

that all announcements from the family or the police would come from Trenton, I had my chauffeur take me back to my telephone.

Big as the story was, days passed with little developing except rumors. George McGurk, who moved to Trenton to cover the official announcements, came up with a story that we thought might break the case. The Jersey City police had nabbed a man who was driving his car with two quart bottles of milk beside him on the front seat. When he wouldn't give an explanation for the milk, they began to work on him. He finally confessed that he was on a milk diet for his gonorrhea. A phone call to his doctor confirmed it.

One night I walked into Gebhardt's general store to find a heavily bearded, shabbily dressed old man ordering a list of provisions. My ears pricked up as I heard him ask what was going on in town. Paul Gebhardt asked the man where he had been, that he didn't know of the kidnaping. Trapping back in the mountains, said the old codger, and he'd just come back to town. "Funny thing," he went on, "I was near the Lindbergh place that night on my way out of town, and I seen a strange car headin' for the house. I figgered it was someone goin' there to paint the house 'cause there was a ladder tied to his car."

My hands turned clammy. Could this be the break we had all been looking for? I was the only reporter in the store.

The trapper now had a coughing spell, after which he mentioned that he certainly could use a drink.

I intercepted him at the door, told him I couldn't help overhearing his conversation, and thought I knew where he might find a tumbler of good old Jersey applejack. I then led him to the Smiths' living room, where I had a half gallon of the stuff among my effects, poured him a drink, told him I was a New York newspaper reporter, and poured him another.

Lemuel Dixen—this was his name—became quite talkative. He described the back road on which he had seen the mysterious car, and he gave me a reasonable time for the event, around eight in the evening. He now recalled that the car had carried a New York license plate. Dorothy Ducas had drawn a map of the region, and sure enough the road the old trapper described was on it. Lem had no objections to my reporting his story, told me he'd sure like to see his name in the newspapers, but said emphatically he would not tell the police what he had told me. "I won't have no truck with the police," he said. "I just don't like 'em."

92

With the rest of my half gallon under his arm, Lem departed. I wrote my story. Ordinarily, I would have checked with the police about it, but news was so scarce that I couldn't resist hurrying it to the office. After filing it at Western Union I met a UP man in the drugstore who said he'd noticed me walking with old Lem. "He try to sell you that yarn about that man with the ladder on his car?" he asked. "Yesterday he got a drink out of me with it," he went on. "Then I found out he's no trapper—only the town drunk. The night of March first he went to a wedding at a farm, and by eight o'clock he was so stiff they threw him in a barn to sleep it off."

Having been let down, I returned to the Western Union office. A message from Barry Faris was waiting for me:

FINE STORY ABOUT LEM THE TRAPPER. IS IT EXCLUSIVE? LET ME KNOW SOONEST.

This presented me with a problem. If I said it was exclusive, Barry would copyright it, and no paper except those serviced by INS would be able to use it without giving us credit. But a copyright would indicate that the story was authentic. Other reporters who had listened to Lem would file conflicting stories. I sent Barry my answer:

STORY IS NOT ONLY ONE HUNDRED PER CENT EXCLUSIVE BUT ONE HUNDRED PER CENT PHONY.

Then I walked back to the Smiths' house, telephoned Barry, and told him the details. He liked it anyway, as the story of a city slicker being taken in by a hill-billy, and the next morning the New York *Journal* used it on page one. I took a certain amount of ribbing for it, but at least got some good out of a story that might have been the blunder of the year.

Several times during the next week I went out to the Lindbergh home ever hopeful that I might stumble onto something that would give Barry the big story he wanted. We were never allowed close to the place, but late one night when a driving rain swept over, I saw a light go on in what I knew was the kitchen. A few moments later the outside door opened, and there, silhouetted against the light, was the petite form of Mrs. Lindbergh. I saw her beckon to someone. The sergeant and two of the police guards followed her into the kitchen. Presently they reappeared, and then three more of the guards went inside.

I managed to get the sergeant's attention. He told me what was going on. Mrs. Lindbergh was serving coffee and sandwiches. "She's quite a woman," he said. "She doesn't even complain about the mess our boots and dripping clothes make on her kitchen floor."

The second week, as excitement faded, a string man was hired to cover INS in Hopewell, and Dorothy Ducas and I followed George McGurk to Trenton. Even here the news was scarce, so Dorothy and George were called back to New York, leaving me to make such stories as I could with the police announcements.

Only one reporter in Trenton seemed to be coming up every day with a news story. The rest of us were mystified about his source until a group of us happened to meet him and a girl one night in a Trenton speakeasy. We were puzzled. This colleague was not known to work his charms on any but the fairest, and his Trenton belle certainly did not qualify.

Then someone in our group asked her what kind of work she did, and before her escort could stop her she blurted out, "I work for the phone company."

Sid Boehm of the New York *Journal* turned on the reporter. "I suppose if she happens to get a call to or from the Lindbergh home she listens and tells you all about it?"

The man tried to deny it. None of us were really angry at him. We respected him for his ingenuity and we also sympathized with him for the price he had to pay.

One morning Barry notified me that there was no longer any point to my staying on in Trenton as far as the Lindbergh story was concerned. However, since there was to be an execution at the state prison that night, I would cover that before returning.

While I had never witnessed an execution before, and did not look forward to it, when I looked into the condemned man's story, I was at least sure I would not be troubled by any sympathy for him. He had brutally murdered his young pregnant mistress, then driven her body all the way to South Carolina to conceal it in a swamp.

Several hours before the execution was to take place, the reporters who were to cover it went to the prison warden's office for a briefing. We were told the items the doomed man had requested for his last meal. We were given the names of the three guards who would walk with him from his cell, and of the attending priest and physician. We were told the number of volts that executioner Robert Elliott would send through the condemned.

The casual way in which all this was announced gave me a moderate shaking, and when I went back to my hotel with my notes it occurred to me that I should write my story ahead of the event, instead of later when I might be under some emotional strain. Sitting at my typewriter, I knocked out 750 words that seemed not bad. I was especially pleased with my lead: "Harry Andrews, convicted slayer of his mistress, walked into the death chamber of Trenton Prison at nine this evening and sat down in the only unoccupied chair in the room."

With the story in my pocket, I returned to the warden's office at the appointed time, eight-thirty. I looked around at my dozen colleagues. While most of them looked outwardly calm, as though waiting to cover a hockey game or a horse show, I noticed that quite a few of them were sampling flasks of applejack. The warden himself, Colonel Mark Kimberling, was very subdued. At eight forty-five he led us into the death chamber. We had been told that once in the chamber, no one would be permitted to leave until the business was finished. Purposely, I entered last, expecting I would take a rear seat. To my dismay, the rear seats were filled. The only one left was in the front row, only about twelve feet from the chair. I hoped I would not become sick.

The wait for the main character in this drama of death seemed interminable. Then, at one minute to nine, Robert Elliott appeared and took his place at the switch. "Please remain quiet, everyone," a guard said. Needlessly—no one was saying a word.

Then a small door opened and the cassocked priest appeared, chanting in Latin, "Depart, O Christian soul, out of this sinful world." Behind him came Andrews, a frail but not unattractive-looking man. He wore a small mustache and was smoking a cigarette. The three guards made no attempt to support him. Obviously they felt that this was a man who could make it on his own. Andrews stopped in front of the chair and looked at us. He smiled faintly. I felt that he might be saying to himself, "I hope I'll put on a good show for you boys."

Then he saw the warden. He took one more deep pull on his cigarette, dropped it to the floor, stepped on it, and said, "OK, Colonel, let's go."

He sat down in the chair. The guards secured the straps and electrodes. They placed the black hood over his head, stepped back, nodded. Robert Elliott closed the switch. I heard a buzzing. Andrews' body strained against the straps. Elliott released the current for a few seconds, then sent a second charge through Andrews. I saw a curl of smoke rise. The chamber filled with the odor of burning flesh and hair.

Then Doctor Gerold Eiber stepped forward and put his stethoscope to Andrews' heart. "I pronounce this man dead," he said quietly.

The guards removed the straps. The body slumped forward. The guards lifted it onto a stretcher and wheeled it out of sight through the same door the living man had entered a few moments before.

We witnesses went out a door that led us to the prison yard and fresh air—and none too soon. The performance I had seen left me nauseated and horrified, and also convinced that the commandment "Thou shalt not kill" did not exempt the state. No matter what Andrews had done in his moment of mental aberration, it seemed to me no less a crime that society, with premeditation and "justice" had deliberately and callously killed a human being. Years later I was to see civilians die in the London Blitz, and soldiers die on many fronts, but I cannot remember that the sight of any death in war, no matter how tragic, filled me with the kind of revulsion I experienced in watching this ritual execution of a worthless criminal in the name of the law.

One of the other reporters, who had covered executions before, assured me that he and I were just spectators watching the sentence of the court being carried out. I couldn't buy that. I felt as guilty as, in my opinion, society was for killing the man. Reading over the story I had written earlier, I felt thoroughly ashamed—especially of its facetious lead. I sat down at one of the Western Union typewriters and wrote a new and wholly factual piece. At the end I added a memo to Barry Faris. "If you ever assign me to another execution, I'll quit."

For me, the Lindbergh case had another chapter before the tragic discovery of the baby's body on May 12. Soon after the case began, newspaper offices everywhere, but especially in New York, began to receive tips—usually anonymous and more or less fantastic—as to who the kidnaper was and where the baby was hidden. When William Randolph Hearst posted a reward for anyone furnishing information that would lead to the child's safe return, INS became a heavy receiver of these tips. On the slim chance that one of them might

96

lead to something, practically every one of them had to be checked.

When someone in Detroit wrote a rational-sounding claim that he had evidence that his city's Purple Gang was holding the baby, Jim Kilgallen packed his bag and took off to keep the street-corner appointment.

Another man, who signed his name and gave a telephone number, told Joe Connolly that three men who were holding the baby in Massachusetts had approached him to be their intermediary. If INS would pay the ransom, he would lead anyone Connolly designated to where the child was being held. Connolly telephoned the man, Daniel Wilson, and asked him to come into the office. He was a small, soft-spoken, neat-looking fellow of about thirty-five who said he had once been a rumrunner. His story was that three of his old-time associates had kidnaped the baby and were keeping him on a boat. The wife of one of the men had once been a nurse; she was taking good care of the child. The ransom arrangement was simple. Mr. Hearst was to deposit one hundred thousand dollars in a Boston bank. After the baby and the Hearst representative were brought together, Wilson would go to the bank with a letter authorizing the withdrawal of the the money. As soon as Wilson returned with the money, the Hearst representative and the baby would be allowed to leave the boat.

Connolly, Faris, and I were at first impressed by Wilson's seeming candor, but Connolly soon spotted the flaw in the plan. "Suppose I sent Reynolds with you. What's to keep the three men from taking the letter from him and sending you to the bank to collect? They might not even have the baby. You would show up at the bank, grab the money, and the four of you would disappear."

"This is no hoax," Wilson said calmly. "Your man will have pictures of the baby with him. When he sees the baby on the boat and is satisfied that it is the Lindbergh baby, he will be taken ashore. There he will telephone you and give his report. When you are satisfied, you will telephone the bank and notify them that I will be picking up the money."

Barry Faris raised another point. "What makes you think we won't turn you over to the police or the FBI right now, or at least give them all this information?"

"Colonel Lindbergh and Mr. Hearst have announced that they are only interested in getting the baby back safely," Wilson replied coolly. "If you report this, you will be jeopardizing his life. Besides, I don't know exactly where the baby is. I am to call the others at three tomorrow from Boston, tell them the coast is clear, and learn exactly where the boat will be moored."

The man had an answer for everything. The three of us already knew that Jim Kilgallen was on his way home from his fruitless quest in Detroit. "It looks as if you're going to Boston, Quent," Connolly said to me.

Mr. Wilson promised to return early the following morning, shook hands all around, and left.

"He's a fake," Barry Faris declared. "We'll never see him again. He's had his little hour of excitement right here in this office."

Conceding that it was a hundred-to-one shot, Connolly began making the necessary preparations. "If it's true, we would never forgive ourselves for not believing him," he reasoned. "If it's a hoax, all we'll be out is a couple of hundred in expenses."

Barry was considerably more optimistic next morning when Daniel Wilson reappeared, carrying an overnight bag.

Joe Connolly had a last word of warning to the dapper little man: "You understand that as soon as the baby is returned, I will immediately turn over all the information you've given us to the police, including your name?"

"That's all right with me," Wilson said cheerfully. "I'm not an accomplice in this crime. I'm just the go-between."

With that, he and I took the train to Boston. The night before, noting my preoccupation, Mom had asked me if something special was going on at INS. For fear she might worry about me if she knew what I was about to get into, I had simply told her that a development in the case might take me out of town for another night or two. If I brought the Lindbergh baby back to New York, she would know the truth soon enough, for I would be sitting on top of what might be the greatest exclusive story of my time. (For those who may wonder why I don't say "scoop," the answer is that I have never heard a newspaperman use that word, which seems to be the exclusive property of novelists and playwrights.)

Wilson read a magazine most of the way to Boston, and I made no effort to question him. When we reached our double room at the Somerset Hotel, for the first time he seemed a little nervous. "I could sure go for a drink," he said. "Did Mr. Connolly give you enough to take care of a bottle of Scotch?"

I told him I would buy him a bottle if he didn't mind drinking alone. If this show proved real, I was going to need all my wits.

The bell captain would not take my money until I produced my police card, which showed that I was a reporter, not a federal agent. He soon returned with a quart of White Horse, and Wilson calmed himself with a couple of straight shots.

As three o'clock approached, saying our room phone might be tapped, Wilson went down to the lobby to make his contact call from a pay phone. In ten minutes he was back, his eyes shining with excitement. "Everything's OK. I talked to the boss and he wants us to come right down."

"If they're on a boat, how could you telephone him?" I asked.

"The boat's anchored off a dock. He came in at the agreed time and I telephoned him at a diner that's near there."

I had already rented a drive-yourself car. Wilson directed me south. When he were out of the city, he produced a road map. He told me we were going to Cape Cod. "Take your time," he said. "We're not due at the dock till eight o'clock."

A nasty rain began slanting against the windshield. Wilson keeping us on course with his map, we drove onto the Cape. The summer season had not yet begun and the roads were nearly deserted. As I made the turns, I saw we were heading for Hyannis.

Beyond the town, in the wind and rain, we came to a deserted dock. It was nearly dark. The ocean was lashing the shore.

"She's anchored right out there," Wilson said, pointing into the roaring gloom.

Though I could see nothing, I'll admit my heart was thumping. "Where are their lights?" I asked.

"They wouldn't show no lights," he assured me. "Just wait. They'll be here in a dinghy to pick us up at eight o'clock."

We waited, shivering, till eight. Then till eight-thirty.

"Where's that diner?" I asked. "I could use a cup of hot coffee."

"What diner?" Wilson said.

I looked at him. "The diner where you phoned the boss."

"Oh, yeah, that one," he said. "It closes at eight."

We waited another hour. Then Wilson said, "I guess something musta scared them away. We'll go back to Boston and call 'em again tomorrow. Or maybe they'll get in touch with me. They know we're at the Somerset."

I began the long drive back to Boston. My vision of casually accepting the Pulitzer prize for breaking the biggest of all stories was waning.

"We shoulda brought that bottle of Scotch with us," Wilson said through chattering teeth.

When we reached the hotel at two in the morning, he had about six shots and became incoherent. Then he collapsed in his bed and began snoring.

I put in a call to New York, told Barry what had happened, and said that I thought we were being had. "I guess none of us were really sold on him," Barry said. "Call me in the morning if anything more happens."

A couple of hours after I had fallen lightly asleep, I woke to hear Wilson stumbling around the room. I was not exactly astonished to see him heading for the chair over which I had hung my coat. As soon as I felt sure that his hands were in its pockets, I snapped on the lamp by my bed. He straightened up from my coat with a jerk and a gasp.

I ran my hand beneath my pillow, where I had sensibly put my wallet. "If you're looking for my gun," I said, "I've got my hand on it." If I didn't sound exactly nonchalant, I was at least under better control than Wilson was. He tried to convince me that he had been looking for my watch to see what time it was.

"You're just a lousy con man," I said in disgust. "This whole thing is a fake, isn't it?"

He admitted it, protesting that he had meant no harm to anyone.

"Go on back to bed," I told him sharply. "No, wait," I said. "Pick up that bottle and let me see you finish it."

Wilson gurgled off the rest of the liquor and was soon snoring again. It was now my turn to prowl. I found not a single thing in his clothes that would tell me anything about him.

Calling Barry again, waking him from a catnap at his desk, I told him the latest. "Shall I turn him over to the police?" I asked.

"The hell with it," Barry declared. "Come on home."

I took a shower, dressed, and left the comatose swindler a note telling him what I thought of him. To sweeten it a little, I also left him a ten-dollar bill.

100

8

The midget on Morgan's lap

Though I saw him play only one game, it was baseball's great Ty Cobb who started me on a career of sorts as a short-story writer. In 1932, when he was just running out his string, I happened to be in Philadelphia doing a story for INS. Cobb was playing for the Athletics then, and I took the afternoon off to sit in the press box and watch him in action against the Yankees. Cobb was playing from memory but he got three hits and stole a base to put the last-place Philadelphia team ahead by a run. In the ninth, with two Yanks on base and two out, a fly ball was hit to Cobb. It should have been an easy out, but Cobb couldn't quite get to it. The ball hit his glove, bounced out, and both Yanks scored. The crowd laughed. They laughed at Cobb, probably the most talented ball player ever to pull on cleats. I felt sick. So did the others in the press box.

The *World-Telegram*'s Tom Meany grabbed my arm and said angrily, "That's like laughing at God!" Then he thought it over. "Ty's over forty, and I guess there's the answer," he said. "Legs last just so long."

I returned to New York haunted by the picture of the mob laughing at Ty Cobb. During a dull hour at the rewrite desk, I rolled a sheet of paper into my typewriter and began to put down my feelings about an aging baseball star. As I wrote, my feelings were his; I knew the damage that laughter would have done to me. After a while what was coming out of the typewriter began to look less like an article than a short story. I did a second draft, gave it the title Meany had handed me—"Legs Last Just So Long"—and mailed it off to a pulp magazine. It promptly came back to me. After it bounced another three or four times, I took the hint and tossed it in a drawer.

That fall Barry Faris sent me to Chicago to cover the Notre Dame–Northwestern football game. On the train I ran into Bill Corum, and he introduced me to Grantland Rice and then to a young-looking, well-dressed, pleasant man named Charles Colebaugh. Like Corum, Rice had a madly overdeveloped instinct for friendship, and he instantly regarded me as someone he'd known for years. At that time he was the most widely syndicated sports writer in the country, and I found his interest in me quite flattering.

Colebaugh was a less demonstrative type. I learned that he was the managing editor of *Collier's* weekly.

In the club car Rice began grumbling to Colebaugh about his work load. "I'm doing my daily column and then grinding out a weekly piece for you. I love you, Charley, but I need more time at the race track. When I quit you, why don't you give my job to this fellow Reynolds?"

Colebaugh, who was the politest man since Lord Chesterfield, smiled and said, "Granny, you know we would give consideration to any man you recommended."

This was all Bill Corum needed. "Let me tell you about Reynolds, Charley. He does rewrite, features, news stories, sports stories, and I'll be damned if he doesn't even write fiction."

I felt like a fool. Bill knew as well as I knew—because I had told him so—that my one attempt at a short story had taken the count.

When Colebaugh amiably invited me to send him some of my work, I confessed that my only story had already been rejected several times. He suggested that I let him see it anyway, pointing out that *Collier's* might like what a pulp magazine would not—a story that went in for character development as well as action.

On my return to New York, still wondering if Colebaugh hadn't exceeded the demands of politeness in asking to see it, I sent him my story. The next day he telephoned me at work. "Very good, Reynolds. Just as I hoped, you made your man believable. We're taking it, and if you can do more as good, we'll want them too."

While I gripped the phone to keep from dropping it, Colebaugh went on: "I'm putting a check for seven hundred and fifty dollars into the mail for you."

I managed to stammer my thanks and get the phone back on the hook, but for the rest of the day I was no good. What really gave me a chill was to realize I might have taken a different train to Chicago and thus not met Colebaugh.

During the next ten years I sold *Collier's* perhaps forty short stories. Ty Cobb, the man who started me, remained my baseball idol until the night in the late 1950s when I was finally introduced to him. He had attended one of the annual New York Baseball Writers' dinners. When the affair was over, he and several dozen other present and former players, managers, team owners, and writers retired to Toots Shor's saloon on West Fifty-first Street. Every year that was the night that Toots never closed, and anyone who tried to pick up a check would get his wrist broken.

It was Joe DiMaggio who introduced me to Cobb, and I'll admit that for some moments I just stared at him in awe. Cobb was in a good mood and was even gracious enough to say that he had read some of my books. I replied by telling him how he had inspired me to start writing short stories. I reminded him of the day in Philadelphia when he dropped the fly ball. It was the wrong thing to do.

"You lousy bastard," he spat at me, "I never dropped a fly ball in my life!"

Toots and DiMaggio moved quickly between us. They knew Cobb.

I saw him around a few times after that, and found him to be a weird, filthy-mouthed, tight-fisted drunk. Ball players of his era, I discovered, respected him as a player, but they despised him as a cruel and humorless man. When he died in 1961 it was reported that he left an estate of twelve million dollars. Not publicized was the fact that the nurse who found him dead in his hospital bed found a million dollars' worth of negotiable securities and a Luger pistol in his bed. He was trying his best to take it with him. While baseball people are notoriously sentimental and loyal, only three of them attended his funeral.

But I can never write Cobb off. He dropped that ball and gave me a real break.

My next break was given me by a dawdling waiter.

Down the block from INS was Gus and Eddie's, our favorite tavern.

One day early in 1933, after lunching there, Barry Faris, Jim Kilgallen, and I played poker dice for the check. I lost. That much was easy. The harder trick was catching our waiter's eye. "Waiter!" said I, but apparently he was dreaming sweet dreams.

"The poor guy doesn't know English," I remarked. "I'll try another flavor." Then I rapped out, *"Herr Ober, die Rechnung bitte!"* The man snapped to attention, clicked his heels, and came running.

It seemed to me that Barry was unusually quiet as we walked back to the office. An hour or so later I saw Joe Connolly go into Barry's cubicle. They talked for a minute, then called me in. "Barry tells me you speak German," Connolly said.

I laughed. "Doesn't everybody?"

"The point is," said Barry, "our feature writer in Berlin has offended Hitler's press director and got himself kicked out of the country. We hired him from the UP over there, and because we don't know him, we couldn't go to bat for him. We want you to take his place. Then, if you get in trouble, we can back you up."

"Me?" I croaked. "All I talk is saloon German. I can order *Kartoffelpuffer* and recite 'The Lorelei,' but that's about it."

Connolly shook his head at me as though I were a babbling child. "You'll find," he said, "that it's an easy language to pick up."

Five days later I was on my way to Berlin. At first I had been excited at the prospect, but as I got closer to European shores, I had the feeling that INS might be putting its money on the wrong horse. While I had not lied to Connolly about my command of German, he had mistakenly thought my protest to be false modesty. More to the point, I knew little about Germany or Hitler's rise to power. He had made himself the absolute ruler of his country, and he was stirring up feeling against the Jews; this much I knew because everybody knew it, but I had no special grasp of current events, of the sort that was making *The New York Times*' correspondent Walter Duranty, for instance, a glamorous figure in Moscow. I had bluffed my way through my first weeks with the Dodgers, but baseball, after all, was a game for boys. Bluffing in Berlin, one of the world's news centers, struck me as a dim possibility.

In addition to these doubts, I wondered about the awkward situation I might find myself in relation to Hudson Hawley, the man who ran the INS bureau in Berlin and reported the routine news. I was being sent to write the features and big news, and Barry had notified

104

Hawley to this effect, telling him that I would actually be working for, and responsible to, the New York office. However, the more I thought about it, the more it seemed to me that Hawley, a veteran Press Association reporter who had worked previously in London and Paris, wouldn't be human if he didn't resent my intrusion.

On my arrival in Berlin I went to the Adlon, then one of the most luxurious hotels in Europe, where a room had been reserved for me. I was hardly in it before the phone rang. It was Hawley, warmly welcoming me and telling me that he had arranged a dinner party for that night so that I might meet some of the other Berlin correspondents.

A couple of hours later I met them in one of the Adlon's private dining rooms: Hawley himself—a short, plump man with an eyebrow mustache, and entirely cordial to me despite my fears—and H. R. Knickerbocker of the New York *Post,* Sigrid Schultz of the Chicago *Daily News,* Ed Beattie of the UP, Louis Lochner of the AP, Sefton Delmer of the London *Daily Express,* and John Gunther, also of the Chicago *Daily News,* whose post was Vienna but who often came to Berlin. I had met none of them before and rather expected some of them to be prima donnas. After all, they were not the kind of reporters who spent their time trying to make something out of rookie ball players or fakers like old Lem Dixen; they interviewed heads of state and covered political crises and their stories regularly appeared on page one. I soon found out I was wrong. For all their skill and insight, these correspondents were simply doing the work that was assigned to them, and membership in their league was open to anyone who could deliver the goods.

As we ate dinner, most of the talk was for my benefit. Ed Beattie was concerned about what people in the United States were thinking of Hitler. It seemed to him, reading the newspapers from home, that Americans were not really afraid of him yet. I explained that in New York most people seemed to consider Hitler a clown who wouldn't last. This got Knickerbocker started on *Mein Kampf,* which he recommended that I read immediately. "No American I know of has taken the trouble to read it seriously," Knick said, "but it's all there: his plan for the conquest of Europe." Knick, a red-haired Texan with an impish sense of humor, also pointed out that Hitler must be one of the world's wealthiest writers. His book, which he had written in 1924 while being comfortably detained in prison, had sold more than a million copies in Germany in 1932 alone. "He's a silly-looking man with that stare and mustache and lock of hair and outstretched arm," Knick went on, "but he doesn't look silly to the cheering German masses, and he writes and says what they want to hear."

The others made their contributions to my education. Tom Delmer (nobody called him Sefton) had little good to say of Hitler as a public orator—he rambled and ranted and was often ungrammatical—except that if he chose to, he could probably hypnotize any German audience into marching unarmed against France. Lochner and Beattie told me of the unholy alliance between Hitler and the country's financial interests. They pointed out the irony of Hitler's appealing for support from the workers and the unemployed while behind closed doors he convinced the industrialists that only he could keep the workers and their Communist leaders under control—and the irony of the Krupps and others contributing their wealth to increase Hitler's power when it was only a matter of time before he nationalized their industries as he had already nationalized the newspapers.

Sigrid Schultz told me that many wealthy Jews, in spite of the increasing confiscations of their property, still hoped to buy their safety from the regime, and John Gunther spoke of the Nazi movement that he saw growing in Austria.

My feeble comment, as the lesson went on, was that I did not understand how any German, rich or poor, if he had a serviceable mind, could follow so visionary and contradictory a leader. "You might think of Father Charles Coughlin," Knick said. "He's giving several million American radio listeners the very same scapegoats that Hitler is presenting so effectively: the Jews, the bankers, the Communists, and the political leaders he calls traitors."

The parallel had not occurred to me, but it was pointed up when Knick went on to tell me that the *Völkische Beobachter,* the voice of the Nazi party, printed Coughlin's radio talks in full and hailed him in its editorial columns.

After this cram session, I finished my first evening in the new Germany with a capsule lesson in oral German. Knick had been making light of my concern over not being able to make myself understood. When our party broke up and he and I and Hawley went into the bar for a nightcap, he said, "You need only four words to get along in Berlin."

106

Naturally, I wanted to be told what they were. "Wait a minute and you'll probably hear them," Knick said. As we finished the round of drinks, the bartender presented the bill to Knick. Knick waved it toward Hawley, saying, *"Der andere Mann besalt."* He turned to me. "There they are: 'The other man pays.' "

A day or two later I met my first Nazi official, the Harvard-educated piano player, Ernst Hanfstaengl, known to all the correspondents as Putzi. I called on him in his post as Chief of the Foreign Press Department, to present my credentials, and I regret to say that on first acquaintance he struck me as a likable fellow. He was a tremendous man physically, with heavy features, dark eyes, and a mane of coalblack hair that he had to keep tossing back. With an ingratiating manner, he was a compulsive and amusing talker and, unlike other Nazis I later had to do business with, he went out of his way to be cordial to Americans. You had to know Putzi to really dislike him. That came later.

At first we chatted about the United States, where Putzi had spent most of his early life. He laughed uproariously as he told me stories about prominent Americans he had known—his father had run an art gallery in New York—and then professed his esteem for the extraordinary Mr. Hearst and his great International News Service. Then, in what sounded like a confidential disclosure, he told me that it was not he, but Dr. Goebbels who had objected to my predecessor. Learning that I did not know the man, Putzi casually suggested that he might have been emotionally unstable.

"You, I am happy to say, appear to be a man with whom we shall be able to work very well," he told me as our first meeting ended. "I look forward to being your friend and to helping you report to your news service the truth about us."

After that I saw Putzi often, for unlike the Nazis of higher rank, the press chief loved to be one of the boys. Hawley and Knick and I were dining at the Taverne a week after my arrival—the Taverne was the good, inexpensive restaurant that was our evening headquarters the way the Adlon was our headquarters for lunch—when Putzi came in. He charged down on us, delightedly crying our names, and made himself at home. "Quent," he said after a few moments, beaming like a fond father about to take his son to a ball game, "I've fixed it for you to talk with Rudolf." (The day before, I had asked Putzi if Rudolf

Diels, the head of the Gestapo, might consent to being interviewed.) This was the Foreign Press Chief: informal, hail-fellow-well-met, charming. The trouble was that the picture he offered me of the Nazi regime never squared with the evidence I saw so easily with my own eyes.

The Adlon, delightful as it was, was no place for a ninety-dollar-a-week man, and when I mentioned my problem to Sigrid Schultz, she knew of just the thing for me, a beautifully furnished nine-room apartment at 36 Brücken Allee, overlooking the Tiergarten.

"I particularly want you to rent this place," Sigrid told me as we took a taxi there the day after she had brought it up. "The tenant, Professor Hans Lederer, late of the University of Berlin, is a Jew. He has just been discharged from the faculty."

I met the professor and his wife, a gentle, quiet-spoken couple, and they led me through the apartment. It was, as Sigrid had expected, not only within my means but much to my taste, since it even had a spacious balcony.

"Here are my books, Herr Reynolds," said the professor at one point. "Sigrid especially wants you to see my books." As I stared at the solidly lined walls of his library, he said casually, "There are five thousand of them here. Some, I dare say, would not be of much use to you." Smiling, he took a sample from the shelf and presented it to me. "Japanese," he said. "I am an orientalist."

After the tour, I rejoined Sigrid in the large living room. The Lederers then left us and we stood by the grand piano that I would never play. Sigrid told me that Lederer could probably get a teaching job in New York. Her problem was to get him there before it became impossible for him and other Jews to leave Germany. Sigrid had helped the Lederers obtain exit permits. All that was now preventing their departure was money. "I want you to buy his books for a dollar a volume," she told me.

"Sigrid!" I protested. "I have about four hundred dollars to my name. Besides, I don't read Japanese."

She shook her head. "You don't get me. You buy them with a rubber check. That's just to satisfy the American authorities that Lederer is solvent. When he gets to New York, you'll send him his books and he will tear up your check."

Thus it was that I learned about Sigrid's double life. When she brought a lawyer to my room at the Adlon to make up a legitimate-

108

looking bill of sale, and I signed the biggest check of my life, I had the feeling that I was buying stock in her personal underground railroad.

A couple of weeks after I moved into the Lederers' apartment, a veiled message came from New York suggesting that I start sending the books. As it happened, the evening that the first box went off, I ran into Putzi in the Adlon bar. He was in one of his supercharged moods, and with a grin and a slap on the back, he said, "You've been here a month now, and you haven't asked me about our so-called Jewish problem or written anything about it to annoy me. How come, Quent?"

"Give me time, Putzi," I replied. "I haven't been here long enough to know what's going on."

Congratulating me on my good sense, Putzi went on to say that of course there was no Jewish problem in the Third Reich. There were, perhaps, a few objectionable individuals who would sooner or later find themselves in trouble, just as they would run into trouble in any other country. But a problem as such there was not.

I had come to Berlin with the idea of getting out of the city as much as possible, and I was blessed with an expense account for the purpose. One of my trips took me to Heidelberg, a town I fell in love with at first sight. After checking into a lovely old hotel on a street that looked like the stage set for *The Student Prince,* I learned that Hitler's Minister of Enlightenment and Propaganda, Dr. Paul Joseph Goebbels, was to address the university students the following night. It seemed to me this might offer something for a story.

During the afternoon and evening I did my background work in several of the *Bierstuben,* talking with a dozen or more of the English-speaking students. Handsome blond youths and girls, superficially like students at any American university, they were happy to be interviewed by an American journalist. (I had learned not to introduce myself as a "newspaperman"; in Europe, he's the fellow that sells the papers.)

Along the way, for a few marks, I hired Greta Gershon, a very attractive blonde who had time on her hands and was delighted to guide me around for the chance of practicing her second language. We spent the next day sightseeing and discussing the temper of the Heidelberg students. Greta assured me—confirming my impressions of the day before—that almost none of them were interested in political matters. "Like me, they do not think much beyond their studies," she said, adding, "however, you must understand that we are Germans, and that we respect our government even as you Americans respect yours."

That evening, in the packed university auditorium, I had my first view of Goebbels. He was a small, dark, rather sinisterly attractive man. His limp, the result of a childhood disease, tended to make him an interesting figure. Unlike most of the Nazi hierarchy, he did not wear a uniform; his clothes came from Savile Row. When he was introduced, I noticed that he received only a lukewarm greeting.

Speaking to university students, Goebbels, the holder of seven university degrees, was in his element. Greta whispered a running translation to me. He began with anecdotes of his college days, leading to the emotional climax of his receiving a doctorate in philosophy from Heidelberg University in 1920, which he called the greatest day of his life. Within minutes he had commanded the respectful attention of every listener. He then went on to his main business: a defense of National Socialism, an exposition of the greatness of Adolf Hitler, and an attack upon the Treaty of Versailles.

Only toward the end did he begin to raise his voice, launching into his thesis that it was the Jews, individually and collectively, who were to blame for all of Germany's ills. I watched and listened to this obviously brilliant man in amazement and cold horror. A few years later he was to say, in an unguarded moment: "If you repeat a lie often enough, people will believe it." He was lying now, but his audience was entranced by his apparent sincerity.

"Repeat it and repeat it until it rings in your ears, 'The Jews are to blame!'" he declaimed at the end. "Repeat it and repeat it until you hear it in your dreams, 'The Jews are to blame.' Every Jew in Germany is the enemy of our state. Repeat this and repeat this and repeat this, 'The Jews are to blame.'"

He was given a tremendous ovation, and while he waited motionless the cry surged through the auditorium: *"Die Juden sind schuldig!"* When it had become an overwhelming roar, Goebbels smiled, bowed, and limped from the stage. Disregarding the dreadful thesis and result, it was one of the most effective pieces of public speaking I had ever heard.

I looked closely at the faces around me. Faces that had appeared friendly before the speech now looked stern and angry, like those of

110

the brown-shirted storm troopers I had several times seen marching in Berlin.

Even my sophisticated, supposedly nonpolitical Greta had changed. She clutched my arm and cried, "Wonderful!"

We followed the chanting crowd to the street. Part of it surged off toward the town's main street. Later, I learned that this contingent of boys spent several hours in smashing the windows of stores known to be owned by Jews. The rest marched off to the *Bierstuben* to sing the Horst Wessel song, the anthem of the National Socialist Party.

The story seemed too important to mail, which was the way most of my stuff had been going to New York. I therefore wrote it in cabelese, telephoned Berlin, and dictated it. My hunch was right. The next day it appeared in the New York *Journal,* and Barry sent me a cable of congratulations.

I decided to prolong my stay in Heidelberg. Although Greta's enthusiasm for the gospel as preached by St. Goebbels had eliminated any idea I'd had of making our relationship more personal, I kept her on as interpreter. A good thing, too, for it was through her that I managed to witness the first student duel held in Heidelberg in many years. Such duels, a tradition going back to the eighteenth century, had been outlawed by the Weimar Republic during the 1920s as an objectionable relic of Teutonic barbarism. Now, Hitler wanted the nation's youth to learn how to be cruel without remorse, and how to take punishment without whimpering, and the university had recently and quietly lifted the ban.

Greta was not clear about the cause of the forthcoming duel. It was possible that one of the fraternity boys had insulted the other, but more likely that a simple challenge had been issued between fraternities, the contests being considered above all tests of courage.

At five-thirty, the morning of the event, I was waiting at the spot Greta had suggested, on the bridge crossing the Neckar. A blood-red sun was rising, and beautiful old Heidelberg was lifting a thousand moss-dappled bright-red roofs to an incredibly blue sky. Down the still-shadowy street toward me came marching two groups of silent students. Half wore caps of one color, half of another. Marching at the heads of their respective corps were the two principals.

The boys crossed the bridge heading for the Hirschgasse, the inn that was the traditional scene for the duels. I fell in at the end of the procession. Greta had told me that while outsiders were not invited to these affairs, I might be able to slip in. The marchers stopped once, before an ancient statue of St. Nepomuk, the patron of duelists. The boys who were to fight lifted their caps and offered their prayers. In silence, then, we proceeded to the Hirschsgasse.

The dueling room, ordinarily the inn's dance hall, had a high, vaulted roof. From its rafters hung tattered, dusty flags—the banners of the oldest Heidelberg student corps. In this consecrated setting I watched the contestants, Fritz Schmidt and Karl von Gruendal, strip to the waist. Then, standing near a table presided over by a white-smocked surgeon, I saw their necks wound with heavy bandages. This was to prevent a saber slash from reaching the neck veins, and it was one of two concessions to longevity. The other was the heavy leather sleeve into which each duelist slipped his saber arm.

The referee, the president of a neutral corps, summoned the duelists to the center of the floor and handed them their sabers. They looked at one another with impassive faces. I wondered if in their hearts they were feeling the fear their expressions contemptuously denied. Both were fine physical specimens. The sun, streaming through the open windows, played on the muscles of their backs and shoulders as they saluted one another.

"Los!" [Go!] cried the referee, and the *Mensur*—Latin for measure—was on. Sabers clashing, the boys clashed furiously at one another. Neither moved on the floor, neither moved his head. Ducking a blow, Greta had told me, would be grounds for expulsion from the corps. Now and then, as one of the weapons just missed, there would be an involuntary exclamation from the spectators. Periodically the duelists were ordered to step back. Their seconds would quickly wipe the sweat from their bodies, and then they would go at it again.

As the boys tired, their sabers moved less vigorously. Suddenly, with a terrific downward slash, Schmidt broke through Von Gruendal's guard and creased his chest. Both men stepped back and Von Gruendal looked down at the dripping gash. He seemed to be sneering at his body for not being as strong as his spirit.

The surgeon closed the wound temporarily with strips of adhesive. The duel resumed.

Both men, exhausted, were now gasping. It seemed obvious that Von Gruendal was the weaker. He wasn't getting his saber up high enough to deflect Schmidt's heavy blows.

And then it happened. Schmidt's yard-long saber, flashing down,

112

opened flesh near Von Gruendal's eye. There was an "Ahhh!" from the spectators as blood spurted from the wound. Von Gruendal swayed and his seconds ran to support him. The referee nodded to Schmidt. The duel was over.

They helped Von Gruendal to the chair in front of the surgeon's table. I heard the surgeon humming softly. He poured iodine into the ugly wound that had missed the eye by less than an inch. He reached for a needle that was threaded with fine silk. He began to sew up the wound. Von Gruendal, white-faced, clutched the arms of his chair. A waiter from the inn's taproom appeared with a bottle of Weinbrand and a glass. He filled the glass and offered it. Von Gruendal looked at him coldly and shook his head. The waiter, uncertain, placed the glass of brandy on the table. Since no one else seemed to want it, I downed it.

After sewing the boy's face, the surgeon took several stitches in his chest wound. Schmidt, an interested spectator, now shook hands with Von Gruendal and invited him to have a drink. With a dozen of their corps members the duelists left the hall and went to the taproom. Lifting steins of beer, Von Gruendal and Schmidt toasted each other. The insult—if there had been one—was avenged, and the boys were not only friends again but equals. Both had come out of the duel with honor. The winner had shown exceptional skill; the loser, exceptional fortitude and ability to withstand what must have been terrible pain.

Walking back to my hotel, I recalled a comment Knickerbocker had made in Berlin: "In Texas we have a saying, 'Give a man a whip and he'll use it.' " He had been speaking of the guns of the brown-shirted Storm Troopers and the black-shirted SS men. At first I had thought Knick's fears exaggerated. Not any more. Within the short space of two days I had seen Goebbels stir an audience to a frenzy of nationalistic and anti-Semitic passion, and seen the blood code revived in the dueling ceremony. I could now believe that what Knick called the *Wehrwillen*—the will to war—was being systematically encouraged.

Greta was waiting for me at the hotel. She wanted to hear every gory detail, and her eyes gleamed when I told her how stoically Von Gruendal had taken his torture from the surgeon.

"He is the kind of man Hitler wants to help build the new Germany!" she exclaimed.

I pointed out that she had recently called herself and the rest of the students nonpolitical.

113

"That was before we heard Dr. Goebbels speak," she said simply. "He explained everything so beautifully that now, for the first time in my life, I am proud to be a German."

Writing my story of the duel, I took the line that it seemed to be the expression of Hitler's new commandments, which were replacing the catechism of Luther. I then telephoned Hawley in Berlin and told him I was ready with something to cable.

"You'll have to mail it," Hawley said sadly. "Here's the cable Barry just sent us: 'Hold down everything. Midget sat on Morgan's lap. No room wires except biggest stories.' "

"Now what in hell is that all about?" I asked. Hawley gave me a few details about the press agent's midget who had broken up a Senate committee hearing by climbing onto the lap of the witness, J. P. Morgan, and getting herself photographed there. Obviously the meeting between Schmidt and Von Gruendal couldn't trump that.

When my dispatch finally appeared, there were repercussions. I had expected that Putzi Hanfstaengl might be upset, but when next I saw him he congratulated me warmly on both my Heidelberg stories. Evidently their implications escaped him. "You see," he said, "even the young intellectuals embrace National Socialism when it is properly explained to them. And that duel is a fine symbol of today's Germany. To use an American phrase, our youth is learning to take it."

Charley Colebaugh of *Collier's* was another who liked what I wrote, though for clearer reasons. I got a letter from him suggesting that I gather some further material proving that German youth was being conditioned for war and make it into an article for him. To egg me on, he reported that Joe Connolly had told him he had no objection to my doing outside magazine work. Encouragement was hardly needed, however, since in addition to the pay, there was the obvious fact that an article in *Collier's,* then one of America's leading magazines, would give me and INS a certain prestige.

Accordingly, one Sunday morning I went marching with the *Jugend,* which outwardly was Hitler's version of the Boy Scouts. The boys, fourteen and older, wore uniforms in the style of Ernst Roehm's Storm Troopers, and met for their outing at ten o'clock, the hour that for decades had meant the opening of Sunday school in the Lutheran church.

As they marched out some eight miles to the wooded Grunewald,

114

they sang songs in which I heard praise of *Der Fuehrer* and of the ideal of healthy minds and healthy bodies. At the recreation field, while the boys drilled in formation, did calisthenics, and put on wrestling matches, I gathered some surprisingly outspoken statements from one of their leaders. Telling me of their summer activities, which would include mountain climbing with rifles and packs and learning to live on emergency rations, he said that Germany would become strong and free only when its young people learned to endure suffering. "We teach these boys," he said, "that they may one day even have to die for their fatherland. This training leads to loyalty."

I saw another angle of the training when I visited Wertheim's department store (which had been taken over from its Jewish owners and awarded to one of Hitler's friends), and discovered that the toy department was specializing in tanks, submarines, airplanes, and guns. Even the dolls had the military image, many of them dressed in SA or SS or nurses' uniforms.

Finally, someone called my attention to the press treatment of a cross-country motorcycle race. The winner received little attention. The hero was the man who had taken a bad spill about five miles before the finish. Despite a broken shoulder, two broken ribs, and a broken nose, he had remounted and managed to come in second. For this, his picture was on page one of the *Völkische Beobachter,* and an editorial lauded him as a model citizen of the Third Reich.

I called my article, thanks in part to Putzi Hanfstaengl, "Trained To Take It." It appeared in *Collier's* as the first of the three hundred and eighty-four articles I would write for that magazine during the next fifteen years.

Not long after my return from Heidelberg I had a verbal skirmish with the Nazis in my own living room. Along with the Lederers' apartment I had acquired a servant named Martha, a pink-cheeked, doll-like Bavarian of tender age. Each morning after the postman handed Martha my mail, he would click his heels and give out with the conventional *"Heil Hitler."* Little Martha would reply with the traditional Bavarian *"Grüss Gott,"* really meaning, if not literally, "May God be with you." She probably added a scornful look along with it.

I was only half aware of this daily contest. Then one morning two brown-uniformed Storm Troopers appeared at the door. One, speaking English, informed me that he had come to take my servant to SA headquarters for questioning. It appeared that she had been reported

115

as a person unfriendly to the regime. Martha, standing beside me at the door, blanched but looked through the two troopers as if they were glass.

Dismissing her, I invited the men to enter and make themselves at home, indicating chairs, a bottle of brandy, and glasses. Then, sitting where they could hear me, I telephoned the Chief of the Foreign Press Department. I told Putzi exactly what had happened. I explained that Martha was a peasant girl from the south who had not been exposed to the tenets of National Socialism and was therefore ignorant of the prevailing customs. I added that for generations the people of her village had undoubtedly greeted one another with *"Grüss Gott"* and that it had never implied disrespect for Kaiser Wilhelm II, and did not now indicate disrespect for Hitler.

"Let me speak to one of those nitwits," said Putzi.

I handed the phone to the English-speaking Storm Trooper. Putzi blasted him. "Have you nothing better to do," I could hear him roar, "than to annoy a simple peasant girl who works for the representative of the great Hearst organization? If you ever bother her again, I will complain personally to Ernst Roehm and he will take care of you." The SA man paled at the mention of his notoriously unpredictable commander and stammered an apology. When he hung up, he mopped his brow and said humbly, "I am sorry, Herr Reynolds. It was all a misunderstanding." Then he said, "May I please have another drink?"

It was probably not a coincidence that we soon had a new and less-assertive postman.

Today it is sometimes difficult to credit how early Hitler began sending his enemies to concentration camps. The horrors of the camps as they were discovered to the world in 1945 left an image that dims the historical fact that nearly thirty thousand Germans were in *Schutzhaft*—protective custody—in some fifty camps by the end of 1933, and that camp guards were already getting away with killing their prisoners out of hand.

Most of this knowledge was rumor in Berlin in 1933, but thanks to the persistence of H. R. Knickerbocker, he and I saw one of the camps. While we were the first members of the foreign press corps to see such evidence, we wrote no story about it—for a very good reason.

Carl von Ossietzky, the well-known editor of the weekly *Weltbühne*, had disappeared early in the year as "an enemy of the state." Actually,

116

his only crime was his continuing opposition to German militarism; he had been one of the leaders of the peace movement all through the 1920s. He wasn't even a Jew or a Communist—just an idealist. Knick and the German editor were close friends, and when Knick learned that he was being held in Oranienburg, not far from Berlin, he badgered Putzi into giving us passes to visit him. Putzi also supplied us with an official car and an English-speaking guide.

The camp itself had once been a brewery. Attached to the huge stone building was a stone-walled yard where beer trucks had, in a happier day, backed to the loading platforms. This yard was now the prisoners' exercise ground. We reached the gates at noon to find several hundred gray-clad men milling about in the sunshine.

A guard, after verifying our documents, disappeared into the eddies of men and a few moments later returned with Ossietzky. He was a thin, sensitive-looking man of thirty-five, appearing a good deal older, perhaps because he was already ill with the tuberculosis that was to kill him some five years later. Since our guide and the guard both stood by as monitors, Knick and Ossietzky conversed in a kind of elevated double talk.

"I imagine that you are getting enough to eat, Carl."

There was a mocking look in the German's eyes. "Of course, Knick. And as you know, I have never been interested in good or expensive food."

"It seems that the accommodations here should not be unpleasant."

Ossietzky nodded. "I have learned quite easily how to sleep on straw."

The talk went on like this for several minutes. The guard then signaled enough. We shook hands with the man whose treatment by the Germans was soon to become an international issue.

As we turned away, Knick asked a last question: "Carl, is there anything you think I could send you from Berlin?"

"No, thank you. I can think of nothing you could send me. Oh, yes—" Ossietzky called after us. "There is one book you might send me. *The History of Germany in the Dark Ages.*"

That night in Berlin, Knick and I discussed the handling of this story. Oranienburg was probably not the worst place the Nazis could keep a man, but if we said this in our stories we would be indirectly justifying the existence of such camps and implying that political prisoners were being well treated, which was probably in Putzi's mind

117

when he gave us our passes. On the other hand, if we described Ossietzky as we had seen him, and repeated his ironic request for *Germany in the Dark Ages,* this could do nothing but make his life worse. Reluctantly, we decided to kill the story.

So far as I know, Knick never saw his friend again, but Carl von Ossietzky became a name in headlines around the world in 1936 when he was awarded the Nobel Peace Prize. The Nazis had removed him from the camp to a TB hospital shortly before the announcement was made. Not only was Carl not allowed to receive the prize, but word went out that no Nobel Prize could ever again be granted a citizen of the Third Reich.

But if I wrote nothing about Ossietzky, I sent a dispatch from the famous toy-making town of Nuremberg that eventually took me into a press conference with Dr. Goebbels himself and earned me his flattering hatred. It happened when Bill and Martha Dodd, the son and daughter of our Ambassador, invited me to drive to Austria with them to attend the Salzburg music festival. We stopped in Nuremberg to spend the night. I had been there once before and knew it as a town that went to sleep early. When we arrived at our hotel on the Königstrasse about midnight, and found the street filled with an excited, happy crowd, we wondered if we had stumbled into a toy-makers' festival.

"Is there going to be a parade?" I asked the hotel clerk as we registered.

He was a pleasant fellow, and he laughed until the tips of his mustache quivered. Then he said, "It will be a kind of parade. They are teaching someone a lesson."

Martha and Bill and I walked out and joined the crowd. Everyone was keyed up, laughing, talking. The Nurembergers seemed much friendlier than the Berliners. Here, when you bumped into someone in the crush, he would smile and say politely, *"Verzeihen."*

We began to hear music, loud and brassy. The people around me pressed to the curb, laughing in anticipation. We could hear the roar of the crowd three blocks away, a laughing roar that swelled toward us with the music.

The band, I now saw, was one of Storm Troopers, not doll makers. Preceded by torchlights and swastika banners, it marched past. Behind it came two six-foot troopers, half supporting, half dragging a human figure. I could not at first tell if it was a man or a woman. Its head

118

had been clipped bald, and face and head had been coated with white powder. Even though the figure wore a skirt, it might have been a man dressed as a clown. The crowd around me roared at the spectacle of this figure being dragged along. And then, as the SA men suddenly lifted it to its full height, we could read the placard hung around its neck: *I wanted to live with a Jew.*

I still could not be sure if it was a man or a woman, and the people around me were too busy laughing to hear my questions. After the figure had passed, I was propelled into the street with the crowd. A two-decker bus lumbered up and got stalled in the crush, the driver good-naturedly holding up his hands in surrender. Faces poked from the windows of the bus. On the upper deck people laughed and pointed. The SA men lifted their toy so that they could see it better.

Then someone got the idea of marching the thing into the lobby of our hotel. In it went, followed by part of the crowd. In the street the band played on. By now I had learned that the thing was a girl, and that her name was Anna Rath. The troopers brought her to the street again, and the mob surged forward, toward the next hotel.

Then, suddenly, everyone seemed a little tired of the fun. It was getting late. There were toys to be made tomorrow. The band began to play the Horst Wessel song. Up and down the Königstrasse perhaps five thousand people stood at attention, with right arm thrust out, their voices massed. Then the party was over. The banners and the band and the marchers disappeared down the street.

In the bar attached to our hotel, after the late drinkers had left, the Dodds and I asked the bartender about Anna Rath. He whispered her story and the part played in it by Herr S. "You have heard of Herr S., whose home is here?" he asked.

We nodded. He was speaking of Julius Streicher, Hitler's circus master of anti-Semitism. In Berlin it was said that Jews and other undesirables were tortured in the basement of the police building, near the Tomb of the Unknown Soldier. If so, their cries did not reach the street. In Nuremberg, the astute Streicher gave the people the entertainment they wanted.

Anna Rath, we learned, had made the mistake of attempting to marry her Jewish fiancé after the ban on Aryan–Jewish marriages.

I went up to my room and telephoned Hawley in Berlin. The Nazis had all along been denying the atrocities that were occasionally reported abroad, but here was concrete evidence. No other correspond-

119

ent had witnessed any atrocities. Hawley agreed that I had a big story but doubted that it would be allowed to go out on the wire. He recommended that I mail it. Further, he suggested that I should leave out mention of the Dodds, so as not to involve the Ambassador.

Writing the story, I found myself trembling. The grotesque white face of Anna Rath haunted me. In the morning, I posted the story to Barry Faris.

We drove on, then, and had our week in Austria. Among the messages waiting for me when I returned to Berlin was a cable from Barry saying that my story had received a big play. There was also a request for me to report immediately to the office of Ernst Hanfstaengl.

Putzi, not to my surprise, was furious. "There isn't one damned word of truth in your story!" he shouted at me. "I've talked with our people in Nuremberg and they say nothing of the sort happened there."

This was a moment to enjoy. I grinned at Putzi. "You're dead right," I said. "I just wanted to impress my New York office so I faked that story from beginning to end."

Putzi began raving the way he played the piano—loud. I stopped him with the announcement that I had watched the affair in the company of two unimpeachable witnesses. When I told him their names, Putzi looked stricken. He slumped into his chair and clutched his head, grumbling that I should not have led him on. When I asked if he wouldn't like to telephone the Dodds and confirm it, he said it would not be necessary.

A few days later, Dr. Goebbels held a press conference. It drew at least forty reporters. Goebbels, who could be very disarming when he wanted to make the effort, himself brought up the question of atrocities against the Jews, saying that they were only isolated examples of behavior by irresponsible individuals.

In the front row of reporters I saw Norman Ebbutt, the head of the London *Times'* Berlin bureau, a mild-mannered man but relentless at follow-ups. "But Herr Minister," I heard him say, "you must surely have heard of the Aryan girl, Anna Rath, who was paraded through Nuremberg just for wanting to marry a Jew?"

Goebbels smiled. "I know that The Hearst Press and your paper, among others, has been interested in that story. Let me explain how such a thing might occasionally happen. All during the twelve years

120

of the Weimar Republic our people were virtually in jail. Now our party is in charge and they are free again. When a man has been in jail for twelve years and he is suddenly freed, in his joy he may do something irrational, perhaps even brutal. Is that not a possibility in your country also?"

"If it should happen," Ebbutt said calmly, "we would throw the man right back in jail."

Goebbels' face clouded. Then he smiled again and asked, "Are there any more questions?"

That was the end of the press conference, but not quite the end of the Anna Rath story. Norman Ebbutt gave me that when he told me that one of his men had gone to Nuremberg and found her confined in a hospital for the insane.

When a reporter reminisces, he likes to dwell on the few exclusive stories he managed to obtain, conveniently forgetting those he missed. Following this tradition of my craft, I shall not mention the occasions when I was beaten to the punch by other reporters, but to this day I regret my failure to see one truly big German story that practically hit me in the face.

It happened when Margaret Lane of the London *Daily Express* came to Berlin and her colleague Tom Delmer arranged for her to interview the wife of Dr. Goebbels, who lived in Warnemuende on the Baltic. To get there, Margaret flew in a chartered plane. I went with her, having promised to hold up my story until Margaret's had appeared.

We found Magda Goebbels a charming woman. She talked to us in excellent English, while serving us tea. Before her marriage she had been an actress. Now she appeared to be a happy wife and mother, despite her husband's well-known way with other women. Yes, she knew Hitler well. A fascinating man, she called him. And so on—nothing productive of a good lead. But of course there were depths to this woman that we could not guess. Eleven years later our gracious hostess would be among Hitler's last companions in his bunker beneath the Chancellery, and there, before having herself shot in the back of the head, she would give the word for the murder of her six unsuspecting children, declaring that they belonged to the Third Reich.

But the big story was not in the home of Frau Goebbels. When we went back to the airport for the return flight to Berlin, our flight clearance was unexpectedly delayed. For several minutes we had to wait at the start of the runway. At least twenty-five small planes were using the field, taking off, circling, and landing again. When I asked our hired pilot about them, he shrugged. "These are just sport planes. This is where our youngsters learn to fly. They do it just for fun."

I should have known better. A year or two later, when I was back in New York, I learned that the "youngsters" I had seen in training at Warnemuende were in actuality the nucleus of what would become the *Luftwaffe*. A Knickerbocker or a John Gunther would have spotted the possibility at once and started asking questions. Me? I had one of the best stories of the year just begging to be written, and I muffed it.

Occasionally some events took place in Berlin to make us forget the grim reality of Hitler's tightening control over all phases of German life. One such was the arrival of Wiley Post during his historic first solo airplane flight around the world. On Sunday morning, July 16, 1933, I went out to Tempelhof Airfield to witness his first touchdown since leaving America. I went not as a newsman but simply as a rubbernecking spectator, since *The New York Times* had an exclusive contract for the flier's story.

As soon as the *Winnie Mae,* Post's red and white Lockheed Vega, landed, a tremendous crowd of Berliners surged onto the field for a close look at the airman who had taken off from New York seventeen hours before. The police did their best to control the mob, but there were not enough of them. I pushed through to the front, showed my press card, and when the one-eyed flier climbed down from his plane, I was the first to greet him.

"You the *New York Times* man?" he asked.

"Of course," I said, more or less for the hell of it. The *Times* man was submerged somewhere in the crowd.

"I'm not supposed to talk to anyone but you," he said. "Keep the other guys away from me, will you?"

"Sure," I said. I turned to a couple of the policemen and snapped in my most officious German: "Let no one come near!"

Then Post clutched my arm. "For God's sake, where's the can?"

I turned again to the police. "Emergency—this man is in a hurry."

With instant understanding they drove a wedge through the crowd for us. The *Times* man was still lost. When we reached the men's room, I ordered the policemen to keep everyone else out. It worked. We had twenty minutes of privacy while the mechanics were refueling

122

the plane, and I got the story of Post's crossing of the Atlantic. At one point, completely lost, he had picked up a radio signal from London.

"If it hadn't been for that signal," he said, "I'd probably be in the North Sea right now."

After dousing his head under a cold tap, Post dashed for his plane and within minutes was off on the next leg of his flight.

Because the INS wires were shut on Sunday until nearly midnight, the exclusive story I had was of no use to me. I therefore phoned it to Tom Delmer, playing up the angle of the radio signal. By the time I returned to my apartment my conscience was troubling me. I got the *Times* man on the phone, was relieved to learn that he had not yet reported his failure to his bureau chief, then gave him what was really his story as if it had been my intention all along.

There were some further lighthearted moments when my family— Pop, Mom, and my sister Marge—used my presence in Berlin as an excuse for a European vacation. Pop circled in via Munich, Hamburg, and Leipzig, studying the school systems, but Mom and my sister came directly to Berlin, and for a week I had a good time showing them the city.

There was an awkward moment the day Mom arrived. As soon as she saw the lovely Martha, she asked me where the girl lived.

"She has the room next to the kitchen, just beyond yours," I replied, knowing what was in Mom's mind, and knowing also that nothing I could say was apt to reassure her.

Mom then wanted to know where the nearest church was. I gave her a choice: the small one just around the corner or St. Hedwig's cathedral on Unter den Linden. Mom, who went to mass every morning that it was possible for her to do so, walked around the corner next morning. When she came back to the apartment at breakfast time, she was bursting with happiness. "Who do you think was the first person at the rail for communion?" she asked.

"Dr. Goebbels," I suggested.

"Martha! We walked back together, and she tells me she goes to seven o'clock mass every morning."

Until that moment I hadn't paid enough attention to the girl even to know she was a Catholic.

"You're lucky to have her working for you," Mom said, and that was her last word on the subject.

Two days after Pop arrived, gloomy about the Nazification of youth he had seen in classrooms, I threw a big dinner party. To be sure it was a success, I enlisted the aid of Tom Delmer, the press corps' best party-giver. Tom not only lent me his cook and his butler for the evening, he chose the menu, picked the right wines, and even made a few suggestions about people Pop and Mom might like to meet. We got together quite a cast, including Martha and Bill Dodd, Sigrid Schultz, Knickerbocker and his fiancée, and Prince Louis-Ferdinand, the son of the former Crown Prince of Germany. Louis-Ferdinand was one of our favorites; he had refused to have anything to do with the Nazi Party, which was quite a courageous act for a man of his prominence.

A last-minute addition to the party was correspondent Walter Duranty, who undoubtedly had a better reason for being in Berlin but insisted that he had come from Moscow simply to replace his old and warped wooden leg with one of the new aluminum legs the Germans were making. During dinner Walter held forth about life in Moscow, making it seem fairly grim, though different in certain important respects from life in Berlin. For one thing, he said, there was still private wealth to be found in Germany, and the power that went with it. For another, it was still possible to send a letter in Germany without having it opened. Further, one could eat well in Berlin, whereas in Moscow the only good food was the caviar. As for the leaders, though their states were run on different principles, Duranty felt that Stalin and Hitler were alike in that they both had supreme control and both were masters of propaganda.

This sort of discussion died out after dinner and my second wave of guests appeared. Among them were Putzi Hanfstaengl and Count Felix von Luckner—the fabulous Sea Devil who in World War I had sunk thousands of tons of Allied shipping without causing the loss of one life. Putzi soon consented to play the piano—not that it ever took much to get him started—and with his usual flair played and sang several innocuous ditties. Then, hearing me translating part of one for Mom's benefit, he turned to her and asked quietly, "You do not understand German, Mrs. Reynolds?" He smiled—and I sensed that he was up to something. "For you, then, I shall sing a song I wrote myself."

And at the piano Professor Lederer had once played, Putzi serenaded my mother with a foul song in which the Third Reich's enemies were jingled out as Jews, Catholics, and Negroes. Perhaps this was

124

Putzi's way of paying me back for the Anna Rath story. Whatever his excuse might have been, the fact that he lowered his voice so that only those of us close around the piano could hear him showed me he damned well knew what he was doing. Fortunately, Pop and Knick and Duranty were not close enough to hear what was going on. I had an impulse to slug Putzi in the middle of it and throw him out. Louis-Ferdinand, sitting next to me and reading my thoughts, said quietly, "What could you prove, Quent? After all, bad manners are bad weapons." I relaxed.

Luckner, the Sea Devil, saved the evening for me. Before Mom, unknowing, could compliment Putzi for his filthy trick, Luckner broke in with, "Mrs. Reynolds, I want you and your daughter to come with me and witness the spectacle of Berlin being divided through the middle." So saying, he drew Mom and Marge away from the piano. "No doubt you good people crossed the Atlantic just in the hopes of seeing this, so I must not disappoint you." Luckner led the way into the dining room. At least half of the party followed to see what he was up to.

He found my telephone directory, a volume as large as a Montgomery Ward catalogue. After carefully drying his hands he gripped the book at the front edge. "Ready? Here goes Berlin!" He strained for a moment, then shook his head, smiling. "My coat," he apologized. "May I remove it?"

In his shirt sleeves he again took up the directory. "This time, good-by Berlin," he said—and ripped the book in two.

One hears of men who can do this stunt, but Old Luckner is the only man I've ever seen do it.

Putzi had taken a telephone call while Luckner was performing, and now he came to announce that *Der Fuehrer* wanted him to come to the Chancellery and play some Liszt. I went to the door with him and, controlling myself, said pleasantly, "Never come to my home again, you louse."

A little later, as Count von Luckner took his leave, I thanked him for his efforts. He laughed and winked. "Hah, you thought I had to take off my coat. That was only for what you call the build-up."

Not for some years later did I have a chance to repay Putzi for his malice. One day in 1942, when I was in New York, I received a letter from him. Two years earlier he had fallen into disfavor with Goebbels, and even his long intimacy with Hitler was not enough to save him.

125

Fleeing to Spain, he had made his way to Canada, where he was now interned as a prisoner of war.

His letter, which began "My dear Quent," suggested that I knew influential men in the government and suggested that I prevail upon them to get him released so that he could come to the United States and make himself useful in the American war effort. I thought about it. Putzi I had known only as a dedicated Nazi. Now apparently he wanted to be a turncoat. For some reason a line of Goethe came to me: *Menschlich ist es bloss zu strafen, aber Göttlich zu verzeihen.* (It is manlike to punish, but Godlike to forgive.) I thought this noble sentiment over, rejected it, and tore Putzi's letter into small pieces.

Apparently he wrote a good many more letters of the same type and some credulous soul eventually went to bat for him. After the war ended I learned that Putzi had been sent secretly to Washington to advise the government on Germany. It was a depressing thought that he had been able to fool high-ranking defense officials into believing that his advice on anything but Liszt, nineteenth-century painting, or the wines of the Rhineland would be worth considering.

As for me, in 1933, at a time when I needed it, I got an education from Putzi and his colleagues.

Late in the year Grantland Rice finally made good his threat to quit *Collier's,* and Charley Colebaugh quite honestly and amicably hired me away from INS as his replacement. When I took the boat home, thanks to what I had seen and learned in the Third Reich, Hitler was no longer just a story. He was a threat.

126

9

The easy years

Charley Colebaugh was on hand to make me feel at home when I walked into the *Collier's* offices on Park Avenue for the first time late in 1933. As an associate editor—meaning that I might be called on to produce an article on practically any subject of current interest—I was assigned a cubicle containing a desk, a couple of chairs, and a typewriter. However, Colebaugh immediately made it clear that I was not expected to occupy this cozy base if I preferred to work elsewhere. It appeared that the other staff men did much of their writing at home or on the road.

Colebaugh then took me in to meet the magazine's publisher, Thomas Hambly Beck. Tall, bald, and pot-bellied, Beck was certainly no Adonis, but his expressive gray eyes, ready smile, authoritative voice, and occasional roars of laughter combined to make him a vivid personality. He had started his business career as a soap salesman, peddling the stuff from door to door. Though he was still primarily a salesman, even as president of the Crowell-Collier Publishing Company, I was to learn that he also had an instinct for what made a good magazine story. As proof of his acumen, *Collier's* was flourishing despite the fact that other magazines had been floundering and disappearing ever since the onset of the Depression.

"So you're Reynolds," Beck boomed when Colebaugh told him my

127

name. "Never heard of you, but Charley and Ed Anthony convinced me I ought to hire you. What ship did you come back on?

"The *President Harding!*" he echoed. The way he said it, I might as well have admitted setting fire to an orphanage. "Always remember this, young fella, when you travel for *Collier's* you travel first class."

I explained that since I had shelled out for my passage, I had returned on the cheapest ship available.

"God damn it," he yelled, "you've been on our payroll ever since you told Charley you'd work for us." He turned to Colebaugh. "Find out what Reynolds paid to travel on that tramp steamer and give him an expense check."

Beck looked back at me. "Satisfied with the salary we're giving you?"

I blinked. This detail Colebaugh had neglected to mention during his long-distance telephone call to me in Berlin. "I don't know what it is, Mr. Beck."

"Don't call me Mr. Beck!" he exploded. "You're in the family now. I'm Tom." Then he summoned the magazine's editor, William Chenery, a tall distinguished-looking Virginian with a Phi Beta Kappa key hanging from his watch chain. "What have you and Charley decided to pay Reynolds?" Beck demanded.

As I watched, Chenery and Colebaugh exchanged questioning looks, it seemed likely the subject had not even been discussed. Chenery looked at me with a pleasant smile and asked quietly, "How is twelve thousand a year to start with, Quentin?"

I had difficulty in even replying. It was nearly three times what I had been making in Berlin.

"One word of advice, Reynolds," Tom Beck said as the session neared its end. "Don't spend too much time in the office we're giving you. *Collier's* stories don't walk in the door."

The next order of business, lunch, was conducted, as hundreds of my *Collier's* lunches were to be, in the Marguery Restaurant, next door to the offices. Beck, who kept an ulcer and usually lunched at the desk on milk and Graham crackers, begged off, but in addition to Colebaugh and Chenery our table included Walter Davenport, considered the magazine's top writer, Bill Courtney, a foreign correspondent and aviation specialist, Kenneth Littauer, the magazine's fiction editor, his assistant, Max Wilkinson, Edward Anthony, the Crowell-Collier public relations man, Frank Gervasi, another recent recruit

128

from INS, and finally Kyle Crichton, who could and did write about anything for *Collier's*, and held the record for versatility by interviewing Henry Ford, the Marx Brothers, and Marlene Dietrich all in the same week.

I found them quite a crew, especially the bluff-spoken Crichton who, under the name of Robert Forsyth, regularly wrote for the *New Masses*. This case of split personality had once caused loud squawks from *Collier's* big advertisers, many of whom made no secret of their belief that another well-known Communist, Franklin Roosevelt, had taken over the White House. Bill Chenery, a conservative Republican but a man with an iron code of fair play, successfully defended Crichton before the magazine's board of directors, a regrettably business-minded bunch who took the advertisers' boycott threats seriously. He did it by handing them every article Crichton had ever written for *Collier's* and challenging them to find one subversive statement in the lot. They of course found none, and Crichton and Chenery stayed on, greatly to the magazine's benefit.

The first drink of the day was pledged to me, the newcomer; the second was lifted in memory of the recent settling of what someone referred to as *l'affaire* Wilkinson. Max, it seemed, had been pleading for two years to have his name added to the *Collier's* masthead as Assistant Fiction Editor, so that when Ken Littauer sent him around the country to tempt authors to submit their stuff, he could exert some leverage. But no sooner had his name appeared than a sheriff had turned up with a seven-year-old judgment against Max for unpaid rent in Greenwich Village. While this was dramatic proof that *Collier's* was a widely read magazine, Max was still smarting under the sting of having to ante up $318.40 on a moment's notice. "Things like this couldn't happen," he told me darkly, "if we'd won the war." Max, like Chenery, was a Southerner, and I presently discovered that his war was the one involving Robert E. Lee, Stonewall Jackson, and J. E. B. Stuart, all of whom Max claimed vaguely as kin.

We were practically through lunch when Heywood Broun lumbered in, welcomed me home, and sat down. A hush fell over our table as the waiter brought his order: a dish of vanilla ice cream and a double gin. Heywood poured the gin over the cream and carefully mashed it in with a spoon.

"Makes a good breakfast," he explained cheerfully, "and the gin kills the taste of the ice cream."

129

Some of the others were more disturbed than I, who already knew of Heywood's contempt for the ordinary rules of drinking. Like as not, he would follow a Manhattan with a Scotch sour, and that with a stinger—and show no harmful effects from the mixing. Heywood may have suffered from indigestion now and then, but in all the years I knew him, I never saw him troubled by a hangover.

Colebaugh was the first at the table who did anything about returning to the office. Heywood stopped him as he was leaving. "You could make life a lot easier for me today if you would send down a portable typewriter and some paper," he said. "I've got to knock out a column."

Ten minutes later an office boy appeared in the restaurant with typewriter and paper. Heywood tipped him five dollars (he usually spent his money as though it was about to be recalled from circulation), excused himself, set up on an empty table, and went to work. He was the only columnist I knew who never had to worry about a lead. Scowling at the machine as though it were an enemy he had to subdue, he kept playing the keys until, in about fifteen minutes, he had finished his day's work. He came back to our table.

"Is it true you're picking up the bill for all this?" he asked Ed Anthony.

Ed smiled. "It's Quent's welcome-aboard party and it's on the house," he said.

"In that case I'd like a green *crème de menthe* and another dish of vanilla ice cream," Heywood told our waiter.

Kyle Crichton asked in awe: "How can you stand a combination like that?"

"I like its color," Heywood said mildly.

It was four-thirty when Heywood went off to deliver his column to the *World-Telegram* and my first *Collier's* luncheon ended. As I walked back to the office I asked Frank Gervasi if this was the normal procedure.

"Don't kid yourself," he said. "It's like this occasionally, but the magazine comes out fifty-two times a year, and you and I and the rest of these characters are the ones who get it out. You'll see."

And see, I did. Charley Colebaugh would say casually, "Quent, we need a few sports stories, one for May fifteenth and the rest for inventory. See what you can dig up."

Sometimes I had the ideas, sometimes they were Colebaugh's or

130

Chenery's. I went to Florida and did an article about jockey Eddie Arcaro and another about a young golfer named Sam Snead. I went to Wisconsin and reported the story of a village that made its winter living by fishing for smelt through the ice. I did stories about Broadway personalities, Hollywood guys and dolls, football players, and about Black Gold, the deceased winner of the 1924 Kentucky Derby. On a tip from Bill Corum, I went to Detroit and watched a little-known heavyweight in action; "Dark Dynamite" I called the piece I wrote about Joe Louis.

I had not been with the magazine long before it took me all of two minutes to sell Colebaugh on the idea of my going to Havana to interview the new Cuban dictator, Colonel Batista. Actually, I had no real interest in talking to Batista; I simply wanted to spend a couple of weeks with the New York Giants while they trained in Havana. Doubting that this would be enough of an excuse, I had gone to the Cuban tourist agency in New York to see what they might suggest for a *Collier's* story. Eager for the kind of publicity that would lure American tourists, the agency gave me several ideas and the promise of cooperation. While I doubted my ability to dramatize Cuba's sugar industry or oil wells, I thought I might be able to do something with her Strong Man.

Colebaugh liked the idea. As I was leaving his office he said drily, "You forgot to mention, Quent, that the Giants are in Havana. I hope you'll have a chance to spend some time with them."

"As a matter of fact," I said, feeling mildly guilty, "Horace Stoneham and a few of the writers are going down on the *Oriente* tomorrow night. I might as well go with them."

Colebaugh laughed. "You do that."

Young Horace Stoneham, who had inherited the Giants from his father, was already well-known as an open-handed host with a special fondness for the writers who traveled with his club. Accordingly, I felt somewhat gloomy when I got to the *Oriente* and my cabin mate, Jim Kahn of the New York *Sun,* told me that Horace's doctors had placed him on the wagon. Kahn's information soon proved to be exaggerated, and it was Horace himself who put us straight. "It's a champagne wagon, not a water wagon," he told us in his cabin. "Champagne never hurt anyone." Backing his faith in this proposition, the chubby, moon-faced baseball mogul had brought several cases of Veuve Cliquot with him. Among the convivial souls who helped dispose of it was

131

Joseph Hergesheimer, the novelist, a chance passenger on the ship. Though the owl-eyed Hergesheimer was seventy-two, and by a long count the senior member of the party, he stayed up as late as any of us.

In Havana the party, now including Tom Meany of the *World-Telegram,* continued. Our guide to the city's night life was Hergesheimer, who knew Havana the way I once knew Flatbush Avenue. One night he took us to see what he claimed was the best rhumba team in the business. The rhumba had just become the craze in the States, but the version one saw in New York night clubs was tame stuff compared with what Hergesheimer showed us—a point I made in the story I sent Colebaugh.

Another night we went en masse to the Sans Souci, a combination night club and gambling house, and contributed, I assume, to Batista's coffers via the crap table. Hergesheimer left us around midnight, explaining with some pride that he had a date. When he joined us next morning at breakfast, he was furious. The girl had turned out to be a hustler, and she had rolled him for a hundred dollars while he slept. In light of our sporting friend's age, some of us looked at him more with awe than sympathy.

Through Edmund Chester, the head of the Cuban AP bureau and the dictator's favorite newspaperman, Jim Kahn and I were able to have lunch with Batista at his Camp Columbia headquarters. We found him an impressive man: handsome, confident, smiling often, gesturing with the strong hands of the professional fighter. His even white teeth gleamed. His uniform was bedecked with campaign ribbons. Occasionally he would take a cigarette from a gold case of which he was very proud. On it were engraved the names of the men who had conspired in the military coup that put him in power. He gave us a good lunch and, through his interpreter, answered our questions with a great display of ease. Actually, he spoke English well, but the pretext of needing an interpreter gave him the chance to polish his answers.

Predictably he denied being a dictator. He aspired to no office, he said, except that which he now held, Army Chief of Staff. Yes, he would hold free elections just as soon as conditions permitted. He spoke eloquently of the economic and social programs that would soon contribute to Cuba's uplift. He expressed admiration for the United States and assured us that Cuba would eventually have a democratic system of government much like her neighbor's. It was

132

all lip service, of course, but as we toyed with our chicken and pineapple, he made it sound great.

I learned an important lesson from this meeting, which is that the closer a reporter gets to news, the more deceiving it may become. Ordinary people rarely spend time in the company of bland, black-hearted liars. Consequently, they tend to go along with the good show even if they are not entirely taken in by it. And Batista was a superb showman. So, a few years later, was Rafael Trujillo when I interviewed him in Santo Domingo, and still later Josef Stalin when I watched him in action in the Kremlin. In such suave presences a reporter—and anyone else who is interested in the truth—has to work hard not to be swept along.

After lunch, learning that we had never seen a cockfight, Batista promised us the finest sport in Cuba, swept us into his car, and took us to a shed where a lot of exuberant and rough-looking characters seemed to be on a first-name basis with him. The pit itself was a fenced circle of packed earth perhaps fifteen feet across, with rows of wooden benches rising on all sides. As we arrived, the odds were being called out for the first event. Batista, forgetting us, inspected the cocks and made his bets. Then a whistle blew and the birds were released. They flew at each other savagely, slashing with the razor-sharp steel spurs that had been tied to their feet. The crowd went hysterical with excitement, but no one shouted louder than our host. I looked at Jim. His face was white. I knew how he felt.

The first fight ended when one of the birds tried to crawl away from the center of the pit. His handler, acknowledging defeat, clapped a hood over its bleeding head and left the pit. White sand was sprinkled over the blood-spattered earth, and the next fight began. Batista had thrown off his tunic, removed his tie, unbuttoned his shirt. His eyes were ablaze with excitement as he screamed encouragement to the bird he was backing. The second fight ended with one cock dead, the other standing with an eye ripped out.

Feeling that the demands of politeness had been adequately met, Jim Kahn and I left and took a taxi back to Havana. Before I wrote my story I went into a huddle with Joseph Hergesheimer, who introduced me to a couple of Cuban businessmen he knew well. That they viewed Batista's promises with skepticism is putting it mildly. "It is easier for us to operate now than it was under Machado," one of them said bitterly. "We used to have to pay graft to everyone. Now we pay it to just one man—the Colonel—and that makes our bookkeeping simpler."

I sent Colebaugh what we called at *Collier's* a personality piece, a story that dwelt less on the background facts than on the flamboyant man. At that, the screaming, wild-eyed, sweating Cuban who enjoyed seeing cocks slash each other to death was probably closer to the real Batista than the ingratiating fraud who had entertained us at lunch.

There was sometimes the feeling at *Collier's* that we were running a weekly newspaper, and among Bill Chenery's happiest moments were those when he beat the AP and UP to a sensational story. This happened in a big way in 1937, and I was the lucky reporter. One morning Chenery handed me a ten-line clipping from the New York *Times*. It said that there had been fighting on the border between Haiti and Santo Domingo. Although the story contained no details, Chenery had a hunch that I ought to fly to Haiti and do some investigating.

Two days later, in Port au Prince, I hired a former U.S. Marine, Al Perry, as interpreter and guide. We drove to Ouanaminthe, on the northern border, and here, from a French-speaking priest, *Père* Emile Robert, I heard a tale of horror.

For many years the back-country Haitians had been crossing the border to work the sugar plantations of Monte Cristi and Santiago provinces, and thousands of them had become squatters there. In recent years the cane crops had failed, and with not enough work to keep even the Dominicans busy, there had been attempts to drive the Haitians off the land. There had been some killings, but it remained for President Trujillo, in an unreported speech he made at Dagabon, in the back country, to put the slaughter on an official, though of course secret, basis.

When I expressed disbelief that as many as two thousand people could have been massacred without the outside world having an inkling of it, *Père* Robert gave me a copy of his list of named dead or seriously wounded. He himself, and other priests in the area, had collected the names from the survivors as they testified under oath.

Trujillo's soldiers had done their work with machetes and knives, rather than bullets, Robert told me, to make it appear that only the Dominican peasants were involved. After listening to this grisly story, I visited a hospital where a Dr. Leveque led me through wards crowded with bandaged patients, all of whom had barely escaped death.

134

Still unable to accept the enormity of what I was being shown, I asked to see an actual wound rather than a bandage.

"Thomas doubted, too," Leveque said, and drew me to the nearest bed. On it lay an eight-year-old boy. The doctor gently eased the dressings away to show me an ugly slice down the boy's head and his ear half severed. "If you still doubt, you may touch the wounds," he said.

I shook my head. Leveque nodded at the boy's bandaged hand. "Three fingers gone," he said. "His brother is in the next bed. Machete wounds. A third brother was killed."

For several days I listened to the appalling stories of about two hundred survivors, and collected as well copies of the affidavits they had previously made. One old man named Joseph, who was recovering from pneumonia, described how, from a hiding place near a road, he had watched a squad of Dominican soldiers hack eighty-eight bound and screaming prisoners to death. I had my interpreter, Perry, tell the old man I could not believe this.

"By God and Saint Jacques I swear that what I have told you is the truth," the old man said with great dignity—and Perry, who had lived in Haiti twenty years, assured me that anyone invoking such an oath would be telling the truth.

After talking with others who had escaped across the Massacre River (not named for this tragedy, but so apt!), leaving their dead children or wives or husbands behind, I then went on to Ciudad Trujillo, the capital of Santo Domingo, and with the help of the AP stringer there, got an introduction to the dictator's public relations man. I explained that I had just arrived from New York to investigate a report that there had been a massacre on the Haitian border.

Trujillo, of course, was eager to enjoy the good will and material blessings of the United States; I soon received an invitation to lunch with him at his home. He was a charming man in that particular setting, and his food and wine were excellent. His bogus sincerity recalled Batista's.

"It is certainly no secret that a regrettable incident occurred on our border, and I am glad that you have come here to learn the facts about it," he said. "A few Haitians crossed the border to steal cattle. Some of our people discovered this and drove them off. Several were killed on both sides, I understand."

135

"There is a rumor in the United States that your army did this killing," I suggested.

Trujillo's gray eyes twinkled and he shook his head. "According to the reports that have come to me, Señor Reynolds, a few men were stabbed to death. My army is equipped with rifles."

"May I quote your denial that your army had anything to do with it?"

"But of course!" said the dictator.

The story I wrote when I got back to New York, published as "Murder in the Tropics," caused quite a stir. Newspapers had to pick it up, giving *Collier's* as their source, and it was read into the *Congressional Record*. Even as AP and UP reporters were hurrying to Haiti and Santo Domingo, I was being summoned to Washington for a meeting with Under Secretary of State Sumner Welles. "You and your magazine have raised hell with our relations with Santo Domingo," the tall and dapper Welles informed me coldly.

A little annoyed at being given the treatment by a top man on our own side, I said mildly, "Mr. Secretary, is your department more interested in good relations with a dictator or in a true account of what's going on down there?" And with that I placed on his desk the affidavits I had collected, as well as *Père* Robert's list of the two thousand named victims. Welles seemed as eager to examine this material as I would have been to unpack a case of nitroglycerine, but there was no way the State Department could duck the facts. The follow-up stories from Haiti revealed that mine had been conservative. Under Trujillo's direction, Dominican soldiers had actually crossed into Haitian territory, and before their work was finished had killed or maimed upwards of ten thousand Haitians.

As a writer I was no specialist before World War II began, and *Collier's* was a hungry animal that had to be fed. One year I made an office record by having thirty-six articles and short stories in the magazine. On one occasion when Ken Littauer was running a short story of mine, Colebaugh discovered that he needed to run two of my articles that he had in reserve. One was about Leo Durocher, the other about a sandhog. To kill the impression that I had written most of the issue, it was suggested that I put phony names on the articles. I signed the piece about the tunnel-builder with my brother's given names, Donald Charles, and on the Durocher piece I put the name of a friend, John Durant.

John was a member of the New York Stock Exchange. "Don't give it away," he begged me, "And I'll have a lot of fun with the boys on the floor."

As it turned out, John not only got a rise out of his financial colleagues, he changed careers. Soon after the article appeared, I ran into an old newspaper friend, now an editor of the *Saturday Evening Post*. He asked me if I could recommend a free-lancer to do a sports article. With a straight face I suggested the author of the Durocher piece, and then talked John into keeping up the masquerade and trying his hand at writing. It worked. While I know plenty of writers who would gladly forsake their trade if offered a seat on the Stock Exchange, John is the only man I know of who went the other way and made good, both as a magazine and book writer. I'm not telling a tale out of school; John long ago acknowledged that my impulse steered him to a better life.

Ken Littauer kept after me to make a short story of anything that wouldn't shape up as an article, and since his hook was attractively baited—I sold *Collier's* my fiction on a free-lance basis—I turned out quite a number over the years. Most of them were solidly based on fact, though they often reached giddy heights thereafter. One of my favorites developed from a midnight conversation I had with a criminal-court judge at the Stork Club. Heywood Broun and I ran into him there one night when he was sitting alone, completely fractured. Since we both knew him as a very moderate drinker, the picture was shocking.

"You've never sent a boy to the chair," he said defensively, as we had a drink with him. He patted the telephone that waited on his table. "Maybe his lawyer is going to call me with some new evidence. He knows I'm here. If he does, I can call Governor Lehman and ask him for a stay."

"Was your man guilty?" I asked.

The judge shook his head as if parrying my question. "The jury was out twenty minutes," he said. "They came back with no recommendation for mercy. Damn it all, first-degree murder. I had no alternative but to sentence him to death. A West Side boy. I'd give anything for his lawyer to phone me right now with something that would save him."

137

"Judge," I said, "you're looking for a West Side miracle."

He nodded. The minutes ticked on toward midnight, then past. "I can go home now," the judge said bitterly, "Warden Lawes has done his duty."

Heywood and I watched the judge disappear. " 'West Side Miracle' might not be a bad title for a short story," I suggested.

"It's all yours," Heywood said, averting his eyes from the silent telephone.

The story I wrote and handed to Littauer was one the judge would never have recognized. My boy in the death house was innocent, the lawyer found his evidence, and the judge got his call at eleven-fifty, just in time to reach the governor. That's fiction for you—it can make everyone happy in the last few paragraphs. But even this little fable was considered too grim for America's movie public, as I learned when Warner Brothers bought the property for a picture. Along with their check for five thousand dollars came a letter explaining that what the studio was principally interested in was my title.

About a year later I went to see a quite awful picture in which the only thing I could recognize was the credit line: "From an Original Story by Quentin Reynolds." Even the title had disappeared. It was now called "Secrets of a Nurse." I left long before the girl's secrets were disclosed.

In the writing business you get to know interesting people. This is not only a great old cliché but a fact so solid that it used to be a potent argument for keeping reporters' salaries low. I think it was never said to me more than once, and that long before I reached *Collier's,* but the line went like this: "We can't afford to pay you any more, son, but just look at all the interesting people you're meeting." I met my share during the thirties in New York, and wrote about many of them.

One was George Brown, to whose gym on Broadway my pal John McClain and I often went to keep in shape. A quiet fellow, George had been well on his way toward winning the middleweight boxing championship when a scaffolding fell on him and nearly killed him. It took him three years to recover. He then opened his gym. At about this time he discovered that his religion could be an everyday concern. Somewhere in the Broadway neighborhood there was always a noon mass being conducted by a missionary, or some out-of-town priest giving a retreat. As the years went by, I think George listened to more

138

sermons than any man in New York. He "discovered" Fulton J. Sheen long before that gentleman became known to a wide audience. I remember going into the gym one morning and finding George quite upset. There were two sermons he wanted to hear that day. To settle the matter, he flipped a coin.

Practically the least thing you could say of George's customers was that they were interesting. Some days I found myself playing paddle-ball in a foursome that included a theatrical producer, some anonymous mobster, and Father John Shanley, a mean hitter. Or my partner might be Deems Taylor, playing against Buzzy Appleton and Champ Segal, a horse-player and former prize fighter who had had his difficulties with the police. Hurrying after a ball, McClain crashed into Segal and sent him flying to land against a wall. While George Brown looked on approvingly, Champ picked himself up, shook the cobwebs out of his mind, and said mildly, "Hey, Big John, why don't you pick on someone your own size?"

A few minutes later I drew my paddle back to smash a ball and hit Segal square across the mouth. To my horror, five of his teeth fell out.

"My God, I'm sorry, Champ!" I gasped.

"So what?" he said. "I'll have a new set tomorrow." Champ nonchalantly scooped his property off the floor and our game continued.

Another of George Brown's characters—and I think that in this context I am not abusing the term—was Ernest Hemingway. Ernest would appear in the gym any time he came through New York on his way to or from Europe. He never wanted any part of paddle-ball but he would punch the bags, heavy and light, for half an hour, and then box. He sometimes wanted McClain and me to go in the ring with him but George wouldn't hear of it.

"Ernest knows only one way to box," he told us. "For keeps. You and John might jab him silly and make him bleed. Then he'd start to fight, and the two of you'd end up hating each other. He wouldn't allow any fighting in here."

The only man who boxed with the novelist was George himself. George never hit him or any of his other clients a solid blow. He would jab effectively, cross light rights to your chin, and clinch and tug you around a bit, but his working theory was that gym boxing was a conditioner, not a contest.

But don't get the idea that Ernest was no fighter—or that his writing was the cover-up of a synthetic he-man. He was no Fancy Dan but he had the courage of a bull and he could hit like a mule. His belly was like a washboard, and it was just about as vulnerable to a punch. Usually, he and George would go four rounds. George's hair wouldn't even be mussed at the end of it, but again that's no reflection on Ernest—George was one of the most skillful defensive fighters I've ever watched.

"Come on, one more round," Ernest would plead.

George would shake his head and, like a father denying a child, say, "You've had enough. Take a steam bath and a shower and I'll give you a rubdown."

In the late 1930s Ernest and his wife Pauline lived in Key West, and once when I happened to be in Miami doing a story, I telephoned him and was invited over for a day and a night that stretched well beyond that. In those days Ernest usually got up to do his writing at 6 A.M. About nine-thirty he would knock off and he and Pauline and I would have breakfast together. She and I had coffee and toast; Ernest doted on broiled fish. One morning I remarked that, though awake early, I had heard no typewriter.

"I write too damn fast on a typewriter," he explained. "If I use a mill I have to rewrite and rewrite. Writing with a pencil slows me down good."

During breakfast Ernest would read his mail, often aloud and with irreverent comments. One morning he took up a letter that made him boil. It was from two recent Princeton graduates who apparently hadn't learned much. With enough capital to start a small magazine, they wanted Ernest to send them a short story or an article for their first issue. Their pitch ran about like this: "Your name on our list of contributors will insure our success. Of course we can't afford to pay for material used, but we feel sure that you will be interested in helping us provide a new forum for the best in American literature."

Ernest crumpled the letter and fired it across the room. "God damn these kids: What do they think I am—an *amateur?* Nobody asks the butcher for free meat or the grocer for free bread."

"Easy now," Pauline said calmly. "I'll answer that one and just say you're too busy."

"They must think I'm a God damn artist!" Ernest grumbled.

In all the years I knew Hemingway, I think that was the closest I ever heard him come to discussing his attitude about his work. For

140

me he was first of all a nice guy to stay up late with, and after that a writer. Thinking about him, I think of another pro, Jack Dempsey. Jack never talks about the left hook that he could throw faster and more accurately than any other fighter who ever lived. Jack talks about his children or his friends or the charity he is shilling for. The Hemingway I knew removed the fat from English prose and discovered the simple declarative sentence as the basis of literary art, but I never heard him make speeches about these accomplishmnts.

When it came to his fishing, though, it took little to start Ernest talking, and I must say he bored the hell out of me any number of times with his tales of the big ones he had killed. (It was Ernest who explained to me that you "catch" ordinary fish but "kill" game fish.)

I can live without fishing. I will go further. To me, fishing is about as stimulating a pastime as golf or bird watching. As long as you can buy halibut or swordfish for less than a dollar a pound, cleaned, I see no reason to take chances with the sun and the vicious rolling of the Gulf Stream. And from the fish's point of view the alleged sport seems so one-sided. Once the poor fish is hooked, I don't see how he's going to get away, or maybe even want to get away, since it's a cinch he's going to leave half his profile.

The first morning Ernest took me out in his beautiful thirty-foot power boat, it was with his guarantee that I would kill a sailfish. Sitting beside me while I occupied the fishing chair, a contrivance that swiveled like something in a barber shop, he fed me extensive instruction:

"When the big one strikes, let the line run out. The sail will think he has killed the bait. He will back away. Then he will rush for it. He will swallow it. You count ten. Then you jerk your rod high to hook him good. Then you begin to work him in. Understand, Quent?"

I nodded.

"You'll lose the first few," Ernest added complacently, "but you'll get the hang of it."

The ice chest of Ernest's boat contained not only beer but conch salad marinated in lime juice. He carried this as a precaution for guests who might get seasick, and he made quite a point of putting it aboard the first morning he took me out. For all I know, conch salad may be the perfect antidote he said it was, but since seasickness is one of the few afflictions that never bother me, I can only report that Ernest's salad and beer made a happy combination.

141

We were about fifteen miles off shore, and mighty rough it was too, when the promised sail took my hook. Forgetting all the briefing, I worked the reel and in a couple of minutes there was the fish, six feet long, gasping in the boat.

Hemingway frowned. "That's no way to kill a sail," he said.

"Well, I caught him," I said. "Will we eat him for dinner?"

"You don't eat sails," he said.

"Then what the hell do you do with them?" I asked.

"You can have it mounted—at ten dollars a foot."

One of the crew baited my hook and tossed it overside. Presently, there was a jolt.

"A barracuda!" Hemingway screamed. "A big one! Take it easy. Don't get excited. Play him—play him!"

I reeled as before, an operation that seemed simple enough, and had the poor fish in the boat in all of thirty seconds.

So it went. That first morning we knocked off ten barracuda, several kingfish, six mackerel, one wahoo, and my one sail. Actually I killed more fish than Ernest, but that was only because he spent most of his time giving me unnecessary instructions.

As we went back to port, Ernest was very excited about the wahoo I had caught. "You don't get them often," he said. "They're great eating."

"We'll have it?" I asked.

"I always give the kill to the crew," he said. "We buy what we eat."

Properly hatted, coated, and gloved, I went out with the big fisherman every day for a week. Ernest was then finishing *To Have and Have Not*. When he killed a lot of fish, he went home happy, in a good mood for writing the next morning. If the killing was poor, the genial Ernest turned morose. This accounts, I am sure, for the unevenness of the last chapters of *To Have and Have Not*. The passages that flash across the pages like meteors were written on the good mornings. The duller sections, my hunch is, were ground out after we had killed nothing but mackerel.

I could go on about Hemingway at great length but it seems to me a rather distasteful way to gain a vicarious reputation by boasting of one's friendship with a man of great stature who is now dead. I'll leave it at this; I knew him well, liked him enormously, and am proud of my close friendship with his widow, Mary Hemingway, who is a fine person in her own right.

142

My *Collier's* office, small as it was, was often shared informally by Heywood Broun and John McClain. Heywood liked to write his columns there, where he could always hire a delivery boy if he was short of time, and McClain, after touring the waterfronts, found Park Avenue a convenient part of town to write his stuff for the *Sun*. My quarters sometimes got a little crowded, but the company was good.

One afternoon Heywood invited everyone in sight to a cocktail party Sinclair Lewis was throwing at the Essex House. John and I had nothing better to do, and the price recommended it. Kyle Crichton, who was finishing an article in the adjoining cubicle, begged off. He had once been quite close to Lewis and his wife, but distance had intervened when both the Lewises went for his scalp in print, and Kyle publicly and wittily retaliated by portraying Dorothy Thompson as President of the United States.

"While I can overlook a lot in a man of Lewis' talent," Kyle told Heywood, "I no longer feel able to drink his liquor."

By the time Heywood and John and I reached Lewis' suite, the party was in full cry and the host was looking and acting like a rewarmed cadaver. Sober, he may have been a companion of qualities, as many have maintained, but since I never saw him except this once, I can only report him as a completely obnoxious man. When he greeted Heywood as "you fat son of bitch," there was nothing in it but meanness. And when he rolled his eyes at me and added obstreperously, "Who in hell are you?" I was ready to take my trade elsewhere.

Another of Lewis' guests was also getting the treatment, and though he was a large man physically, he was visibly wilting. "Fat boy," I heard Lewis snarl at him, "do you think anyone but your editor ever finished reading a book of yours?"

I watched Heywood, who seemed to know the big man, detach him and lead him to the bar. John and I followed. The big man downed a bourbon with a trembling hand, then said quite unhappily that he would like to escape. When Heywood suggested that we all go to the Stork Club, he brightened immediately. Then a shy smile spread over his face. As though confessing a mortal sin to a priest, he said, "I've never been to a night club in my life. Do you think we can get into one?"

"I think so," Heywood said gravely. "These boys and I know Sherman Billingsley pretty well."

A few minutes later the four of us were in a cab, fitting rather

143

snugly, when the big man said apologetically to John and me, "We really haven't met, have we? My name is Tom Wolfe." He said it humbly, as though sure that the name would mean nothing to us.

At the Stork we sat at Billingsley's Table 50, in the middle of things, and Tom, a real country boy, reminding me of some of the rookie Dodgers I had known, was entranced with the music and the beautiful women. When Heywood ordered champagne, Tom was aghast at the extravagance. He felt better when Billingsley was also able to produce a supply of Jack Daniels.

We spent a pleasant hour together, and then Tom turned to Heywood and said in some concern, "I live in Brooklyn, as you know, and so I spend a lot of time on the subways, and it seems to me about every time I come to New York someone comes up to me and says, 'Aren't you Heywood Broun?' I'll bet no one ever says to you, 'Aren't you Thomas Wolfe?'"

Heywood slipped an arm around Wolfe's broad shoulders. "It happens all the time," he said.

As our party broke up, Wolfe asked us where to find his subway. Heywood, who would sooner have walked on hot coals than ride a subway train, ordered a Carey Cadillac for Tom and had Billingsley add it to his bill. We saw Tom into the limousine and watched it drive off.

"There goes a great man," said Heywood, almost reverently.

Not all of my favorite characters of the thirties are still around, alas, but one of them, the tavern keeper with the face but not the manner of a cherub, is going stronger than ever. I refer to the Philadelphia boy who began life with the name Bernard but was soon and ever afterward called Toots because his baby sister couldn't say the longer one. During my first years on *Collier's,* Toots Shor was managing Billy LaHiff's Tavern on West Forty-eighth Street, a couple of blocks from the new or uptown Madison Square Garden. When I say *managing,* I mean Toots was operating the place to suit himself. One night I was sitting with him and his wife Marian when Jack Spooner, the headwaiter, approached with a problem. The fights had just let out at the Garden, and the place was filling up.

"I've got six real big spenders from Chicago who want a table," Jack told Toots, "and all I got is the two you're saving in case some of the fight writers drop in. How about I give this party one?"

"Do I know these guys?" Toots demanded.

"No, but I used to take care of them at the Stork Club," Jack said. "They're big wheels."

"Tell them to get lost!" Toots roared. "Remind them I run this place for my friends. Who wants strangers in here?"

Baby—as the petite Mrs. Shor was usually called—smiled her approval, but I pointed out that Toots would never get rich by turning down trade.

"I don't want to be a millionaire," Toots declared cheerily. "I just wanna live like one."

This rough and ready philosophy was not Toots' only contribution to friendly living. He also had humanitarian impulses, and one of them, in 1939, led to my writing a *Collier's* piece that almost got us both killed. My subject was Mickey Walker, the last of the ring gladiators who loved to fight because they had hearts and brains that were only happy when they were fighting. If Mickey, the Toy Bulldog, was paid to battle before a mob of screaming fans at the Garden or the Polo Grounds, so much the better, but if the fracas happened to occur in a night club or a hotel room, that was all right too.

The welterweight champion, after retiring, had opened a tavern just across the street from the Garden. His place was jammed on fight nights but at the end of the business week there was seldom much loot to show for it. Trouble was, Mickey was a notoriously easy touch, especially after a few beers. His place of business got to be known unofficially as the Tavern of the Bite.

Toots, with his palship and civic concern, told me that something in *Collier's* about Mickey might bring a lot of out-of-the-neighborhood trade to his place and turn a sagging operation into a success. For two or three nights I sat in a booth at Mickey's and reviewed his wild and woolly career with him, including his near knockout of heavyweight Jack Sharkey, and his crazy win over heavyweight Paul Swiderski, when he climbed into the ring orry-eyed drunk under the misapprehension that the bout had been canceled. I also heard about Mickey's seven marriages and the fortune he had made and squandered during his seventeen years in the ring. I didn't quite say it in my story, but the Toy Bulldog seemed to me a perfect symbol of the Wide-open Twenties.

The week after my story appeared, I went into Billy LaHiff's and found Toots beaming. "Good story on Mickey, Quent. He and Doc

145

Kearns and Joe Benjamin are inside and they think it's great. Let's go in and have a powder with them."

We went in. The three men thanked me for the story as if I had done them all a personal favor. Jack "Doc" Kearns, a scrawny, hoarse-voiced, one-time brawler, had managed Mickey throughout his fighting career. Joe Benjamin was a slender, good-looking man who had just missed the lightweight championship and had retired to spar now and then with the bottle.

The five of us had several drinks, which Mickey and his two pals certainly did not need, and suddenly Mickey turned his slightly flattened nose my way and snarled, "How much did you get for that article?"

I told him I couldn't be sure, since I worked on a salary.

"What's it break down to?" he insisted.

When I told him maybe eight hundred dollars, he said, "You cheap bum—you might at least split it with me!"

Toots and I were shocked. "OK, Mickey, if that's how you feel about it," I said. "Toots, get four hundred out of the damper and see if it will make Mickey happy."

It seemed to me that Kearns and Benjamin were embarrassed by Mickey's bad behavior. However, they said nothing.

Jack Spooner, having cased the register, came back and reported to Toots that there was not more than fifty dollars in it.

"There's only one way to settle this," the five-and-a-half-foot Mickey growled. "We'll go out in the street and I'll take care of you."

"Quent and I go as an entry," Toots warned.

"So do Doc and Joe and me," Walker replied.

The few patrons in the place stared in wonderment as they saw the five of us heading for the door. I was still too angry at Walker to be as frightened as I should have been. Toots and I were up against three of the best barroom fighters in America. There wasn't a dirty trick Kearns didn't know, and as for Benjamin, legend had it that he and Jack Dempsey had once engaged in a free-for-all and the lightweight had won. I had asked Dempsey about this and while he had neither confirmed nor denied, he had assured me that Benjamin could flatten any man alive.

Toots, who had more sense about what we were getting into than I did, nudged me as we neared the door. "Watch Benjamin," he whispered. "He's in better shape than the others."

Then Benjamin laughed. Grabbing Mickey by the shoulder, he swung him around. "This is crazy, Mike. Quent and Toots are our pals. What are we doing, fighting with our friends?"

Mickey looked uncertainly at Benjamin, then at Toots and me, then again at Benjamin. "Yeah. You got a point. Okay, let's go back and have a drink on me."

"Not a chance!" Toots barked. "This is my joint. Come to the bar and have a drink on me!"

That was the end of it, except that next day when I realized how close I'd come to being smeared all over Forty-eighth Street, I said a prayer of thanks to Joe Benjamin for turning the tide with a little common sense.

Quite a few years ago, that happened. Today, Mickey, a long-time passenger on the wagon, is an artist who has had four one-man shows and sells his paintings for substantial sums. Doc Kearns, now well over seventy, still manages fighters. He makes more money than I ever will and spends a good part of it on orange juice, no longer touching the other stuff. Joe Benjamin, still handsome, is now a liquor salesman.

One night not long ago Benjamin and I were talking about the evening when he and his pals were close to eliminating Toots and me from the human race.

"I don't know," Joe said thoughtfully. "You and Toots might have taken us. You were both sober. We were stoned."

I looked at him sternly. "Joe, you're a damned liar."

"I'm not a liar," he replied with a gentle smile. "I'm a salesman."

Any writer who worked around New York during the years I'm writing about inevitably has a favorite story to tell about Mark Hellinger, who was a wit, everybody's friend, and the gifted and industrious author of a daily eight-hundred-word fiction piece in the *News*. My offering concerns the night I watched him—and in part helped him— get conned out of fifty dollars.

It was impossible to buy Mark a drink. He was a generous man to begin with. Further, his stories emerged from the fact that he was an excellent listener, and that the mob guys, stage stars, fighters, cops, chorus girls, and others that he got his material from told their best stories with a drink in hand. One might expect Mark, after a working lifetime spent in such company, to be quite sharp. And he himself thought he knew all the answers. He and I were in The Tavern one night, chatting with Sullivan, one of Toots' bartenders, when a seedy stranger came up, cackled happily, slapped Mark on the back, and said, "How are you, boy? Come on, you and Reynolds have a drink with me. Set 'em up, Sully."

Mark looked faintly puzzled, and I was certainly puzzled, but he nodded, and Sullivan served us the drinks. "On my check, Sully," Mark said, at which the stranger protested forcefully but without altering the matter. Then he said:

"Mark, you know, and Reynolds knows, that I don't drink much, but this a tough night for me. My wife had a baby last week. I just now went to the hospital to take her and the kid home, but the hospital told me I owed 'em fifty bucks and they won't let my wife go till I got it up. It happens I got the shorts today. The laugh is, I bet ten on a horse that won at Jamaica and paid ten to one, but you know these local bookies don't pay up till the day after the race, so the old lady and the kid gotta stay in that lousy hospital another night —just because of a lousy fifty dollars."

Mark was concerned. "Look, pally, if a quick fifty will help you, here it is."

"Oh, I couldn't take your money, Mark," said the man. But by now Mark had stuck a few bills into his coat pocket. With tears of gratitude the man left.

"Who's your friend?" I asked Mark.

"*My* friend? He mentioned your name."

"I never saw him in my life," I said. "Sully, you know the guy?"

"Never saw him before," Sullivan said in disgust. "I tried to get your eye, Mr. Hellinger, but you was too busy giving him your money. If Mr. Shor was in tonight, he'd have thrown the freeloading bum out on his can. You really got took."

Mark thought it over. "Well, no, I didn't," he decided. "Maybe he didn't need it to bail his old lady and baby out of the hospital. Maybe he needed it to get square with a bookie or to buy some broad a meal. What's the difference?—he needed it. I'm glad I had it to help him out."

Sullivan didn't even blink—he was accustomed to Mark's whims while I knew that Mark was not covering up—that his charity was genuine.

I'm lingering over memories, of course, but it's because all these friends helped make wonderful years for me—the last careless, casual

148

years of my life. I couldn't foresee it then, but soon I was to be writing about man's inhumanity to man, about the death of a French city named Beauvais, about the heroic spirit of the English during the Blitz. Life was not again to be so simple and full of fun as it was in the Thirties, and today it seems constantly harder to find replacements for a Mark Hellinger, a Hemingway, or a Heywood Broun. Or—to draw in one more peerless character—a Robert Benchley.

While Benchley was a humorist, those of us who knew him well sometimes find it difficult to remember one devastatingly funny thing he said. It was the general outlook, rather than the individual remark that mattered. We are more apt to recall how much fun it was to be around him.

It was Mr. Benchley—all I ever called him except perhaps Benchley, though a few called him Bob, Bobby, or even Fred, for no discernible reason—who introduced me to St. Claire Pollock. He made it an occasion. John McClain and Benchley and I were up quite late one night. Well into the new day McClain went home on the flimsy excuse that he had to meet an early boat in order to interview Winston Churchill. When I suggested to Benchley that he and I should also call it a night, he said anxiously, "You've got to help me out, Quent. My son Nat is coming down from school right now, and I promised to meet him at Grand Central Station at seven. If I go to sleep, I'll never wake up in time to meet him, and that would be a hell of a way for a father to behave. You'll have to stay up with me."

His appeal was not to be denied. We played through one more after-hours bistro and then invaded an all-night restaurant and had a very early breakfast. Afterward, we sat glumly looking at one another.

"I wish you had sent your son to CCNY or Columbia," I said. "Because you sent him to Harvard, we have two more hours to kill."

"There must be something I can do for you," Benchley said, shading his watch and listening to it. Then he raised his head sharply. "Have you ever been to see St. Claire Pollock?" Before I could speak, he went on: "This is a privilege I claim. Come along, Quent."

He climbed into a cab. "Grant's Tomb, please." The startled driver recognized the authority in Benchley's voice and aimed his cab northward without a word.

"Just who is this guy that we can call on at an hour like this?" I ventured.

149

Benchley was not telling. All he said was, "It's odd how few people have ever heard of St. Claire Pollock."

At the Tomb, in the gray, silent dawn, Benchley told our driver to wait. We climbed a low iron fence and went through some shrubbery to a gravestone. Benchley found it unerringly. Later, I learned that he came here quite often.

I read the stone:

ERECTED TO THE MEMORY OF AN AMIABLE CHILD
ST. CLAIRE POLLOCK
DIED 15 JULY 1797
IN THE FIFTH YEAR OF HIS AGE

We didn't say much on our trip downtown to the station, but I could sense beneath Benchley's obvious satisfaction at introducing me to something rare, a warm parental feeling for the amiable child—dead so long, but still remembered. It pleases me to recall Benchley thus, touched by his own feeling for someone gone.

And there it is, the six years I spent writing about race horses and rhumba dancers, pitchers and prize fighters, golfers and tavern keepers—while Mussolini's black shirts overran Abyssinia and Franco's conquered Spain, while the Nazis took over Austria and Hitler conned Neville Chamberlain and Edouard Daladier into handing him the beating heart of Czechoslovakia. Sometimes, when I thought back to my experiences in Germany in 1933, I wondered what some of my later journalism was worth. It was not easy to remember my mood of indignation the day the midget climbing onto J. P. Morgan's lap got in the way of my dispatch from Heidelberg. The excuse I found for what I was doing at *Collier's* was that I was having an awfully good time gathering the information, and that I was being well paid. And, of course, that I was writing the kind of stories the American public wanted to read. It was easy to read—and easy to forget.

10

The wounded don't cry

Eddie Cantor and Rudy Vallee ranked high on Mom's list of favorite entertainers. Both happened to be appearing in Brooklyn the first week in November, 1939—Eddie at the Metropolitan, Rudy at the Paramount.

Mom went to see Eddie on Monday, Rudy on Tuesday. Ordinarily, that would have been the start of a great week for her. Late Tuesday afternoon she telephoned me at my office and told me she would be cooking veal birds, my favorite dinner dish, next day. That was all. She didn't *ask* me to come home, she just let me know what I would find on the table. Though Mom never quite said it, I think she sincerely doubted that I, a bachelor, living in Manhattan, knew how to take care of myself.

I went home early on Wednesday and found Mom alone. While we waited for Pop and my brother Don to come in, Mom told me what a wonderful time she had had watching Cantor and Vallee. She knew that I had written stories about both of them. "Why don't you ask those boys to come have dinner with us some time?" she suggested.

I explained that entertainers doing three shows a day usually stuck close to their theaters.

"That Eddie is such a good man," she went on. "Do you know, he even makes speeches for Catholic charities? I'd love to meet him."

151

"I'll fix it, Mom," I said casually.

"Now I have something to tell you, Quentin." Even though she said it lightly, there was a change in her tone that warned me. "Tomorrow, I'm going to have a slight operation."

"Operation for what?" I gasped. At sixty-six, Mom looked the picture of health. She had never been hospitalized in her life. She had never even been really sick.

She blushed. "A silly thing, really. It's just a minor condition that happens to people of my age. I find it embarrassing to talk about it. Dr. Zimmerman says he's only going to do an exploratory operation. A real operation probably won't even be necessary."

When I heard this, I felt easier. For years we had regarded Victor Zimmerman not only as the best of doctors but as a well-loved friend. If anything serious had been wrong with Mom, I was sure he would have let me know. Nevertheless, I suggested telephoning my brother Jim, who was now working in a steel plant in Alabama.

"Don't you dare!" said Mom. "The poor boy will only worry, and there isn't a thing for him or any of you to worry about."

Next day Mom entered Brooklyn Hospital. My sisters, both of them married now, and my brother Don, a reporter for the *Herald Tribune,* filled her room with flowers. Pop, to whom Mom's illness was a shock, had a hard time keeping up with her good spirits and complete confidence. When I visited her, a few hours after the biopsy was done, she seemed as cheerful as always. She told us she enjoyed being in a hospital. "I'm getting to see so much of you all," she said with a twinkle.

Then I went to Dr. Zimmerman's office to get his report. He broke the bad news as gently as he could. Mom had cancer. He and the consulting surgeon were going ahead with the operation to remove it. Mom had a good chance, he thought, for a complete recovery.

I asked if Mom knew what was wrong with her. He thought not. "You're going to have to tell Pop," I said. "I don't see how I can break it to him."

"Let's not tell him yet," he said. "And I think it's best to wait a bit before you tell Con and Marge. It may be easier on your mother if they don't know."

I telephoned Jim in Alabama and told him everything we knew. "I'll get the next plane out of here," Jim said. "Tell Mom the plant gave me a vacation."

152

I don't think we fooled Mom on that one. Next morning Jim and I were in her room as she was about to go up to surgery. "You know what the trouble is, don't you, dear?" she asked Jim softly.

Jim looked at Mom. She was smiling as always, and he could not lie. "Yes, I know, Mom. And I know you're going to be all right."

"Of course I will. I'll see you again before you know it."

The first part of the two-stage operation went well. After it was over, Dr. Zimmerman was confident of its success. For ten days Mom maintained her sunny disposition, never complaining. Jim and I, still the only ones in the family who knew the truth, went along with the pretense that this was all just a minor illness. Pop, so far as I could tell, honestly believed that Mom soon would be well again. We made plans for the big Thanksgiving dinner we would all have at home before Jim went back to Alabama.

Perhaps it took this illness to make some of us truly realize what a remarkable woman Mom was. She had so subordinated herself in her role as mother and housewife that we were inclined to forget how important a person she was in her own right. When she and Pop were married, she had of course given up any thought of teaching. Then, when we were grown up, she had filled the void left by our decreasing need of her by returning to college to earn her degree in education. Not content with that, she had entered Fordham University Graduate School and when she was sixty had received her master's degree, which was something none of her children ever earned. We were all proud of Mom, but somehow we took her too much for granted.

During the days when we were waiting for the second operation, I suddenly remembered my casual promise about Eddie Cantor and Rudy Vallee. I made two phone calls. We were all in Mom's room the evening before the operation when a sharp knock sounded on her door. "Hey, Mom—can I come in?" a bright voice demanded.

Mom looked wonderingly around at us. Not a Reynolds was missing. "Who is it?" she asked.

Instead of answering, Eddie Cantor began to sing, "If you knew Susie . . . Oh, oh, oh what a girl . . ." Still singing, he opened the door and pranced in. "I hear you like candy, Mom." Putting a large, gaily wrapped package on the table next to her bed, Eddie leaned down and kissed her on the forehead. Then for half an hour he regaled her with songs and jokes.

Just as Eddie was departing, Dr. Zimmerman and a nurse came in.

153

"Jim," he said to Pop with mock sternness, "get these noisy kids of yours out of here. I want Katherine to have a good sleep tonight."

While the nurse was giving Mom a sleeping pill, the telephone rang. Don answered it. "It's for you, Mom, but the man wouldn't tell me his name." Mom took the phone. We could all hear the voice at the other end singing "My time is your time. . . ." Rudy followed it with "The Maine Stein Song." Then, while Mom and Rudy chatted, the sleeping pill took effect. When Rudy said, "Good night," she was already asleep.

The second operation went well, and for a week all of us were full of hope. Then Mom died.

I found her death almost impossible to accept. Several times during the next week Heywood Broun took me to lunch. He had recently finished his instruction with Monsignor Fulton Sheen and had been baptized. I continued to be a sullen companion, but Heywood was not much impressed by this. One day he said sternly, "Quent, listen to me. You can't live with a ghost—even with the ghost of someone you loved. Get hold of yourself."

I thought that over and it began to make sense. That's what I told myself, but actually I've never gotten over her death. I never will.

Then, a month after Mom's death, Heywood himself was dead, struck down by pneumonia. Those who knew him could hardly believe it. Heywood had seemed indestructible. He was the man who could stay up all night singing the Harvard songs he loved so much, and then without sleep, hurry to Newark to march on a picket line. He was the man who could spend a day writing columns to get ahead of his deadlines, then attend a dinner and without any preparation or notes, make a magnificently witty or emotional speech.

Heywood was a man of many talents and interests, but it was the quality of his friendship that counted most to those of us he left to mourn him. Writers, ball players, actors, cabinet members, labor leaders, businessmen, night club owners, cab drivers, waiters, doormen, ex-convicts—all had known and loved him, and sat elbow to elbow in the vastness of St. Patrick's Cathedral, listening to Monsignor Sheen's eulogy. I sat with Heywood's second wife, Connie, and with his son Heywood, Junior.

Connie's grief for the man she had affectionately called the Commodore had shattered her. As we left the pew, she suddenly sagged.

154

Mayor LaGuardia, seated just behind us, slipped out of his pew to walk on Connie's other side, and together we supported her on the seemingly endless walk up the long aisle.

I rode to the cemetery with Connie, young Heywood, and Monsignor Sheen. As Connie sobbed quietly, I tried to comfort her. "Connie," I said, almost hearing Heywood's voice, "you can't live with a ghost."

Monsignor Sheen patted her hand. "Quent is right, Connie," he said gently. The sedative Connie's doctor had given her finally took hold and she slept all the way to the cemetery.

It was a long time before I could resign myself to Mom's death and, to a lesser degree, to Heywood's death. Not even my work could fill the void. The war in Europe had begun, but I wasn't much interested in it even if *Collier's* was. It still seemed remote to me in March, 1940, the day Charley Colebaugh suggested that I go to Europe and get accredited to either the German or Allied armies. Since the Germans had been making most of the news, he favored my going to Berlin.

I went to the German Consulate to apply for a visa. Returning a couple of days later to pick up my papers, I was told politely that my request had been turned down. When I mentioned that I had had no difficulty in being admitted to Germany in 1933, the consul-general looked unhappy. "Perhaps, Herr Reynolds, you wrote something uncomplimentary about us," he suggested.

I hung on till I learned that my application had provoked a one-word response from the German Foreign office: "UNDESIRABLE." There was no appeal from that. Soon afterward I was on my way to Paris by way of Naples. I went on the *Conte di Savoia*. There were only a handful of passengers aboard that lovely ship, and each of us had a steward to wait on him. Though I could not guess it, this was the last luxury traveling I was to do for some years.

One of my doubtful talents seems to be attracting odd characters, and I found one on the *Conte di Savoia*. Besides being an American rubber magnate, he was almost the only passenger beside myself who enjoyed sitting up after dark. In the course of our crossing I learned some interesting things about the rubber business. My man, Graves Smith, was on his way to England to buy all the rubber he could find, a proposition so completely open-ended as to make no sense to me, especially when he told me he had already sold most of what he had not yet bought. The trick in rubber, it appeared, was to sell it for future delivery while it was still oozing out of trees in Malaya and other picturesque places, and then hustle around the world buying it at a lower price. It is a truism that many otherwise intelligent people cannot understand why or how writers make their livings, but alongside this man's operation my trade seemed abjectly rational.

Besides brokering the stuff, Smith had a sideline—manufacturing rubber falsies for glamour girls. He named several film beauties who were using his product. The older types, it seemed, had to be strapped in place; his were hollow and adhered by suction, making possible the well-developed front in conjunction with the backless evening dress. "Gravy" Smith then practically kayoed me with the information that his gay deceivers were chocolate flavored. Rubber in its refined state, he explained, had a disagreeable odor, but this was cancelled by a judicious addition of chocolate and a little peppermint. . . .

Gravy had me on the ropes. "There's a rock outside," I said. "Let's go out and have a look at it."

"What's a rock doing out in the ocean?" Gravy asked warily.

"It's one the Prudential boys put up," I said—and we carried our drinks out on deck and admired Gibraltar.

It was like that all the way to Naples. Life was good. In April, 1940, a month before Dunkirk, it was still, for many who were not yet close to it, a comfortable war. The news had come, of course, that the Germans had taken Denmark and Norway, but it never occurred to me or anyone I talked with that they would dare attack Belgium or the Netherlands. And of course the Maginot Line, that incredibly well-publicized piece of French engineering, would keep the Germans out of France. On that score there could be no doubt.

I looked forward to having my base in Paris, and was glad, now, that I had been turned down by the Germans. Berlin would have been a war capital. But even being at war, Paris would be Paris. After I had written a few stories there, I would probably cross to London before returning to New York. I had first become acquainted with Fleet Street when I stopped in London on the way to Berlin in 1933. It would be good to visit there again and renew my contacts with the men and women of the *Express* and the *Daily Mail*. And all this on an expense account. It seemed too good to be true, that spring of 1940. And, of course, it was.

156

In Paris, after checking into the Ritz, I looked up an old friend, Ken Downs, who ran the INS bureau, hoping that he could show me the ropes. He and another correspondent I knew, Bob Cooper of the *Times* of London, took me to the Hotel Continental, the headquarters of the foreign press section, with the idea of getting me accredited to the French Army. Without accreditation, I would not be allowed to go outside Paris.

I presented my *Collier's* credentials to Pierre Comert, a charming official who was obviously determined to make the deal as hard as possible. Before I could be accredited, he told me, I would have to have a recommendation and certification from the American Ambassador, William Bullitt. Further, I would have to submit six photographs of myself and outfit myself with a uniform.

I had expected the uniform. The French—and all other armies—insisted that correspondents visiting the front go in uniform. The reasoning was sound enough. The fronts were under constant observation. If the enemy saw a man in civilian clothes mingling with the troops, he might be taken for a VIP, say a Cabinet Minister, leading to special efforts to eliminate him and the surrounding troops. But I had not expected the rest of Comert's run-around. The Nazis turned a correspondent down with less fuss than the French.

Accompanied by Downs and Cooper, I soon returned to the Continental with all the required trophies, including a tailor's receipt for a uniform in progress. "Ah, you Americans!" M. Comert exclaimed, obviously impressed as well as dejected by my speedy reappearance. "Now, I shall send all this information through the required channels," he explained, warming to his task. "Your application will go first to the *Deuxième Bureau,* and if it clears itself there, it will go to the War Office. In all, you may expect to hear one way or another in, let us say, three weeks. You are prepared to wait for this accreditation?"

"So this is the way it is?" I said, staring him in the eye.

"This is the way it is," Comert agreed sweetly.

I had one more card in my hand. "May I remind you, Monsieur Comert, that the American magazine I represent had a weekly circulation of three million people, and that it is entirely sympathetic to the French cause?"

Comert bristled. "May I remind you, Monsieur Reynolds, that France declared war without consulting your admirable magazine?

157

France does not regard the esteem of *Collier's* magazine as of the first importance."

In the face of this, Cooper, Downs, and I regrouped at the Ritz bar for a conference. "What in hell is the *Deuxième Bureau?*" I asked.

"They're the boys in charge of propaganda, censorship, internal security, and of course the foreign press," Downs told me. "We've got to play ball with them."

"Things must be bad at the front," Cooper commented. "Even though I'm accredited, I have yet to see any fighting."

Thinking I might have an angle, I asked George, the Ritz's bartender, for a cable blank. After composing my message with some care, I showed it to Downs and Cooper. They both laughed. "What the hell, all you can do is try it on him," Ken said.

We returned to the Hotel Continental. M. Comert looked a little pained as we walked into his office so soon again.

"A simple and friendly request," I said humbly. "I am about to send President Roosevelt a cable asking him to facilitate my accreditation with Premier Reynaud. Naturally I do not wish to go over your head, and so I have brought the message to you for your approval."

I handed him the cable. He read it, as well he might, with popping eyes:

DEAR UNCLE FRANKLIN, AM HAVING DIFFICULTY GETTING ACCREDITED TO FRENCH ARMY. TIME IS IMPORTANT. WOULD YOU PHONE OR CABLE PREMIER REYNAUD AND ASK HIM TO HURRY THINGS UP? IT WAS GRAND OF YOU TO PHONE ME LAST NIGHT. PLEASE GIVE MY LOVE TO AUNT ELEANOR.

QUENT

"You," said M. Comert in awe, "are a nephew of the President?" I smiled but said nothing. He appeared to undergo a great awakening. "Ah, but of course—Quentin Reynolds, Quentin Roosevelt. A family name, *sans doute*."

"I never talk about it," I said modestly. "Really, monsieur, I would prefer that you mentioned it to no one."

"But you understand that this places a new face upon our transaction?" Comert assured me earnestly. "I shall telephone for your accreditation at once."

158

"In that case," I suggested, "I will not bother to send my cable."
I made a move to retrieve it.

"Not at all!" Comert placed it in his desk drawer. "Allow me to dispatch it for you. Through our facilities, it should reach your uncle more swiftly than by the ordinary route."

Downs, Cooper, and I played it deadpan to the end, but as I left Comert's office my sensation was one of rapid sinking. During the next twenty-four hours I expected the worst. What would it be? A summons to the Embassy? A cable conveying the White House's puzzlement or annoyance? FBI agents dropping into the Ritz to investigate me? Thankfully, none of these things happened, although I confirmed that the obnoxious M. Comert had sent the cable as promised. Perhaps they had wastebaskets at the White House for that sort of message. I fervently hoped so.

I was handed, soon, the precious pink card that allowed me to "circulate in the zone of the French armies." Now, like Downs and Cooper, all I lacked was the pass that would enable me to travel to the front.

Waiting for it, I went on several short tours with guides assigned by the French public relations forces. At the Chantilly airdrome I interviewed some of the French fighter pilots and inspected their Morane, Potez, and Bloch fighter planes. On a hilltop north of Paris I watched my first plane duel, between a short, stub-winged Messerschmitt and a Morane. The lighter, inferior French plane fought bravely, but it was not a match for the invader, and down it went. I tried to write something about these interviews and episodes that would be worth the cable tolls but with the censor cutting half my words, little of value got through.

My ire against the bureaucrats increased when I discovered that my old pal H. R. Knickerbocker, who had succeeded me as an INS correspondent in 1933 and was now in France, was going practically anywhere he wanted to go. He and another of my correspondent friends from Berlin, Tom Delmer, were good friends of Premier Reynaud and Defense Minister Georges Mandel; as a result, they got every facility they wanted. Ken Downs was annoyed about this. Even though he and Knick were both INS men, Ken had the instinct that burns in the heart of any good reporter to be first man at the fire. Bob Cooper was more than annoyed. In his refined way he was out-

159

raged that Delmer's *Daily Express,* called by many "The Harlot of Fleet Street," should have privileges that were denied to the *Times.* Although Bob was virtually incapable of expressing anger, it seemed to me that his protest, if I could bring him to make it, might be all the more effective for its gentlemanly passion. I proposed a simple strategy that made sense to Ken, and we took Bob to lunch at Maxim's, starting him off with a couple of stiff cocktails. Through the meal we kept his wine glass filled.

"When I was in Berlin," I remarked over the salad, "I remember that Norman Ebutt and Douglas Reed of the *Times* got every facility they asked for. But they were two tough cookies. They stood up for their rights even to the Nazis."

"I stand up for my rights," Cooper said sullenly.

"Of course you do," I said soothingly. "Anyway, it doesn't matter to me if Tom Delmer is up at the front, and the *Express* gets an exclusive story every day."

"It's certainly funny-looking, though," Downs said, "to see a lousy rag like the *Express* printing stories that the greatest paper in England—maybe in the world—can't get."

"Oh, well, it's something that can't be helped," I said. "Let's forget about it."

Like a couple of Borgias, Ken and I watched our poison take effect. Finally our victim banged his glass on the table. "They can't do this to me," he muttered. "I represent the *Times.* If I don't get it this try, I'll see Mandel and Reynaud myself."

Skipping dessert, we bundled Cooper into a cab and headed for the Hotel Continental. Cooper was still grumbling. "The Prime Minister always gives his speeches to the *Times* in advance. The *Times* is more than a newspaper. The *Times* is England. It's the spirit of—" He groped for a crusher.

"Of Nelson," I supplied. "The French can't insult the *Times* like this, Bob."

As we went into the Continental, Ken planted one more harpoon. "Tell Comert the three of us have to travel together. Tell him I own a car and we all want passes. Tell him if he refuses, you'll make a formal protest to Neville Chamberlain. Get tough, Bob."

"Damn right I will!"

I think this was the only time I ever heard the mild-mannered Cooper swear. When he reappeared from Comert's office, he had a

160

letter with a pass for each of us. For a period of five days, beginning immediately, we could visit whatever parts of France we wished. If it was not a total victory, the spirit of England had at least achieved an impressive breakthrough.

An hour later, wearing our uniforms, we piled into Ken's French Ford station wagon at the INS office and headed northeast toward Nancy. We traveled light. Besides linen and a toilet kit, our musette bags—following Ken's suggestion—contained only a half-dozen cans of sardines and chicken, a carton of cigarettes, and two bottles of brandy. Downs thought that the smokes and liquor might generate some good will with the officers at the front.

As we drove north on a beautiful spring afternoon we had little idea of what we might find. The only news that had been coming to Paris was the official daily communiqué, and it was invariably optimistic. Downs had just received word from Barry Faris that the tightness of the censorship had prompted Knickerbocker to switch from the French to the British forces. Tom Delmer had switched with him. The lack of information argued that things must be going badly. For the past week every communiqué had been to the effect that the French had repulsed another German attack, inflicting heavy losses. No French attack was ever mentioned, but apparently this didn't worry the Parisians. We had seen Maxim's and the Tour d'Argent and other restaurants crowded every night, to say nothing of the Montmartre night clubs and the Ritz, Crillon, and George V bars. Though the poilus were dying less than three hundred miles from Paris, it all seemed remote.

Downs, who had been working in France for several years, knew the roads almost as well as he knew those of his native Montana. Some four hours out of Paris, during which time we had seen little to suggest that we were traveling through a country at war, we heard an angry buzzing ahead of us. Heinkels in a V formation were flying toward us at low altitude, using the road the way hounds use a trail.

Ken pulled out his ignition key and we tumbled into the roadside ditch, but the planes zoomed over us without pressing a trigger. Though we learned later that their mission was to strafe anything moving in an effort to stop supplies from reaching the front, a single stalled car on an otherwise empty road was apparently not worth a burst.

We spent the first of our five nights in Nancy, and here we began

161

to see ambulances filled with wounded. Travel restrictions, air-raid warnings, censors and bureaucrats, enemy planes in the sky—all these signified war, in some degree or other, but it was the sight of wounded men being trucked back to Paris that brought the actuality home to me with an impact I hadn't felt before.

Next day in Verdun, Downs, always the epicure, found us a three-star restaurant, and while French soldiers and civilians died not many miles ahead of us, we ate an excellent lunch, starting with *pâté de foie gras* and ending with *fraises de bois*. With the entrée we sipped Nuits Saint-George; with the strawberries, champagne. Then, while we listened to the throaty roar of distant artillery fire, Ken introduced me to *framboise,* a raspberry derivative. Ever since 1940 it has remained a good friend of mine, but I never drink it without recalling the somewhat unreal setting in which I first encountered it.

Our second morning out from Paris we reached the headquarters of General Charles Huntziger at Montmédy. When we presented our credentials to the colonel in charge of press relations, Downs asked if there were any officers available to show us the front.

"We have several press officers," said the colonel dryly, "but no correspondents. No doubt the correspondents find Paris more comfortable and interesting than our part of France."

"That," said Downs, "is the fault of your *Deuxième Bureau,* which apparently wishes to keep your war a secret."

The colonel nodded sadly.

Ken, Bob, and I were each assigned an officer and conducted forward to different combat units. My English-speaking lieutenant, Charles LeBrun, announced that he would take me to a pillbox, as yet undiscovered by the enemy, from which I would have an excellent view of the enemy line.

The distance was five kilometers. At first we walked through a dense wood, part of the Ardennes Forest. Then we advanced into a meadow. Occasionally a German shell would land near us. I say "near" because that was my opinion. Lieutenant LeBrun assured me they were landing half a mile away. Nonetheless, I dropped to the ground at every explosion.

"It is not necessary to worry about the explosions you hear," he explained. Being then an amateur, I could not properly evaluate his comforting theory that one is hit only by the shell or fragment he does not hear. Later, after some experience, I learned that a shell

162

can throw lethal fragments at least four hundred yards and that men certainly do hear the scream of scrap metal coming their way, as well as the explosion of a shell landing as close as fifty yards away.

The last kilometer of our walk seemed longer than all the rest. We had to cross two open fields that were, LeBrun told me, under direct observation by the enemy. He should have kept it a secret. My instant impulse was to charge forward, but this was old stuff to the lieutenant. Not in the least increasing his pace, he asked if the Tour d'Argent was still serving great food, and if the fish was still good at Armenonville in the Bois. As calmly as possible I assured him that both restaurants were up to par.

I was sweating when we reached the advance outpost, a well-buttressed dugout on the French side of a steep hill. The major in command told me that fifteen thousand Germans, a full division, were facing the French line here. "We captured a few this morning," he said, "and in the pocket of each was this." He showed me a slip of paper reading, in German: "Soldiers of the Reich, stand fast. If you retreat you will be court-martialed. Your Fuehrer."

"We have a tough fight on our hands," the major told me. Thinking it would only worry him if I disclosed that very few people in Paris or anywhere else knew anything at all about his situation, I said only, "I hope you will win it," and then left the dugout with LeBrun and entered a tunnel halfway up the hill. After walking perhaps sixty yards in darkness, we emerged into the pillbox on the exposed side of the hill.

I was introduced to the two observers, Pierre and André, and then the three men suggested that I look out through the box's slits. My view was of a lovely green valley perhaps half a mile across, with a ridge of hills on the opposite side. At first I noticed nothing to indicate this was the actual spot where two nations were at war. Then, down the valley, I saw flashes of the German artillery. A moment later a roar spread up the valley toward us, muffled as it entered the narrow slits of our box.

"You are actually between the lines," LeBrun informed me nonchalantly. "Our troops and artillery are three kilometers back. This box is beautifully camouflaged, you understand, or I should not have brought you here."

André lifted the phone from its wall bracket and spoke to the dugout at the base of our hill. "All quiet. Nothing to report. The American journalist is here."

163

Then Pierre said, excitement in his voice, *"Le Boche!"*

Peering through one of the slits, I did not at first see what had alerted the observer. Then I heard a plane, its sound rapidly growing louder. A Messerschmitt flashed by, so close I felt I could have reached out of the box and touched it. It traversed the valley and returned. Two more planes materialized. Moranes. The Messerschmitt did not flee. Obviously it was willing to take them both on. As if by signal, both the German and French guns stopped firing. Save for the sound of the planes, the valley was silent. I had the impression that hundreds, perhaps thousands of hidden men were watching the air duel.

We could see the golden flashes from the four guns the Messerschmitt carried in its wings. One of the slower-flying Moranes was hit. I expected to see a spectacular death—a cloud of flame and smoke, the way it happened in the movies—but the plane died slowly. It wobbled, its motor choking, and heading for home, it passed over our heads at low altitude. That evening, after I left the pillbox, I learned that it had landed in an open field and that the pilot had walked away from the wreckage unhurt.

Now it was one against one. The German dived at the Frenchman, but the Frenchman, untouched, climbed and got on the tail of the Messerschmitt. We watched tensely, knowing that within a minute or two one or both of these pilots would probably die. Now the Morane was firing. Smoke began spiraling up from the Messerschmitt's engine. As it wheeled toward the German lines the Morane kept on its tail. Smoke trailed from the Messerschmitt's wings. A dot dropped from the dying plane and a moment later a parachute opened. The pilotless plane flew on, engulfed in flames, and disappeared. The Morane flew the length of the valley, impudently tipping its wings like an actor taking a bow from an enthusiastic audience.

When it disappeared, the quiet in our valley persisted for a time. Ridiculously, I heard birds singing. Several of them flew by our pillbox, perhaps feeling that the valley once more belonged to them.

It came time for me to leave the box. LeBrun led me back through the tunnel. We waited in the dugout for darkness. It fell like a blanket, and with it came rain. It was a long walk back to headquarters. We could not use a light. Twice we ran into barbed wire and had to work around it.

At headquarters I found Downs and Cooper waiting for me. Downs

164

had spent the day with the artillery; Cooper, with the infantry. We were invited to mess with the officers. Surprisingly, they had excellent omelets and vegetables. Even under the most difficult conditions, the French seem incapable of making bad omelets. The officers, lean and hard-looking, struck us as determined, dedicated men, tired though they obviously were from their day's work. It was not difficult to be impressed by such officers.

After our meal, we were given mattresses, blankets, and a floor to sleep on. We spent two more days watching the troops in action—and arriving at our conclusion that probably we were seeing France's best-trained, best-equipped land forces in action. Then it was time for us to return to Paris.

Driving back, we passed many ambulances. We discussed our separate findings. The plane battle I had watched from the pillbox had given me confidence in the French ability and the French fighting spirit. If a light Morane could shoot down a Messerschmitt within a couple of minutes, it seemed to me the much-vaunted Nazi air strength might yet prove to be illusory. Ken Downs felt less optimistic. He had managed to draw out a liaison officer and learn that things were not as good as they looked. Everything that mattered was in short supply, Ken had been told: tanks, air cover, transportation, even ammunition.

Cooper, too, was less optimistic than I. "Huntziger may be the best of the generals," he said thoughtfully, "but it's going to take more than a few great generals to stop the Germans when they get moving."

In a mood of admiration for the spirit of the fighting men and apprehension about their chances of living long, we returned to Paris and found the optimism there very hard to take. Obviously, this was the pattern the French political leaders wanted their Pierre Comerts to create: indifference, obliviousness, confidence. When I went into the Ritz and saw it full of elegant people completely unaware of the ambulances streaming toward the city, I thought again of André and Pierre on duty in their isolated pillbox—the victims as well as the saviors of a disunited country. The story I tried to send *Collier's* about all this, needless to say, was emasculated by the censor.

Bob Cooper, who was accredited to the British Army as well as to the French, now left the city in an attempt to reach the British units. Downs and I resumed our agitation to have our passes extended, but in a state of what seemed to be almost panic, the authorities kept turning us down. Incongruously enough, it was an American movie

165

actor who freed us from the enchanted forest of red tape. Robert Montgomery had come to France as a member of the American Field Service to drive an ambulance. Downs and I met him just as he was leaving town. Bob, who seemed so appropriately cast as a dashing figure in white tie and tails in his movie roles, appeared equally well cast in his new role as volunteer lifesaver. He hated dealing with French officialdom almost as much as he hated the Germans.

"I don't know if there's any action where I'm going—Beauvais," he told Downs and me, "but if you want to take the chance, you can stow away in my ambulance."

That was all the invitation we needed. If there was no action to be found around Beauvais, perhaps we could find someone else to take us farther forward. With our musette bags replenished, Ken and I climbed into Bob's brand new ambulance, reclined on a couple of the stretchers, and drew concealing blankets to our chins.

"How much do you think Bob earns in Hollywood?" I asked as our conveyance gathered speed.

"Oh, ten thousand a week, maybe," Downs said. "What's on your mind?"

"I'm just wondering who else could afford to see France with him as chauffeur," I said.

None of us had any idea that we were going to Beauvais to see it destroyed. The historic little city of some seventeen thousand people was proud of its beautiful cathedral and of the tapestries and toys it manufactured. There were no plants in Beauvais making guns, munitions, or other war material, there was no military base there, and yet for some unexplained reason the Germans decided to wipe out the city. When Downs and I and Montgomery arrived there at ten o'clock that night, nearly a third of Beauvais was in flames. The Germans had been bombing it all day.

At the American Field Service headquarters on a hill overlooking the city, Peter Muir, in charge, told us that one of the first bombs had scored a direct hit on a home for the aged, and another one had landed on a hospital filled to capacity with wounded soldiers evacuated from the front. A boys' school had been turned into an emergency hospital and Bob was to go there immediately and help shift the dressed cases to the railway station, where a train was waiting to move them to Paris.

Without bothering to ask, we climbed aboard Bob's ambulance and went with him into the stricken city. Now, for the first time in my life, I breathed the smell of war's destruction. There was no breeze and the ashes from the fires rained down and seeped into our lungs. The smoke hung low over the city; it was so thick that I felt I could chew it. The ashes and the smoke were bitter on my tongue. The roar of the fires was frightening; one knew that no fire-fighting apparatus, even if it had been available, could have helped. Now and then explosions broke through the roar of the flames—fuel supplies going up. Sometimes a tremendous crash would tell us that roofs had given way or that walls had collapsed.

The emergency hospital was on a small hill up a winding road. The street lights were out, but the burning city lighted our way. Downs stayed outside with Montgomery. I walked into the building and found myself in the operating room. Until a few hours before it had been a schoolhouse playroom. The walls were covered with children's pictures. Among them I noticed Michel Souris, the French kids' name for Mickey Mouse, and a very un-Gallic-looking Popeye eating his can of spinach. Three surgeons were working in silence at three long tables—possibly the children's lunch tables. Each surgeon had three assistants who were not doctors but hastily recruited orderlies.

A surgeon would examine the nearest wounded man waiting on the floor. A glance, an exploring hand, a question or two, then at the surgeon's nod his assistants would lift the man onto the table. The ether cone would be clapped over his nose and mouth, his uniform would be scissored open, and the surgeon would go quickly to work.

An artillery captain was lifted onto the table nearest me. He was talking in bursts, very fast. "It was good. It was good." He laughed as he caught my questioning eye. "Ten to one we got. There were only a few of us with our seventy-fives. The tanks came at us and fired and fired and we destroyed those tanks as fast they came at us. Each of our seventy-fives got ten tanks before they got us. Our general had said, 'Hold your place or die.'"

While the assistants cut away the captain's uniform, he lifted his hand and kissed his fingers at me. "I tasted Boche blood," he said happily. Then he laughed, much too loud. He was still laughing when the surgeon emptied a hypodermic into his upper arm and motioned for him to be removed from the table. There was nothing they could do for him except to let him die without pain.

The three surgeons had been operating without a break since early

167

afternoon. Every motion of their bodies told of their exhaustion, but they continued to work quickly, surely. The rubber gloves had long since given out. They worked barehanded, dipping their hands frequently into pails of disinfectant.

A huge black Senegalese infantryman was placed on the table before me. He looked at me and grinned. I grinned back. When I looked at his mangled lower right leg I stopped smiling. The surgeon felt the man's thigh and nodded. It was firm there. He took a pot of iodine and swabbed the thigh with it. At first I didn't understand. Then I saw the assistants tying the soldier's hands to the table. He began to howl. Holding his head down, they held the ether cone on his face. When the surgeon placed his saw in readiness, steadied the knee with his free hand, and laid the thigh open with his knife, I left the room. Amputations had never bothered me when I was a surgical orderly, probably because they could be rationalized as the ultimate treatment of a medical situation. Here in Beauvais, where the need to saw off a man's leg had been produced by the arbitrary and frightful action of bombs, I suddenly found the sight too much for me.

Outside the operating room I encountered two old women waiting for their turn on the tables. They had survived the leveling of the home for the aged. I tried to talk to them, but they only looked apathetically at me. Dry-eyed and dignified, they sat watching the coming and going of the laden stretchers, the orderlies, the nurses. "The soldiers must be helped first," said one of the old women. It was certainly not a complaint, but it was also not a declaration of self-sacrifice. It was simply her explanation to me of why she and her friend happened to be waiting in this place at midnight. The wounded did not cry, neither the men nor the women, the soldiers or the civilians.

Outside the school the night was bright with the city's fires. In the unsteady light I made out the covered forms of the dead lying in rows near a shed. I went into the shed where the wounded waited. Some eighty soldiers and a few civilians were sitting on chairs and benches or lying on the floor while three nurses and a doctor moved around by lantern light, dressing their wounds. Three wounded women were lying among the soldiers. When one of the nurses stopped to rest a moment, she told me proudly that she and the other two nurses had been born in Beauvais. They would die here if necessary, was what she seemed to be saying.

168

The AFS ambulances returned to the hospital one after another to take the wounded soldiers down to the train. Well past midnight I saw Bob Montgomery drive up again. It was not easy to recognize in the untidy apparition—grease and dirt and blood on uniform, hands, face—the dapper Bob who had chauffeured Downs and me out of Paris.

"The train is about full," he told me. "Pete Muir says this will be my last trip. The rest of these poor devils will have to stay here."

I helped Montgomery load his stretchers and went down to the station with him. The long dark train stood waiting. Perhaps a hundred soldiers were lying on the platform. Only the most urgent cases were now being admitted to the train. Jack James, one of the Field Service boys, and I unloaded the men from Bob's ambulance and passed them to others who carried them into the train. Only one of our load remained in the ambulance when the terse word came from the train: "No more room."

"We'll find some room," James said. I boarded the train after him and followed him through the cars. Each one was filled to capacity. We reported the news to Montgomery. There was nothing we could do but drive our last man back up the hill to the hospital and leave him in the shed.

"I don't have the nerve to tell him," James said. He and Montgomery looked hopefully at me.

"He'd never understand my French," I said.

Montgomery took a deep breath, lit a cigarette, and climbed into the ambulance. I watched him put the cigarette between the soldier's lips and heard him say, "There will be another train in a few hours. You may be sure of this. You will be all right." He repeated it several times to make sure the man understood. Then we drove him back to the hospital and gently lifted him out.

There was a glimmer of gray in the east when the ambulances finally returned to their hillside headquarters. We were physically tired and emotionally drained as we flopped down in the strawpile to sleep. The next thing I knew, a bugle was blowing, echoed by others in the distance. In the dying city of Beauvais there were no longer any sirens to sound the alert.

It was five-thirty: the day already bright. I heard the drone of the two-motor Dorniers before I saw them. Six of them were flying in a rough triangle, two on the sides, two at the base. Then, in the sky beyond, I saw another triangle of six—and another and another. . . .

They started dropping their bombs, big ones that whistled shrilly and then exploded in the city. On our hill all we could do was hug the earth and watch. There were no ditches or holes to hide in. Some of the bombs dropped close to us. They made a heavy noise, and you shook your head to clear it of the concussion effect. The bombs fell forever. Five minutes of that can be forever. A few antiaircraft guns began to bark. So far as I could see, they fired entirely without effect. Then the planes moved off in their triangles, the morning sun glinting on their wings until they disappeared. I had pushed my tally close to a hundred when one of the ambulance boys announced "One hundred and twenty." That was a lot of planes for one little city that had already been bombed.

The boys made coffee. A French artilleryman who had been manning an antiaircraft gun near us came over when the coffee was ready. By his count there had been one hundred and twenty-six planes.

Jack James, a big, tough, hard-working boy, with gentleness underneath his outward appearance, said, "Anyone on this hill who claims he isn't scared is either a liar or a damn fool."

There were nods of agreement. We all felt better for Jack's saying that, and we could lift our coffee cups without spilling more than a few drops.

The planes returned to drop more bombs on our city three times within the next two hours. In disgust, James, Montgomery, and several more of the weary drivers pulled straw over themselves and went back to sleep.

Two hours after the planes had left for the last time, a dull explosion sounded in the burning ruins. The planes had planted delayed-action bombs. This was a new hazard for the ambulance drivers. You might go into a wrecked building to bring out an injured person only to have a bomb explode beneath your feet. One of the men, Edwin Watts, was getting survivors out of a battered house when a delayed-action went off nearby. The wall of the house began to totter. Watts braced himself against it and held it upright until others of his team had removed the injured residents.

In midafternoon, orders came from the French Army that the AFS was to move its ambulances to another town. All the men I spoke to

170

told me they hated to leave. They felt they might still be able to help. They had developed personal affections for Beauvais. I felt the bond, too.

While Downs and I were watching the boys pack up, an orderly appeared and told me that the colonel in charge wished to see us at his headquarters *toute de suite*. Feeling like schoolboys caught playing hooky, we shouldered our bags, said good-by to the ambulance boys, and reported. The colonel knew we had no permission to be here, and he knew we knew he knew it. He had no time to waste on us.

"You will proceed immediately to Lyons-la-Forêt and report to the officer in charge," he said.

We said we could not leave; we had no means of transportation.

"You can walk," he said abruptly. "It is only forty kilometers."

I pointed to what was probably the healthiest ankle in France. *"Mais, mon colonel, la cheville . . ."*

The colonel assigned us a car and a driver.

When we had gone only a little way from the city, we had the driver stop. We wanted to take one more look at our city. It was dying, all right. Great ugly columns of black smoke were lifting away its life. Watching, I wondered what had become of the wounded man James and I had been unable to place on the last train to Paris. I wondered what had become of the nurse who had told me she would die in Beauvais rather than leave it. In a military sense, Beauvais had no meaning. There was no base there, no essential manufacture. It was simply an insignificant city in the Oise Valley that fate had tossed into the path of the god of war. The leveling of Beauvais did not help the German cause in the slightest, unless the cruel demoralization of innocent people could be called a military objective.

Turning our backs on a city that now seemed almost a part of us, we told the driver to proceed. He confessed the need of a map, being unsure where, precisely, Lyons-la-Forêt was. Downs produced a map and confirmed the fact that we were headed in the right direction. After our night and day in Beauvais, the countryside was strangely peaceful. The blue sky was herringboned with ripples of fleecy clouds. We relaxed and began to enjoy the ride. To the right we could hear the French guns.

"Listen to that echo," I told Ken. "Do you know what makes it?"

Ken admitted he did not.

171

"Mountains," I said, pulling my superior knowledge. "There must be mountains off there somewhere, and the sound hits them and bounces back."

Some ten kilometers from Beauvais we approached a village. It was warm. We were all thirsty. Our driver approved my suggestion that we stop for a cool drink. However, we found the village's one café closed and deserted. As we looked around a bit, we discovered that the whole village had been deserted. We didn't see even a dog or a chicken wandering about. Uneasy, we checked our map. No mistake had been made—we were on the direct road to Lyons-la-Forêt. We drove on, somewhat faster. There was no one we could ask about our direction. The road was deserted. We met no cars, saw not one tank or ammunition wagon. I thought again about the echo of the French guns that continued to travel with us. Somehow, it seemed unwise for me to disclose my revised thoughts about it, especially after Downs asked petulantly, "Where the hell is everybody?"

Reaching our destination, a lovely, secluded village half-hidden by heavy trees, we drove to headquarters. The general was not there but his aide-de-camp, an amiable type, took an immediate interest in the fact that we had come from Beauvais.

"By which road?" he inquired.

We showed it to him on our map. After a preliminary *"Mon Dieu!"* he dissolved in laughter. *"Mes amis,* I congratulate you on your crossing of no man's land!"

Downs sank limply into a chair, turning as pale as I'm sure I did. The aide, still laughing merrily, poured three brandies. He lifted his glass to us. "Messieurs, may you always be so favored by fortune!"

We were having a good time with the aide when an officious major came in, heard the main points of our story, and proceeded to give us a tongue-lashing for daring to be in his sector of the front without permission. We listened to him in some amusement but also anger. His country was coming apart at the seams but his biggest concern seemed to be that we were unable to produce the required slip of paper from the *Deuxième Bureau.*

"You will return to Paris immediately!" he snarled.

And within ten minutes we were on our way in another army car.

In Paris we heard the sad news of the German breakthrough at Sedan, the smashing of Huntziger's army at Montmédy, and the retreat of the British Army from Dunkirk. None of this news was in the

172

Paris papers nor was it aired by the French radio. It all came from the BBC. Now we knew that the war, as far as France was concerned, was just about over. But still the crowd at Maxim's and the Ritz bar didn't seem to get the message.

Perhaps since our trip to Montmédy, Downs and I had subconsciously felt that it was merely a matter of time, but the finality of it came as a shock. We had never really believed that the British Army would be overwhelmed. Then there was always the faint, unexpressed hope that America might enter the war. The question now was: "Would the French defend Paris in a last-ditch fight?" Colonel Horace Fuller, the American military attaché, thought they would not.

Finally, even the French who had sat the war out in the Paris bistros realized that the handwriting was on the wall. They stormed the railroad stations trying to get on any train that was heading south. Gasoline stations began to close—no fuel was reaching the city. Automobiles began to disappear from the streets.

With communications breaking down and little news coming into the city, the American correspondents became increasingly dependent on the American Embassy. Every day we went there to learn the latest from Colonel Fuller, and to see the red pins on his map creeping closer to the capital. The last-ditch defense efforts of General Maxime Weygand were coming to nothing. Two thousand enemy tanks were now racing across French soil toward the capital. On June 10 Fuller told us that Paris would not be defended. Appalled by the ruthless destruction of Rotterdam after it had been declared an open city, the French government was pulling out to Tours, virtually offering northern France and the capital to the enemy. Fuller advised us to follow the government, the censors, and Press Wireless, our cable service.

Ken Downs and his INS crew loaded three cars with provisions, gasoline, clothing, and typewriters, and hit the road. Although Ken and Knickerbocker urged me to go with them, I declined. The British correspondents left, and the remaining American writers followed. Shops were closing, hotels were emptying, and the chefs were packing the duck presses. The last trains had left and thousands were now crowding the roads which pointed south. Not a car nor a bicycle was to be seen on the streets.

Even though there were no communications, I decided to stay on. The story of the occupation of Paris by the German Army would be a good one, and the first thing the Germans would do would be to establish communications with the outside world. They would want the world to know of their great triumph.

I soon found that my decision was more than a little foolish. Colonel Fuller made it clear when I went to the Embassy on the morning of July 13 for another look at the red pins on his map. He was amazed that I was still in the city.

"The arrival of Hitler to accept the keys to the city will certainly make a great story," he said grimly, "but you won't be able to report it. Only correspondents accompanying the German Army will be allowed to use the cables and wireless. And as for your plea that you are a neutral correspondent," Fuller went on, "you are on their black list. They'll be here tonight or early tomorrow, and if you don't want to be interned somewhere or sent to Spain, I suggest you get out of here while you can."

This was easier suggested than accomplished, now that there were no more exasperated commanders to supply me with cars and drivers. Leaving the Embassy, I walked to the Café de la Paix, took my choice of the empty tables, and ordered the only fare available: brioches and coffee. The waiter read the shoulder patch on my uniform— American War Correspondent—and asked me why I was still in Paris. I mentioned the shortage of transportation.

"Perhaps you would like an auto?" said the waiter. "There is one here for sale." And he pointed to the only other table that was occupied. An attractive woman in her early thirties sat there alone. Even now I remember the chic black suit she was wearing and her pert little hat. She looked very thoughtful and a little downcast. I walked toward her table, but with no hope in my heart. Lady Luck had been good to me over the years, but now I was asking too much of her.

"Will you have a cup of coffee with me?" I asked.

She looked up, saw the correspondent's patch on my shoulder, and smiled. "I would be glad to," she said in perfect English. I ordered more coffee. She told me that she was English, but married to a French neurosurgeon.

"We cannot leave Paris," she said. "My husband's hospital is filled with wounded and he is operating eleven hours a day. We feel that when the Germans come in, it will be more important to have money than a car, which they will probably requisition."

When I asked her how much she wanted for it, she shook her

174

head uncertainly. "I have never sold a car before, so I really don't know."

"I'll give you all the money I have," I said. In my pockets I had $450 in traveler's checks and about a hundred dollars in French and American money.

"That seems enough," she said gratefully—and handed me the key to a baby Austin that was standing at the curb not far away. The tank was full, she said, and ought to take me to Tours.

She offered to pay for the coffee I had ordered, I wished her and her husband luck, and hummed off through empty streets to the Ritz. Having paid my bill with a check drawn on my bank in New York, I went to my room, filled my musette bag with linen and two cans of boneless chicken left over from the trip to Montmédy. With the bag, sleeping bag, and my typewriter, I headed for the elevator.

Then I had a second thought. A very pretty Swedish-American girl lived down the hall from me. She and I had been seeing Paris after dark and telling each other pleasant lies which neither of us believed or was supposed to believe. Now it occurred to me that Ingrid and her equally attractive friend Joan were probably still in the hotel, without any means of leaving.

I knocked and was admitted to the sitting room of their suite. The girls seemed unworried. They were breakfasting on champagne and would hear none of my proposal to take at least one of them—all my Austin would hold—to Tours. Ingrid laughed as she spoke of her unwillingness to abandon two closets full of new clothes, but beneath her and her friend's banter I caught the suggestion that they were looking forward with excitement to the advent of the Germans. Both girls had been profitably divorced. I suggested that as a precaution I should take their jewelry with me and store it for them in a bank vault in New York or London.

"Darling, we'd be naked without our jewels," Ingrid protested. "Now kiss us good-by and run along."

Not till after the war did I learn that the girls' confidence had not been misplaced. They were handled very gently by the German officers who were billeted at the Ritz. And I need not have worried about their jewels. They didn't lose them, they added to them.

I drove out of Paris on quiet, empty streets, my Austin purring like a cat. At Versailles I caught up with the refugees. They rode in cars and trucks, in horse-drawn wagons, on bicycles—in or on anything

175

that would move, including an occasional hearse. Thousands upon thousands of vehicles were on that road, crawling in the direction of Tours. And thousands of people were plodding along with packs on their backs or pushing handcarts. Those on bicycles made the best time, for they could wind through the massed traffic. Those on foot moved just about as quickly as the cars.

This was a quiet army. The people seemed dazed rather than frightened. They seldom spoke. Occasionally we would be stopped by a knot of French soldiers, and run through a cursory check. God knows what they were looking for in that tide of misery. My uniform, passport, and military pass got me through. I talked to one of the soldiers for a moment and learned that some of the refugees from the north of France and the Netherlands and Belgium had been on the road for two weeks or more.

In four hours I covered twenty-five miles. Then night fell and a cold rain began. Without lights, without rest, the army of the hopeful traveled on. Then a whisper came to us from up ahead: ". . . *Alerte* . . . *alerte!*" Perhaps it had started miles ahead of us. German planes were flying somewhere in the darkness overhead, high up. All movement on the road stopped. Trucks and cars turned their motors off. Faintly we heard the hum of the planes. Near me in the blackness I heard children whimpering.

We were lucky. The hum of the planes died away.

As the tragic march resumed, we were held up again and again by vehicles that had broken down or run out of gas. While the daylight lasted, I had gained quarter miles by driving off the road and bumping through fields, but this could not be done safely after dark. Having made fifty miles in eight hours, I gave up, drove off the road, and tried to sleep. It was impossible. I sat in my little car and listened to the eerily quiet sounds of the people moving past me. In some strange way, that massed sound had the effect of overpowering noise. All through the night the people kept passing me, and in the morning there were as many as ever.

Preparing in the murky dawn to breakfast on a can of chicken, I discovered that by some mischance the key had disappeared. I found nothing else in the Austin that would open a can, so I went hungry.

Soon after I resumed my place in the procession, I saw people pushing their cars. We were nearing a town where people hoped to find a little gasoline. As we inched through the town, I saw hundreds of cars

176

and trucks waiting in line at a gas pump, their owners hoping that the supply would by some miracle be replenished. Nor was there any food to be bought in that town—neither a loaf of bread nor the key to a can of chicken.

We waited for the planes to reappear, but that day there were none. In the north, they had repeatedly strafed the refugee-crowded roads, increasing the civilian panic and slowing down the retreating French Army. In the wrecks of automobiles and wagons in the fields I sometimes saw human bodies. They were not victims of air attack. When an old woman died of exhaustion, when a father died of heart failure, there was seldom anyone who could carry the body to the next cemetery.

In Tours I drove to the Hôtel de l'Univers and there found Ken Downs and his entire INS staff. They invited me to rebuild myself from their food cache—cheese, sausage, bread—and while I was pitching in, H. R. Knickerbocker told me that Louis Huat, who ran Press Wireless, the service we had all used in Paris, was now operating from an office in the town hall. Brushing the crumbs aside, I tapped out a quick story for Colebaugh about the army of despair I had seen on the road to Tours. I took it to the town hall and introduced myself to the censor, a frosty-looking colonel sitting behind an untidy desk.

"I am anxious to get this right off," I told him—and I was, since it had been four days since Colebaugh or anyone else outside France had heard from me.

"*Parlez français s'il vous plaît,*" said the colonel curtly.

"*Est-ce que vous n'êtes pas le censeur pour la presse américaine?*" I asked.

"*Oui,*" he said sharply. "*Je ne parle pas l'anglais mais je peux le lire.*"

I wondered again about France and the French. With typically beautiful French logic this man who didn't know English would censor my copy. He was the censor, wasn't he?—What right had I to object?

I sat down in front of him, much to his annoyance, while he read my story. A censor hesitates to use his blue pencil if you are sitting there. You don't have to say anything: just sit and watch him. I found this technique effective everywhere but in Russia.

The colonel came to the last page, stamped it, said "*Bon!*" and handed it back to me. I doubt if he had understood twenty words of it.

177

Press Wireless was just across the hall. When I handed Louis Huat my story I knew it was as good as on Colebaugh's desk. We correspondents took Louis' achievements very much as a matter of course, but he was a gifted man. Tours was now one of the news centers of the world, and it was Louis' transmitters that got our stories to London, whence they were relayed to New York.

Back at the Univers, Downs and I went into the bar hoping to find some sandwiches. There were no sandwiches and nothing to drink except champagne. This hardly seemed the proper drink for a death-hour vigil, but we ordered it. At the far end of the bar a familiar voice was roaring that its owner had been the only man to pick someone in some fight in Philadelphia.

"Who did you pick, Bob?" I asked.

Bob Casey of the Chicago *Daily News* turned, saw us, and promptly left his one-man audience, a waiter who didn't know a word of English. "I picked Gene Tunney—that's who," Casey went on, as if it hadn't been weeks since Downs and I had last seen him in Paris. "And I mean in the first Tunney-Dempsey fight at Philadelphia. I was the only one." Casey looked like a fat, bald, tough leprechaun, but there was nothing tough about him: at heart he was a pixie.

"I know another one who picked him," I said. "Fellow named Gene Tunney. And Bernard Gimbel picked him and won a nice bet on the fight."

We had finished our arguments about fights and were just getting onto Ty Cobb when the air-raid sirens began screaming. They were good in Tours, like dentists' drills wired for sound. A few moments later we heard the bombs. "They're after the bridges you crossed coming in," Casey said. By now, with the exception of the bartender, we had the bar to ourselves. Some of the bombs landed unpleasantly close to the hotel and we stiffened a little. Later in London we became reasonably accustomed to bombs, but at this point few of us were able to take them casually. The young bartender had an inspiration. He hurried to the windows that faced the courtyard, closed them, and fastened the latches.

"That will certainly keep them out," I told him. He smiled gratefully.

Bob Casey, who had a supreme belief in two things—his wife and his luck—lifted his champagne glass without a tremor as an explosion made Ken and me go rigid. "When I was in the artillery in the last

178

war," he said mildly, "we learned that if a bomb falls and your windows are *open,* there's a good chance the glass won't even crack."

"Don't tell the kid," I begged. "It will only make him unhappy."

The all-clear was sounding when Mickey Wilson, one of Ken's men, came running in with word that a nearby gasoline station had just been given a consignment. My little car was sitting at the curb with about a pint of the gasoline left in her. I would like to say I leaped into her and sped to the oasis, but no one but a jockey ever leaped into a baby Austin. I counted the cars ahead of me. I was the fortieth. It took me two hours to inch my way to the sacred font. When I got there, at least one hundred cars were in line behind me. Sadly assuring me that the tank was already dry, the buxom dame who was turning the pump managed to produce the full allowance of ten liters—enough to take me another sixty miles.

No one in Tours slept much that night. While the German bombers droned overhead, rumors went around the streets like cats chasing their own tails. Paris had fallen. Paris hadn't fallen. The United States had entered the war. The United States had not entered the war. Mussolini's legions, attempting to invade France, had been thrown back with staggering losses. Most sensational of all was the report that Winston Churchill, England's new Prime Minister, had flown to France to urge Premier Reynaud not to capitulate but to carry on the struggle from North Africa. Reynaud, we heard, was in favor of honoring France's promise not to sue for a separate peace, but most of his cabinet felt that the situation was hopeless. General Weygand was supposed to have told Churchill that Hitler would wring England's neck like a chicken's. Later, of course, this mission of Churchill's and its failure were confirmed, but during that baffling night in Tours it was just another rumor.

In the morning we learned that the government had left secretly for Bordeaux at 5 A.M. Louis Huat, his eyes bloodshot, a four-day beard on his face, said "I'll get to Bordeaux somehow and be ready for you boys when you get there." Within half an hour we were on the road again, I in my Austin, Ken's bunch in the three INS cars, carrying their office equipment and food. At first we found ourselves struggling in the crawl of southward-moving refugees. Then Mickey Wilson worked out a back-roads route, and our little cavalcade swung off the main line. Driving conditions became saner and we were even able to find a couple of places where we could eat.

179

The only thing that was out of the question was a hotel. At midnight, we pulled up in front of the Château de Candé, headquarters of that part of the American Embassy that had been sent out of Paris. We rang for some time. Finally, an ancient bundle of plumpness appeared out of the night and asked us crossly what we wanted. When we explained to her that we wanted to spread our sleeping bags on the Château's floors, she went away and did not return. We were in no mood for further ceremony. Knickerbocker and Downs scaled the iron fence and walked the quarter mile to the house. In due time they reappeared with a youthful member of the Embassy staff who took one look at us through the bars and then thought better of unlocking. Even the sight of the two women in Downs' group—Lucy McVane and Jacqueline de Moduit—did not soften him.

"If Bill Bullitt were here," Knickerbocker said sharply, "he'd open those gates and share anything he had with us."

"The Ambassador is in Paris," the staff member said stiffly.

"Tony Biddle is acting as his deputy in Bordeaux. Phone him and tell him the situation," Knick urged.

"I couldn't wake him at this hour," the Embassy representative said.

Dead tired and irritable, I thought it was time for direct action.

"Let's get some tools out of these cars," I told Mickey Wilson. "We'll smash this lock and when we get inside I want first crack at that silly bastard."

"OK," Mickey said happily, "but I want first crack. You can have what's left."

When the Embassy man heard the tools rattling and realized we meant business, he opened the gate, assuring us that he wanted no trouble. He then led us to the stable and suggested that we make ourselves comfortable on the straw. This gracious gesture was augmented a few moments later when he reappeared with a blanket for each of us. The girls, John McVane, and a couple of the others settled for the straw; the rest of us spread our bags on a well-trimmed lawn near the house. It proved a much pleasanter night than the one I had spent in Tours. No rumors, no German planes. Just stars overhead.

The sun woke us early. We decided to ask for a few gallons of gasoline. After tossing pebbles against a couple of the high windows of the old house and getting no response, we went to the garage, found a length of hose, and siphoned off a modest helping from each of the three cars sitting there. Ambassador Bullitt or Tony Biddle either one, we told ourselves, would have given us anything we needed, had they been around.

When we got to Bordeaux, normally a city of two hundred and fifty thousand, it was jammed with more than two million people. Pain, misery, and bewilderment—there seemed to be no end to it. Abandoned cars clogged the streets. There was no gasoline. Thousands stood outside the restaurants and food stores. When told there was no food, they continued to stand there. Where were these people going next? They didn't know. For days and weeks they had endured this twentieth-century Gethsemane. Why?—They were not sure. What crime had they committed? Surely this country that they had loved and sacrificed for could not die almost overnight? What had the leaders of France done—or failed to do—to bring about this situation?

In Bordeaux as in Tours one heard rumor after rumor. On June 16 came the word, quickly verified, that Reynaud had resigned. Marshal Pétain was the new Premier; Pierre Laval, the new Foreign Secretary. People in the streets, clutching at straws, cheered. The Hero of Verdun would put things to rights. He was the very man needed—a tough old army general.

In the loft building that had become our press headquarters and temporary home, we were not so sure that the news was good. Ken Downs recalled that Pétain, despite his heroic reputation, had always been more of a calculator than a man of action. "Before we become hopeful about him," suggested a French journalist we talked with, "let us see what move he makes."

The period of waiting was brief. Next day came Pétain's sickening broadcast to the people of France and to the world: "It is futile to continue the struggle. . . . It is with heavy heart that I say we must cease the fight. . . ." And the old Marshal surrendered his nation without even waiting to learn what the terms for an armistice might be!

That day Downs, Knickerbocker, and I had lunch at the Chapon Fin, one of the world's great restaurants. We got in by showing our military passes. Once seated, we looked around at our fellow diners. Our Acting Ambassador, Tony Biddle, was host at one table—urbane, smiling, though under a terrific strain. Nearby sat the dapper Pierre Laval, gnawing his mustache. As usual he wore a white tie. It was already being said of him that the white tie was to cover his black heart. Beyond Laval, at a third table, we saw Reynaud's Minister of the Interior, Georges Mandel, his face lined with fatigue and worry, his weary eyes peering out of his heavy glasses.

Mandel was one of the most respected of the recent Cabinet ministers. Following World War I, he had been a protégé of Clemenceau, and his loyalty to the old man had earned him the nickname of the Tiger's Cub. It was known in Bordeaux that until the moment of capitulation, he had tried to persuade his colleagues to continue the fight until help would come from England, and eventually from the United States.

Downs, taking no back seat to any gourmet, even at a moment like this, discussed with the *sommelier* the problem of which white Bordeaux we should have with our fish, which Burgundy with our entrée. We hadn't slept in a bed for days, we hadn't had a bath, our uniforms were filthy—but we drank a good Bordeaux with our sole Marguery, and after that we ate steaks with a delicious wine sauce. And Ken saw to it that we finished with a brandy of 1856—not quite Napoleon, but choice.

"The condemned men ate a hearty meal," Knick commented happily.

Ken called our attention to Georges Mandel. We watched him rise from his table and make his way past Pierre Laval. Neither man looked at the other. Knick, who knew Mandel, got up from our table and had a brief conversation with him just before he went out. He returned to tell us what Mandel, the Jew, had said: "If my name were Du Pont, I could still save France. But it is Mandel."

Among the defeatists, incompetents, cowards, and traitors, Mandel was magnificent to the end, but his voice could not be heard above the rustle of red tape, above the clink of gold that found its way to the pockets of some in power, above the babble of incoherent minds.

That was a bitter night in Bordeaux. At dusk Downs and I were sitting at a table outside a café, watching the endless procession of refugees passing ghostlike in the gloom. Now and then someone noticed our shoulder patches and we would hear muttered remarks. *Les États-Unis* had promised so much and had done so little. Speeches by prominent Americans pledging help for France had been printed almost every day in the French papers, and the people had been foolish enough to take hope from what they read. We saw a few soldiers mixed in with the passing civilians. Some were more than a little drunk. Their gaunt faces reflected their despair and bitterness.

182

Next day, because no American was likely to board a refugee ship without the Acting Ambassador's stamp of approval on his passport, Downs and I went to see Tony Biddle. Ken had known Biddle for years. He was now going to put their friendship to a test.

"Including Reynolds, we have a party of eight," Ken said. "Can you get us on a ship for England?"

"You've left it till rather late," Biddle replied, "but a Dutch ship is due at Point de Grave sometime tonight. Let's have your passports. Maybe you can make it."

Ken handed them over. Stamping them, Biddle said in surprise, "There are only six here."

"Two of my staff left Paris in such a hurry that they couldn't go home for their papers," Ken said. "Can't you give them some kind of emergency permit?"

Biddle nodded. "I have a form, as long as you can vouch for their American citizenship. Give me their names."

"Paul LaCoste and Jacqueline de Moduit," Ken said steadily.

Biddle hesitated a moment, smiled faintly, then began filling in the forms.

"Two fine old American names, very common in Louisiana," he said suavely. "I presume both these people were born in New Orleans?"

"Yes, Tony, they were," Ken answered with a straight face.

Biddle signed the two precious papers and handed them over. "Ken," he said, shaking his head, "if I'm ever fired from the State Department I hope you can get me a job with INS."

As a matter of fact, Tony Biddle probably saved two lives that day by forgetting the rules. Paul LaCoste, a fifteen-year-old INS office boy, was a Jew, and Jackie's husband was Count Alain de Moduit, whom the Germans had condemned to death for spying. He had escaped some weeks before, and was hiding somewhere in France. A message had come from him to Downs, asking him to use every effort to get Jackie out of the country.

At dusk on June 18, Ken's caravan and I reached Point de Grave, at the mouth of the Gironde, sixty miles from Bordeaux. Here we met an English naval officer who was in charge of getting British and American citizens out of France. We showed him our papers. Though he could not say for sure, he thought we might be put aboard the Dutch ship *Benekon* in the morning.

183

We decided to sleep on the dock. The mosquitoes were bad but most of us could shut them out by pulling the flaps of our sleeping bags over our heads. This technique was inadequate for the squadron of German planes that began to sing above us around midnight. A couple of freight cars stood on a siding at the end of the dock. We crawled under them with our bedding. In our snug quarters, chain-smoking the last of our cigarettes to make things harder for the mosquitoes, we watched the flares being placed and then listened to the bombs. Some of us thought they were falling rather close, but the Germans were actually concentrating on the harbor. After forty minutes of it the planes left, and we went to sleep to the music of the sea lapping on the shore.

The English officer appeared soon after dawn and told us that we were to board the *Benekom,* which was due to sail at noon. Ken offered him his car. "Thanks, no," replied the officer. "In the past week I think I've been offered half the automobiles in southern France."

Leaving my Austin with the ignition key in place for the next person who might need it, I said a prayer for the dear lady, whose surgeon-husband was now taking orders from German commanders. But for her sturdy little car, I might still be in Paris, sitting on stories I couldn't cable.

The *Benekom,* a freighter, looked as handsome to us as a transatlantic liner when we went out to her on a tender. We were welcomed aboard by the chief engineer, who was fluent in English. His first beautiful gesture was to conduct us to the galley for a hot breakfast. He confirmed what we had been told ashore—that the ship was waiting only to pick up a few more refugees who were supposed to be arriving any minute from Bordeaux by train. It turned out that we did not wait for them. After breakfast a group of us were smoking some of the chief's cigarettes by the rail, enjoying the peace of the perfect south-of-France morning, when fifty yards away a geyser shot into the sky, acompanied by a detonation even louder than those I had so much disliked in Tours. The *Benekom* swayed, the geyser subsided, and all was silent again.

This, the chief told us, was a magnetic mine, probably one that had been dropped during the previous night's attack. Apparently the *Benekom*'s metallic attraction had been countered by that of another freighter lying some two hundred yards away, and the mine had spent

184

a miserable night shifting back and forth before relieving its frustration in suicide. The captain declined to risk his ship in the harbor any longer, and an hour later we were at sea.

Because we were unarmed and traveling alone, the captain followed an evasive route of his own choosing, and it took us four days to reach England. Twice during the trip we were told that submarines were in the vicinity, but these proved to be the only exciting moments in a dull trip. After what we had been through in France, we liked it dull. Two mornings I peeled potatoes, our main article of diet, and enjoyed that simple-minded routine. Lucy McVane and Jackie de Moduit managed to wash some clothes for themselves and us, and even to appear for supper the first night with coiffures worthy of a beauty shop. They took the hardships, as I remember it, with grace better than we men.

Once the shock of our recent experiences had worn off, we began looking for answers to the question, Why had France fallen so quickly? The supposedly invincible Maginot Line, for some inexplicable reason, had proved weakest where one would have supposed it would be strongest: in the Ardennes Forest region where the German ground forces had broken through. But it was also easy to see that even the impregnable sections of the line had been no deterrent to the *Luftwaffe*'s bombers. The French General Staff, infused with overconfidence in defensive positions, had for years underrated the role of air power. Later, I learned that as late as 1939, when Germany was producing ten thousand planes a month, France was producing less than fifty. Even to us on the *Benekom* it was obvious that the French had been reluctant to spend the huge sums required for offensive weapons like tanks, heavy bombers, and adequate fighter planes. Finally, we knew that the nation had been weakened by years of inadequate leadership. The French leaders, like the English under Neville Chamberlain, had counted in part on something called "the pressure of world opinion" to stop Hitler. When I recalled the bombers I had seen leveling Beauvais, world opinion seemed to me a pitifully inadequate counterforce.

But if we were concerned with explanations for the debacle as we neared England, the question of the future was also in our minds. With France, Belgium, the Netherlands, Denmark, and Norway fallen so swiftly into Hitler's hands, and Hitler, Mussolini, and Stalin dividing up the corpse of eastern Europe, where would the next action be? We

185

were reporters, not second-sight artists, but there was no doubt among us that England would be the next Axis target.

Falmouth Harbor, congested with dingy and battered refugee ships, looked mighty good to us. As we debarked, we paid off the chief engineer, who had been very good to us, with the last of our assets. I remember that part of the offering was my well-traveled and still keyless cans of chicken.

Ashore, to our astonishment, we promptly found a taxicab. Somehow we thought they might have disappeared in England the way they had in Paris. Did the driver know of a hotel that might put all eight of us up? Yes, indeed. He would take us to it in two trips. I accompanied the girls, John McVane, and Downs in the first load. We drove to a sprawling wooden building with a flower-dotted lawn stretching down to the water's edge. It looked too good to be true. We walked in and asked for rooms, fully expecting to be turned away. Yes, there were rooms.

Ken and I were given an enormous suite overlooking the water. We pulled back the covers of the beds and fingered the snow-white sheets. We touched the starched window curtains. We counted the hangers in the closet, the rugs on the floor. It was almost too much.

I won the toss for the first bath. At the phone Ken ordered sandwiches and a bottle of Scotch, soda, and ice. I stepped into a tub that had been manufactured in the days of old when people thought big about such matters. The water was marvelously hot. I submerged to the nostrils and planned on staying there until ordered out.

Unbelievably, a waiter came bearing Ken's order. Ken fixed me a drink and brought it to the tub. I prolonged what I now recall as a blissful moment. In the other room Ken was already at work typing a story for INS.

"I want to ask you an important question," said I.

"What is it?"

"What can heaven have that we haven't got here, right now?"

Ken thought for a moment, then called back: "No typewriters."

186

11

London could take it

Next day we all went on to London. There I discovered an astonishing calmness about the war. In a way it was inspiring to find people going about their business and pleasure in normal fashion, but it was also a bit frightening, a month after Dunkirk, to see them behaving as if death might not drop from the sky at any moment. That an improvised fleet of tugs, fireboats, motor launches, yachts, and fishing vessels had crossed the Channel to rescue some 338,000 Allied troops from annihilation was a magnificent achievement, no doubt, but it seemed to me that too few Londoners realized the ominous truth about Operation Dynamo, as it was called. This greatest single action yet achieved against the enemy was, after all, a retreat, and it had been carried out not by the military forces, most of which were helpless, but by civilian volunteers. To call Dynamo, as the Admiralty did, "a triumph of Allied sea and air power," seemed to me dangerous. What worried me even more was that the British appeared not to realize the true extent of their loss at Dunkirk, which was much more than the 40,000 troops captured by the Germans. In addition to abandoning the Continent itself, the British had left on the French shore the equipment needed for the protection of Britain.

After I had seen with my own eyes what the military men were

187

calling their "defenses" on the beaches at Dover and Brighton, I marveled at their confidence. Except for some mangy barbed-wire barricades and some concrete antitank construction, I saw little that would delay an invader. Yet the military spokesmen kept reassuring me (so they thought!) with such comments as "We still have our Navy, Mr. Reynolds," and "The Channel will stop Hitler"—the Channel that a month before had not stopped a thousand English small craft from bringing the beaten armies to safety. Hearing what I heard, seeing what I saw, I found it a time to wonder about British sanity.

Hardly had I opened my typewriter in London before I found another American correspondent to team up with: Robert Low, who wrote for *Liberty* magazine. Bob was liked by all our profession in London and he already had good connections with the War Office, the Admiralty, and the RAF. When I pooled my Fleet Street sources with what Bob could offer, we were in pretty good shape. One night Arthur Christiansen, the editor of Lord Beaverbrook's *Daily Express,* told us that he was sending two men to Ireland (I wasn't used to calling it Eire then, and I'm still not!) to be ready for a possible invasion attempt there. That was notice enough. If Beaverbrook, the new Minister of Aircraft Production, figured the Germans might pull another Norway in Ireland, it was time for Low and me to move. Under the circumstances, I though it quite sporting of Christiansen to write a letter of introduction to Prime Minister De Valera's press officer, suggesting that Low and I be granted an interview with the Irish leader.

We took the boat from Liverpool the next day. As a man whose ancestors had lost their skin pigment in the drab old peat bogs of Donegal, it occurred to me that I might experience a sentimental reaction when first setting foot on the Emerald Isle. Nothing of the kind took place. In fact, beyond finding Ireland a very pretty country and the Irish a very friendly people, I must confess that I found little to be enthusiastic about—and the longer I stayed, the more the people disgusted me with their insularity. Hatred of the English, rather than fear of the Germans, was the pervading note. Beyond declaring their neutrality and putting their small army on the alert, the Irish were sticking their heads in the sand, entirely forgetting that when the ostrich did this, he left a highly vulnerable part of his anatomy exposed.

"If either one of them invades us, by the living Lord, we'll kick them

188

right out!" a Dail (parliament) member assured me during an excellent lunch of unrationed food at Dublin's best French restaurant. "If the Germans invade us, we might allow the English to help us kick them out. If England invades us, well, we've been fighting England for seven hundred years, and we know how to handle her."

With variations, Low and I heard this attitude expressed in Dublin homes, pubs in Cork, village inns in Tipperary, and in a centuries-old castle in Galway. No matter what the tall, anxious-looking De Valera said about other matters, no matter what my umbrella-carrying friend of New York days, William Cosgrove, the leader of the Opposition, said—or William Norton, leader of the Labor Party, or gentle, scholarly President Douglas Hyde—neutrality was one issue on which the Irish were united. Their country would stay neutral if they had to fight everyone in Europe to keep it that way.

Low and I began to wonder if anyone in Ireland knew what was going on in the world. One night we walked into the bar of the Royal Hibernian Hotel. It was full of men deep in form charts, figuring out possible winners at Phoenix Park. The bartender, giving us our tipple, winked at the man standing next to us. "These fellows," he said, "are here for the invasion."

"Never mind the invasion," the man said. "We'll take care of those blighters if they ever show their noses."

Some of the men were interested to hear that I had been in France, and listened attentively to my account of the hordes fleeing from Paris. "Oh, the poor devils!" one commented, glancing up from his study of the next day's entries.

Another man's interest quickened when I told how the German tanks had made hash of the defenses around Montmédy. Then he laughed. "Some of our lads with rifles would have picked their eyes out," he said.

"This is not a war between men and men, but men and machines," I said. "The German parachutists land with machine guns and devices that throw flame a hundred yards."

"Come now, have a spot with me and forget your machines," said another man. "Do you know that I went to school with James Joyce?"

This was the Dublin—the Ireland—of July, 1940. Far more real than the peril of the present was the glory of the past. Unless I mentioned it, no one offered a word about the collapse of France or England's rout at Dunkirk, but I heard a good bit about how the

Dalcassians of County Clare drove the Danes out in 1014. The Germans' crushing of Belgium in seventeen days and the Netherlands in five was a shadow. What was substantial was that Michael Collins, when he had a price of forty thousand pounds on his head in 1920, walked gaily along O'Connell Street rubbing elbows with the Black and Tans.

One afternoon, still waiting for our interview with De Valera, Low and I missed by a hair's breadth acquiring a race horse The Irish don't have claiming races the way we do in the United States, but after certain races they put the winner up for auction, which amounts to much the same thing. Bob, a knowing horse player, and I, in this case a pure hunch player, had gone to the Phoenix track, put a pound on Donegal, a small and lovely piece of horseflesh, and seen him win. After the race, Bob steered me to where the horse was being auctioned. It had not been a stake race, so the bidding was not high. Still, when Bob called out "Eighty pounds!" I was horrified, picturing us taking the horse back to London. Bob's bid, amounting to some $320, had been pure impulse. He told me afterward that he had always wanted to own a sailing ship and a race horse.

I clapped my hand over Bob's mouth and maintained it there with some difficulty while Donegal was knocked down to the next bidder. Today, now that Bob has quit writing and succeeded in business by really trying, he concedes that the horse would quickly have broken us both. "But what a mascot he would have made!" he says wistfully, still resenting the fact that I shut him off at the crucial moment. The point is, money didn't seem to matter much to us in those days. Being on expense accounts, we had no worries. This wartime state of mind about money was not peculiar to American correspondents. In England and North Africa I was to see British army privates and RAF pilots shooting their month's pay on a roll of the dice. Still later, I was to see our GIs gambling in the combat zones as though the end of the world was only ten passes away.

One morning the call came to our hotel, the Shelbourne, for our meeting with the *Taoiseach* (the Leader), as practically everyone called De Valera when he wasn't simply called Dev. His smile was pleasant, his voice soft, as he greeted us in his office. His clothes hung on him as if they had been made for somebody else. I think of him now as an older, gaunter Estes Kefauver.

In large part, it was Dev who interviewed us. Bob answered his questions about Dunkirk; I told him of the collapse of France as I had seen it. He smiled good-naturedly from time to time. Conditioned, now, to the Irish mentality, I could almost hear him thinking: You are two nice young men, but I'll not be impressed with your wild stories.

I mentioned my conviction that the Germans would love to possess Cobh on the south coast, Lough Swilly on the northwest, and Killarny Harbor in Galway, not to mention Bantry Bay in Cork and Dun Laoghaire in County Dublin. This would give Hitler a Gibraltar from which to keep a conquered England in order.

Dev leaned back in his chair and chuckled. "Ah, but if the Germans come here, we have a tidy little air force of our own," he said.

When we left, after spending nearly an hour with Dev, Patrick Gallagher, his press officer, stunned us by saying: "Of course you boys realize that everything the *Taoiseach* said was off the record. He never gives interviews. He was just giving you background information."

So there went the big story on which we had been counting. Gallagher softened the blow by promising that we should see Ireland's "tidy little air force." Next day we were driven to an airdrome not far from Dublin. A pilot himself, Bob gasped when he caught sight of the planes lined up on the field—all twenty-four of them. To me, they looked suspiciously like leftover biplanes from World War I days.

"My God, think of one of those meeting a Messerschmitt!" Bob whispered.

I had seen enough of Ireland and was ready to go home. Home, to me, was London. I was already thinking of it that way.

An incident having to do with a beautiful young redhead named Sheila hastened our departure. Convent-educated and as sweet a girl as I ever met, Sheila had set her sights on becoming an actress, and she had already appeared in bit parts with the Abbey Players. She and a friend of hers had spent several evenings with us seeing Dublin. The girls' interest in me was based entirely on the fact that I knew a good many show-business people in the United States. I told Sheila that her peaches-and-cream complexion and graceful figure, not to mention her intelligence, might well be marketable in Hollywood. This was not entirely the blarney of a man on the make: I honestly saw myself as the means by which a beautiful and possibly talented girl could get out of Dublin, which seemed the goal of every young man or woman we met.

191

When Sheila told me her father might pay her way to the United States, I gladly handed her a batch of letters of introduction to various producers and directors I knew. The four of us were out later than usual the same night, going from a party at the American Embassy to the Elm Park Country Club, and last of all to one of Dublin's few late spots. Pretty Sheila, who usually drank nothing, consented to try champagne halfway through the evening and found it much to her taste. It was 3 A.M. when Bob took his lass home in one direction and I went the other way with Sheila. I left her on her doorstep with a promise to pick her up for dinner the next evening.

It took me perhaps half an hour to get back to our hotel. To my surprise, Bob was packing. "Hop to it, chum," he said sharply. "That is, unless you want to marry Sheila. Her father was waiting up for her," Bob went on, "and as he pointed out on the telephone a few minutes ago, Sheila has never been out this late in life. She has also never been tipsy before, but what really did it was when she showed him all those letters to your Hollywood pals. He's convinced that you've seduced her."

"But, my God, Bob, I—"

"Tell your story to her father when he shows up in the morning to discuss your future."

By this time I was really nervous. "Damn it, she's a very good Catholic," I protested.

"So's her old man," Bob commented. "And in case you're having a memory blackout, may I remind you that he's Dublin's Public Prosecutor?"

I finished my packing a lap ahead of Bob.

Of course this proved to be a story that Bob greatly enjoyed repeating to all our colleagues in London, and I might add that it grew handsomely in the telling. When a week or so had passed and I had received no communiqué either from the irate father or from his daughter, wondering why I had walked out on our dinner date, it dawned on me that Bob might have made the whole thing up, either because he was a frustrated dramatist at heart or because he was eager to return to London. With an innocent face he denied both charges, insisting that it was only his quick reflexes that saved me from respectable married life in Dublin and a dreary career in Irish journalism.

Despite the fact that in July, 1940, there weren't enough antiaircraft guns in London to hold off a squadron of Piper Cubs, Low and I and the rest of the American correspondents developed a strong faith in England's ability to fight back and survive. I'm afraid this was at first an emotional rather than a rational conclusion, especially when American military, naval, and air spokesmen were not hiding their opinion that England was going to be overrun like France. In part, my growing confidence in the English may have been a reaction to my experience with the Irish. What had once struck me as the Briton's foolish aplomb now began to look like his quiet determination to resist. Then came Churchill's inspiring speech in the House of Commons, with its climax of: "Let us therefore brace ourselves to our duties and so bear ourselves that, if the British Empire and its Commonwealth last for a thousand years, men will still say, 'This was their finest hour.' " No one heard this speech outside the House of Commons, since it was not broadcast, but everyone in England drew strength from it when it was printed in the newspapers.

On Sunday nights the BBC had a forum often used by Churchill or other national figures. Called the "Postscript to the Nine O'clock News," it was listened to on every ship at sea, in every army encampment, and in every home in the country. The Prime Minister was a virtuoso when he sat before a microphone. If he said something funny, you could hear him chuckling, and the chuckle was infectious. When he referred to Hitler, there was loathing and contempt in his voice, and always there was his dogged confidence that communicated itself to the millions of listeners. One Sunday night I was in a noisy Fleet Street pub as the "Postscript" came on. The place fell silent as Churchill began to speak. I watched the faces of the listeners. It has been said that the man in the pub is England herself. At that moment, certainly, the idea did not seem strained. All eyes were glued on the loud speaker, almost as if the listeners believed that by concentrating, they could see Churchill's face. "Little does Hitler know the spirit of the British nation," the familiar voice rasped, and each man seemed to tighten his jaw. One of Churchill's secrets was that he never talked down. He often used extraordinary language, but only to create verbal images that anyone could understand. As I listened to him and watched his rapt audience, I realized that England had the leader that France had lacked. Churchill was not only speaking to his people; he was speaking for them. When he finished with the thought that the Old World and the New would eventually join hands to rebuild the temples of man's freedom and man's honor, the pub rang with enthusiastic yells—from an audience that was half blasé reporters and editors and half truck drivers and shopkeepers.

"I don't know how in hell we're going to win this war," Frank Owen of the *Evening Standard* told me after the cheering died down, "but if the Old Man says we can, I guess we can."

When Colebaugh got a story from me entitled "England Can't Lose," he cabled: YOU ARE PROBABLY CRAZY BUT CALL SHOTS AS YOU SEE THEM. WE WILL PRINT EVERYTHING YOU WRITE. And *Collier's* continued to do so, in spite of the sometimes abusive letters it received from its readers.

My new-found optimism about the British spirit was bolstered by several experiences I had away from London, in places where the dirty part of the war was going on. I found that the English were fighting, and fighting well.

Under orders to sweep British shipping from the Channel and British planes from the skies, the *Luftwaffe* was at this time bombing hell out of the Channel ports and the coal and coke convoys going into them. England's overburdened railway system could deliver only a fraction of the needed fuel to the war industry plants in the south, and forty thousand tons a week were supposed to be delivered by sea. A lot of it was going to the bottom. Almost every night one could hear Lord Haw-Haw gleefully broadcasting from Berlin that another convoy had failed to get through. At first this nasal-voiced British traitor, William Joyce, frightened some of his tremendous radio audience in England with his eerie knowledge. One night, for example, he advised the people of Brighton to adjust their town clock, telling them it was running twenty minutes slow, which it was. Later, when the Blitz began, Joyce's communication lines, whatever they were, broke down, and the inane things his boss, Dr. Goebbels, made him say provided comedy relief. After one raid, I recall, he announced that the Savoy Hotel, which happened to be our press headquarters in London, had been demolished. Those of us who were in the Savoy bar listening to this raised our glasses to him with jeers.

But if Lord Haw-Haw was an unreliable informant, the fact was that in the summer of 1940 the convoys were being sunk. The Admiralty admitted that the losses were severe, adding the hopeful note that Lord Beaverbrook was getting the new Spitfire plane off the drawing board and into the air. It was expected to turn the tide.

194

To look into this story of supply and protection, I received the Air Ministry's blessing for a four-day visit to an air base near Dover. I might add that most of the Air Ministry's public relations officers had been plucked from Fleet Street, and as reporters they knew the value of creating a favorable public image for their service. Actually, giving a writer access to the information was all that was needed; the favorable image created itself.

There were four squadrons of fighter planes at the base I visited, and of the squadron leaders the one who immediately stood out for me and became the central figure of my story was A. G. Malan, a South African called "Sailor" because he had spent most of his short life as a seaman. Six months later, after the worst of the Channel fighting was over, Sailor Malan was generally acknowledged to be the greatest of all RAF fighter pilots. Much later, when the American Eighth Air Force came to England, they borrowed Sailor as an instructor. When I met him he was still just another squadron leader, though with an enviable record of twelve enemy planes downed. At thirty he was older than the other pilots, but it was not simply his seniority that made the younger men look up to him. There was something compelling about the stocky South African's calmness. He was almost phlegmatic. My first revealing experience with him was in the matter of some books. I had half a dozen paperback mysteries in my bag and I asked Malan if he would like to borrow a couple of them. "No thanks," he said, then added, "I've never read a book in my life for pleasure. To enjoy reading, it seems to me a man requires a lot of imagination. I have no imagination at all. Maybe that's why I'm still alive."

He had pitched me a curve. I asked him what he meant.

"When you're up there fighting, you've got to be realistic," he said, "and when you come back, you've got to put it all out of your mind. A lot of these youngsters go to bed at night and refight the scrambles. Thank God I'm not the worrying kind. They're the first to go."

I soon found that Malan's simple division of the pilots into the worriers and the nonworriers was not enough. Some were exuberant believers in the idea that "The Jerries may get everyone else but they'll never get me." Others knew that the death rate in the RAF was high and felt that they had virtually written themselves off by joining up. It was this group that went to the village pubs at night to drink quietly, a bit sullenly. Some of the pilots felt a fierce hatred toward the Germans. Others looked with detachment upon the dirty business of killing them. Each time I talked with another of these men, I found a new combination of the basic attitudes that in effect made him a special case. Malan was simply more special than the rest.

The first two days I was at the field it rained heavily, and the *Luftwaffe* didn't show itself. The third morning began with a beautiful dawn, and at five-thirty the pilots were in readiness on the field. Three of the four squadrons were flying Hurricanes, the other—Sailor Malan's squadron—had the new Spitfire II. The new plane, like a thin needle, could climb faster, fly higher, and maneuver better than the Hurricane, which looked a bit humpbacked by comparison.

On the field were two large tents, one near the Spitfires, one near the Hurricanes. Phones connected them with the operations room. At six o'clock, bells clanged in the tents. As the pilots hurried to their planes, a calm voice announced over the loudspeakers: "Twelve plus bandits heading for convoy off Dover at fourteen thousand feet. All squadrons take off."

In a matter of seconds the engines of the Spitfires were roaring. Across the field the Hurricanes joined in. The squadrons took off in flights of three. They had done this so often there was no need for orders. Malan's squadron of twelve planes took off first. Within minutes all forty-eight planes were in the air. They circled the field once, gaining altitude, hoping to be above the Germans when they reached the Dover area, some eight minutes away. Then as the sound of the engines faded, an unnatural stillness hung over the field. It was soon broken by the shouts of the mechanics as they began a soccer game.

This was my first experience in waiting for pilots to come back. I was to learn that no one ever really becomes used to it. I went into the Spitfire tent and asked the officer who was manning the phone what the dispatcher's "Twelve plus" might mean.

"At least twelve Jerry planes were picked up by our radar," said the officer, "but that was only the first wave. We've got a big convoy coming down, and they'll be making an effort."

I asked about the chances of our squadrons running into a superior number, and learned that planes had been sent up from other fields all over the south of England.

A little over an hour after they left, the planes returned, circled the field, and landed in a predetermined sequence. To my inexperienced eye, they were all there. I watched them taxi quickly to the sides of the

196

field, saw the gasoline trucks rush to refuel them, the mechanics to swarm over them. Then I went back into the Spitfire tent. Intelligence officers were there now, and each squadron leader and then each of his pilots tersely, and in somewhat technical language, reported his version of what had happened in the flap.

By the time all the pilots had been heard from, the intelligence officers had a good idea of the net results. One of them summed it up for me: "Our boys sighted them halfway across the Channel. They were at fourteen thousand feet as expected. Twenty Heinkels and Dorniers and at least twenty ME-109s and 110s. Our boys came out of the sun and got fairly close. I'm reporting eight enemy planes down and four unconfirmed. Not bad. Your friend Malan got a Heinkel and an unconfirmed Messerschmitt. We lost two of our boys." The officer snapped his note book shut. "That's it," he said briskly. "But the day's young."

It was indeed. Twice more before noon the squadrons went up to save that same convoy. After the second return of the planes, I spent some time talking to a nineteen-year-old, Cecil Douglas. He was one happy kid, for he had downed his first German plane.

"I wish I could buy you a drink to celebrate it," I told him.

"Save it for tonight!" he said. "I hope the one I got today is the one that got me last week."

"You were shot down?"

He nodded. "Twelve miles off Folkstone. A twenty-millimeter hit my engine and, like that, the whole damn thing was in flames. I slipped back my greenhouse, turned her over, and just fell out. That Channel is cold, let me tell you." A boat had picked him up. "Know what my squadron leader said when I got back? He had the nerve to say I bailed out because I wanted a new uniform. That's the rule, you know. If you go into the drink and make it back, they give you a new uniform."

Young Douglas was very proud of his Spitfire. Just before the bells rang for the third sortie, he invited me to stand on the wing while he explained the cockpit to me. He had gotten through half the twenty-four dials on his panel when the loudspeakers ordered him to action. The bandits were still after that convoy. Douglas started his engine. The prop wash nearly blew me off the wing.

I watched his Spitfire disappear toward Dover. Twenty minutes later Cecil Douglas was dead.

My sojourn with the fighter pilots gave me only a distant picture of what was going on in the Channel. Obviously a ringside seat was needed. I went to the Admiralty and asked permission to go on a convoy. A night or two earlier Göring had proudly announced from Berlin: "The German Air Force now dominates the North Sea and the English Channel." Naturally, I doubted this, and so I had quite a shock when the public relations officer at the Admiralty told me off the record that the convoying had been suspended. Twenty-four thousand tons of shipping had been lost during July, he told me, in large part because the Hurricanes were not adequate against the *Luftwaffe*'s high-flying 109s. It was expected that the problem would not be solved until the new Spitfires were available in quantity.

Three weeks later I was summoned, given my credentials, and at midnight sent to Southend in the Thames estuary. There I boarded the large trawler and introduced myself to Captain Hugh West, a stocky, gray-haired veteran of the coastal run and commodore of the convoy. Busy with getting his night-concealed colliers properly prepared for sailing, he said somewhat gruffly: "You have the run of the ship, Mr. Reynolds. I have only three orders to give you. Always wear your tin hat. Always wear your Mae West. And report to the messroom as soon as the sun is over the yardarm. Good trip." With that he disappeared.

We moved out of the river before dawn, twenty-six small ships. All were heavily laden and our top speed was six knots. After the sun rose, I could see them strung out behind us: trawlers, freighters—anything that could be made to carry coal. On either side of the line, at midpoint, steamed a destroyer. The sea was as calm as cream in a saucer, the sky empty.

I was on deck several hours later, enjoying the cruise and reflecting that the *Luftwaffe* seemed to be taking a holiday, when the First Officer nudged me. "Sun's over the yardarm," he said, nodding aloft. "Come, we can't keep the skipper waiting."

I followed him below to the officers' mess. West and three of his officers were already there, gathered around a green-baize-covered table on which stood a bottle of Plymouth gin and some glasses. I was asked my preference: with water or bitters.

It would have been sacrilege to suggest a chunk of ice. Even worse would have been asking for a Scotch and soda. Room-temperature gin was the Navy drink. A naval officer would no more be seen drinking whisky than he would be seen painting a mustache on the statue of Nelson in Trafalgar Square.

I settled for bitters. West dashed six or seven drops into a glass, swished it around to coat the inside, filled it to the brim with gin; and gave it to me. "God bless," he said, when all of us were armed.

The drink was not at all unpleasant, leading me to suspect that the Navy brand is not nearly so corrosive as the English gins exported to the United States. We had a second, and now there was nothing gruff about Captain West. He told me that he had formerly been a submarine commander. I asked him if he had been in combat.

"Peacetime skipper only," he said. "Worst experience I ever had was cabbage on the 167. The bloody cook thought he'd feed us some. We were submerged at the time. Smell of cabbage cooking, foulest smell imaginable. Reported it to the Admiralty. Order went out to the fleet never again to cook cabbage aboard submarine."

The captain looked at his watch. "We're off Ramsgate, just entering the Straits of Dover. Come up to the bridge, if you want. You might see a show."

We went up. Far ahead, almost as I had first seen them as a boy on the *K. I. Luckenbach,* were the Dover cliffs, a glorious sight in the sun-splashed morning. Then our lookout in the crow's nest called out, "Enemy aircraft approaching."

Faintly, we could hear the hum. Even with my binoculars I had a hard time seeing the planes. They were so high they looked like silver splinters, almost transparent. Then from the coast to our right came a lovely sound, the singing note of the Rolls Royce motors that meant Spitfires. I counted twelve as they raced aloft.

The German planes, closer now, turned out to be twin-engine bombers. Surprisingly, there were only six of them. If they had a fighter escort, it was so high we could not see it. Then the bombers, flying three and three in close formation, wheeled and headed back toward France. The Spitfires circled over us and headed home.

"They must have orders not to chase," West said. "Possible those Jerry planes were decoys." Then he told me the code name of our convoy: Bacon. "Many of the Channel fishermen use bacon for bait," he said, "and that's what we are—bait. I shan't say we hope to be attacked, but we expect to be."

As we approached Dover I saw remains of previous convoys. In toward shore the masts of a dozen ships stuck up out of the water.

199

I left the bridge and went aft to our antiaircraft guns. The two gunners had been fishermen before the war.

"You're on a lucky ship," one of them assured me. "We've a lucky captain and I'm a very lucky bloke myself."

I said quite sincerely that I hoped our luck would hold.

"You don't believe me," the gunner said angrily. He fished in his pocket. "Here—lookit. The bloke with the beard is the patron saint of seamen."

I examined his medal. On the back of it there was an inscription in French. "Do you understand French?" I asked. "Not a word," replied the gunner. I returned his medal with my best wishes. What was the use of telling him that it was dedicated to St. Bernard and that St. Bernard was identified on it as the patron saint of skiers?

As I went back to the bridge, three Spitfires flew over us at two thousand feet, and began lazily to circle the convoy.

"They're up there to prevent a dive bomber from sneaking through and taking a crack at us," West said. "We'll be off Hell's Corner in a bit."

That was the name I had seen mentioned in the London newspapers. The turn the convoys made off Dover was called the most dangerous ten-mile stretch in the world. I found it hard to believe. The sun was painting the Channel here a deep purple, there a burnished copper, farther on a flashing gold. Once, the boats of fishermen had dotted this water, and once Gertrude Ederle had made it a headline place by swimming from Cap Gris-Nez to Dover. Now, save for our boats, the water was deserted. Ahead of us, flanked by white cliffs, bright green at the top, was Dover itself, looking like a toy village with its red-gabled roofs and its two tall white church steeples. Far to the left, through my glasses, I could see Calais and Boulogne where the Germans had twelve-inch guns.

Save for the droning of the Spitfires overhead, all was quiet. The tide was now heavy against us. We were making less than four knots. Then came the lookout's "Enemy aircraft approaching."

We heard the singing of a Spitfire squadron coming from behind Dover. Obviously, the radar installations ashore had picked up the German planes before we saw them. The squadron roared over us at twelve thousand feet. Our small protecting umbrella of three stayed with us.

To the left, I saw Heinkel bombers, flanked by fighters. Our two

200

destroyers opened up, but the white puffs from their exploding shells blossomed far below the oncoming planes. Then, as the Spitfires closed in, our guns stopped. Now it was up to the RAF.

The Spitfires were a little above the German planes. As they dove, they left vapor trails across the deep blue of the afternoon sky. The glistening German fighters and the Spitfires twisted and turned and their red and gold tracer streaks wove fantastic patterns as the planes crossed and recrossed their vapor trails.

The bombers came steadily on toward us. Then a bright golden burst appeared at the nose of the leader. It dived majestically, trailing black smoke. Three dots detached themselves from the plane. Parachutes mushroomed above them.

The rest of the bombers came on. While they were being harried by the persistent Spitfires, they dropped their bombs. A bomb does not drop straight down, of course, and as I watched them curving toward us, I wished that this immutable law of physics might just for once be suspended. But even though we were not on the ski slopes, perhaps the good St. Bernard had his eye on us: the bombs ripped up a lot of water but didn't touch the convoy.

A burst of black smoke came from one of the Heinkels as the rest wheeled for home. The plane headed for the water, but at about a thousand feet it recovered and straightened out. Then suddenly it disintegrated and shattered junk rained into the sea, a sight that cheered me immensely. A moment later another bomber went down. The German fighter planes streaked toward the French coast. The Dover Spitfires turned toward their base. As they went over, we counted them. There were still twelve.

Dusk stole over the Channel. Our Spitfire escort left us. As we steamed on, four squat motorboats hurried toward us. At the stern of each I saw a red and white flag indicating that the craft was manned by Poles. Captain West told me that these boats carried torpedos and depth charges and that they would be with us all night. The dusk deepened. We went on with not a light showing.

The crew and officers ate dinner in relays. It was a good spread: steak, Brussels sprouts, mashed potatoes, peach cobbler, coffee. In the months to come I was to eat much less well in London's best restaurants.

When I went back on the bridge, the tide had turned our way. We were now doing eight knots. The night was clear. Presently, I noticed

201

our bow shifting across the star-scape. A few moments later, in the blackness, Captain West said, "That's the last of Hell's Corner, Mr. Reynolds."

Just before midnight we heard the roar of motors over the English coast. Our bombers were en route to France, or perhaps Germany. "There they go!" said West. He could see them against the stars. "Ten," he said. Even with my glasses, I couldn't spot them.

A few minutes later searchlights pointed golden fingers above the French coast all the way from Calais to Boulogne. Tracer bullets knifed upward. It was a beautiful sight. I found it hard to realize that what looked like a magnificent fireworks display was in fact tons of steel and explosives being hurled at our bombers.

Then the searchlights died, the tracers stopped, and we were again alone with the stars. Beside me on the bridge a seaman wore ear-phones. He was in charge of the submarine detection instruments. Now and then we heard the powerful motors of our escorting torpedo boats. It was comforting to know that they, too, had listening devices. Twice, as the hours passed, the instruments showed that subs were somewhere about.

"I almost wish they'd try us," West said, during one tense moment. "The RAF laid a devil's nest of mines to port last night." It was then that I learned we were steaming down a precise course between mine fields.

Around four, far behind us, we heard our bombers returning from their task of discouraging Hitler's invasion fleet. A golden dawn crept in from the east. No German E-boats had appeared to do battle with our torpedo boats. No submarines were in the neighborhood. No more planes appeared. A few hours later West pointed ahead and said, "Pompey," which is the naval man's name for Portsmouth. Our trawler led the way into the harbor, rather proudly, it seemed to me. Twenty-six ships had started from Southend; twenty-six were about to anchor.

"Sorry Bacon couldn't have shown you a bit more excitement," West said as our hook went over. "I suppose you journalists feel rather cheated when things go right."

I assured him I had seen enough to make a story, and that it would be called, "It's Still Churchill's Channel."

The Blitz might better have been called the Siege of London. "Blitz" implies a quick lethal punch. What Hitler began in September 1940

202

was a wearing-down process, designed to reduce the defenses of London to impotency, to destroy the vital dock and railway areas, and to cause the collapse of civilian morale.

Despite appearances, all had not been going well for the Germans in the air. During the week of which the great air attack of August 15 was the climax, the *Luftwaffe* lost 256 planes to the RAF's 130. It was this magnificent effort on the part of the RAF fighters that inspired Churchill's statement in the House of Commons: "Never in the field of human conflict was so much owed by so many to so few."

But Hitler had smashed Warsaw and Rotterdam from the air, and he saw no reason why he should not succeed in the same way with London. His effort began shortly after five o'clock on the evening of Saturday, September 7, when approximately 320 bombers hit a dozen important installations, badly damaged three railroad terminals, and started serious fires in the East End dock area. At first, the reaction of many Londoners was curiosity. Thousands stood on the roofs of hotels and apartment houses to watch the show. I was among them, on the roof of Lansdowne House, where Bob Low and I lived. We couldn't know, then, that the show would go on, more and more horribly, until the end of June, 1941, with the only intermissions those enforced by bad weather.

In the next raids a hospital was hit, then a school, and one began to hear bitter talk of the Germans' inhumanity. Had we been thinking more deeply, we would have realized that London was a legitimate military target, crammed with docks and warehouses devoted to the transport and storage of weapons of war and food. We would have remembered that most rail lines passed through London. Quite literally, London was the heart of England, and if that heart stopped beating, its arteries stretching out everywhere would wither and die.

Ironically, it was the increasing efficiency of the English antiaircraft fire that made the Blitz worse. The German bombers were seldom able to get through to specific targets, and so dropped their death and terror indiscriminately. This was especially true when the city was blacked out. The Thames, pointing the way to London, was easy to find. After that, the bombs rained down anywhere.

The night of September 9 was a bad one. In New York a less epic event was taking place, though it was one of considerable personal interest to me. Toots Shor was opening his new bistro on West Fifty-first Street, and on that sentimental evening a number of my friends had gathered to wish Toots success. When I walked into the Savoy Hotel just before midnight, I was handed a cable signed by night-club comedian Joe E. Lewis: WE ARE MISSING YOU HERE. WE HOPE THEY ARE MISSING YOU THERE.

In the Savoy lobby I met Noel Coward. He had just returned from a government mission in Australia. This was his first experience with an air attack. When he insisted that he had to have a front row seat, I reluctantly took him to the Embankment side of the Savoy. Less than a quarter of a mile away, across the river, the warehouses were a roaring sheet of flame. The noise of the fire was so great that had a bomb fallen a block away, we wouldn't have heard it. Noel was entranced. There was nothing callous in his attitude—he was simply watching a spectacle no dramatist could ever have envisioned.

"It's almost impossible to believe that it's really happening!" he shouted above the noise.

"Let's get the hell back in the hotel," I said. Spent steel from anti-aircraft shells was dropping all around us.

Noel, arms folded, gazing at the flames, said, "I feel part of it now. This is my city. I've been away too long."

Then, in the light from the flames, I saw a huge green parachute coming down with a land mine clinging to it. This was the weapon we feared the most, because it exploded on contact and its concussion would kill up to four hundred yards away. I threw myself on the ground and yelled to Noel to drop.

He merely looked at the settling parachute. "Magnificent!" he declared.

The mine landed on our side of the river. For some unaccountable reason it didn't explode. I practically dragged Noel back into the hotel, ignoring his protests that I was interfering with his pleasure on his first night home.

Living in London became as exciting an ordeal as I imagine living in the Athens of Pericles must have been. The constant threat of death seemed to make people really alive. Every person you passed on the street had a story that he was living. They would take their beatings, and in the morning shake the noise of the night from their heads and face the new day with a calm display of fortitude. The growing terror Hitler hoped for never appeared. In its place there developed an implacable anger against the Germans and a determina-

204

tion in the face of disasters that never failed to astonish me. Sometimes, too, there was an almost unearthly detachment. I remember just before Christmas going to a dinner party given by a poet. He was one of the more esoteric literary types, and his flat in Chelsea was in itself almost a work of art. Between the time his invitations were issued and the evening of his party, bombs made rubble of every house in his block except his. Bob Low and I and the other guests, making our way through the devastation, were astonished as well as relieved to find our host alive and intact. His greatest concern, as we sat down to eat, was that the black olives—which he had managed by some extraordinary maneuver to procure—did not look right on his Oriental china. He had hoped to serve us green olives.

"Hitler thinks he can break a spirit like this?" Bob Low muttered to me.

I'll confess that I never really learned to enjoy the almost nightly raids. I hated and dreaded them, but like everyone else I learned to live with them. Fortunately, my friendship with Sidney Bernstein, the Deputy Director of the Film Division of the Ministry of Information, led to my having an occasional weekend vacation. Sidney owned a farm in Kent, and there was a period when I went there nearly every week end. If I could not forget what was happening in London, I could at least think about it from a distance. Some nights the bombers would pass directly over us on their way to London, and a few moments later we would see the searchlights stabbing the sky. Then, perhaps an hour later, they would return. Those that had been hit would jettison their bombs. One night, I remember, several of them landed on Sidney's property, scaring his three dogs thoroughly and annoying his prize bull, who bellowed angrily in his stall.

Sidney's job at the Ministry was the production of documentary films. One day he proposed that I do the narration for an opus he expected to release as *London in the Blitz*. The film itself was a stark record, and Sidney felt that what he called my "lazy, tired" voice would, by underplaying, make the presentation more effective than would the polished style of the conventional English commentator. Since it seemed to me that the title should be as informal as the narrative, I suggested a revision to *London Can Take It*. So named, the film was shown in the United States, and presently I heard from Pop that he and my sisters had seen it and been much moved by it. "Take care of yourself, boy," Pop's letter ended, leading me to wonder if he thought I had gone into the crumbling buildings to record my commentary on the spot. I felt like writing back, "How?"

Because Bob Low and I occupied a large apartment at Lansdowne House and were looked after by a valet-cook-houseman who was able to find such things as eggs for us once in a while, we frequently had guests staying with us. One was Arthur Christiansen, the editor of the *Daily Express.* As had so many Londoners, Chris had sent his wife and children to the country for the duration. Three days after he had seen them off, a bomb had destroyed his home. After that, he either slept on a cot at his office or bunked with us. Late one night when Chris was with us, we were awakened by a terrific thump. Lansdowne House, until then having lived a charmed life, had finally been hit by a fire bomb. While the sirens blew, we found our slippers and bathrobes, and rushed down six darkened flights of stairs (the elevator had been knocked out) to the street.

The fire apparatus was already rounding the corner from Savile Row, and air raid wardens were dashing through the building, evacuating everyone. As we waited in the chill air, watching the flames on the roof, it became obvious that we had not dressed wisely. In fact, my teeth were chattering. Bob Low said earnestly, "A drink wouldn't go so bad right now."

The remark snapped Chris to action. From the pocket of his robe he lifted a bottle of brandy. "It's yours," he said simply. "I caught it up as we went out the door."

"This," Bob commented to me, "is why Chris is an editor and you and I are only reporters."

After perhaps an hour, we were allowed to return to our smoky but otherwise undamaged quarters. Two apartments on the top floor had been burned out, but without loss of life. Before going back to sleep I removed a bomb fragment that had burned a hole in my pillow. No Londoner ever really believed the adage about lightning never striking twice in the same place, but it was often mentioned, since it was the cheapest tranquilizer available. But as a matter of fact, this was the only time that Lansdowne House, though it was only a quarter of a mile from the Houses of Parliament, a prime target, was ever hit.

It was the Prime Minister who finally put into words the Londoner's basic contempt for Hitler's bombs. One day, noting that London's pigeons numbered in the hundreds of thousands, he observed that he had yet to lose a hat from their aerial depradations. This got around and gave us all a pretty sensible outlook, except that I wasn't as comforted as most because I rarely wore a hat. I remember getting into a taxi one day and hearing the driver grumbling about his chances. This was shortly after Churchill's comment, so I told him to shut up. "If your name's on the bomb, you're going to get it," I said, "and if it's not, you're not." His unhappy answer to that was, "My name is Smith."

One of the most popular Americans in London when the Blitz began was our Ambassador, Joseph Kennedy. As a token of esteem for this man who had until now expressed himself as confident that England would hold out, Beaverbrook had named a new fighter-bomber the Boston, for Kennedy's home town. I myself found Kennedy so agreeable that I felt free to involve him in a correspondent's joke. Every time any of us went on some operational trip that might be, but seldom was, dangerous, we had to sign what we called a "blood sheet," absolving the authorities of any responsibility in case the trip had an unhappy ending. In the space marked "next of kin," I took to writing "Ambassador Joseph P. Kennedy, Grosvenor Square, London." This was usually good for a laugh with the press relations officers, but Kennedy, hearing about it, objected.

"What the hell, Joe?" I said. "I've got no kin within three thousand miles, and if I should ever get it, I have every faith in you. I know you'd make a nice speech about me, see I had a proper funeral service, and ship me home to Brooklyn. Why, you might even foot the bill."

I noticed that my kidding was not amusing the Ambassador. Then, bluntly, he advised me to go back to New York while I still could. He himself was leaving his post, he told me, and with the conviction that it was time for the United States to face up to reality and not be left holding the bag. Kennedy was very clear about the reality he had in mind. It was the defeat of England.

So Joe Kennedy went home and shocked the British government and a lot of Americans by talking publicly against a declaration of war by the United States. To my further dismay, I found that Kennedy's views were shared by Tom Beck, the publisher of *Collier's*. When I heard the defeatist speeches Beck was making, I cabled Bill Chenery: SUGGEST TOM BECK READ STORIES I AM SENDING YOU. While Beck, like Kennedy, remained an isolationist until we entered

207

the war, I must add that not one line of my optimistic dispatches was ever suppressed in *Collier's*. Colebaugh had told me to call the shots as I saw them, and he never went back on that.

One day I received a cable from a New York friend, literary agent Mark Hanna, suggesting that I fashion *Collier's* war articles into a book, revising where necessary to give the pieces continuity and bring them up to date. The firm of Dutton, Hanna said, would publish such a book if I could deliver it. A night or two later I happened to be alone in my apartment, typing near the front window, when a bomb landed in nearby Stratton Street and knocked out the electricity. While I sat at my desk trying to remember where the nearest flashlight was, I heard the unholy screech of another bomb. This one was dropping in my direction. We were all afraid of glass; the concussion of a bomb landing even a block away could shatter a window and drive the splinters into you. Hastily retreating from the window in the dark, I took a beautiful fall over a table. The bomb, landing in Berkeley Square, bothered practically nobody since it was a dud, but it was some time before I could get off the floor.

Next day, when I took my aching side to a doctor, the diagnosis was two broken ribs. He taped them and suggested that the only sensible way to hurry their healing would be to stay in bed for a week. I recalled Mark Hanna's cable. Perhaps I could do my convalescing at Sidney Bernstein's farm and at the same time whip the book into shape. But how to get to the farm carrying the usual luggage plus typewriter and briefcase filled with my *Collier's* articles? I could hardly stand upright, and the thought of a train ride made me wince. It was Bob Low, the angle-worker, who solved my problem. He called some helpful soul in the Admiralty, greatly exaggerated my physical condition and my importance as a correspondent, and within half an hour an official naval car was carrying me to Kent.

For a week, with the help of a part-time secretary from the village, I labored with shears and paste pot. The result, *The Wounded Don't Cry,* I sent air mail to New York, wondering if it would sell enough copies to recoup the fifteen dollars postage. Three or four months later the happy answer arrived. Either there was a minor Reynolds boom in the States or else the war itself had become a hot topic for American readers. The book was at the top of the best-seller lists.

An experience I had soon after I returned from my week in Kent seemed to sum up all the examples of courage and fortitude that I had been encountering in London's battered streets. It happened the night I went to watch the work of the Auxiliary Ambulance Service— a service staffed almost entirely by women.

When I reported to one of the ambulance garages in the East End, not far from the docks, the blue-uniformed girls were making tea. Shortly after I was introduced to their leader, a Mrs. Evans, we heard the German planes approaching. Then, through the noise of the anti- aircraft fire, we heard the bombs begin to drop. One landed not far away, shaking the garage. Dust from the inside walls of sandbags drifted into our eyes. More important to the AAS women, it went into their tea.

"Really, this is going too far!" said one of them angrily.

Then a slim young girl in uniform entered the garage. I heard her tell Mrs. Evans that she wished to go on duty even though it was her night off.

"But Ethel, dear," said Mrs. Evans. "You should be at home to- night." Then she looked more closely at the girl's stricken face, as did the rest of us. We all braced ourselves for Ethel's disclosure. She had neither home nor family. A direct hit the night before had wiped them out.

There was a moment of silence. Then Mrs. Evans said quietly, "All right, Ethel. Plan to go out first call."

Nor was there long to wait. The telephone rang, Mrs. Evans lis- tened, made notes, then announced: "Fire, East End Avenue and Wyndham Street. Residential. Street filled with glass. Ethel, you and Pringle go along; Harris, you and Foster accompany."

I went, too, sitting in the front seat of the ambulance. Ethel was a first-rate driver. She not only took us through the blacked-out streets at a good clip, but knew precisely where she was going. When we reached the address, we found two adjoining houses burning fiercely. Firemen were playing water on them. One of the houses, they told us, had been empty. It was thought there was a family in the second. Shielding their faces from the heat, two firemen inched their way into the building and disappeared. I crouched on the sidewalk and peered through a broken window into the cellar. Presently we could see the firemen flashing their lights about.

"All dead!" one shouted through the window.

"No!" his partner called. "Stretcher, girls!"

Ethel and Pringle passed two rolled stretchers through the window.

A few moments later, one of the stretchers was passed out to us. A middle-aged woman lay on it. Though she did not move, she did not seem to me to be dead.

By now, from somewhere, a doctor had joined us. A tall young man, he opened his bag and found a needle of adrenalin. After injecting it into the woman's heart, he began artificial respiration. Pringle handed him his stethoscope. The instrument was painted white to make it easier to find in the dark. After listening and trying to find the woman's pulse, the doctor rose to his feet. "Suffocated by smoke," he said.

He hardly glanced at the second corpse brought from the cellar—that of another woman, blackened by the flames.

Then one of the firemen came out of the house with a burden for which no stretcher was needed. He carried a little girl. Her hair and clothing had not even been singed. She had a faint frown on her face, as though daring anyone to wake her up. When the doctor took up his needle, I had to look away. As he began artificial respiration on the child, a woman from a neighboring house told me the story of this family of mother, daughter, and granddaughter. The younger woman's husband had been lost at Dunkirk. Gloria, the little girl, was their only child.

Watching the doctor at his work, I found myself praying, "Wake up, Gloria, wake up."

As the doctor picked up his stethoscope and tried the child's heart, the sirens sounded, telling us that the German planes had left. "They've done their work," said the doctor to no one in particular. "Why shouldn't they go home now?" Then he lifted the child's body onto a stretcher and pulled a blanket over it.

"Shall I drive her to the hospital?" Ethel asked, as the stretcher joined the first two in the ambulance.

"Take her to the morgue with the others," the doctor said.

I climbed into the front alongside Ethel and we started off. Neither of us spoke for a time. I suppose that she was also thinking of the horror of these unnatural deaths and of the death that had visited her family the night before. As we drove along, I wondered what the child would have had to face had she lived. Growing up in an orphanage? When we reached our destination, I put my feeling about it all into words.

"What did you say?" Ethel asked sharply.

210

"I guess little Gloria is better off dead," I repeated.

Ethel turned to me in the dim light, and I saw contempt in her eyes.

"Nobody's better off dead," she said harshly.

Whether she was thinking of her own family or of those who lay in our ambulance I was not sure, but her comment made me feel very small.

12

Yours faithfully, Winston Churchill

The first phase of the Blitz ended with the onset of bad flying weather, and when the RAF predicted (correctly, as it turned out) that there would be comparatively little activity through the winter months, I accepted Charley Colebaugh's suggestion that I return to the States for a holiday. Only government officials with high priorities were crossing by air, and to get home I first had to go to Portugal. After waiting around Lisbon for ten days, I finally managed to get aboard the crowded *Exeter* and was one of a hundred passengers who slept on cots in the main dining room. The crossing took fourteen days. Several times I thought wistfully back to my relaxed crossing on the *Conte di Savoia*.

To my surprise, as the *Exeter* entered New York harbor, several newspaper reporters appeared to interview me. One of the group was my old INS friend Jim Kilgallen. From him I learned that *London Can Take It* had been a big hit all over the country and had raised a large sum of money for Britain's war charities. "You're almost a celebrity," Jim said. I doubted that until I discovered that Mark Hanna, in cooperation with *Collier's,* had booked me for a country-wide lecture tour for British War Relief.

Off I went, speaking to club, church, school, and other groups. My theme was, "While I can't tell you exactly how England is going to survive, I can tell you that she will not be defeated." I enjoyed the speaking, even though the attitude of the audiences was often discouraging. They came and listened and sometimes questioned me, but for the most part they were not vitally concerned. It was still not their war. However, they were generous. I raised nearly two hundred thousand dollars on the tour, twenty thousand of it at an actors' hundred-dollar-a-plate affair in Hollywood.

That Hollywood engagement was the only real bright light of my country-wide tour. John McClain's talent had finally been recognized by MGM, and he was now one of their high-bracket screen writers. He had a nice house, with guest room for me, and a wonderful Negro man-of-all-work named Gene. Gene made breakfast for us, and if his experienced eye saw that we'd had a late night he made us superb Bloody Marys instead of serving us orange juice. He washed and ironed our shirts and pressed our clothes (so help me, each morning he even pressed our money). And at night, equipped with uniform, he drove us wherever we were heading in John's huge Dusenberg. McClain had always been a car buff. He had picked this one up cheap, worked weeks on it, had it painted, and now it belied its fifteen years.

"A silly investment," I told John.

"Not so silly," slow-talking John said. "It's the only serviceable Dusenberg in town. I rent it out to various studios for a hundred dollars a day. It just so happens that some studio needs a Dusenberg at least three days a week, so I'm about a thousand dollars ahead on the deal."

I had many old friends in Hollywood and those I didn't know, John knew. There was some sort of party every night and my visit was climaxed by the affair Dave Chasen gave at his restaurant. Every name actor in Hollywood was there and a good many of them got up and did their acts. Chaplin did a parody on his own *The Dictator;* elegant Fred Astaire sang and wore out a pair of shoes dancing; Jimmy Stewart did an imitation of someone imitating him; Jim Cagney, Pat O'Brien, Phil Silvers, Clark Gable, and several others broke their backs and tonsils to entertain. It was the greatest show I've ever seen in my life.

When I returned to New York, I autographed some advance copies of *The Wounded Don't Cry* for Pop and my close friends, including,

213

naturally, Toots Shor. Carrying on the tradition of the genial insult on which our mutual affection was based, I wrote in his copy:

To TOOTSIE BOY: What a pity it is you are too iliterate to read this book. My esteem and affection.   QUENT.

Toots scanned these sentiments, then roared, "Why, you bum— you don't even know illiterate's got two l's in it!"

That's one word I now know how to spell.

My return trip to England, early in 1941, began in St. John, New Brunswick, where I boarded a British freighter. Although it already seemed to be carrying a considerable load of aircraft and tractors, not to mention two tons of Canadian cheese, our first stop was Halifax, where we took several hundred crates aboard with great care. The mate kept saying "Easy! Easy!" as he directed the stowing, and for a while I thought we must be loading fresh eggs for the English breakfast table. Then one of the hands drew my attention to the red flags fluttering on the cargo barges and at our masthead. "When you see that on a ship," he said, "give her a wide berth. That means explosives."

The next morning, when we were out of sight of land, we were put through an abandon ship drill. It was not the perfunctory affair such drills usually are. The other passengers and I were handed emergency rations, shown the supplies of crackers and water in the boats, and issued old-fashioned cork life savers. "Must be careful not to jump overboard with these things on you," the chief steward was good enough to tell us. "When you land, the front will hit your chin and knock you out."

"Will they float?" asked one of the three British passengers.

"Will they float!" echoed the steward indignantly. "Long after you're gone, man! Why, I've seen 'em pick bodies out of the water that have been there a fortnight, and the old ring as good as ever!"

We thanked the steward for making us feel so well equipped. The life rings, which had been purchased as salvage in Hong Kong, were stamped with the name of a Chinese ship, and it seemed to me this ought to confuse any possible rescuers in case our ship, the *Talthybius,* was torpedoed.

"I keep meaning to have them rings relettered," the steward said earnestly when I pointed out the matter to him, "but you know it takes either a stencil or a steady hand. Lettering's got to be neat, you

214

know." I agreed that it would never do to have a corpse picked up from a poorly lettered ring.

We crossed in a convoy of some eighty ships, sailing three abreast. Four destroyers went with us, and during daylight hours we were looked after by a patrol of land-based planes. The seventh day out we hit fog. This made our skipper quite happy. A sub, he said, would now have difficulty in spotting us. The fog was succeeded by a storm, which made him even happier. For three days I had visions of the explosives breaking loose and rolling around our holds until they blew cheese, aircraft, and innocent travelers all over the North Atlantic, but it seemed that our little ship had been skillfully packed against just such a possibility.

One of my messmates, a British aircraft specialist, was voluble on his absolute conviction that England was going to win the war. It was based on Scripture—or at least Scripture as he understood it. "In the Book," he told me, "you'll find the expression 'the isles far off,' of which the Lord said, 'I will appoint a place for my people.' Or you'll find it as 'isles to the west and to the north.' It could hardly be plainer. Draw a line due west from the Holy Land, and the only isles you'll come to, west and north, are the British."

Since the Book also indicated that the ultimate battle against the might of Hell was going to be fought in Palestine, it was easy to conclude that Hitler was not going to prevail in the isles to the west. I found the faith of this man, who had been in Canada bringing the aircraft industry up to date on the lessons of the Battle of Britain, somehow very touching. I asked him what he thought our chances were of being torpedoed before we reached Liverpool. He patted his Bible affectionately. "Were we to be," he said calmly, "we should think of it as a triviality. You and I are, essentially, details in the supreme plan."

Details or not, we finished the crossing uneventfully, and nineteen days after clearing Halifax I was again in London, though in a new residence. The Ministry of Food had taken over Lansdowne House, and Arthur Christiansen and Bob Low had moved my belongings to a suite at the Savoy. Low himself had gone to Libya to cover the battle against General Rommel and his *Afrika Korps,* but Chris assured me there would always be plenty of applicants to use the second bedroom. When a large group of correspondents and Fleet Street characters gave me a welcome-home dinner in the Savoy's Mikado

215

Room and then let me pick up the check for my expense account, I knew that my vacation was over and that I was back where I belonged.

To my surprise, the English edition of *The Wounded Don't Cry,* which had come out during my absence, was selling very well. I wondered how the Blitz-weary Britons could enjoy reading about experiences that could be neither new nor pleasant to them. A London literary expert offered me this explanation: "Partly, it's a matter of the timing. Yours is the first book out describing the fall of France and the Blitz. Partly, it's you. You were personally involved in both, and the British love first-person accounts. And of course you tell us how brave we are. Coming from an American, that pleases us no end. We are so accustomed to Americans criticizing us."

One day I received an unexpected written invitation from Nancy Astor, whom I had never met, asking me to lunch at Cliveden. At first I thought of declining her invitation. Not only had she advocated appeasing Hitler in the Neville Chamberlain days, she was also a militant prohibitionist, and I doubted that I should be very happy as her guest.

Ed Murrow, the CBS correspondent in London, had also received an invitation, and he talked away my objections. "She serves wonderful food," he said, "and her cast is usually all-star. You may meet people there who can be helpful to you."

Ed and I went to Cliveden together. Cliveden itself, one of the traditional stately homes of England, was magnificent, and Nancy Astor's guests lived up to Ed's billing. Among others present were Brendan Bracken, Parliamentary Secretary to Churchill; Alfred Duff-Cooper, Minister of Information; A. V. Alexander, First Lord of the Admiralty; and Sir Walter Monckton, a member of Duff-Cooper's ministry. Monckton, as it turned out, became one of my best and most helpful friends.

There were twenty of us at table, but the delicious cold salmon, which had been sent to the Astors by one of their friends in Scotland, was more than enough for all of us. As we were having dessert, Nancy Astor called imperiously down the table to me:

"I hear you have written a book, Mr. Reynolds. Of course you are going to send me an autographed copy."

Much as I was enjoying myself in the company of England's VIP's, this rubbed me the wrong way. "Lady Astor," I said, "books are

216

written to be sold, not given away. My book costs only ten shillings. Now surely you can afford that."

There probably would have been a moment of embarrassment around the table except that the lady was quick on the riposte. "I never buy books written by my friends," she said—and how could I answer that one?

That evening when I returned to the Savoy, I bought a copy of my book at the stall and before I lost my nerve (and remembering the Astors' library, a huge room lined with leather-bound volumes and first editions of the classics) I wrote:

To LADY ASTOR—Congratulations on this magnificent addition to your otherwise worthless library   QUENTIN REYNOLDS.

The receipt of this offering and its addition to the Astor collection—if added it was—were not acknowledged.

The Sunday-night "Postscript to the Nine O'Clock News," when it did not present Winston Churchill or a Cabinet minister, usually offered a combat hero telling of his experiences. It was Sidney Bernstein who suggested to his superior, Duff-Cooper, the Minister of Information, that it might be a good idea to vary the flavor by introducing an American correspondent, and he suggested me.

The fifteen-minute broadcast was a responsibility I did not take lightly. It seemed to me that my best hope would be to disregard the usual format of a talk. I therefore composed an open letter to Dr. Goebbels, ridiculing his boss, whom I called Mr. Schickelgruber. I was impressed by the comic possibilities in that unfortunate name.

Sidney was delighted with my script, as was Duff-Cooper, but you could have knocked me down with a broiled kipper when the BBC declared it unacceptable. "We fear that your language is rather rude," the program manager explained. "Especially at an hour when our people are coming away from their churches."

I supposed "rude" to mean irreverent and in bad taste. That my script was irreverent to the Nazis I granted, but I pointed out that its good or bad taste was hardly the issue. I was not proposing to address the House of Lords, but to communicate with the man in the pub, the men and women building aircraft, the service men huddled in trenches in Africa or Burma.

An ex-Fleet Street man who was then in the script department of the BBC said privately he hoped I would hold out for the right to present my talk as it stood. He mentioned some of the specific objections that had been made. "They think your attitude toward Rudolph Hess is unpardonable. You tell Goebbels that Hess should be flown back to Germany and dropped by parachute. That much is tolerable, but not, 'And I would very much like to be the man who folded that parachute.' And they balk at your close when you say, 'Take good care of yourself, Doctor. We'll be seeing you one of these days. And when we do see you, Doctor, we want you to be in very good health.' They think that sounds sinister."

"The BBC doesn't want anyone to hate Goebbels?" I asked.

The script man laughed. "Not on Sunday night, old boy."

The question of censorship became academic when Winston Churchill pre-empted the "Postscript" of June 22 to call Adolf Hitler, among other things, "a bloodthirsty guttersnipe." After listening to that, I went over my script and made it a little stronger. Meantime, I had taken my case against the BBC to Arthur Christiansen, and he had called on one of his boys to write a scathing article about the matter under the heading BBC IS SO KIND TO HITLER.

The forces of rudeness prevailed and I delivered my open letter on June 29. The only person in the small studio was the announcer, who sat across a table from me and listened with an expression of refined horror while I used every vocal trick I knew to create the effect of a prosecutor summing up his case against a murderer. When it was over, the announcer, master of himself, said nothing. No one else came around to say if I had sounded effective or if it might have been better, or even to shake hands or say good night. I walked out of the place through deserted corridors.

The planes had come over while I was broadcasting. It was dark night. I could find no cab. I made the long walk through Leiscester Square to the Strand and then to the Savoy. Several times I ducked into doorways as bombs exploded in and near the Strand.

The Savoy's lobby was deserted. Everyone in London who could possibly leave the city on a Sunday did so. I went to the desk for my key, feeling weary and discouraged. The clerk told me that I had received several telephone calls. I told him they would keep, and not to ring my phone until morning. Convinced that my impudent stunt had not come off and that I had let my friends down badly, I fell into my bed and went to sleep.

While I was having breakfast early the next morning my secretary, Betty Marais, came bounding into the suite, her eyes gleaming with excitement. She showed me the morning papers. Every one had a page-one article about the Postscript, and the *Express* had printed the text in full. Then we went through the fifty or so telephone messages that had been gathering at the desk: calls from Lord Beaverbrook, Brendan Bracken, Duff-Cooper, and others. There were telegrams from all over England, including a wildly enthusiastic message from Sailor Malan, and this from Sidney Bernstein in Kent: TRIED TO PHONE YOU LAST NIGHT JUST TO SAY YOU PULLED IT OFF BEAUTIFULLY.

Then the BBC began forwarding letters. Seven thousand were delivered over the next few days, and Betty had to hire help to handle them. "God bless you, Yank," said one. "You had the whole Elephant and Castle Underground Station roaring. It seemed easier to face the rest of the night after you finished off Mr. Schickelgruber." Another—and Betty shrieked when she discovered it—read thus:

> MY DEAR SIR,
> I should like you to know how admirable I thought your broadcast last Sunday. I know that I was far from being alone in my enjoyment of it and that your words have given real pleasure and encouragement to a great many people in this island.
> Yours faithfully,
> WINSTON CHURCHILL

Like all the American correspondents in London I had sought to have an interview with the Prime Minister, but Brendan Bracken, his Parliamentary Secretary, had put me off, like all the rest, with the word that he was too busy. He also argued that Churchill was being interviewed to the limit already. "In Washington," Bracken pointed out, "your President sees you and answers your questions. Here, Parliament represents the public, and the Prime Minister submits to questions from the members a couple of times a week. We feel no need for additional conferences." I pointed out that Americans wanted to know about the human side of Churchill: what his home life was like, how he spent his few leisure hours, what books he read, what he ate and drank. Bracken waved all this aside as unimportant.

Giving up the frontal attack, I approached Averell Harriman, who happened to be in London on a mission for President Roosevelt. Harriman had been one of Heywood Broun's pals, and I knew him well. As an example of what I meant, I told him how the Palace had let me go along when the King inspected the bomb damage in Plymouth. I had just tagged along and listened while the King talked with the wardens, firemen, doctors, and others who were still digging people out of the rubble. The King had been so interested in what he was seeing that he had forgotten his stammer—a point that I had included in my story of the tour. "I certainly didn't rush up to His Majesty and say 'Hey, George, how about a few words for *Collier's!'* " I told Harriman, "and I'm not about to try that with Churchill either."

Laughing, Harriman said he would do what he could for me. It turned out to be quite a bit.

On July 24, Commander Charles Thompson, Churchill's aide, telephoned from Downing Street and told me that the Prime Minister was going out of town the following morning to observe some tank maneuvers. "He has invited you to go along and spend the day with him," Thompson said.

I was at Paddington Station at the time stipulated, and Thompson, a dapper, pleasant, but constantly worried-looking man, took me past the Scotland Yard inspectors to the platform where the special train was waiting. Except for three or four policemen, there was no one else about. The brilliant morning sunlight filtered down through the open spaces of a roof that had once been glass.

Two large black cars drove up. Harriman climbed out of one, Churchill out of the other. He was smiling. When he saw a Scotland Yard man standing with a watch in his hand, he glanced up at the big station clock and broke into a laugh. The clock read eight fifty-nine. Churchill was a minute ahead of schedule.

Besides Churchill and Harriman, there were seven in the party I was joining: General Sir Hastings Ismay, Commander Thompson, Major John Churchill (the PM's brother), two American generals in England as observers, and Churchill's two personal secretaries. I was the only one not yet known to Churchill. Harriman gave me a satisfied smile as he introduced us.

Churchill eyed me closely: "So," he said, "you're the lad who did that 'Postscript.' You have a style, Mr. Reynolds."

With this, he waved us all toward the train. "In with you!" he cried. He himself boarded last of all.

Playing the perfect host, a role he obviously enjoyed, Churchill

220

saw to it that everyone had cigars and drinks. Then he said, "It's awfully hot. Let's take off our coats." He then excused himself and with his secretaries at one end of the car went to work on the morning mail.

Later, while the train slipped through the summer countryside, we had a good enough lunch of rationed food. Through most of it Churchill talked about tanks with the two Americans.

When we reached our destination, at least a thousand soldiers were drawn up waiting for us. The general and his staff saluted smartly. As we stepped off the train, each one of us had to be introduced to the officers. Then the Prime Minister nodded at the ranks of soldiers. "I supposed they've been waiting for us a long time," he commented. "Let's walk along and say hello to them."

The general in command could not conceal his delight. We all trailed after the Prime Minister who, apparently unaware of the wilting sun, chatted with many of the soldiers as he walked past them. Somehow, he gave each man he spoke to the impression that he had come down from London especially to see him.

We then climbed into cars and drove to Salisbury Plain to watch the maneuvers. Now, I can take a tank or leave it alone, and one, to me, looks and acts much like another. Not so with Churchill or Harriman. Harriman had become an authority on the subject, and we were watching American-made tanks on maneuvers.

After two hours of it in the hot sun, we got back in our cars and headed for the station. The five-mile way was lined with cheering troops, and Churchill smiled, waved, and made V-for-victory signs all the way. Just before the station, our cars stopped. A long table had been set up beside the road, and soldiers stood behind it ready to serve us drinks and sandwiches. From my car I watched the general suggesting that we refresh ourselves before taking the train back to London. I saw Churchill waver. He was probably thinking that he would be more comfortable aboard the train with his coat off. Then he looked at the soldiers waiting behind the long table. I saw him smile and nod.

"Come on, come on," he said to us, like a hen clucking her chicks to her side. We followed him to the table. I heard him speak to every one of the men who stood there serving, and he said something different to each. He spread his charm upon officer and private, and the charm was contagious.

At the station, the troops were lined up once more, and a band was playing "For He's a Jolly Good Fellow." The villagers, who had gathered behind the troops, began to sing, and then the troops joined in. Churchill stood there with his hat off, a broad smile on his face. Then he waved and we entered the train.

Most of us were weary, but Churchill, after seeing that we were again supplied with drinks and cigars, sat with his secretaries, dictating, his voice rising and falling, all the way back to London.

In the station, as I was thanking him for my day's experiences, he shook my hand and said earnestly, "You'll come to Chequers and have lunch with us tomorrow, I hope." Before I could stammer an acceptance, Churchill added, "I have an American visiting who I am sure can use your help."

I assured the PM that I would be on hand. Next day, Harriman picked me up and we drove to the Prime Minister's official country seat. On the way I learned the name of Churchill's American visitor: Harry Hopkins. It appeared that Harry was working on a "Postscript to the News" speech and Churchill thought I might be helpful with the phrasing of it.

I had first met Harry in the 1930s at a racetrack. Like Heywood Broun, Harry was an enthusiastic but unorthodox horse player. During one race, as the closely bunched horses swung into the home stretch, Heywood and I heard Harry yelling, "Come on, Somethin'!" When the race ended, he told us triumphantly, "I had the winner!"

A look at the program showed us that there was no horse named Somethin' in the race. I asked Harry, who was a wisp of a man with a quick grin, how he could have the winner. "I bet two dollars on every horse in the race," he told us. "Somethin' had to win."

Impressed by the madness in his method, Heywood asked him how he made out. He explained it quite seriously: "There were six horses, so I bet twelve dollars. The horse that won paid ten, so I got my two dollars back, plus eight. Of course my other ten went down the drain, but I've only lost two dollars. Not bad, eh?"

Heywood and I looked at each other.

"I seldom have a winning day unless a lot of long shots come in," Harry told us, but I always get plenty of action, always cash a winning ticket, and I can't lose much."

"I know a guy who says he beats the stock market by buying on Monday and selling on Friday," I said.

222

Harry shook his head. "That seems a very unscientific way to go at it," he said.

Mrs. Churchill and her pretty eighteen-year-old daughter, Mary, greeted Harriman and me at the door and had some difficulty controlling Mary's dog Sukie, who loudly resented our intrusion into the family circle. "She's a Free French poodle," Mary informed me proudly. "Have you a dog?"

I told her that the Savoy Hotel would take a dim view of a guest who kept a dog. "However, I do keep pets that the hotel doesn't mind," I said. "They're goldfish, and their names are Adolf, Herman, and the Doctor."

Mary wrinkled her nose. "I shouldn't think they would be much fun," she said. Then she led us into the big, high-ceilinged drawing room. Harry Hopkins, though it was summer, was dressed warmly. He mentioned a touch of grippe, but it seemed to me he was looking quite fit. Later he told me he considered Chequers the coldest house in England. "If you want to read in comfort," he said, "the downstairs bathroom is the only place."

Churchill, smoking a cigar, was wearing what the press called his siren suit and what his staff called his rompers—a blue, one-piece, zipper-closing coverall. Many great public figures, I have found, seem to dwindle in stature when one finally meets them informally. Churchill was not one of these. It was impossible to miss his aura of strength and confidence, even when he was chatting about trivialities. At that time, when almost the only good news for the public was Britain's victory in the skies, the whole burden of preserving the free world seemed to rest upon Churchill's shoulders, and yet even in the privacy of his home I heard no word from him that suggested either weariness or exasperation.

Mrs. Churchill—her husband called her Clemmie—soon asked us in to lunch.

"You're a friend of Nancy Astor's?" Churchill said to me as we sat down.

I replied that I had lunched at Cliveden once.

"You sent her your book." Churchill chuckled. "She told me about it the other day. That's the way to handle Nancy, all right."

I told him I hoped the inscription hadn't been too offensive.

"Not a bit," said Churchill. "She loved it."

During the meal Mrs. Churchill made several references to Harry

Hopkins's poor health, and at one point Harry gave me a despairing look that suggested he had been receiving some excessive mothering since his arrival in England.

After lunch, Churchill and Harriman went off for a discussion of their own and Hopkins and I went up to his bedroom, where a typewriter had been provided. Lying on his bed, Harry read me the mass of notes he had made for his talk, which was to be on Lend Lease. Congress had recently approved the Lend Lease legislation but as yet the English had seen no tangible benefits. It was Harry's task, as President Roosevelt's spokesman, to reassure them that any delay was caused by the fact that hundreds of American factories had to be retooled to produce war weapons. At the same time, he could not be specific about the big things that were on the way because this information would have further agitated the American isolationists.

"We want to make this hopeful but not wildly optimistic," Harry told me.

While I worked typing a draft of the speech, Harry fell asleep. Presently there was a soft rap on the door. Mrs. Churchill opened it, saw Harry on the bed, and looked reproachfully at me. "You should have put a cover on him," she said. "He catches cold so easily." She opened a closet, pulled down a blanket, draped it over Harry, smiled at me, and tiptoed out.

I worked on for a couple of hours, and thought I had done a pretty good job, but when Harry finally read the draft, he said, "My God, Quent, you've got me declaring war against the Nazis!"

My rejoinder was that we should have done it long before. (Harry read the speech—having toned it down—over Churchill's Chequers' microphone the following night.)

About the time Harry and I had finished revising and timing the speech, Commander Thompson, Churchill's aide, appeared with word that I was to stay on for dinner. I protested that I had no dinner jacket, but the excuse was disallowed. When I went down to the drawing room, I discovered that Harry was the only one of us who had dressed. Churchill had changed, but only to another siren suit. "It's easy to see," Churchill said, with an impish look in Hopkins's direction, "which of us worked all afternoon."

Mary Churchill acted as hostess. I made the blunder of asking for a martini. Vermouth was a war-shortage item, and there was none in Churchill's house. It was Averell Harriman who rescued me from my

224

embarrassment. As a frequent visitor to Chequers, he had discovered that a South African wine Churchill stocked enabled one to create an acceptable ersatz martini.

As we lifted our glasses, from out of a dark corner of the drawing room, stalked a huge, baleful-eyed black cat. This was Nelson. He ignored the rest of us but allowed Churchill to stroke him. He even listened patronizingly to the PM's attempts to draw him into the conversation.

"Bravest cat you ever saw," Churchill told me. "I once saw him chase a big dog right out of the Admiralty."

Nelson yawned and majestically led us toward the dining room. "He knows we're having salmon," Mary revealed, "and he's hoping that Pa will feed him."

It was a family dinner. Without conscious effort the Churchills made you feel entirely at home. We began with the smoked salmon Nelson knew about and proceeded to what Mrs. Churchill announced, with some pride, as lamb. Churchill took a bite of it and grunted. "This isn't lamb, it's mutton," he said. "Clemmie, can't you get us better meat than this?"

Mrs. Churchill smiled and said, "Remember, Winston, there is a war on."

We talked of many things through the meal, none of them of world-shaking importance. Of food, for instance, which was the number-one conversational topic that summer, and of cigarettes. "Thank goodness I smoke only cigars," was Churchill's summary of *that* problem. And of course we talked of the war. Churchill spoke freely, as one who trusted his guests. Nor did he preface what he said with "This is off the record"—the stricture that we correspondents heard so often. I understood, without its being mentioned, that being the Prime Minister's guest called for self-imposed responsibility. However, this did not discourage me from later making a good many notes about what was said.

After dessert, Mary and her mother left us to our cigars and brandy. Mrs. Churchill could not resist cautioning her husband about a limit. Churchill was not impressed. "Always remember, Clemmie," he said affectionately, "that I have taken more out of alcohol than alcohol has taken out of me."

When we were alone, Churchill spoke again of the war—at first of the dark days of Dunkirk, now a year in the past. His face clouded

225

at the memory. "That was bad," he admitted. "We needed the Spitfires most of all. I said to Beaverbrook, 'Get those Spitfires into the sky,' and Max said, 'If God will give me three months, you shall have them.' Well, God gave him his three months, but there still weren't enough planes. I said, 'Max, we need more Spitfires,' and he replied, 'If God will give me two months more, I shall have them for you.' " Churchill smiled at us. "God gave him two more months, and when the *Luftwaffe* came over in force, we were ready."

It seemed to me that Churchill spoke in private much as he spoke in public. I heard the same beautifully paced sentences, the occasional "armchair phrases," the use of repetition and alliteration.

"Now we are getting stronger," he went on, "and that evil man, Hitler, knows it. He knows his days are numbered, even at this moment when his submarines are sinking our vessels in the North Atlantic, even now when his planes are bombing this island."

Churchill lit a fresh cigar and gazed reflectively through the clouds of smoke. He pointed to the chair his wife had occupied. "Your Mr. Schickelgruber would like to be sitting there right now," he said to me. "He would like to be talking to me and asking if there was not some way out for him. Aye, and he'd like to meet me alone somewhere."

"If you ever have an appointment to meet him alone," I said, "please be sure the Beaver is nearby with a club in his hand."

"Good! Good!" Churchill laughed. "Max would come in handy then. Ah, that Hitler!"—his tone turned serious again—"When I think of the crimes he has committed! When this war has come to a successful conclusion, something must be done about that man. If my allies agree, I would favor trying him and exterminating him. If he should be victorious—a possibility I do not for one moment entertain—I feel sure that he would have me shot. I would not like that"—he looked at us archly—"but I cannot say that my sense of righteousness would be outraged."

"Do you know why I hate the Nazis?" he demanded suddenly. "I hate them because they frown when they fight. They are grim. They are dull-faced. They do not go into battle with a song in their hearts. Now, take our magnificent RAF lads. They grin when they fight. I like a man who grins when he fights."

It was noteworthy that, sitting with three Americans, Churchill did not directly refer to the possibility of the United States' entry into the war. "We have a long way to go," he commented at one point, "but

226

with the help of our great friends across the sea, we shall get there." This could have meant our declaration of war; it could also have referred simply to our Lend Lease aid. None of us felt comfortable just then, and I'm sure our host sensed it. "I am not overoptimistic, I hope," Churchill said lightly, "but then at heart I am an optimistic person." With that, the conversation turned.

I asked Churchill what sort of world he thought we would be seeing when the war was over.

"Same old world with just a bit of the gingerbread knocked off it," he said without hesitation.

I looked at Hopkins. He shrugged and said nothing. For me it was a jolt to find this attitude in the man who had galvanized his nation and swept away the archaic attitudes of the Chamberlain era. Churchill seemed unaware that he had surprised us.

His conversation darted like a chameleon on a rock. He touched on the situation in Greece and Crete—now occupied by the Germans— and that reminded him of a canto of *Don Juan* and he talked of Byron. Then India was mentioned, and that reminded him of Kipling. "Ah, there was a singer of songs!" he told us. "I've got a lot from Kipling." But it appeared that the greatest poet was Shakespeare, a point Churchill attempted to prove by reciting Hamlet's "To be or not to be," acting the part and never groping for a word. It was an impressive performance.

Harry Hopkins commented that no poet of importance had yet been inspired by the war. Churchill agreed. "And there were very few in the last war," he said, "though there was one who died too soon. Rupert Brooke. Do you remember that lovely thing he wrote called 'The Fish?'

> " 'In a cool curving world he lies
> And ripples with dark ecstasies.'

"And further on—

> " 'The dark fire leaps along his blood;
> Dateless and deathless, blind and still,
> The intricate impulse works its will;
> His woven world drops back; and he,
> Sans providence, sans memory,
> Unconscious and directly driven,
> Fades to some dank sufficient heaven.'

227

"And how about these lines today?" Churchill asked us gleefully, "Can you fit them to anyone?

> " 'But there the night is close, and there
> Darkness is cold and strange and bare;
> And the secret depths are whisperless . . .'

"That was a poet," Churchill said softly.

Something Hopkins said awakened another of Churchill's memories, and there came forth stanza after stanza of Thomas Moore. And then, amazingly, a passage from Bret Harte, and Churchill laughed at Harriman and Hopkins because neither of them could identify the author.

It was hard to remember that outside this quiet room, dominated by the resonant voice, the superbly confident personality, a murderous conflict continued with its heartbreak and terror and grinding hardship. For me, that hour of respite ended too soon when the Prime Minister said ruefully, "Gentlemen, I'm sure we're wearing Mary's patience thin." In the long run, fathers, even Prime Ministers, are bossed by their daughters.

Churchill led us upstairs to a motion picture projection room where Mary and her mother were already waiting. The film we saw was *Target for Tonight*. Enveloped in his cloud of cigar smoke, Churchill was as tense as any movie fan when things looked bad for the bomber that was over Germany. He chuckled when its bombs hit their target.

When the picture was over it was time for Harriman and me to return to London. We said our good nights, but Churchill walked on to the door with us. "It's been nice having you, and you must come again," he told me, for a moment sounding like any country host bidding a casual guest farewell.

I looked back from our car. Churchill, disobeying the blackout, was standing in the doorway, silhouetted in the light from the hall, rocklike, his cigar projecting from his mouth at a jaunty angle. As our car began to move, he drew a hand from his rompers pocket and waved.

228

13

Potluck at the Kremlin

When Hitler turned on his partner and invaded Russia on June 22, 1941, Moscow became the story, and I soon received a cable from *Collier's* suggesting that I move on from the Savoy to Red Square. Armed with this, I went to see Ivan Maisky, the Soviet Ambassador to England. A genial little man with a tidy black goatee, he looked like someone I had once known but could not place. He warned me apologetically that at such a critical period for his country a request like mine might take some time to process. When three weeks passed without result, I went back to see what the trouble was. This time, shaking his head sadly, Maisky told me that the Kremlin had rejected my application. *Collier's* already had a representative in Moscow, Alice Leon-Moats, and it was deemed unnecessary to admit another.

When Colebaugh notified me that he was getting a similar runaround from the Soviet Ambassador in Washington, I trotted once again to Averell Harriman, the man who knew how to get things done. I learned that he and Beaverbrook, following up the mission of Harry Hopkins, were just about to leave for Moscow to work out Lend-Lease details with the Russians. Averell thought he might be able to get me into Russia as his press officer.

Leaving the problem in Harriman's capable hands, I turned my attention to another pressing matter: the wake for my goldfish. These pets, ensconced in the gleaming *bidet* in my bathroom at the Savoy, had given me companionship during some of the loneliest hours of the Blitz. Now they were dead, struck down by the carelessness of a maid who, after changing their water, had neglected to stopper the *bidet* tightly. As a tragedy it was hardly global, but as an excuse for a party in wartime London it was ideal. Arthur Christiansen helped me send out the invitations, and we filled my quarters at the Savoy with enthusiastic mourners. Several RAF pilots and a couple of Americans who were flying in the volunteer group known as the Eagle Squadron were allowed to attend in uniform. For the rest it was a black tie affair. Afterward, I thought it only proper that *Collier's* should foot the bill, for in a sense my companions had died in the line of duty. Along with an article not urgent enough to cable, I mailed this expense account:

Purchase of three goldfish to combat extreme loneliness	$ 3.
Feeding of goldfish	$ 8.
Medical care for goldfish	$15.
Entertainment for friends of dead goldfish at wake	$40.
Hire of Carrol Gibbons and his orchestra to play Handel's *Messiah* at wake	$90.
Church services for late departed at St. Paul's	$60.
Interment of late departed at St. Martin's-in-the-Fields	$30.
Headstone for grave	$25.
Present for bereaved parents of goldfish	$75.

Charley Colebaugh read the article and the expense account (I learned later) and handed them to Bill Chenery saying, "Which one of these do you think we ought to publish?"

Three days after Harriman went to work on the Russians for me I was invited to call again at the Soviet Embassy. This time, beaming, Maisky handed me my passport with the visa neatly stamped upon it. He offered no explanation for his government's about-face, and I, determined to be just as good a sport as Britain's new ally, asked for none.

With Maisky was Constantine Oumansky, the Soviet Ambassador to the United States, who happened to be on his way home to Moscow. He was a chubby little man, black-haired and clean shaven. His smile turned on and off with the precision of a neon sign and seemed just about that warm. To celebrate the success of my application, we had a drink together, Maisky pouring us slugs from a bottle of Haig & Haig of which he was touchingly proud. I noticed that both Russians drank a mighty good glass of whisky.

Ever since my first meeting with Maisky, I had been troubled by his resemblance to someone I had once known. Now it came to me. I asked him if by any chance he had lived in Brooklyn in 1911. He declined the honor. Wearing a *yarmulka* he would have been a dead ringer for the rabbi who used to give me fifteen cents a week for turning on his sabbath lights.

Reporting my good news to Harriman, I learned that he and Beaverbrook had officially borrowed me from *Collier's* for the duration of their mission. How long I might be allowed to remain in the Soviet Union after that was problematical, but that bridge could be crossed later. As the mission's press attaché, I was handed transportation orders stamped by our State Department. Harriman and Beaverbrook and a few of their aides would be going on a British cruiser. I and the other members of the mission, and Ambassador Oumansky as supercargo, would fly from Scotland in two B-24 bombers. Harriman warned me to take warm clothing. "You'll be flying the northern route," he said, "and it will not exactly be tropical."

As it happened, an American volunteer pilot who spent his leaves as my guest at the Savoy had recently made me a present of a fleece-lined RAF flying suit, complete with boots, gloves, and helmet. It had been the spare suit of another pilot I knew who had gone down over France. Adding this to my usual luggage, I reported to Euston Station to take the night train to Prestwick. My compartment mate turned out to be Ambassador Oumansky. Evidently less experienced than I in wartime travel, he had brought no food, whereas my secretary, Betty Marais, had had the Savoy pack me a cold chicken and sandwiches. Oumansky's neon grin flashed on at the sight of this, and again when he produced a bottle of Haig & Haig that his pal Maisky had given him. Between his beverage and my groceries, we had a pleasant supper as the blacked-out train sped north.

At first Oumansky entertained me with chitchat about diplomatic life in Washington. Principally, I remember the barter system he had used to obtain Scotch whisky from the British Embassy: one case of vodka and five pounds of Volga caviar for a case of the precious Scotch. Recalling that the British Ambassador, Lord Halifax, was not only a teetotaler but a believer in austerity for austerity's sake, I won-

231

dered what use his Embassy would have for vodka. Oumansky told me that it was traded, unopened, to the Argentine Embassy for beef.

Then we fell to discussing the flight we were about to make. Somehow, its dimensions had not yet broken through to me. Oumansky made it clear that it was to be anything but a routine venture. Archangel, the refueling stop, was nearly three thousand miles from Prestwick, and most of our course would be over water, made necessary by the fact that the Germans had fighter planes based in Norway. Not only would we fly unescorted, blacked out, and in radio silence—save for one tail gun each, our planes would be unarmed. Of necessity loaded to the gills with gasoline, they could not carry the weight of additional guns.

When I remarked that all this hardly made it sound like a picnic, Oumansky casually produced a small box and flipped it open. "These are what make me a perfect flier," he said rolling the capsules about. "Seconal." Then he told me that, although he seldom dreamed, he had a recurring vision of being in a plane that crashed and killed all on board.

Perhaps to throw off my own feelings of uneasiness about the forthcoming flight. I told Oumansky he ought to have himself psychoanalyzed and learn the meaning of his fears. He did not take it as a joke. "This is what will help a man to die properly," he said, patting his box of pills.

In Prestwick the weather kept us waiting around the airport for four days. Oumansky and I had one good afternoon visiting the Robert Burns Museum in nearby Ayr. This Russian, who knew many things I would not have looked for in either an ambassador or a Socialist realist, was aware (as I was not, until then) that the museum housed Burns' unpublished pornographic verses. A small bribe to our guard and the material was placed in our hands. On the way over from Prestwick, Oumansky had given me quite a lecture about the Soviet people's veneration of Burns as a poet of the masses, an artist of unique cultural worth in a period when most other English-speaking poets had been landed gentry or aristocrats. The cultural angle aside, Oumansky, as communism's representative in the West, presented quite a spectacle, laughing at the bawdy verses.

The next day at dusk we began what would be—if we finished it—the longest flight ever made over water by an Army plane. With its extra load of fuel, our huge plane weighed twenty-eight tons, but it lumbered down the runway and was airborne in only fifteen seconds. It was evident that our pilot, Major Al Harvey, had been practicing.

At first I sat between mission members Colonel Philip Faymonville and Admiral William Standley. Faymonville, who had been stationed in Moscow several years earlier and spoke Russian fluently, was along as Harriman's military adviser. He was one of the few Americans I had met who doubted that the Germans would conquer Russia. The sixty-eight-year-old Standley, who had retired in 1936, had been recalled to serve as Harriman's naval adviser. He and many of the rest, including Ambassador Oumansky, fell asleep soon after we were airborne. I found the bucket seats too uncomfortable. Until the cabin lights were switched off for the night, I passed the hours reading Peter Cheney's *It Couldn't Matter Less*, a very tough detective story indeed.

When a numbing cold crept into the cabin, I donned my flying suit. Still finding it impossible to sleep, I made my way back to the tail compartment, where we had been told we might smoke. Sergeant Jerry Green, who was tending our only gun, told me he had seen nothing but black night since we left Scotland. I asked him where he thought we might be.

"I don't know and I don't care," he replied. "The skipper knows. That's good enough for me. You got nothing to worry about. You're riding in the best airplane in the world with the best damn pilot in the world, and it ain't costin' you a dime. What more do you want?"

"A temperature of about eighty degrees," I said.

Green presently went forward, leaving me with his gun, which I eyed nervously until he returned, bearing a Thermos of tea and a box of sandwiches. The tea was steaming, but when I bit into a sandwich, I nearly broke a tooth. The roast beef was frozen stiff, the lettuce was ice.

"What is it doing, being so cold?" I complained.

"When I was up in the cockpit just now I asked Major Harvey the same question," Green said. "We're less than six hundred miles from the North Pole, so why shouldn't we be cold?"

The hours crept by, and then, like a reprieve, we saw the light of dawn.

"There's a plane!" Green cried excitedly. "Two! My God, don't those Red Stars look good!"

The two Russian fighter planes, which looked to me much like our P-40's, stayed with us the rest of the way to Archangel. We arrived there earlier than expected, thanks to a helpful tail wind during the second part of the trip. Twice Major Harvey flew over the muddy Archangel field. Then he made his decision. Rather than land and get stuck, we would go on, counting on the fuel we had saved with the tail wind to get us through.

Gradually the bleak countryside below us turned to farmland. Then we saw Moscow in the friendly morning sun. Harvey set us down without a jolt and we climbed out, stiff-legged and still half frozen. I congratulated Major Harvey on the good trip he had given us. He regarded me pityingly. "There was nothing good about that trip," he said. "Thirty-two hundred miles in fifteen hours without one radio signal. And twice we iced up badly. A good trip, you call it. Me, I've been flying twenty years and I didn't like that flight one bit."

Disregarding this, I signed a wire to Harry Hopkins in Washington in which all of us suggested that Distinguished Flying Crosses be awarded to Harvey and Lieutenant Reichers, the pilot of the second plane. Both pilots eventually received the decorations.

Being given VIP treatment as press attaché, I was housed at the National Hotel, not in a simple room but in a two-room suite. Philip Jordan of the London *News Chronicle* and Llewellyn Thompson, the second secretary of the American Embassy, acted as installation committee. Thompson told me that mine was not just any two-room suite. "Trotsky once lived here," he said. "It was from your balcony that he made his last speech in Moscow and was shouted down by the crowd, angered by his break with Stalin and inflamed by the fact that he had not attended Lenin's funeral, which was probably one of the greatest mistakes in political history."

Jordan pointed out that he and Thompson had not gotten me this lodging for its historical association but rather because of the large round table in the sitting room. He called it the best poker table in the National Hotel.

While waiting for Harriman and Beaverbrook to arrive, I did a good deal of walking around Moscow to get the feel of the place. Sometimes my guide was my *Collier's* colleague, Alice Leon-Moats, who spoke Russian; sometimes I went alone. At this point the Nazis had overrun sixty thousand square miles of Russian soil, and were only a little over two hundred miles away. This much the foreign correspondents knew, but little more, since none of them were being allowed anywhere near the fighting.

A few streets away from the Kremlin and Red Square, I found Moscow shabby. Long lines of would-be customers waited in front of every food store. I saw no able-bodied men in these lines, and for that matter very few young or even middle-aged women. Moats told me that Marshal Voroshilov had raised a new army for the last-ditch stand to keep the Germans out of Moscow, and that thousands of the city's men and women had gone out to dig trenches, gun emplacements, and tank traps. I could not help but contrast this resolution to save Moscow with the collapse I had seen in Paris in June, 1940.

The people I passed on the streets, all of them poorly dressed, looked anything but frightened. Every day one saw groups of recruits training in Red Square. Many were very young, many were over normal military age, all looked determined, and when they marched off to their barracks they sang lustily. If at that moment there was no rational reason for thinking Moscow would stand against General Von Boch's Panzer forces, I felt at least as confident as I thought the Moscovites felt. It was as though they had whispered their secret to me.

Then Harriman and Beaverbrook appeared, and for a week there was one conference after another. The question, basically, was what was wanted and what could be supplied. After the Russian negotiators stated their needs, Harriman and the Beaver consulted with their military, naval, and economic advisers to see if the United States and Britain could, in safety, spare the required material. In a few cases the Russians made demands that were considered unreasonable. They wanted heavy bombers, fighter planes, and anti-aircraft guns, all of which were of course badly needed in England. In other cases, especially in regard to certain raw materials, the Russians surprised us by the modesty of their requests. Nearly every night, after the work of their various committees was done, Beaverbrook and Harriman conferred with Stalin himself. They told me after their first meeting with him that they were impressed by his knowledge of technical matters. When I asked for an example, Beaverbrook told me how Stalin had caught him up on a detail about the Hurricane motor:

"When I said it had thirteen hundred fifty horsepower, he smiled and said, 'No, it has only twelve hundred fifty.' And he was right."

This struck me as a revealing little story to give out to the cor-

235

respondents, and with Beaverbrook's OK, I passed it along. It was immediately censored. I went to the Soviet Foreign Office and protested to Solomon Lozovsky, the censors' head man. He replied that it would be discourteous to Lord Beaverbrook to let that item go out.

"But Beaverbrook told me the story," I said, "and he himself said it was all right to let the correspondents have it."

Lozovsky, a cold type who wore rimless glasses, answered that point by ignoring it. He assured me that Stalin would not wish to appear superior in knowledge to the English minister who had come to help Russia.

"But it is a great tribute to Stalin that he can correct Beaverbrook on anything to do with British airplanes," I said. "It was a good joke on Beaverbrook, and he himself laughed at it."

Lozovsky looked at me steadily. "The story would serve no useful purpose. We will not pass it."

Practically every night the mission was in Moscow, there was an air raid of sorts. To those of us who had been brought up on the London raids, so to speak, they didn't amount to much, but the Russians took all the alarms with utmost seriousness. The moment the sirens sounded, everyone had to get off the streets.

One evening, just as I was sitting down with Harriman and several other members of the mission to have dinner at the National, the sirens began to sing. The hotel manager appeared and told us politely but firmly to go into the subway across the square. Our dinner, he said, would be served to us there.

Accompanied as usual by a squad of NKVD men—or YMCA boys, as we called these always obtrusive secret policemen—we hurried through the blackout and took an escalator down to the train platform, perhaps a hundred and fifty feet below the street. Resigned to the thought of dining to the accompaniment of passing trains, I got a new slant on the Russian way when we were ushered into a sumptuous marble-walled room, lit by crystal chandeliers, and much handsomer than the dining room of the hotel. I learned that this haven had been reserved for our mission against just such a contingency. Several of our members were already there, feasting on kasha and mushrooms while an intense-looking trio of pianist, violinist, and cellist soothed their spirits with strains from Tchaikovsky. It was astonishing, of course, but a little absurd for the sort of raid that would not have caused a ripple at the Savoy.

236

As the finish to the week of work, Stalin invited the entire mission to a state dinner at the Kremlin. This was a big deal; there hadn't been an affair of such size or importance in years. An entourage of embassy cars, each one containing a YMCA boy to protect us from God knows whom, swept us into the Kremlin through a huge archway. The great buildings within the wall were ugly in their futile camouflage—futile in that the Moskva River flows right by the Kremlin and on a night with a moon would point the way as unerringly as the Thames pointed to central London.

Entering what had once been the palace of the czars, we made our way up a mountainside of white marble steps and past several sets of guards to the banquet hall. The guards, incidentally, were all army officers. Guarding the Kremlin was apparently not a suitable assignment for the proletarian soldier. The banquet hall, set for one hundred, was a beautiful sight with its three massive crystal chandeliers aglow and its red tapestried walls and gilt trimmings. In all that splendor, one could truly feel that the Russian working class had lost its chains. I thought of trying this observation out on Constantine Oumansky, who was present, greeting the guests, but somehow I felt that his sense of humor, even after his sojourn in the free world, might not be equal to it.

While the gathering ate pastry sticks from passing trays and waited for Comrade Stalin to arrive last of all, I moved around, sizing up our hosts. For one, there was the fat, smiling Maxim Litvinov, chatting with Beaverbrook. He had acted as interpreter for Harriman and Beaverbrook during their meetings with Stalin. Once he had been Russia's representative in London, Berlin, Washington and Paris, and he had been admired by many Westerners for his affability and good sense; he had impressed people as a Russian who could think like a European. When he could not manage even the pretense of happiness at the signing of the Hitler-Stalin nonagression pact in 1939, he had disappeared—some thought for good. Now that Germany and Russia were at war, he was again bobbing to the top, looking as if he had never missed a day at work.

Representing the military was Marshal Voroshilov. Resplendent in his dove-gray uniform with red and green collar tabs, his red marshal's sash, and his chestful of what the correspondents called sardine tins, he looked every inch the general. Only he and his newly raised army now stood between the Germans and Moscow, yet he was chat-

237

ting genially with Colonel **Faymonville** as though he hadn't a care in the world. Physically, he was a small man with noticeably small feet. Though we understood that he had not had the military training of either Budenny or Timoshenko, he seemed to have become Stalin's favorite. A marshal in Russia wore a splendid uniform and people cheered him when he reviewed troops, and the press of the free world acclaimed him as a military genius when his men won an important victory, but within the Soviet Union it was recognized that there was only one military genius, just as there was only one political genius—Stalin.

When I caught sight of Molotov, the regime's Number Two man (if a dictatorship can be said to have one), he was standing alone, apparently finding no one worth talking to. He wore a Groucho Marx mustache and most of the time looked as if he were watching someone sucking a lemon. When he smiled, a rare event, the crust of his face seemed to crack reluctantly, and you felt that the display cost him physical effort. To a man, the correspondents disliked and distrusted Molotov; most thought that he had been the chief engineer of the nonaggression pact with Germany, and all of us still remembered his praise of the Germans for their glorious conquest of France.

Another important official present was the soft-spoken Lavrenti Beria, who looked like a family physician until you got close to him, and whose innocent-sounding title, Commissar for Internal Affairs, meant among other things that he was boss of the YMCA boys. I watched plump, rosy-cheeked Andrei Vishinsky chatting in French with Harriman, and found it difficult to realize that this benign-looking man was the one who had been in charge of the purge trials in 1938 that had sent to death or imprisonment at least one hundred thousand of his countrymen. Everything about him was warm—except his eyes which looked like two bits of coal in the snow.

Then the hum of talk faded. The big boss was approaching. This was the first time I had seen him. I was amazed. In all his pictures, and on the thousands of posters around Moscow, he had seemed to me huge, forbidding, surly—though of course any Russian would have told me the term I wanted was "inspiring." The rather bowlegged little man who walked toward us, his face a broad grin when he caught sight of Beaverbrook and Harriman, was a shattering contradiction of the public image. I gathered that he wore elevator shoes. Somewhat later a British correspondent wrote this of Stalin: "He looks like the

238

kindly Italian gardener you have in twice a week." It couldn't have been put better.

Oumansky led the dictator around, introducing him to everyone he didn't already know. He shook hands with each of us, and murmured a pleasantry that Oumansky translated. I found his grip firm. According to Oumansky, his deathless remark to me was, "I hope you like Moscow." Stalin carried his atrophied left arm close to his body to minimize the defect. He wore the military-style tunic in which he was always pictured, but there was nothing sloppy about his appearance. The simple gray suit fitted him beautifully. Beaverbrook said he was the best-dressed man he had seen in Russia.

At the banquet table I was placed between a Russian admiral and and a Soviet Foreign Office man. Eddie Page, a Russian-speaking member of Harriman's staff, sat on the admiral's other side and was my closest source of language help. The caviar, which led off our twenty-three course orgy, was on the table in huge bowls. Not being one who can take caviar or leave it alone, I kept on taking. Eddie Page, alarmed, spoke to me past the admiral: "Lay off the aviarcay. This goes on for hours and you can't refuse anything."

Vodka was on the table in carafes—white vodka, yellow vodka, and red vodka with peppers in it. As soon as a carafe began to look low, a waiter would replace it. Every time my glass was half empty, the admiral, with whom I was making out in German, would refill it, professing great consternation at the lack of hospitality being shown me by the Foreign Office character on my other flank. We would then lift glasses, murmur *"Vashe Zdorovie,"* and belt the stuff down.

Meanwhile, course succeeded course on the same large gold-rimmed plate. You were expected to finish everything. At first this was no problem because the food was fantastically good. But about the time you leaned back in your chair to relax and establish further capacity, the waiter would be hovering over you with the next course. For me, the high points were the mushrooms sautéed in sour cream, the sturgeon in champagne sauce, and the pilaf of quail. Feasting thus, I found it a little difficult to remember that the Germans were now less than a hundred miles from Moscow—or to recall the lines of the hungry of this classless society doubtless even now waiting at the doors of food stores. I glanced down the table to where Stalin sat between Harriman and the Beaver, chatting and laughing. As Number One man, was he, I wondered, preoccupied with the ominous situation at the front and

239

simply going through with this social pageant because he thought it was required, or, after all, was he able to forget the harrowing realities for a few hours' relaxation with his new friends?

No speeches were made, only toasts. Stalin led off by toasting Beaverbrook and Harriman. By the time we reached the borscht, half-way through the menu, there must have been twenty toasts, all of them applauded and cheered. Some of the offerings, as translated, had little connection that I could see with Lend Lease, but they were wildly received all the same. Apparently anyone who felt the spirit could rise and lift his glass. I almost offered a few words in praise of Toots Shor. I'm sorry now that I thought better of it. Stalin, I noticed, drank each toast in red wine, but sparingly. Vodka *nyet*. The master of Russia might be called many things behind his back, but from what I saw no one could fairly call him a boozer.

When we reached the coffee stage, Stalin rose again and lifted his glass. After he spoke, Oumansky translated:

"Comrade Stalin says that he would like to propose a toast to the President of the United States. Comrade Stalin says President Roosevelt has the very difficult task of leading a country which is a nonbelligerent and yet which wants to do all it can to help the two great democracies of Europe in their fight against fascism. Comrade Stalin says may God help him in his most difficult task."

It was an interesting moment for those of us who thought of the Russian dictator as the anti-Christ. Harriman gripped Stalin's hand, thanking him. Later I asked Harriman if he thought Stalin had been sincere. "No one can read that man's mind," he said.

I would willingly have called it quits when we finally rose from the table at midnight, but Stalin now led us into the Kremlin's motion picture theater, a beautifully paneled room with seats for about two hundred. At each comfortable chair was a small table, and even as we sank wearily into our places, waiters began serving us champagne and sweet pastry. The first film, the heavy one, was an eerie number called *War of the Future*. Made in 1938, it showed the Germans invading the Soviet Union. While it was technically poor, the miniature battle shots being especially crude, the prophecy was everything. The Red Army and a rather large actor made up to look like our host predictably triumphed before the fade-out. I waited in vain for someone in our group to ask Stalin where this film had been playing between August, 1939, and June, 1941.

240

The second item on the Kremlin's double-feature bill was *Volga, Volga*, a boy-meets-girl number that seemed as long as the river it vaguely celebrated. At three in the morning, when we thanked our host for his delightful party, he still looked as fresh as he had at the start of the evening. I commented on this to Oumansky, and he told me that Stalin was simply waiting for us to leave so that he could go to his office and study the latest dispatches from the fronts. The kindly Italian gardner had staying power.

I was allowed to stay on in Moscow after Harriman and Beaverbrook left, but without my privileged status as press attaché I became just one more of the terriers who tried to worry something out of Vice-Commissar Lozovsky at his twice-weekly press conferences. Always graciously inviting us to ask him any questions we wished, he succeeded in answering none. Actually, most of our news about what was going on came from American and British Embassies or from the German radio. At one conference I recall Arch Steele of the Chicago *Daily News* asking Lozovsky if there was any truth in the German boast that their armies had broken through in the south and were now pressing on toward Moscow.

"Mr. Steele, you know the German radio," said Lozovsky. "Can you ever believe it? As for what Goebbels says, we Russians have a proverb: 'If loud braying counted for anything, the ass would be king of the animal world.' "

Out of such evasions and proverbs, plus the two brief daily communiqués and an occasional tour of a factory or hospital or ballet school, correspondents had to write their stories.

We knew that the Germans were getting closer and the people of Moscow knew it, but as one watched them in the streets or at the theaters no increase in tension could be detected. One night Alice Leon-Moats and I went to see the great Galina Ulanova dance in *Swan Lake*. During the intermission we circulated in the lobby and Moats listened in on some of the conversations. The only topic was Ulanova. She was being compared with great ballerinas of the past, and winning hands down. We heard not one word about the war. I was reminded of Stalin's poker-faced performance at the Kremlin.

Moats, who had been stationed in Moscow a year, had a word of advice for me. "Don't try to understand these people or you'll go nuts."

241

As the situation became worse, only two of the people I knew personally remained confident that Moscow would not fall. One was the American Colonel Faymonville, who had stayed on as Lend Lease representative and saw the matter in military terms. The other was my Russian interpreter and secretary, Tina Sofiano. Her conviction seemed to have a purely mystic base. "You Westerners do not understand our country," she said to me. "In *War and Peace* Tolstoy said of Napoleon's campaign, 'The maggot may gnaw at the cabbage, but the maggot dies before it has killed the cabbage.' That is what will happen."

None of the correspondents' secretaries were young or pretty—I think the Kremlin's press bureau, which furnished them to us, saw to that—and Sofiano, as we all called her, a big, matronly, slow-talking soul, was no exception to the rule. However, she had a serene good nature, despite the fact that her husband and both her sons were at the front, and she was one of the finest scroungers I met in Russia. One day I deliberately asked her what she thought would happen when the Germans entered Moscow. Handing me a carton of Lucky Strikes obtained heaven knows where, she brushed the possibility off with, "More than a hundred years ago Tutchev gave us this proverb: 'You cannot understand Russia with your reason; you cannot measure Russia with your yardstick; you can only believe in Russia.' "

On the morning of October 15, it appeared that even the steadfast faith of Sofiano might not be enough. Ambassador Laurence Steinhardt summoned all the American correspondents to the Embassy, and advised us that most of the Soviet government was in the process of moving six hundred miles east to Kuibyshev, and that the entire diplomatic corps and others would follow on the evening train. We were also to go, along with censors. "You have no discretion in the matter," Steinhardt told us, assuming that some of us might be tempted to linger behind in what now seemed to be another doomed capital.

Soon after five we began gathering at the huge Kazan Station. We carried only hand luggage and what food our secretaries could find for us. Thanks to Sofiano, I had a roast chicken, some radishes, and two bottles of vodka. The first snow of the year was swirling down in large dry flakes, turning to slush as it hit the pavements. For a while I stood near the main door watching the ambassadors and ministers trudge in: Haidar Atkar, the Turkish Ambassador; anxious-eyed Vladimir Kot, once a college professor, now the Polish Ambassador;

242

Shao Li-tze, the Chinese Ambassador, one of the best-liked diplomats in Moscow; Japanese Ambassador General Tatekawa, apple-faced and shriveled, fastidiously brushing the snow from his uniform; Greek Minister Pipinellis; Yugoslav Minister Milar Gavrilovitch; Fierlinger, the tired-eyed Czech to whom evacuations were old stories; roly-poly Mohammed Saed of Iran, who smiled because it was his nature to smile even though empires tottered. Tight-lipped Sir Stafford Cripps, the British Ambassador, looked suddenly old as he sat alone, stroking the head of his Airedale, Joe, Moscow's best known dog-about-town. Steinhardt and his aides appeared: Llewelyn Thompson, Charlie Thayer, Walter Thurston, all of whom were carrying crates of food.

The smoke from hundreds of cigarettes grayed the air, and as the hours of waiting for the train passed, the individuals became part of a mass of humanity. An evacuation is a great leveler. Although this was my first evacuation by train, the rest of the picture was familiar.

At last, word came that the train was ready. Carrying our baggage, we stumbled through the heavy slush and boarded. In the classless society of Russia you traveled on trains either "soft" or "hard." The diplomats got the soft coaches, which were almost as good as those in the best American trains. The rest of us traveled hard.

My compartment mates were Cy Sulzberger of *The New York Times,* and Henry Cassidy and Robert Magidoff of the AP. For an hour we sat on the wooden bunks of our unlighted compartment on the motionless train and discussed the lack of heat. It was very noticeable. The only one in the crowd who hadn't yet ridden on a Russian train, I thought surely that the heating system must be connected with the locomotive—that we would be warm as soon as we started moving. At 1:30 A.M., five hours after the announced starting time, the train crept out of the station. The seeping Russian cold immediately lowered the temperature of our compartment still further. I slept in my RAF suit, which was regarded by my companions with some envy.

Dawn found us traveling slowly across a drab plain. Occasionally we stopped briefly at a station. The villages looked uniformly primitive and unattractive. We rolled past one that had been hit by German planes during the night. None of us could figure out why this remote spot had been bombed, but Henry Cassidy probably came the closest when he suggested that the Germans may have been looking for us.

Ours was a long train, thirty-three coaches, and our one locomotive

243

seemed to tire frequently. Once we sat on a siding for seven hours, not at all cheered by the spectacle of a bomb- and machine-gun–scarred train on the next track. At other times we went onto sidings while trains laden with troops and guns passed en route to Moscow.

The first morning out, the Embassy's Charlie Thayer called us to a breakfast of sorts in a heated coach. After we had thawed out there, we refused to return to our compartment. Moats, the only woman correspondent aboard, had, we learned, been given a soft compartment all to herself. We hard-compartment exiles agreed that this tasteless excess of Slavic gallantry should be rectified immediately, and Sulzberger, Cassidy, and I laid claim to her three unoccupied berths, assuring the loser, Magidoff, that Moats ought not to have more than one AP man in her quarters.

After that first day there was no drinking water on the train. Those of us who could made out with vodka and similar potions. Others took their chances with the tap water to be found when we stopped at stations. At intervals Charlie Thayer passed out cans of salmon and beans, which we ate cold. The second morning we stopped at a large, well-kept station and found waiting for us a hot breakfast of cabbage soup, fried eggs, and boiled beef. Along with the diplomats of Europe and Asia we ate our fill. Someone suggested that this bounty must mean we were nearing Kuibyshev, but Thayer consulted his map and straightened us out on that one. We had another three hundred miles to go.

All day long in our soft compartment, until the early darkness made us stop, we played poker, the only cultural facility available. Once we persuaded Ambassador Steinhardt to join us and were happy to plunge him a thousand rubles in the red. He recouped and then some, long before we reached our destination.

Moats earned our admiration by her fortitude and her lack of the usual feminine insistence on cleanliness and tidiness; as well as being a top correspondent, she was a very attractive girl of impressive spirit. Some months earlier, Ambassador Steinhardt, one of the many Americans who had no faith in the ability of the Russians to defend Moscow, had sent his wife to Sweden. He had tried to send Moats with her, but she had defied him. She and Steinhardt were now operating under an uneasy truce.

The refusal of Moatsie to trade on her sex during that endless train ride was something unforgettable. She complained only once. Early

244

one morning, she snapped out our names. Sleep was precious, and to have it stolen so unceremoniously did not make any of us cheerful.

"You three have been snoring very loud!" she announced.

"You should be used to it by now," Cassidy grumbled.

"I am," Moats said witheringly, "but now you're yodeling!"

We reached Kuibyshev before dawn on the fifth day. A sprawling city on the Volga River, it was so far east of the war zone that it was not blacked out. For those of us who had been living for months in night-time darkness, the beauty of Kuibyshev's twinkling lights was almost shocking.

There were two hotels in the city. I hoped the National, which was already occupied by the advance Russian contingent, had more to offer than the Grand, which was where we correspondents landed, along with most of the foreign diplomats and an overflow of high-ranking Russians. The Grand had neither bathtubs nor central heat. But I complain unduly. The room Arch Steele and I were given contained a small electric heater that worked nearly every day. Across the hall my old friend Oumansky, sharing his room with three other Soviet functionaries, apparently had to depend on the warmth given off by a samovar. The great Andrei Vishinsky lived down the hall, and there was never any mistake about which door was his, since it was guarded day and night by two NKVD men. Vishinsky smiled readily enough when we met him in the hall, and while he looked and acted like the dean of some small American college, there was in his pale blue eyes a hint of winter that suggested an inadequately heated hotel room was the least of his concerns.

The dining room of the Grand was filled all day long with men in Russian, British, Czech, and Polish uniforms. One of them was bald-headed General Vladislas Anders, now the Commander in Chief of the Polish Army in Russia, whose cheerful air quite concealed the fact that he had only recently been released from a Soviet prison. Anders and his poorly equipped forces had bravely fought both the Nazis and the Russians when they overran Poland in 1939. Ever since, about a hundred thousand survivors had been in Russian labor camps or prisons. Now that the Germans were threatening Moscow, the Polish general and the remains of his army had made their reappearance. Anders himself was being wooed as a great Polish hero. To us who knew his story he was a good deal more of a hero than the Russians would publicly admit.

245

Prior to the exodus from Moscow, Kuibyshev had been a city of two hundred thousand. Now, suddenly, it contained a million people. As a result there was a good deal of hardship, but not even the man or woman waiting hours in line for a bowl of soup and a chunk of bread complained or felt that the situation was hopeless. Sofiano, my secretary, had come on to Kuibyshev by a later train, and with her help I interviewed a number of the refugees in the snowy streets. Though many believed that the city of Moscow might now be taken, they scoffed at the idea that Russia would ever be subjugated. For Stalin, the heroic leader who had stayed on in the beleaguered capital, I found a feeling akin to deification.

Real news was in short supply in Kuibyshev, and the censors were letting very few stories go out. Hoping that we had found a noncontroversial minor subject, Arch Steele and I one day persuaded Comrade Lozovsky to let us visit a munitions plant we had heard about. It was some fifty miles off, and we were driven there by an English-speaking army lieutenant. The wintry landscape to the east of Kuibyshev was of a piece with what we had seen from the train: flat, empty and discouraging. Two days of rain had melted recent snow. Our road was a mud track.

About thirty miles out, we drove past a cluster of bleak wooden buildings surrounded by a wire fence. Our guide readily identified it as a concentration camp. His willingness surprised me until I realized that, as Lozovsky's deputy, he knew we would be unable to write anything about it. This particular camp, he told us, was for political offenders.

A mile or so beyond the camp we came to a large group of prisoners working on the road with picks and shovels. A few soldiers with rifles were guarding the group quite carelessly. It was obvious that there was no place for any of the prisoners to run or hide. Dressed in their shapeless gray clothing, they stood just off the road and watched us pass, their faces expressionless. Steele and I looked at one another. All of them were women.

When you have toured one munitions plant—and I had, in England—you've seen them all. For me, the most interesting feature of our visit was the lunch we were served. We had not only the inevitable cabbage soup in which pieces of boiled beef floated, we had steak, fresh tomatoes, beans, onions, and potatoes, not to mention all the milk we wanted. I told the director of the plant that he was eating a lot better than Comrade Vishinsky was at the Grand Hotel in Kuiby-shev. The director replied proudly that the plant maintained its own farm and dairy, and that every one of the workers was enjoying the same fare that we were having. Furthermore, the plant had its own store in which the workers were able to buy their clothes at prices far below Moscow's.

Steele and I returned to Kuibyshev in a thoughtful mood. Neither of us had ever seen a better-run plant, or more cheerful and industrious workers. As at the concentration camp, we had been vouchsafed a glimpse behind the veil, but this time at something attractive. I wrote three thousand words about the munitions plant and its unusual spirit. Hoping it might get by the watery eye of censor Nikolai Pulganov, I added a mention of the prisoners who had been repairing the road. Pulganov not only struck out the prisoners but practically everything else. My gutted article in hand, I called on Pulganov's boss. "I am not," I told Lozovsky, "writing articles for *Pravda!*"

Far from reeling at this insult, the commissar urbanely conveyed his conviction that I lacked the objective, scientific point of view that would make my journalism of interest to readers in the USSR.

Though further argument was actually useless, I said that there were influential people in America who hated the thought of giving the Russians even a can of C rations because in effect it would be an aid to communism. These were the people we correspondents hoped to reach with our stories. None of us gave a damn for communism, but we knew that Communists were killing Nazis, and we knew that victories now by the Red Army would make it that much easier for the British troops when it came time for their invasion of Europe. By dramatizing the story of the Russians' suffering and defeats and victories, I told Lozovsky, we would be creating climate favorable for increased material aid to Russia.

Perhaps it was the free-enterprise spirit of the correspondents that was finally too much for Lozovsky and those who stood above him. The United States newspapers and radio networks were using the news bulletins issued by Tass, the Soviet news agency, and according to Lozovsky, Tass was telling the people of America all they had to know.

I knew I was licked. With Moats' approval, I composed a service message to Colebaugh. Service messages were not censored, since it was understood that their contents would never be published so I

247

wrote: MOATS AND I WOULD LIKE TO REMAIN TO WRITE ABOUT THE HEROIC RUSSIAN PEOPLE AND THE GREAT RED ARMY BUT STUPID CENSORSHIP PREVENTS US FROM DOING THIS. MOATS WANTS TO GO TO INDIA. I WANT TO GO TO LONDON. WHAT DO YOU THINK? Hoping he would show the message to Lozovsky, I handed it to Pulganov. He glanced at it, nodded, and the message went through as written.

Within twelve hours Colebaugh replied: YOU TWO GO WHEREVER YOU CAN FIND STORIES. IF YOU NEED MONEY, CABLE. MY ESTEEM AND AFFECTION.

Our only problem now was getting out of Russia, a big place with no transportation facilities for foreigners. Then we heard that Sir Walter Monckton, whom I had met at Cliveden, was soon to arrive for a meeting with Commissar of Foreign Affairs Molotov. With some confidence I told Moats that we would be flying back to London with Monckton.

Before he arrived, there came a day when I thought maybe I wasn't going anywhere, except possibly to a morgue. Having survived dysentery and scabies, two routine afflictions in Kuibyshev, I came down with carbuncles, one on my knee, the other under my arm. Irwin Norman, the Embassy doctor, examined them daily until satisfied of their ripeness, then summoned me to his dispensary.

A select audience gathered to watch. Ambassador Larry Steinhardt shook his head in disbelief. "Only two of them, Quent? Don't you know they always come in sevens?"

Lieutenant Charles Olsen, one of Colonel Faymonville's assistants, administered what I assumed was a local anesthetic: a severely cooling spray from a can. Afterward I learned that it was simply something to freeze the skin and render it easier to cut.

As Dr. Norman moved toward my knee with his little knife he suggested that I might like to look the other way. Having the idea that he was simply going to stick a needle into me, as one does with a boil, I was not prepared for what followed. The yell I let out must have been heard by a large part of Kuibyshev.

"You wrote a book called *The Wounded Don't Cry*," the surgeon said dryly. "Where did you ever get that silly title?"

I started to tell him I would have the title changed immediately. Instead, I fainted.

The eggplant under my arm was good for some further witticisms

248

from the callous onlookers. Then, after suitable bandaging, I started off for the hotel. Since the Embassy's one car was off somewhere, I walked, if you could call it walking. It was snowing hard and the streets were slippery. They were also dark, for Kuibyshev had lights only on its main thoroughfares. Philip Jordan accompanied me. Clinging to him with one hand, I felt my way along the building fronts with the other like a blind man. Suddenly, I stepped into nothingness. When I finally stopped falling, I was halfway down an open grating. Jordan got me back on my feet and we resumed our stroll.

"How much money have you in your pocket?" he asked abruptly.

It seemed the silliest question of 1941. Maybe I was delirious and not really hearing what he said. "About fifteen hundred rubles," I replied.

"That's approximately a hundred dollars," he mused. "And I have the same. Yet here we are in a snowstorm, wading in slush, and there isn't a taxi to be had. We'll get to the hotel wet and freezing, but with two hundred dollars between us we'll still have a problem finding a hot drink for you. Norman told you to eat fresh vegetables and fruit for the next few days, but with two hundred dollars we still can't buy you an orange. You'll go to bed for a few days. In London, that would be a pleasure. You'd send out for a dozen detective stories and enjoy your holiday. Here, with all our capital, we can't buy a sixpenny thriller because they don't exist. And yet," Jordan concluded, "there are people who think war correspondents lead glamorous lives."

Next morning I was awakened from a sleeping-pill and codeine haze by a brisk knocking at my door. It was Oumansky, with news. Maxim Litvinov had just replaced him as Ambassador to the United States and he, Oumansky, had just been made director of Tass.

I perked up at once, telling him that this would make a nice little story for the press association boys, though it would be of no use to me personally. Oumansky then handed me the crusher. The two appointments had already been announced by Tass.

"That's just fine!" I said bitterly. "And you fellows can't understand why we hate your methods of giving out and holding back news. We correspondents sit here going through carbuncles and all the rest of it, and the first time a decent story breaks, every one of us is beaten by some radio announcer five thousand miles from here."

Tass's new boss treated me to one of his on-off smiles, but it was

249

obvious that he no more understood what made me tick, a scheming lackey of the West's decadent capitalist press, than I understood him, the complete Communist.

In 1945, soon after Oumansky was made Soviet Ambassador to Mexico, he was killed there in a plane crash. Much as I hated all that he represented, I recalled the chubby little man with his box of pills, and I hoped that he had been able to load up before his nightmare came true.

When Monckton arrived for his meeting with Molotov, we learned that his mission was to encourage a better give and take between British and Russian sources of information. The two representatives did a lot of conferring, but I gathered later that little of a practical nature resulted. The Russians just preferred to play with their cards held close. Much more noteworthy, from the correspondents' point of view, was the cocktail party Phil Jordan and I put on for Monckton on Guy Fawkes Day, November 5. When we explained to the manager of our hotel, a little man we knew only as Jack, that Sir Walter was as big a wheel in England as Molotov was in Russia, he fell into the spirit of the thing, assigned us a private dining room, and swore he would provide exceptional food and he outdid himself by producing fried potatoes, a genuine rarity. Thirty-nine out of forty invited guests appeared, including eight ambassadors, and no one really noticed the absence of Sir Stafford Cripps, the eminent vegetarian, who should have been with us if only because he was Monckton's law partner.

What the convivial Monckton may have had in common with Cripps, I never decided. Cripps was a loner, respected but hardly liked. While he professed a great love for humanity, it was obvious to anyone who watched him in action that he had little liking for individual representatives of the species. It was no secret that Cripps had a burning desire to be Prime Minister of England, and there were many who believed he might make the grade if the Labour Party ever came to power. My personal opinion was that England would not tolerate a Prime Minister who neither ate nor drank.

Our guests were unanimous in calling our party the best celebration of Guy Fawkes Day ever held in Kuibyshev, and Monckton himself was so pleased that he hardly batted an eye when I told him that Moats and I expected to fly to London with him.

"There'll be room for you on the plane," he said, "but I'm going to

Cairo rather than London. That's the place for you, too, take my word for it."

In my relief at the thought that I would soon be out of the land of the Lozovskys and Oumanskys, I did not ask for an explanation of Monckton's hint.

We left Kuibyshev in a DC-3 in the first real blizzard of the year, our destination Teheran. A last-minute addition to the party was Iran's Ambassador Saed. Others flying out included Larry Steinhardt and Maxim Litvinov and his wife. Charlie Dickerson and Charlie Thayer of the American Embassy came to see Steinhardt and the Litvinovs off, while Cripps and his shivering Airedale came to see Monckton off.

"We should have hired a couple of stooges to say goodby to us," I whispered to Moats. "I'm afraid we're losing face."

After an hour of listening to weather reports in the icy waiting room, we went out through whirling snow to the plane, which was tugging at its moorings. The usual YMCA boys accompanied us to the door of the plane, and Moats finally found a use for them: she had them carry her luggage.

We broke our thirteen-hundred-mile flight with an overnight stop at Astrakhan, and the next day, the weather growing worse, we made an unscheduled stop at Baku. We were flying with silent radio, even though there were no German airplanes within a thousand miles of us. Steinhardt and Monckton were concerned about our grounding because Teheran had been notified of our expected arrival time. However, investigation in Baku showed that a cable directed to Teheran would have to be routed back to Kuibyshev, then Moscow, then London. Steinhardt decided not to cable, figuring we would reach the Iranian capital well ahead of the message.

Baku, meanwhile, had its compensations in the form of a modern hotel with hot baths, good food, and comfortable beds. Moats and I quite cheerfully accepted our share of the VIP treatment that was turned on for the rest of the group. This included a banquet and concert in honor of the Litvinovs, Maxim having once been the commissar in this part of the world.

The bad weather persisted, and four days passed before we at last set down in sun-drenched Teheran. A sizable delegation was on the field to welcome us. The British Ambassador rushed up to Monckton, grasped his hand, and said fervently, "Thank God, you are safe!"

251

Steinhardt's opposite number greeted him with similar warmth, and Ambassador Saed was met by a dozen rejoicing Iranians.

Jim Peters, the local UP man, explained the excitement. A report had come through that our plane had gone down in the Caspian Sea and that only two survivors had been picked up by a fishing craft. Although the report could not be verified, the BBC had announced that hope for other survivors was fading.

While this story had been making headlines around the world, Larry Steinhardt, Ambassador Saed, and some of the rest of us had been playing poker in the best hotel in Baku! It was Monckton who had the last word, turning to Moats and me. "You let us down, I must say. We've been presumed dead, and you two great reporters never even suspected we were missing."

14

Only the stars were neutral

After seeing Moats off to India, I flew on to Cairo, courtesy of an RAF courier pilot, about the middle of November. Meeting Bob Low there, I at last learned the reason for Monckton's comment that Cairo—not London—was where I really wanted to go. The big push was on against the Germans in the desert, and there was the chance I could find some good combat stories. Low, who had now been in the Middle East for several months, knew the proper tailor to take me to for my desert uniforms, and how to facilitate my accreditation at Army Headquarters.

Maddalena, the advance battle headquarters, some two hundred and fifty miles west of Cairo, was simply a surveyor's quadrant point on the desert map. As a place, it didn't exist, but Low and I found some eight thousand men and two hundred fighter planes and bombers stationed there. The RAF was under command of Air Vice-Marshal "Maori" Coningham, and the ground forces were under Major-General Neil Ritchie, whom Sir Claude Auchinleck, Commander in Chief of the British Army in the desert, called proudly a "thrusting general." For once, thanks to Coningham, the RAF had air superiority, and one could lie down to sleep in Maddalena without fear of a bombing attack.

253

Except for the blowing sand and the broiling sun, Maddalena was something of a paradise after Russia. I could go wherever I wished— out on night patrols or flying with the bombers—and I could interview the prisoners; something I had not been allowed to do even in England. The prisoners were Italians as well as Germans. The Italians were a sorry-looking lot, obviously glad to be out of it. The Germans, the elite *Afrika Korps,* were cold and contemptuous.

The nights were bitter cold for men in pup tents, and the shadeless days were unmerciful. Ken Downs, whom I had last seen in England the year before, had beaten me to Maddalena by a couple of weeks. He thought it quite a joke to see me wandering around in a scarf, a long-sleeved shirt, gloves, and with Low proposed to buy me a parasol at the first opportunity. But for me the desert sun was no joke.

It was Downs who introduced me to Colonel Desmond Young, in charge of press relations for the Indian Army. Downs called Young the bravest man in North Africa, which at first struck me as a rather sweeping statement to make about an officer who spent most of his time chaperoning correspondents. However, I detected at once in Young the steadiness, the dedication, that I had encountered in some of my favorite fighter pilots during the Battle for Britain. The quiet, white-mustached colonel knew his wars. After serving in World War I, he had gone to India and had become a newspaper editor. Now he was in his second war, and he hoped it would be his last. "When this is over," he told me quite seriously, "there is only one job I really want. I should like to go to America and become a butler."

It was Young who took me to Sidi Omar where I got my big desert story. He had invited Downs and Low to make the trip, but they preferred something that seemed more promising—a visit to a New Zealand tank outfit that was in combat. "You go along with Desmond," they told me a bit patronizingly. "He'll at least give you a good idea of the desert terrain." So Desmond and I set off one morning in his staff car, a canvas-topped American Ford converted for desert use.

Within two hours we were in the midst of a sea of sand. It was silent, but somehow it seemed to express hatred for intruders like ourselves. When I mentioned this rather absurd thought to Desmond he didn't laugh. "You're right. If a sudden sandstorm were to come up we should have to stop. If it kept up for two days the sand would cover our car. We have food and water for two days—that's all. In this part of the desert there are no oases. I know of no part of India

254

as unfriendly as this damn desert. The whole country seems to say, 'Come here at your own risk.' "

After six hours of eerie driving through the absolute quiet we saw bursts of black smoke far ahead of us on the horizon.

"Ken and Bob may have been wrong in not coming along with us," Desmond said mildly. "My lot is in the thick of that."

As we drove on, the road, such as it was, frequently faded from sight. Our driver, Captain Clive Burt, a barrister in civilian life, used a compass and a map to keep us on course in the vast stretches of sand.

Now we began to hear the bursting of the shells. "They're coming from Sidi Barrani," Young said. "Soon we'll be under enemy observation."

As we went on, it seemed to me that the shells were dropping fairly close to us.

"Italians are doing that firing," Young said. "Not too accurate, is it?"

"The shells aren't exactly landing in Cairo," I ventured.

"It would be silly," Young said thoughtfully, "to be killed by the Italians."

That was typical. The British military men hated the Germans with a healthy honest hatred, but they scorned and despised the Italians.

We came to barbed wire—the outer limit of the mine fields that surrounded Sidi Omar. Burt found one of the gaps through the wire and through the field, and we gingerly began the last part of our drive. The track was said to be thirty feet wide. When Burt assured me the limits were obvious to him, I could only hope he was right.

An artillery shell landed a quarter mile away. "They're aiming at us now," Young said. "That's good, because the Italians seldom hit anything they aim at."

I was not comforted, having visions of a shell touching off a few mines, but Burt drove on as nonchalantly as if he were taking us to a football game.

When we reached Sidi Omar at dusk, and I saw the objective that had already cost hundreds of lives, the whole idea of desert warfare suddenly seemed batty. We were on a plateau of sand perhaps a mile square in the middle of nowhere, and yet everyone wanted it because it was a vantage point.

General Sir Frank Messervy, in charge, received us at his sand-

255

bagged command post and told us the story of the plateau's costly capture from the Italians a few days before. Despite its name, the 4th Indian Division was not an all-Indian outfit, and the principal attackers had been the 1st Royal Sussex, a line regiment of English farmers. Unable to find the gaps in the surrounding mine fields, they had plunged straight through them. Their losses had been heavy, not only from the mines but from the Italian machine guns on the plateau above. Twenty-eight tanks had been blown up as they stormed through the mine fields.

Scratching his five-day growth of beard, Messervy told us that Italian forces were now facing two sides of the plateau; the Germans, the third. Only the fourth side—the one by which we had approached—was still open. "They shelled us most of the day," Messervy said cheerfully, "and I imagine tomorrow will be noisy too."

In the dark, Burt and Young and I made a quick cold supper from the tinned food we had brought. We had hardly finished when, in the distance, we heard a dull boom and then the swish of a shell feathering its way toward us. We dived into a three-foot slit trench beside our car and lay flat. The shell whistled directly over us in the dark and landed with a sharp explosion three hundred yards back.

The gates of hell opened with that sixty-pounder. More shells came over, and while all of them exploded behind us, many dropped unpleasantly close. Whenever the scream turned uncertain and warbling, I was convinced the shell was getting ready to drop on me personally. One exploded near a truck some forty yards from us and the blast in some inexplicable manner drew the air out of its tires, though they were otherwise not touched.

Then the British artillery, which was about a mile to our rear, opened up, and we had two streams of shells whistling overhead. Soon the firing was so heavy that the whining of the shells almost obliterated the sound of the guns.

The barrages stopped before dawn and we slept where we were, in the sand. When the sun was high and the air quite still, Young and I investigated some of the trenches near us. In addition to a great many unexploded Italian hand grenades, we found the remains of several Italians who had missed being buried because of shortage of time.

That night, patrols of black-bearded Sikhs and members of the

1st Royal Sussex went out and brought in more than two hundred Italians. At dawn, happily expecting to be sent to the rear, the prisoners learned that they would have to sweat it out with us, for now there was no rear. Word came from our reconnaissance planes that fifty German tanks were approaching on the fourth side to attack us.

We began to hear the unmistakable bark of tank guns while the tanks themselves were still out of sight, over a mile and a half away. The British artillery began to answer. I watched General Messervy as he stood observing atop a half-ton truck. There was something magnificent about his calmness. Reports came to him every few minutes. At first they were bad. Six of our guns had been put out of action, and the tanks were coming on.

Then a grimy dispatch rider hopped off a motorcycle and blurted out, "We got seven of them!" Messervy smiled and the man repeated his message in more acceptable military language.

"There they are," Messervy said after a while almost casually.

The tanks were approaching in single file, a departure from their usual frontal attack. Now they were only a mile away. I counted twenty-three, most of them the big Mark 4 type, General Rommel's pets. Our shells kept bursting around them, sending up spurts of sand and smoke that hung in the still air. Sharp golden flashes broke from the tanks, followed by lazy puffs of white smoke. The artillery on the other sides of the plateau began shelling us, but we were too engrossed in the drama of the tanks to hide in our trenches.

One of the tanks received a direct hit. Its nose lifted in the air. It leaned drunkenly on its side. A column of black smoke spiraled up from it. All around us on the plateau the soldiers let out derisive yells, much as they might have at a football game. Another tank was hit, and then another, each time to a chorus of triumphant yells. Then five tanks were burning before our eyes. More messages came to the general, but now he needed none. The whole battle was laid out in front of us, less than a mile away. It lasted an hour. By then the Germans had had enough. The surviving tanks crawled away. The shelling stopped, and a heavy, exhausted quiet descended upon the desert.

I felt that I had seen something historic. On paper the heavily armored tanks had every advantage over the vulnerable British guns with their single steel plates protecting their crews. In practice, our guns, supported by nothing more substantial than our enthusiastic cheers, had destroyed seventeen of the best German tanks. It would be something for Rommel to mull over.

After dark our patrols went out to put any wounded tanks out of their misery, lest the Germans return during the night to try first aid. After the excitement of the day, I found it easy to sleep that night, despite the winter cold. My awakening was rude. At first I automatically brushed away what seemed to be a mosquito. Then suddenly I was wide awake. The plane was quite low. Was it one of ours or one of theirs? We were not left in doubt for long. High above us a light blossomed to hand against the blackness—then another and another. In a few minutes our whole plateau was bathed in a penetrating white light. My watch said 3:45.

We were in for a taste of one of the nastiest attacks that warfare had yet devised—dive bombing. The sound of the casually circling plane changed from a steady drone to a high singing whine as the pilot leaned against his stick and pointed his machine earthward. The whine changed to a scream. The plane seemed to be coming directly toward my trench—which was suddenly far too shallow. It dived to what must have been nine hundred feet and then came the antipersonnel bombs. The world shook. Jagged bits of red-hot metal flew in all directions. Sand and rock covered me.

The plane flew off, climbing for another dive, I smelled smoke and heard a new sound, a crackling noise. Sitting up, I saw that a large supply truck, thirty feet away, had received a direct hit. It was burning brightly. Now the Germans could use the fire as a target.

I heard the plane returning. This time it was not alone. Word had gone out that there was good hunting to be had here on the plateau— and that there were few antiaircraft guns to discourage a hunter. The planes dropped more flares and took their time getting into position. I knew that our slit trenches, shallow though they were, would be black lines from the air—standing out like charcoal marks on white paper.

There was a sharp explosion nearby. I stuck my head above the trench. The gas tank of the burning truck had blown up. The truck suddenly came to life: a fantastically beautiful cascade of flares and Very lights, blue, green, and white, shot out of the flaming wreckage. I could imagine the Nazi pilots discussing the spectacle through their radios: "Good joke, eh, Franz? They shoot fireworks at us."

This time five planes dived at once, strafing as well as bombing. Bombs dropped all over the plateau. The blasts swept around me. Bullets and hunks of steel tore into the sides of my trench. The planes climbed and dived again.

There were three- and four-minute intervals when the Nazis seemed bored with their sport. Then we took deep breaths and called to one another, checking to see who was still present, and the medics and stretcher-bearers scurried around picking up the wounded.

I had been through fifty nights of bombing in London, and like everyone else had had my share of near hits, but until now I had never known the demeaning fear that makes the mouth dry and ties the stomach into knots. Although there were five thousand men on the plateau, I had the feeling that I was being attacked personally. Then, during an intermission, I raised my head and saw Desmond Young climbing out of his trench. "Still with us, Quent?" he called. He urged me to climb out, too, and stretch my legs. Then, from another trench, I saw Clive Burt emerge and light a cigarette. The spectacle of such nonchalance gave me the courage to face my fear for what it was—a purely physical reaction. I tried the cigarette routine, and was pleased to find that I could manage it with reasonable calm.

Then the bombers returned, and we went to earth. This time, rather than fear, I felt hatred for the attackers. Hatred seemed to hang in the air. We on the ground were sending up waves of hate, and the Germans were returning it. While smoking my cigarette, I had had a glimpse of the stars—brilliant in the desert sky, and incredibly serene above this man-made nightmare. Now, as I pressed myself closer to the bottom of the trench, trying to become part of the desert, a phrase occurred to me. Only the stars were neutral. It would make a good title—if I ever got to write the story.

In the east a turquoise strip brightened the horizon. One more attack remained, and it was the worst. When a plane dive-bombed it could not drop its heaviest bombs because it might itself be caught in the upward blast. What we had been living with until now were the Nazis' hundred-pounders—small, but each one capable of killing a great many men. Now, without the steep dives, the high-explosive bombs came screaming down. These were the bombs I had heard in London so many times. Each one sounded as if a giant were tearing an enormous sheet of heavy silk.

After the planes left, I lay a while with my face in the sand, dazed

259

and exhausted. Then I climbed out of the trench. I fell twice before I could stand upright. I noticed that the others were also having trouble with their balance. No one said anything for a time, and when the talk began it was disjointed and foolish. The smell of destruction hung heavily in the dawn. I was relieved to find that Young and Burt had come through it all without a scratch.

Then Burt said, "You're bleeding," and pointed to where blood was soaking through my uniform at the knee. For some time it seemed to me that I was looking at someone else's leg. My leg was without pain. Then I noticed that the backs of my hands were also bleeding. I had been cut by flying rock or bomb fragments. The wounds seemed quite unimportant compared to the fact that we were all alive. Young looked for a medic, but they all were busy with more serious cases. Not having any iodine to offer, Young poured a little brandy over my cuts, complaining of the waste, and applied bandages.

Later in the day, when we had pulled ourselves together, we agreed that I now had a story. Young thought it not only worth cabling but, if possible, something that I should report direct to England via the BBC. "The people of England haven't had many victories to cheer about out here," he said, "but these Sussex farmers have shown that Rommel can be stopped. We've got to see that they hear about it."

But both cabling and broadcasting meant first getting back to Cairo, and according to General Messervy this might take some doing. Even though British artillery and tank reinforcements were now on their way to bolster the position at Sidi Omar, and the action on the plateau was about finished, the Germans and Italians had now completely encircled us. Messervy plotted a line for us to the southeast and suggested that we just might get through in that direction during the night.

"I really can't recommend that you try it," the general said, "but I want to send some dispatches to Army Headquarters. If you will take them with you, I shall let you leave. At your own risk," he added hastily.

It was Desmond Young who decided we would make the attempt. Soon after dark, a German flare went up a mile or more to the south. Both Messervy and Young knew that German tanks and armored cars would be scattered across the desert in small units. This was their nighttime tactic. All night long, flares would be going up to help guard against surprise attacks by British patrols. "If you steer clear of the flares, you ought to get through," Messervy said, "but if you

260

run into trouble, turn around and hurry back. I'll be glad to have you again."

Young's Ford had sustained some shrapnel wounds in its torso, but the motor was running. We rolled back the canvas top in order to have a clear view of the sky—in part to watch for enemy planes, in part because Burt expected to steer by the stars as well as by his compass.

We felt our way out through the mine fields. Once past them, we drove at a steady eight miles an hour. Burt found that our motor seemed to make its least noise at this speed and there was less chance of damage to the car. Twice we went into bomb craters; each time the car pulled itself out easily. While Burt drove, periodically checking his compass with a well-shaded flashlight, Young and I stood and acted as lookouts. To our left a flare went up about two hundred yards in the air and hung there, spreading its ersatz daylight for about a quarter of a mile. Then another went up, this time perhaps half a mile to our right. There were Germans on either side of us.

And then two flares burst directly ahead, perhaps half a mile apart. We drove between them. The night was cold but I found myself sweating. Several times I saw what I thought were groups of tanks silhouetted against the horizon, only to find when we reached them that I was looking at the top of a high dune. At one point we passed three tanks lying on their sides—souvenirs of the afternoon battle.

Then, an hour out, three silent but all-too-real tanks loomed out of the darkness to the right of us, less than a hundred yards away. The low half-moon had to pick that moment to creep from behind its clouds. I gripped Young's shoulder, but he had already seen the tanks. We could see no men around them. Probably they were huddled inside to escape the cold. There was nothing for us to do but appear unconcerned. We continued to crawl along, veering slightly to the left.

I kept hoping Young would tell Burt to step on the gas and run for it, but he was too wise. We crept on at our snail's pace.

For another tense two hours we snaked between the flares. After midnight we saw no more. Just before dawn we reached Conference Cairn, a six-foot-high pile of stones some forty miles from Sidi Omar and about a two hours' drive from Maddalena. It seemed to me a fantastic accomplishment that Burt could have brought us through to this pinpoint.

Three very tired men, we sat on the sand drinking hot tea from a Thermos and smoking our first cigarettes since Sidi Omar. Relaxing for a moment, I fell asleep. I awakened sick with sun poisoning.

When we drove into Maddalena about noon, I felt like a pot roast, and my face looked as if rats had been nibbling at it. By one of those miracles granted to knaves and fools and a select few war correspondents, an airplane was leaving for Cairo within an hour. I don't remember much about the trip, but do recall checking into Shepheard's Hotel with Desmond.

While the room seemed slowly to rotate around me, flickering with heat waves as it went, Desmond placed my typewriter in front of me, fed me what he called pep pills and cold lemonade, and at the scheduled time delivered me to the radio station where, it being a Sunday night, I broadcast the saga I had written of Sidi Omar as a "Postscript to the Nine O'Clock News."

"I hope it went well," I remember saying to my handler afterward.

"But of course it went well," he replied rather ungallantly. "That was a story that almost wrote itself."

It must have been true, because during the next few hours of fiery collapse I also managed to write eight thousand words for *Collier's,* which Desmond, acting as censor, filed at the cable office after leaving me at the British Army hospital.

When I was discharged from the hospital—the day was December 7—I found that Desmond had gone back to the desert. He had left a note for me saying that my broadcast had made the hitherto obscure 1st Royal Sussex famous. This made my personal misery seem worth-while.

Ken Downs and Bob Low had just arrived in Cairo. I found them a bit disgruntled about their desert experiences. They had never managed to catch up with their tank outfit.

To celebrate our reunion, the three of us went into Shepherd's dining room and ordered the best dinner to be had. It was a large place and nearly empty, and when Captain Douglas Williams of the Ministry of Information came in a few minutes later, he spotted us and came over.

"What's the news, Douglas?" I asked as he sat down. It was a perfunctory question anyone would put to an Information man.

"We've heard little beyond the first reports," he said.

262

The three of us looked at him. Obviously, he knew something we didn't know.

"*What* first reports?" I asked.

It was Williams' turn to look at us in surprise. "You mean you boys haven't heard?" he asked. "The Japs made a sneak attack on Pearl Harbor, and like it or not, you're now in the war with both feet."

After the first shock, Downs, Low and I found ourselves seized by the same impulse—an overwhelming desire to return to the States as soon as possible. However, it appeared that transportation would be quite a problem. Cairo was full of American military observers and procurement men, all of whom had been ordered back to Washington and had been given Number One priority.

I went to see my friend Sir Walter Monckton, who had remained in Cairo as a representative of the Ministry of Information. With only my Number Three correspondent's priority, I told him I didn't see much chance of getting back to New York. He thought it over for a minute, and asked, "How would you like to go as a King's messenger?"

As a devotee of spy thrillers I knew that a King's Messenger was a man entrusted with the delivery of state documents too precious to be entrusted to diplomatic pouches. Monckton confirmed this as he took my passport. "You'll fit the part nicely, Quent," he said, "though if you want to carry it off even better, you'll buy yourself a bowler."

Two days later he called me in, handed me my passport, now stamped *KING'S MESSENGER,* and an impressive dispatch case. Noting that it had been sealed, I wondered what official communiqué might be resting within.

"This will get you through to London in a hurry," Monckton said. "After that, I'm afraid I can't help you."

With a vision of being sent to 10 Downing Street or to Whitehall, I asked Monckton where he wanted me to deliver his dispatch case.

"Give it to the porter at the Savoy, if you wish," he said. "There's nothing in it."

The dispatch case was a magic carpet as far as London, but from there on the trip was a long one. With the help of the Admiralty I managed to get a berth out of Cardiff on a small freighter that was part of a large convoy.

The first few days were quiet and with nothing else to do I started on a book I called *Only the Stars Are Neutral.* I had kept carbon

263

copies of stories I'd tried to send from Russia as well as copies of the few desert articles I'd done, and with this as a basis I found the going easy. Then one morning I awoke to find that we were in the midst of a real gale. Our little ten-thousand-ton ship lurched and rolled and pitched helplessly. I hurried to the small wardroom where we ate. The purser had hot tea, cheese and biscuits ready for us six passengers.

"Eggs won't stay in the ruddy frying pan this morning," he said cheerfully.

Two hours later we received word that we had run into a hurricane. I clambered to the bridge. Captain Peter Smith nodded and motioned to a heavy seaman's jacket that hung on the wall. I put it on. From the bridge the sight of the angry sea was awe-inspiring.

"Convoy ordered to disperse," the stocky veteran captain shouted above the gale. "It's every man for himself now!"

A sharp rain was coming down, and when it hit the steel plates of the bridge the combination of the rain and the heavy spray sounded like a continuous fusillade from small arms fire. The angry waves rose high as though to brush our little ship right out of the ocean. The fury increased and then a towering wall of water rose above the port bow, toppled and hit the deck with a crash that made the ship tremble all over. Water kept pouring green over the sides, cascading as it hit the bulkheads. We were heading into the wind and when the ship hit the waves directly it shuddered as thousands of tons of green water crashed down upon it. And then the bow would dip sickeningly, the stern would rise, and our twin screws would seem to scream as they encountered nothing but unresistant air for the moment. When this happened the ship twisted as though in agony, the ten thousand tons of steel creaking and groaning.

Captain Smith, who must have been sixty-five, wiped the spray from his eyes and grinned at me. It was a reassuring grin. He was evidently a man who could take a hurricane in his stride.

I'd never been through a hurricane at sea before, but everything that was happening seemed familiar—even the sounds made by the ship when it was hit a particularly shattering blow. And then, of course, I remembered. I'd experienced all this vicariously through the eyes of Joseph Conrad. I'd been through hurricanes in *Almayer's Folly,* and *The Nigger of the Narcissus,* and in the pages of *Lord Jim.* Perhaps that was why I could be reasonably objective watching the

264

sea at its worst—Conrad had taught me that all hurricanes must come to an end.

And, of course, this one did come to an end after three long days and nights. For another two days the sea was sullen. The rain beat down heavily, smoothing out the waves, until at times they looked like the rounded sand dunes I'd seen in the desert. And then one morning we awoke to a calm sea and a bright sunny sky, and the hurricane was only a memory. We had lost two lifeboats but beyond that, little damage had been done. Now I could go back to work on my book. We reached Halifax twenty-three days after leaving Cardiff.

When I reached New York at the end of January, 1942, I had one thought—to get into the war effort. I had visions of becoming a bomber pilot or perhaps a Marine or a naval officer. I went eagerly to my draft board and talked to the chairman, "Johnny" Johnston, who had been a great tackle at Brown in my time.

"Red," said Johnny, using my Brown nickname, even though it had been some time since there was much red in my hair, "we are not yet scraping the bottom of the barrel. Besides being exempt as a war correspondent, you're forty years old. Get lost, you're holding up the line."

I left there feeling very old. In fact, I haven't felt that old since. After brooding for a couple of days, I went to Washington to see Harry Hopkins. We discussed my problem in his office in the new wing of the White House. He told me he could telephone Admiral King or General Marshall or Hap Arnold and any one of them would commission me immediately—but as a public relations officer. My contribution toward winning the war would be writing press handouts or ghost-writing speeches. "And you'll do it all sitting on your rump right here in Washington," Harry warned me.

I told him I thought all my experience with combat troops ought to make me more useful than that to the services.

Harry shook his head. "You shoot bullets with your typewriter," he said. "Keep on doing it, and forget the commission."

Then he suggested that I come back to the White House at the end of the afternoon and meet the President.

As I walked up the steps a couple of hours later, I remembered the "Dear Uncle Franklin" cable of two years before and hoped that it had never been called to the President's attention. Harry met me at the door and took me upstairs to the big, comfortably furnished room in which the President held informal conferences with members of his official family. The President was already there, sitting in his wheel chair behind a desk. He greeted me with a big smile. He looked like his photographs: vital, happy, confident. Before him on the desk sat cocktail ingredients. "What'll you have?" he asked, and when I said a martini, knowing of his reputation for this mixture, he nodded. "Even my political enemies admit that I make a good martini," he said.

I had come into the room keyed up and nervous. In less time than it took the President to mix my drink and hand it to me, all my tension was gone. This man, with his warmth and charm, put you instantly at your ease.

While he went on mixing drinks for the others who were present—Robert Sherwood and Samuel Rosenman, in addition to Hopkins—he began asking me questions about conditions in England and Russia. I was at first flattered. Then I realized he was listening intently to my answers, even those that were general, and it struck me that this desire to hear from others was one big element in the man's magnetism. Though his questions were not about important matters, his attention to my answers was flattering.

We talked of Winston Churchill, for whom Roosevelt obviously had great respect and great affection.

"I wish I could give Winston the destroyers he needs to protect his convoys," he said ruefully, "but we ourselves are fighting a two-ocean war and we can't spread too thin. I have every faith, though, that England will hold out until our protection reaches its peak. What do you think, Quentin?"

He smiled and shook his head approvingly when I told him it was unlikely that England would ever give up under any circumstances.

When the talk turned to the Russians, I offered Roosevelt my impressions of the people and their fighting spirit and then summed it up with the comment that I really didn't understand them very well.

"They're not easy to understand," he said thoughtfully. "Kipling explained why in one of his Indian stories. He said, 'The Russian is the most western of Eastern people and the most eastern of Western people.' But they certainly can fight."

That was a point we all agreed on.

Roosevelt began talking about the Japanese. "Those treacherous people!" he declared bitterly. "They used to come to me and say, 'Mr. President, we are a peace-loving nation.' They would smile and

266

hiss through their teeth"—he treated us to an imitation of the hiss—
"and all the time they were making their plans against us. Well, we'll
make them pay. We're building the greatest navy the world has ever
seen, and when it's ready, we'll take the offensive. Bob, your glass is
empty. Let me have it."

"Thanks, Mr. President." Lanky Bob Sherwood took his glass to
the desk, followed by Judge Rosenman.

Though Sherwood and Rosenman and Hopkins were all very close
to the President, I noticed that even in the highly informal atmosphere
of our gathering he was invariably addressed as "Mr. President."

Hopkins told me later that only Louis Howe, who had been Roosevelt's intimate adviser during his early presidential years, ever called
him Franklin to his face.

An hour passed all too soon, and then Roosevelt said to me with
apparent regret, "I suppose I have to get to work. I have to make a
radio talk and Bob and Sam are going to tell me what to say."

"That will be the day, Mr. President!" Sherwood said, laughing,
and a few moments later Hopkins and I went our way.

Sherwood once told me how speech-writing for the President worked
out in practice. First, Roosevelt would explain the points he wished
to make. Then Sherwood and Rosenman would write a draft of the
speech, working in the supporting evidence. Roosevelt would read
the draft, praise it generously, and immediately ask, "You boys don't
mind if I change just a few things here and there?"

Later I had my own experience with this process. During the Fourth
Term campaign in 1944, Sherwood and Rosenman asked me to come
to Washington and help write the Navy Day speech that Roosevelt
expected to deliver in Philadelphia on October 27. Since this was to
be what Roosevelt called a nonpolitical speech dealing mainly with
the course of the war, Sherwood and Rosenman felt that I might be
able to inject some authentic touches. I not only worked in a lot of
background but composed what I thought was some colorful phrasing. Having knocked myself out on it, I felt very happy when Rosenman told me that the Chief had read it and was delighted.

I settled back complacently before a radio the night Roosevelt
spoke—and not one of my phrases emerged. A lot of my material
was there, but all of it was in the President's words. Fighting down
my author's pride, I had to admit that he had done an excellent rewrite job.

267

When I returned to New York after being discouraged away from the Armed Forces by Hopkins, my agent Mark Hanna gave me a jolt by informing me that I was not only broke but that the Internal Revenue boys were probably going to be after me any minute for a second year's nonpayment of income tax. Since I had long before given Hanna a power of attorney, I was at a loss to understand how the situation could have come about, especially when I had been housekeeping in a musette bag and putting up inexpensively in the neighborhood of German bombs, Russian carbuncles and African sun poisoning. Hanna pointed out that I had also been living on a rather grand scale whenever possible. Specifically, he pointed to what he called my one-man USO canteen at the Savoy, where British and American fighter pilots were still getting free lodging, entertainment, and theater tickets at my expense. My bill there was now up in four figures, none of them tax free. "While I applaud your motives and your generosity," Hanna said, "we can't stick *Collier's* with what is after all your personal venture in international friendship."

As a result of this chilling brush with fiscal reality, I cabled Betty Marais to check me out of the Savoy, began filling in my check stubs for the first time in years, and heeded Hanna's suggestion that I immediately go out for a second time on the American lecture circuit.

While waiting for him to book the dates, I picked up some threads of New York life, making Toots Shor's new place my headquarters. It was like the old Tavern but on a grander scale. I discovered that Toots had periodically been sending a car to Brooklyn to bring Pop and a few of his friends over for dinner at what the regulars called The Store. Pop told me that any time he asked for a check, Toots would bellow, "Quent is loaded. When he comes back I'll give him a bill for everything. You've been supporting the bum all his life; it's time he picked up a tab for you now and then."

Needless to say, Toots never gave me a bill.

If there is a harder, lonelier way to mine gold than a lecture tour, I don't know it. The speaking was the easiest part. What hurt was the traveling—the living in sleepers, the getting into strange cities at dawn, the donning of the big happy smile for the welcoming committees. And that was only the beginning of it. A well-established tradition of the business was that the visiting firemen went, either before the speech or after, to the home of the committee chairwoman,

268

there to eat a bite of supper off his knee and to be introduced to dozens of the locally eminent.

After seven or eight of these soirees, all given me by decent, well-intentioned people, I began to yearn nostalgically for the Libyan desert. Night after night I had to listen to comments on current events that all began to sound the same, and night after night I was obliged to answer the same questions. My answers began to sound as stereotyped as the questions.

"Do you feel that we can really trust the Russians?" someone would ask.

"More than a million of them have been killed by the Nazis," I would reply. "I guess we can trust them somehow."

Someone was bound to ask, "How do you think communism is working out in Russia?"

"Russia is the only country I know of where there is nothing that resembles communism," I would say. Of course, this required elaboration. I would tick off the facts. The Russia I had seen was ruled by an absolute dictator, not the proletariat, and his rule was carried out by martial law. I had seen nothing that looked like the socialism of Marx. I usually added that my personal attitude toward the Russians was the one held by Winston Churchill: as long as they kept on killing the Germans, more power to them.

Inevitably, I would be asked about Churchill's drinking. That gave me the opening for "Churchill has taken more out of alcohol than alcohol has taken out of Churchill." Since many people considered this quite clever, I did not bother to reveal that Churchill had said it first.

As I lectured my way into the Midwest, the questions took a turn for the worse. One night I found myself in an Ohio city, widely known for its isolationist sentiments even three months after Pearl Harbor. At the post-lecture collation, I felt as out of place as the Archbishop of Canterbury speaking to the College of Cardinals in Rome. All around me were people who would have bet ten-to-one that Senator Taft could walk on water. And along with the bourbon they were belting F.D.R.

"The son of a bitch promised he'd never lead us into a foreign war, and now look at us!" said one of the city's intellectual leaders. "My grandpappy told me never to trust a cripple, and by Jesus he was right."

It was all I could do to thank my host and hostess for a delightful evening. In my dreary hotel room, I was too burned up to sleep. I thought of the wonderful people I knew in London and of how much more pro-American they were than these intellectual slaves of the Chicago *Tribune*. Feeling that I had to take my anger and frustration out on someone who could understand my problem, I put in a long distance call to New York and woke a beautiful and witty girl I knew there. Since it was long past midnight in Manhattan, Virginia Peine was not exactly overjoyed to hear from me.

"Ginny," I shouted into the phone, "what in God's name am I doing here?" I described some of the company I was keeping and warned her I would probably disgrace myself by speaking plainly before my tour was finished.

Ginny was an actress. We had met several years earlier when I was in Hollywood writing a *Collier's* piece. Her letters to me had made many of my nights pleasanter in London and Moscow. Supporting herself and her ten-year-old daughter, Ginny was now appearing with Danny Kaye and Gertrude Lawrence in Moss Hart's long-running musical *Lady in the Dark*.

I told her that I missed her badly. She seemed unimpressed, merely suggesting that I relax and go to sleep. I countered with the idea that she ought to marry me. She laughed and told me to put it in writing.

My letter went off first thing in the morning. I called her that night after my lecture in Columbus. I asked her if she had ever been in Columbus. She told me she hadn't. "Well, don't trifle with your luck," I said. I'd had another trying time with the Roosevelt haters. Then I asked her if she'd given further thought to my proposal.

Ginny didn't reply directly. Impishly, she told me she had felt compelled to consult Mother Hanna, as she called Mark, and that he had given his approval. Further, she had telephoned my father, whom she knew and already called Pop. Far from being dismayed at the thought of a black Protestant for a daughter-in-law, Pop, she told me, was looking forward to being our best man.

We were married in New York on March 30, 1942, a few days after I got back from my tour and Ginny's show closed. Pop and my brother Don, driving over from Brooklyn to the Ritz Tower where we were waiting for them, passed the Waldorf a few blocks away. Scores of policemen were guarding the street, and a police car with siren screaming pulled in ahead of Don's car and escorted him out of the way. Pop was deeply impressed. "I know that Quent has a lot of friends," he told Don, "but I never thought that half the police force would turn out for his wedding."

Don let it go at that, though he might have reminded Pop that President Roosevelt was expected at the Waldorf at noon to make a speech.

Our wedding party at the Ritz Tower was quite a gala, attended by the whole *Collier's* gang, Toots Shor, Sherman Billingsley, Jack Dempsey, Averell and Marie Harriman, half the sports writers in town, several Navy and Army figures, and many of Ginny's Broadway and Hollywood friends. Joanie, the daughter I had acquired, a tall dark-haired child who even at ten gave promise of the real beauty she would become, had learned to play "Here Comes the Bride." She proudly sat at the piano and played it over and over until Ginny gently persuaded her to let Eddy Duchin take her place.

We even had an unmistakable Republican at our party, Wendell Willkie, and he danced with every pretty girl there. I had met him for the first time a few weeks before when both of us were speakers at a Freedom House dinner, and had been pleased, then, to learn that he deeply admired Franklin Roosevelt. Later, when Ginny and I had dined with Willkie at his hotel, he had asked me to autograph his copy of *The Wounded Don't Cry*. I inscribed it:

TO WENDELL WILLKIE, WHO WAS GOOD ENOUGH TO FIGHT THE CHAMPION.

Willkie laughed appreciatively as he read this. "Damn it all," he said, "he still is champion."

Ginny and I received quite a wedding present from the Harrimans —the use of their house in Sun Valley, Idaho, for as long as we wanted to. We went out on the train and had two glorious weeks during which we both tried skiing for the first times in our lives. Ginny, who had once ridden jumpers in the Madison Square Garden horse shows, had the sense of balance that enabled her to sail down the slopes with confidence. My overconfidence soon reduced me to being a spectator.

Unfortunately, *Collier's* knew where we were, and one morning Charley Colebaugh telephoned to say that some big, though still secret, operation was about to start in England. The tip had been picked up in Washington by Tom Beck, who had a hunch it might mean the opening of the much-discussed second front.

271

That night Ginny and I were on the train to New York. We were not in the best of moods. I had just telephoned Mark Hanna and learned that my bank account had been cleaned out to keep the government off my neck. The day we were married, I had given Ginny what I then dismissed casually as some walking-around money: a thousand dollars in her own checking account. Now, as nonchalantly as possible, I asked her how much of it she had left.

She pulled her checkbook from her handbag and gave me the figure.

"Well, that's what we've got left between us," I said.

Ginny didn't bat an eye, bless her. It was a source of relief to both of us that she hadn't given up her apartment in New York. While I was in England, she and Joanie would at least have a roof over their heads.

When we got back to New York I went in to see Tom Beck and found him convinced that his tip was valid. Fond of the cloak and dagger manner, he would not tell me its source, though he ruled out the bar of the National Press Club by reminding me that he hadn't had a drink in twenty years.

I attempted to be logical. This was April. We had been in the war not quite five months. I asked Beck how he thought the United States could have transported enough men and equipment to England since December 7 to launch an invasion of Europe.

"If you want to resume your honeymoon," he said a little petulantly, "we can transfer Frank Gervasi from the Middle East. Or we might get Ernest Hemingway to go over for us, or John Steinbeck."

I had a further thought. I would go to Washington and see what could be learned from Harriman or Harry Hopkins, or another man I knew, Secretary of the Navy Forrestal.

Beck shook his head. "Not one of them would confirm it or deny it," he said.

I had little choice. If there was going to be an invasion, I didn't want to miss it. Having got Beck's promise that my wife and child would not be found standing on breadlines while I was away, I set off on my third crossing of the Atlantic by freighter.

This time there was a vast improvement that pointed toward the future. Our triple line of deeply laden ships was convoyed by many American planes and destroyers, and we went the whole way without raising a German submarine.

272

15

In the valley of the shadow

London was talking excitedly about the possibility of a second front. Many people, including Lord Beaverbrook, were saying that a large-scale thrust across the Channel would result in the withdrawal of perhaps a dozen German divisions from the Russian front. At mass meetings sponsored by Beaverbrook's *Daily Express* advocates of immediate military action on the Continent were wildly cheered. Some people noted that these demonstrations paralleled those sponsored by the English Communist Party, but no one suggested that the doughty little Canadian Presbyterian, Max Beaverbrook, was ever the Communists' dupe. While Churchill himself had not been heard on the possibility of an invasion, it seemed to me that Beaverbrook's press campaign indicated the necessary strength might after all be available. Also, there was a newcomer in London: General Eisenhower. His arrival, coupled with the fact that large numbers of American troops were now in Northern Ireland and England, lent further credibility to the matter.

I went to Eisenhower's first press conference, held in a large room at Grosvenor House. Eisenhower, wearing what afterward became known as the Eisenhower jacket, looked very trim and healthy as he strode briskly to a platform and faced us. He grinned in response to our applause; his warm friendliness communicated itself as soon as he

273

began speaking. Glancing about, I saw approving looks on the faces of my colleagues.

Eisenhower began immediately with a matter that was of key importance to us—censorship. "I'm going to use you fellows," he said disarmingly. "You are the links between our GIs and the home front, and the people at home have a right to know how their sons are being trained and cared for. Write anything you want about us as long as you tell the truth. As long as you do that, the censors will stay off your backs. They will be guided by one consideration only: security."

He then startled us by launching into a discussion of a delicate situation existing in the Midlands: the fighting between Negro GIs and the British soldiers who resented their success with the British girls. We all knew the story, but the British censors, on security grounds, had refused to let it be sent. Eisenhower said that a soldier was a soldier, regardless of his color. While he deplored the incidents, he regarded them as personal or community problems and therefore not censorable. He then asked for our comments on this decision. One or two of the correspondents urged that the censors' ban be retained, pointing out that the seriousness of the incidents would certainly be exaggerated by troublemakers at home. I was impressed when Eisenhower stuck to his position that the truth should be told.

While nothing came out of that conference to confirm that Eisenhower was about to lead an expedition across the Channel, I went away feeling good about General Marshall's choice to command our troops in Europe.

I saw the less official side of Eisenhower a short time later when Ed Beattie of the UP and I were spending a country week end with the Tony Biddles. While Tony and his more athletic guests were playing tennis, Beattie and I sat nearby playing two-handed gin under a large umbrella. I looked up from my cards to see General Eisenhower, his aide Harry Butcher, and Averell Harriman emerging from the house. They had lunched with Churchill at Chequers nearby and had decided to drop in.

"If you want to play four-handed," Eisenhower said pleasantly, "Butch and I will be glad to oblige." He sat down and began to deal. Conversation turned to the developments in the Pacific theater. The morning newspapers had carried the story of the invasion of Guadalcanal, and several of them had printed feature stories on Douglas MacArthur. To most of us, MacArthur was an unknown quantity. I

274

had forgotten that Eisenhower had served on MacArthur's staff in Manila. Ed Beattie remembered it and asked if he had known Mac-Arthur well.

"Oh, yes," Eisenhower said. "I studied dramatics under him for twelve years."

He expanded on his point as we continued our game, but not all of it was criticism. Eisenhower summed up his former commander as one of the best military strategists he had ever known.

I discovered another of Eisenhower's qualities soon after Ernie Pyle arrived in England. Ernie had never been in London before, but he was not noticeably enthusiastic when I suggested introducing him to a few Cabinet ministers. The English people Ernie wanted to know were in the streets and shops and pubs. Then Harry Butcher arranged for the two of us to spend a coupie of weeks with the GIs in Ireland. Here I saw Ernie demonstrate his knack of getting plain men to open up and talk about themselves. It was this knack that soon made little Ernie the most widely read and admired war correspondent in America.

When he and I returned to London, Butcher asked us to report to Eisenhower. "My officers tell me that the troops in Ireland are well satisfied," the general said, "but, damn it, troops are never 'well satisfied.' You men have been with them. Tell me what their gripes are."

"Well, for one thing, it's been raining about five days out of seven over there, and they've been doing a lot of marching," Ernie said. "Each man has three pairs of socks. They wash 'em, but because of the rain, they can't dry 'em. They really ought to have more socks."

The man who would soon be named Supreme Commander of the European Theater of Operations not only took notes on this and other details and saw to it that they were taken care of, he had Butch get in touch with us to confirm it.

As the clamor for the second front increased, I began to wonder if other people knew something I hadn't yet discovered. I had seen thousands of GIs in Ireland, but few tanks. I had seen destroyers at the Londonderry docks, but no landing barges. In Scotland, where I went to do a story on Americans in training, I had found only a few hundred paratroopers, not the thousands who would be needed for a big assault. One day I telephoned Butcher and asked if I might ask the general a few off-the-record questions. Butcher had me hold the phone while he got the word. It was to come right over.

Trying to tackle the matter diplomatically, I said to Eisenhower that if there was to be any joint British–American operation in the near future, I would very much like to go along on it.

Ike grinned. "Why not come right out and ask me if we're planning a second front?"

The answer was no. Beside the shortages of men, weapons, supplies, and transportation, Ike told me there were not enough landing craft available to put one fully equipped division across the Channel.

After hearing what the minimum requirements would be for a successful invasion, I suggested that I ought to send *Collier's* a story on why a second front could not be launched. Eisenhower thought this would be a helpful thing, and he had Butcher arrange for me to get my background material from the American air generals Ira Eaker and Tooey Spaatz as well as four of the top British generals.

My story was published as "Second Thoughts on the Second Front," and was immediately picked up by the London newspapers and reprinted in a British magazine. I was amazed by some of the vicious letters it prompted, both at home and in England. The conclusion could only be that many of the proponents of the Second Front were more emotional than rational.

In discussing the picture of what lay ahead for the Allies, Ike had mentioned that the British would continue to harass the Germans with their unpredictable Commando raids. These had already struck at a dozen points from France to Norway. With the thought that such a raid might produce a good story, I got myself an introduction to Vice-Admiral Lord Louis Mountbatten, the head of the Commandos, and suggested that I be added to the correspondents covering his next operation. The tall, handsome vice-admiral shunned the term *Commando,* which Churchill had plucked from his memories of the Boer suicide squads of forty years before. Punctiliously referring to his independent force as Special Service Units, he reminded me that the few correspondents who ever went on their forays were chosen by lot. When he told me that the drawing had already been held for the next operation, I said I would be happy to take my chances on a stand-by basis. Mountbatten neither encouraged nor discouraged my hopes.

The next I heard about the matter was one evening in August when Major Jock Lawrence, an ex-Hollywood publicity man now acting as liaison between Combined Operations and the American Army and the press, was chatting with me at the entrance to the Savoy. As we parted he told me to report at his office at nine the next morning, bringing my uniform in a bag. "You're probably going out of town for a few days," he said, "but of course you're not to mention this to anyone."

Next morning, while breakfasting with Jock at Combined Operations Headquarters, I was briefed by a British Marine colonel. And very brief it was, too. I learned little beyond the fact that I would be the only correspondent aboard the command ship of the imminent action, though there would be other correspondents aboard some of the other ships. I was not told where or when the action would take place.

After breakfast Lawrence drove me to his apartment and here I met an American Air Force colonel, Loren Hillsinger, who was going on the operation as observer. Hillsinger and Lawrence watched approvingly as I changed into the light uniform I had last worn in Egypt. "Good idea," Lawrence said. "In case this develops into a swimming race, you won't be handicapped by heavy clothing." Then he had me give him my shoulder identifications.

"If this weather holds, the show will start tonight," he explained. "But if it is delayed, you and the other correspondents will stay at the port. The wrong people might notice that you are correspondents and figure something is going on. Therefore, you're going as a lieutenant colonel."

He began fastening the silver leaves on my shoulder tabs. "While you're at it, why can't I be a general?" I asked.

Lawrence grinned. "That would be real bad casting."

Leaving Lawrence behind, Hillsinger and I drove to Portsmouth with Wing Commander Eric Roland and Major Alan Newton of the British Army.

We arrived at dusk and I was delivered to the destroyer *Calpe*. My three companions were to board the destroyer *Berkeley*. "When we get back," Wing Commander Roland suggested, "let's meet at the bar in the Queen's Hotel, and then we'll drive back to London together."

It turned out to be a date that only I could keep.

Lieutenant Robert Boyle, a young press officer, welcomed me aboard the *Calpe,* handed me a steel helmet and a Mae West, and introduced me to the three officers who were going to direct the assault: Captain Hughes-Hallett for the naval phases, General John

Hamilton Roberts, a Canadian, commanding the ground forces, and Air Commodore Cole, in charge of the tactical part of the aerial operations.

When it was dark, we left the harbor. Only then did I learn something of the size of our force. Following us in addition to the *Berkeley,* all unseen in the blackness, were six destroyers and dozens of smaller craft: troop ships, barges, LSTs carrying tanks, landing craft, and torpedo boats—a force large enough to put six thousand troops ashore. There had not previously been a Commando raid of anything like this size. In the command room, Boyle showed me aerial photographs of our objective, Dieppe, with its eight-mile stretch of beaches from Berneval on the north to Varengeville on the south. At each of these limit points there was an installation of six-inch guns, and the plan, General Roberts told me, was to knock them out before our main force went ashore in the center, took the city, and held it for the day. "If we move according to our timetable," Roberts said, tensely but happily, "we'll be ashore with our tanks at 7 A.M. I hope you'll come with us."

As he and Cole and young Boyle explained further details, I understood the controlled excitement that pervaded these men. If this raid should prove successful, it would pave the way for bigger landings.

We were perhaps two hours out when word came from Hughes-Hallett on the bridge: "Entering mine field."

Boyle consulted his watch. "On schedule. Now, our first problem is not to get our heads blown off." He took me to the deck. Ahead of us, to my surprise, I saw a small green light bobbing in the choppy water. "We should meet another one every half mile or so," Boyle said. "Our sweepers drop them as they clean the field."

Remembering the caution with which we had traversed the mine fields at Sidi Omar, it seemed to me that the *Calpe* was traveling at a rather brisk pace, especially when Boyle told me that our lane of clearance was only a hundred yards on either side of the lighted buoys.

Boyle laughed at my concern. "When you hit a mine," he said, "twelve knots isn't a bit worse than two knots."

There were two hundred men aboard the *Calpe,* but except for the subdued hum of her engines, there was little sound. I had the impression that everyone was silently sweating it out. Once a sailor stumbled over a stanchion near me. His "Bloody dark!" was comforting to hear.

278

Ahead of us, one green light showed up after another. Hughes-Hallett, upon the bridge, was hitting them right on the nose. It took us an hour to go through the field. Then a bell clanged somewhere, and voices were heard again. The ship seemed to breathe a sigh of relief.

On through the night we went. As we drew close to the French shore, I went to the bridge. Hughes-Hallett called my attention to a blinking lighthouse. " So far, so good," he said. "Had they been expecting us, they would have turned that off."

Our ship and the invisible flotilla on either side moved slower and at last stopped. Five miles to the right of us was Varengeville, with its deadly battery in a camouflaged concrete emplacement; three miles to the left was the battery at Berneval. Somewhere in the night soot-faced knife-wielding Commando forces were already on their way to the beaches to surprise and silence these points.

As we waited aboard the *Calpe* for the next move, a heavy silence seemed to descend. Incongruously, I was reminded of that magic moment in the theater when the lights go down and the audience stills in anticipation of the rise of the curtain. On the bridge, the minutes passed. As far as we could tell, everything was going according to plan. Had the Germans detected our approach, their planes would have been over us by now, dropping flares to reveal us to the shore batteries. Instead, the lighthouse continued to flash. I recalled Mountbatten's comment that a raid like this could be a sticky wicket. It seemed, on the contrary, that we had nothing to worry about.

And then, to the north, the sleeping night awakened in a riot of dazzling green and red streaks that arched across the sky. This was where—according to the timetable—Major Peter White's Commandos were about to land. But the tracers were firing at aircraft, by the looks of it, and we knew that our planes were not due for another hour. For a moment we on the *Calpe* were puzzled. Then one of the air officers suggested that the German radar had picked up our boats and interpreted them as planes. All too soon the tracers lowered their lines to the water.

We soon heard what had gone wrong. By the worst imaginable luck German E-boats—overgrown torpedo craft carrying machine and antiaircraft guns—had been escorting a tanker in the neighborhood, and after firing at a nonexistent plane, they had discovered our landing barges.

279

Hughes-Hallett gave terse orders, and a seaman began working his blinker. Two destroyers to our left got the message and hurried to the scene. We soon saw their tracers and heard the sound of their four-inch guns. This went on for several minutes and then there was silence again. Obviously, the destroyers had done their job on the E-boats and the tanker.

But now, what was happening ashore? Were the Germans tumbling from their beds and hurrying to the gun positions? Undoubtedly. In any case, the element of surprise was gone and the landing schedules were slipping. To our right, in the direction of Varengeville, there was no sign of activity, which seemed to indicate that Colonel Lord Lovat and his No. 4 Commandos had succeeded in their mission.

Now dawn was thinning the night. I looked at my copy of our time-table. One minute more and our destroyers would shell the 1780 yards of beach in front of Dieppe and to the right—the stretch where our aerial surveys had shown machine-gun emplacements. On schedule our guns thundered. The air trembled with the sound. Then day came—and the curtain on this grim drama was finally up. As our guns finished their barrage, our landing craft were putting men and tanks on the beach.

The guns at Berneval started to roar—which could only mean the attacking Commandos had failed.

Then we heard the sound of Spitfires—our air cover. Twenty-one of them began circling above us at three predetermined heights. For the moment, there was nothing more for them to do.

All our ships were moving fast along the beaches now, to prevent the shore guns from firing accurately. Despite our barrage, machine guns were rattling away ashore, and we knew that the Canadians who had landed in front of Dieppe and further to the right were in trouble. When I went to General Roberts' command room to get the sense of the fighting, he was calling for our planes to lay smoke in back of the beaches and over the high ground to the right of Dieppe. "If it hadn't been for that damned German tanker, the beaches would have been secured by now, and our tanks would be taking the city itself," Roberts told me. "As it stands, I doubt that I'll ever get ashore."

I heard the *Calpe's* ack-ack guns begin firing. This meant that the *Luftwaffe* had finally arrived. I went out on deck to have a look. Three Dorniers were above the town and our guns were trying for them. As they came over the harbor at about eight thousand feet, our Spits took over, diving from fifteen thousand feet. One Dornier died in a huge orange flash. Another, trailing black smoke, dived sedately toward us, its crew parachuting. The plane struck the sea with a mighty splash and broke apart. The third plane was also a sitting duck for the Spits, but just before it was knocked out, it dropped its bombs. Some landed close enough to make the *Calpe* quiver.

From then on the *Luftwaffe* was all over us, not only the Dorniers and Junker 88s, but the new and deadly Focke-Wulf 190 fighters, carrying 500-pound bombs. It was not easy to see through the smoke that now shrouded Dieppe to a height of nearly a mile, but our observers estimated there were ninety to a hundred German planes above us. They had nice targets—our two hundred craft. They didn't have to score a direct hit to sink the smaller boats: a near miss would open their seams.

I was standing on deck with Boyle and Air Commodore Cole when a Focke-Wulf dived at us. The ack-ack gun near me went into action. Although there were black bursts all around the plane, it was not hit. At about three hundred feet it leveled off and its eight guns raked us from bow to stern.

The plane dropped a bomb that struck our deck some forty feet from where I was crouching. The concussion was frightful. It threw me several feet against a steel bulkhead, and left me numb, my ears roaring. I wondered if I had been hit. Then I bit on something hard and spit out a gold inlay. That seemed to be the extent of my injuries. I got to my feet with some effort, only to find that both our antiaircraft gunners were dead. Air Commodore Cole staggered past me holding a hand to his blood-covered face. Boyle was bleeding from the neck and scalp. As I helped him down to the first-aid room he said, "This is one hell of a way to celebrate a birthday. I'm twenty-one today."

I went back on deck in time to see a badly wounded Junker pass overhead, heading for the beach. When it was about two hundred yards past us, it jettisoned its bombs. The *Berkeley* chanced to be directly below. A sheet of flame sprang from her bridge and the ship immediately listed and began to go down. Small craft rushed in to take off the survivors.

Now the *Calpe* swerved in toward the beach to begin picking up survivors. General Roberts had reluctantly ordered the men on shore to evacuate. The Dieppe raid was in its last terrible moments.

A dozen of Lovat's Commandos clambered aboard us from a landing barge, grinning and jerking their thumbs up. Their mission at Varengeville had been one of the few successes of the day. Many of the men we picked up from the center beaches were ash-gray from shock, their eyes staring blankly. A great many of them collapsed on our decks and lay in a stupor. The walking wounded were helped below to receive attention. Among them was a correspondent I knew, Wallace Reyburn of the Montreal *Standard*. He, too, had the face of a man in shock.

"I'm hit somewhere," he mumbled as I helped him out of his bloodstained uniform.

I surveyed his minor damage. "Wally, unless you're a contortionist, you'll never be able to admire your scars," I said, and began plucking bits of shrapnel from his buttocks.

But Reyburn was not listening. "What a story! What a story!" he suddenly burst out. The doctor who was now examining him thought he was delirious.

Some forty Canadians lay groaning or silent on the ward-room floor. For some, the shock had anesthetized the pain of their wounds. One man began loudly to recite the Hail Mary. Another suddenly cried, "Why don't we get out of here? Haven't we had enough for one day?"

At last the order came to withdraw, but the *Calpe*, as command ship, would be the last to leave the scene. On deck I watched what was left of our flotilla head for England. Soon we were alone. We continued to race up and down the beaches, picking up the last few survivors we found in the water. All the while machine-gun bullets from the shore beat a tattoo on our bulwarks and found targets among the men on our decks. As the last ship, we had the complete attention of the shore guns. Their six-inch shells threw up geysers on either side of us.

Finally, General Roberts gave the order to go home.

That night in Portsmouth I learned that Wing Commander Roland and Major Newton had been killed when the *Berkeley* was struck. Colonel Hillsinger had lost a leg but was expected to survive.

The reports were not all in by the time I reached London next morning, but it was evident from the silence at Combined Operations Headquarters that no one was about to call the raid a success. Well over half the men who had landed, nearly all of them Canadians, had been killed, wounded, or captured—some 3600 casualties. Further, twenty-eight tanks had been landed and left on the beaches, and the RAF had lost ninety-one planes in downing a hundred German planes. Appalled, I wondered how such losses could be justified, but when I talked to Eisenhower a short time afterward, he said that the raid had been invaluable as a dress rehearsal. For one thing, he said, it proved that intensive bombing and shelling would have to precede any large-scale, permanent landing. For another, it showed that the delivery of airborne troops would need to be an integral part of a big operation. At Dieppe, he said, such troops might have knocked out blockhouses and pillboxes whose existence our aerial photographs had been unable to show.

And so, in the histories of World War II, that rough, tragic day at Dieppe appears as a study piece for the combined operations that were soon to be successful in North Africa, Sicily, Italy, and eventually Normandy. For me, though, as I went through it and as I look back on it, that day was the longest of my life.

The weeks that followed could not help but be dull by comparison, even though the *Luftwaffe* was still giving London occasional attention. After doing some personality pieces on the newer Cabinet ministers and war heroes, I cabled acceptance of Colebaugh's suggestion that I come home in time for Christmas. With Arthur Christiansen's help I had already been working on Ginny's Christmas present—a large silver cigarette case adorned with the engraved signatures of twenty of my London friends, American as well as English. When this souvenir was delivered from the jeweler's, early in November, I found my usual freighter berth and returned to New York.

After my reunion with Ginny, and my vivacious schoolgirl daughter, I got back to my typewriter and finished up a quick book on the Dieppe raid that Bennett Cerf of Random House wanted to publish early in 1943. I gave it the title Eisenhower had given me: *Dress Rehearsal.*

Ginny and Joanie and I had a wonderful Christmas together, and for that brief time the war seemed far away. The cigarette case delighted Ginny as much as I had hoped it would. On the cover, beneath the "Merry Xmas, 1942," appeared the signatures of Churchill and the other Cabinet ministers. Inside were the signatures of Ambassador John Winant, Tony Biddle, Noel Coward, Sailor Malan, Louis Mountbatten, Bea Lillie, and several more, including that of a man who signed himself Philip of Greece. I had to explain that one to Ginny: while his title was Prince Philip of Greece, he was actually Lord Mountbatten's nephew and an officer in the British Navy.

One day early in the new year Tom Beck, the old tip hound, summoned me to his office to hear some interesting news. I went in dedicated to the proposition that I would not believe his latest—and promptly found myself being impressed.

"This is big, Quent, and it comes direct from the White House. Roosevelt and Churchill are soon going to Moscow to meet with Stalin."

Having had my exposure to the Russians, I assured Beck that any such meeting would be surrounded by secrecy thicker than the Kremlin walls, and that no correspondent, not even one from *Collier's,* would be able to file a word about it until long after the President and the Prime Minister had returned home.

"I can tell you something else," Beck said. "Harriman and Hopkins are going with the President. If they can't open the doors for you, who can?"

Loath to break up my home life for another mirage, I insisted this time on going to Washington to check Beck's tip with Hopkins. He admitted cautiously that plans were in the making for a meeting of the Big Three. This was all he would or could say.

My only hope now was that the Russians would reject my visa application. But apparently they were in a forgiving or forgetful frame of mind. It was promptly granted.

Ginny gallantly mastered her disappointment and went with me to Miami Beach to see me onto an Air Transport Command flight to Teheran. Though several flights were going there every week, higher priorities than mine kept filling the planes. For eight days we loafed contentedly at our hotel, swimming early before the sun became angry at me, and in the evenings giving the restaurants and night clubs a play. Aside from the thousands of Air Force boys who were training there, Miami Beach seemed quite remote from the war. We began to think we were on a vacation.

"If this goes on much longer," Ginny suggested one evening as we strolled back to the hotel from a movie, "the Big Three will have had their old meeting, and then you and I can go home."

She shouldn't have said it. The ATC's summons was waiting for me, and off I went on the long trip, via Trinidad, Natal, Ascension

284

Island, the Gold Coast, Khartoum, and Cairo. From Teheran I flew in a Russian plane to Moscow.

As far as the city itself went, it looked much as I remembered it. However, there was a new spirit in the air. The Germans had not taken Moscow, the government and diplomatic and press corps had returned from Kuibyshev some time before, and now, with the counteroffensive succeeding at Stalingrad, it was beginning to seem possible that the Germans' days in Russia were numbered.

It did not take me long to establish that Tom Beck's pipeline to the White House needed an overhauling. Eddy Gilmore of the AP doubted my sanity when I told him I had come to cover the meeting of the Big Three. When I insisted that I had confirmed that such a meeting was in the works, he promised to get me the answer from a confidential Russian contact. He had it within twenty-four hours. Such a meeting had been proposed, but Stalin had turned it down in November.

Two weeks later *Pravda, Izvestia,* and the Soviet radio simultaneously announced the meeting of Roosevelt and Churchill in Casablanca. Hopkins and Harriman were also at the Casablanca conference (at least Beck got *that* part of it right), and months later, when I returned to the States, Hopkins told me that Stalin had been invited to attend but had declined because he was busy calling the shots for his armies.

So I had traveled fourteen thousand miles to a city I didn't like, only to miss the Casablanca meeting. I felt like adding a substantial penalty to my next expense account. Instead, I made a list of four or five stories I wanted to write that would take me out of Moscow, and sent it with exaggerated hope to the Foreign Press Office. For one thing, I wanted to go to the front where I could see American Lend-Lease material in action. For another, I wanted to enter some city that the Red Army was liberating. *Pravda* was full of ghastly stories about the Germans' mistreatment of the Russian civilians, and though I had no doubt of the German capacities in this direction or any cause to doubt the Russian claims, I still wanted to see the evidence of atrocities for myself.

Running short of reading matter while I waited for action on this program, I procured a copy of *War and Peace,* a book I had never read. It seemed the perfect moment to plow into it.

Tania Sofiano, who had been so valuable to me during my first stay in Moscow, was again working for me, and she was delighted when she saw what I was reading. "No one can understand Russia today if he does not read that book," she said.

When I told her I thought she was overdoing it—that Tolstoy had after all written about the Russia of another era—she said, "We are still the same people. You will see."

One afternoon Sofiano brought news that I had been granted permission to visit Vyazma, a city a hundred and twenty miles west of Moscow. It had been retaken only the day before. The Press Office was providing me with a car and driver and something more I could have done without, a conducting officer, but I felt better when Sofiano was allowed to go along as my interpreter. As it turned out, she interpreted more for me than the incidental conversations. At her bidding, I slipped Tolstoy's novel into my bag. "We will travel the very road that Napoleon used in his retreat," she said. "You will see *War and Peace* come to life before your eyes."

A few miles out of Moscow, Sofiano pointed out a hill. "That is Poklonnaya. Napoleon stood there waiting for emissaries to come out and surrender the city to him. But Moscow never surrendered. Had it surrendered, Napoleon would have entered Moscow as an emperor. Instead, he entered merely as an invader."

We drove on, passing through villages where we saw only old men, old women, and small children. The young people, women as well as men, had long since gone to the war fronts or to the faraway industrial plants. We reached Borodino, which probably hadn't changed its appearance much since September 7, 1812, when the Russians fought Napoleon's forces here and were defeated. Sofiano found me the appropriate passage:

A mist hung over the scene, melting, parting, shimmering with light in the bright sunshine and giving fairylike beauty to the shapes seen through it. The smoke of the guns mingled with the mist and everywhere gleams of sunlight sparkled in it from the water, from the dew, from the bayonets of the soldiers crowding on the river. Through this mist could be seen a white church and here and there roofs of cottages in Borodino . . . and the whole scene moved or seemed to move as the mist and smoke trailed over the wide plain.

Napoleon had won his battle but, in losing thirty-two thousand of his troops, he had begun to lose his victory. In Moscow, the conquered had refused to acknowledge that they had been conquered, and at last Napoleon retreated from the burning city, fleeing not so much from the army of General Kutuzov as from the dissolution he carried within his own ranks. Tolstoy wrote:

> There was no general engagement nor even a skirmish of any importance, yet the French Army ceased to exist. . . . Victories are not always an invariable sign of conquest.

As our car rumbled along toward Vyazma, it was as though Tolstoy was conducting me himself. One hundred and thirty years before, the French had hurried along this road, looking over their shoulders, seeing menace in every birch thicket, afraid to straggle lest they fall to the knife or club of a Russian partisan. And not more than a month ago, the Nazis had retreated on this same road, accompanied by the same fear. Yet neither army had suffered a decisive defeat at the hands of the Russians. They had simply found Russia too big for them. The explanation was in *War and Peace:*

> Just as water flowing over dry land is absorbed by the dry land, so did Russia absorb the French Army.

A few miles beyond Borodino, as we were passing through a village, our engine quit. Our driver tinkered with it, then let loose a fast stream of Russian to Nikolai Borisovich, our Press Officer chaperon. Sofiano translated.

"We need a new carburetor. It will be dark when it is replaced, so it will be best to spend the night here. All right?"

"Nitchevo," I said, and Sofiano grinned. *Nitchevo* is a very serviceable Russian word. It means "So what?" It can also mean "What in hell else can we do?"

Borisovich went off to find us lodgings. A little later Sofiano and I followed him across the village square to a small one-story wooden house. Its sole tenant, a plump elderly woman, admitted us without any show of enthusiasm but without hostility. Her name was Maria. Her home, while rather bare, was immaculate. She led us through it: sitting room, bedroom, kitchen, and bathroom—the last containing only a tin tub. Prominent on the sitting-room wall was a framed photograph of three men in uniform. I assumed that they were Maria's grandsons. Sofiano, who had begun to draw her out, corrected me: The oldest one was her husband; the other two, her sons. I looked at the photo again; either it was a very poor likeness or Maria's husband was at least twenty years younger than she was.

We had been in the little house only a few minutes before there came a knock at the door and a smiling soldier delivered some bedding and a box of food, both provided by the local commandant. As we ate this supper in the kitchen, it struck me that Maria was not one to engage in small talk. Beyond a few references to her absent family, all of whom seemed to be well, Sofiano found little to translate for me.

We visitors slept the night comfortably enough in the living room, one on the sofa, one on a cot, the other on the floor. In the morning I tried to give Maria some rubles. She refused them. Sofiano, with a smile, rebuked me. "We have been Maria's guests," she said.

As we said good-by, following Sofiano's example, I kissed the old woman on both cheeks. Later, I brought up the matter of her young-looking husband and sons. Sofiano enlightened me. "She is the same age as her husband, and not yet a grandmother. For seventeen months, German officers were billeted in her home."

Beyond the village our road grew worse. We bumped along the rough surface, sometimes sinking hub-deep in tracks made by giant tanks. The Germans had blown up every one of the bridges leading to Vyazma, but Red Army engineers had already spanned the streams with temporary wooden structures. On either side of the road we saw traces of the Germans; well-fortified dugouts in which they had lived, slit trenches, abandoned tanks, smashed gun carriages, and now and then the barrel of a gun pointing futilely toward Moscow.

Every few miles we were stopped by uniformed women sentries, and there was no slipping past them simply because our car carried an official insignia. One woman would ask sharply for our credentials while others stood with rifles leveled. I thought they were some of the prettiest girls I had seen in Russia. They were young and relatively slender, and their outdoor life had given their cheeks a color very much lacking in the faces one saw in Moscow.

As we drew close to Vyazma, the road became congested. Trucks passed us, traveling fast. We passed lumbering tanks and huge guns that were crawling beyond Vyazma. Red soldiers were still looking for mines on either side of the road and in the woods beyond.

Then we reached the top of a hill and looked down upon what had once been Vyazma. Nothing I had seen in England had prepared me for the total destruction I saw spread below me. In a city that had once housed eighteen thousand human beings, hardly a building stood.

288

We drove down the hill and introduced ourselves to Major Ivan Smolin, who had led the Red Army into the recaptured city. Only twenty-six, he was a veteran in the field. On his tunic there gleamed the Order of the Red Star.

"When we entered," Smolin told me via Sofiano, "we found the cathedral and two large brick warehouses still standing. The Germans had a purpose in leaving them for us. Our doctors and nurses were converting one of the buildings into a hospital when a delayed-action bomb killed them all. Two days later the second building blew up. The survivors in the city wished to hold a service of thanksgiving for their deliverance in the Cathedral. I had my sappers inspect it first. They found another time bomb. It was removed, and the people held their service."

Smolin urged me to walk through the city and talk to as many of the survivors as I wished. I was given only one warning—to walk on the cleared paths. Not all the mines had yet been found.

Most of the city was deathly silent as Sofiano and I began our investigation. Here and there old women sat apathetically in the ruins of what had been their homes, burning rubbish to keep themselves warm. A few children played in the wreckage, occasionally unearthing some household article: a dish, a broken chair, the remains of a stove. The smell of the trapped bodies decaying in the rubble hung nauseatingly in the air. Steeling myself, I questioned groups of the emaciated survivors and heard their stories of shootings and hangings and torture, of rape and starvation and epidemic sickness.

At one point Sofiano and I walked a little way outside the city to where some soldiers were digging in a field. Carts waited near them, and as we went closer, we saw that the harvest they were lifting into the carts was death. The bodies were being separated by size; one cart contained only young children.

"We were looking for mines," the officer in charge told me. "We found this instead. Already we have taken five hundred bodies from this field. Most of them, our doctors say, were hung or shot, though some starved to death."

Sofiano and I walked back to our car in silence. It was evening now, and mobile kitchens were feeding the townspeople hot soup. In the west, in the direction of Smolensk, we could hear the rumble of heavy guns. At length Sofiano asked me, quite seriously, if I felt the trip had been worth the effort and the discomfort. I assured her it had been.

Sick in spirit, I was thinking of war as the book-reader finds it celebrated in poetry and prose. I thought of Byron's stanzas on Waterloo, Tennyson's "The Charge of the Light Brigade," Kipling's *Barrack-Room Ballads,* Winston Churchill's relishing account of his experiences in the Boer War. I thought of what I had read about Pickett's Charge at Gettysburg—accounts that did full justice to the gallant heroism of the Southerners but somehow glossed over the picture of men killed outright or left screaming on the battlefield with gangrenous wounds. In none of these glorifications could I recall having encountered the simple statement that a dead human being emits the same frightful stench as a dead mule.

The war I had come to know was short on glamour and long on tragedy, whether it was the dead on the beaches at Dieppe or the miserable survivors of Vyazma, wearing their masks of death.

Out of these reflections came a sobering realization. I, too, had often been guilty of glamorizing the war in my articles and books.

290

16

They called it bloody Salerno

In allowing me to report the story of Vyazma, the Russians evidently felt that their obligation, if any, had been met. After vainly trying to talk my old opponent Vice-Commissar Lozovsky into giving me another such opportunity, I called it quits and flew out to Teheran, a transfer point now almost as familiar to me as Grand Central Station. From here, lacking any clear instructions from New York, I went to Tel Aviv, produced an article about a rest camp there for American pilots, and then proceeded to Cairo.

It was now July, 1943, and Shepheard's Hotel was full of Americans in uniform. One of them was my *Collier's* colleague Frank Gervasi. He suggested that I had reached a point when I ought to see some American troops in action. Considering this sound advice, and knowing that our forces had just invaded Sicily, I asked Frank how I would go about getting there. What planes were flying?

"You don't fly to Sicily, you go to Tunis," Frank explained. "From there maybe you fly or maybe you swim, but at least you go to Tunis."

The first part of this operation soon fell into place when Eddie Rickenbacker appeared in Cairo, returning to the United States from a mission to Moscow for the Air Force. He had room for me in his plane and the next stop was Tunis. When we arrived there, the cam-

291

paign in Sicily was reaching its climax, and every plane and ship going there was jammed with higher-priority material than correspondents. I hitched a jeep ride north to Bizerte. Here I put my case to a Lieutenant Richard O'Brien, the young skipper of a PT boat that was about to make a night run to Palermo. O'Brien said he would be glad to deliver me there if I had nothing against dirty weather.

Weather at sea was a subject I thought I knew in depth, as a result of my Atlantic convoy crossings. The Mediterranean showed me how wrong I was, and so did that PT boat, which had not been built for comfort. It did not merely pitch and rock like a freighter; it hurled itself into the waves and twisted in them like a wounded thing. My principal activity through that long night was hanging onto anything handy in order not to be demolished against guns, ventilators, or ammunition boxes, and as my collection of bruises increased, my admiration for the stamina of the PT men increased in direct ratio.

In Palermo, after bacon and eggs in the Navy mess, I checked in at press headquarters, the Sole Hotel. Here I met another new arrival, Demaree Bess of the *Saturday Evening Post*. He was getting his bearings from a chubby little veteran of the North African landings, Sammy Schulman, a photographer for International News. When a correspondent arrives in a new theater, it is the unwritten rule that he reports immediately either to the commanding general or to his public relations officer. Sammy volunteered to introduce us to General George Patton.

Even though Sammy announced that he knew Patton quite well, I was not prepared for the action we got when our names were announced at Patton's office. The commander sprang from his chair to greet Sammy as if he were a three-star general, and then turned to Bess and me with effusive cordiality, saying he would be glad to do anything he could for us, and what projects did we have in mind?

Even though the famous pearl-handled revolvers and lacquered helmet were sitting side by side on his desk, it did not seem to me that this was the George S. Patton about whom so many stories were being told.

Sammy let the general know that Bess and I wanted to go forward toward Messina with the Seventh Army, and that we were counting on having a jeep and the freedom to move where we wanted. All of this was news to me; I had discussed no such plans with Sammy.

Patton nodded. "I think we can fix that," he said.

Sammy had another suggestion. "Gen, these boys just got here, why not bring them up to date on what the picture is?"

"Of course, Sammy." Patton strode to his wall map, picked up a pointer, and gave us a dramatic description of the landings and the subsequent developments. His pointer lingered on Gela, where the American First Division, under General Terry Allen, had landed. "Surely you recall what happened at Gela, gentlemen? It was there that the Greek playwright Aeschylus met his death. An eagle, mistaking his bald dome for a rock, dropped a tortoise on it and fractured his skull." After this flash of erudition, Patton returned to the present.

"Terry Allen had worse than the onshore wind to contend with at Gela; he had the whole goddam Hermann Göring Division, tough sons-of-bitches loaded with tanks." At the mention of tanks, the tank expert's eyes sparkled. "Two of our cruisers, the *Savannah* and the *Boise,* opened up on them and added something new to military history—the first engagement between tanks and cruisers."

I was astonished to see Sammy Schulman yawning and not even bothering to conceal it.

"You were there, Sammy," Patton said. "It was touch and go for a while, wasn't it?"

"Right," Sammy agreed. He then asked Patton for a cigarette.

Patton put half a carton on his desk. Sammy took a pack and urged us to do likewise, warning us that American cigarettes were scarce in Sicily.

Patton went on with our briefing, giving us the historical background on Agrigento, which, it seemed, had first been conquered in 406 B.C. by the Carthaginian general, Hamilcar, and then, eleven centuries later, had succumbed to the Saracens. "Before our 3rd Division got through with the goddam place," Patton said merrily, "I'll bet the Nazis wished they'd never heard of it. And now look at this." He tapped Ribera with his pointer. "Palermo to Ribera is seventy-two miles. The 3rd Division made it there in two days. That would have been a hell of a feat in maneuvers. They'll be studying that one in the goddam textbooks when we're all dead."

This was Patton, the man I was soon to see roaring in and out of Palermo in his command car or jeep or sedan, escorted by a dozen white-helmeted MP's on motorcycles—and the man who, all too soon, would come close to finishing his career by his impulsive slapping of a GI. I found there were at least two views of Patton in the field. His military successes gave most of the men of the Seventh Army an intense pride in their service and his leadership, but the famous "Patton discipline," which saw even advance patrols wearing neckties, infuriated many. Said one, "He likes to be called Blood and Guts Patton—his guts and our blood." Better men than I have attempted to explain Patton. Just when I thought I had him figured as a naughty boy who never quite grew up, I heard that he wrote religious poetry in his off hours, and that really set me back.

Our briefing went on and an, and it was ended at last not by General Patton but by Sammy Schulman, who rose to his feet saying it was time he took Bess and me back to the hotel for a cold lemonade.

"On the way out," said Patton, "tell my PR man to give Bess and Reynolds PX cards and a jeep and driver."

"Will do, Bossman," said Sammy.

Outside, I almost felt it my duty to salute Sammy, "Where's the body buried?" I asked. Sammy looked at us innocently. "You boys don't understand," he said. "He just loves to have his picture taken."

During my stay in Palermo I got to know a badly damaged destroyer, the *Mayrand*. She came limping into port on July 27. The afternoon I walked down to the waterfront to say hello to her, she was leaning against a dock and looking mighty tired. Emergency repairs were already under way, and when I went aboard I had to shout to make myself heard above the hammering and the shrieking of winches. I asked a seaman if the executive officer was around.

"Big Pancho? Yeah, forward." The seaman pointed. "Big guy in the dungarees."

I picked my way toward the incredibly dirty but still familiar figure whom I had last seen in New York at my wedding party. "Hi there, Big Pancho!" I said, enjoyed his startled look of recognition, and then shook hands with Franklin Roosevelt, Jr.

A few minutes later I was sitting with Frank and the skipper, Commander Edward Walker, in the wardroom, hearing about what had happened after enemy aircraft left the *Mayrand* with her port deck only four inches above water. The order had been given to jettison weight, and along with nine hundred rounds of heavy ammunition and the depth charges had gone eight torpedoes, each weighing a ton, and each costing eight thousand dollars. But it was not just these losses that had depressed young Roosevelt; what had hurt him was tossing overboard everything that made his ship an instrument of war. Helpless, with three holes in her side that a man could have walked through, the Mighty May, as her crew affectionately called her, would remain in Palermo until patched up enough to stand towing to Malta, where she could be drydocked.

A few nights after I met the *Mayrand,* the harbor was given a pasting by German bombers. They came late, dropped their flares, and worked the place over until nearly dawn. When we heard explosions continuing after the all clear had sounded, we knew that ammunition supplies had been hit.

I went down to see how the *Mayrand* had made out. She had not been struck, but there were two bomb craters in her stone dock, and shells and bullets from a still-burning ammunition train had been whizzing in her direction for hours. Her sides and bridge were scarred where the fragments had hit. Big Pancho was directing the clean-up. Though he was obviously weary, I heard no sound of fatigue in his voice as he barked his orders, nor did the crew fail to respond. "Some of our boys got it from fragments," he told me. "Now I know what it is to be a sitting duck."

In the wardroom I drank coffee with the skipper. "It was a bad night," he admitted. "Young Frank did a hell of a job getting our wounded off the ship. He's been a fine combat man right along, and if he wasn't the President's son, I'd recommend him for one of the big medals."

Later in the morning I went along with Big Pancho as he cased back streets of Palermo to find living quarters for his crew. The idea was to get everyone off the ship except a skeleton crew in case the Germans returned. After an hour of poking around, we found a large empty house that had not as yet been requisitioned by the Army. Giving the owner a slip that would permit him to collect rent from the port commander, Roosevelt lettered a sheet of cardboard with the words BARRACKS FOR MEN OF U.S.S. MAYRAND. Signing his name to it in large letters, he stuck the notice on the door.

"You made the 'Junior' about as small as you could," I said.

Big Pancho grinned. "Self-defense. Maybe the Army won't grab the place away from us."

When I moved on from Palermo, it was to hook up for a couple of days with the 1st Division, whose commander, Terry Allen, I had met the previous summer in London. Allen's second in command, Brigadier General Theodore Roosevelt, was another London friend.

At Enna, where I found Allen and Ted Roosevelt in tents, the 1st Division was ahead of its timetable, catching its breath for a few days while other units came up on the flanks. I found another friend at Enna. Allen, as he greeted me, told me his aide was off scrounging some fresh vegetables for dinner. With a grin, he declined to reveal his name. Thus, both of us had a good surprise when Major Ken Downs appeared.

The second day I was at Enna, we had a sudden visit by German planes, requiring us to dive into our slit trenches. Happily, they had made only a couple of passes at us before our planes appeared and chased them away. This was the closest thing to action I had yet seen in Sicily. The thought occurred to me that I had perhaps arrived too late, and that I would have to go elsewhere to see Americans in real combat. A couple of days later, when Terry Allen received orders to report to General Eisenhower in Algiers, I decided to hitch a ride with him.

We found Palermo buzzing about Patton's slapping of the hospitalized soldier. Demaree Bess and Merrill Mueller of NBC had the story cold, supported with signed statements from doctors and patients who had witnessed the affair, but even with their ample proof, neither of them felt like reporting it. Since Terry Allen had room on his plane, I suggested to Bess and Mueller that they come along to headquarters and see what Eisenhower might have to say about the situation.

In Algiers, when I telephoned Harry Butcher for an appointment, he said, "I know what you're coming to see him about. The general hasn't slept for two nights, worrying about it."

Eisenhower listened most unhappily while Mueller and Bess recounted what the witnesses had told them. Then he managed a smile. "You men have got yourselves good stories," he said, "and as you know, there's no question of censorship involved."

"Quent and Mueller and I have been discussing what would happen if we report this," Bess said quietly, "and our conclusion is that we're Americans first and correspondents second. Every mother would figure her son is next."

Then Mueller said that we were not only going to kill the story but deny it if any of the other correspondents broke it. Eisenhower seemed to draw new life from this. Only then, after we had committed ourselves, did he reveal that the British correspondents had already decided to deny the story. Then he told us what would follow if the

296

story was printed: "Georgie, the best armor man we've got, would be destroyed."

As we listened to the rest, it seemed to me that Eisenhower had handled the ugly business about as well as any commander could hope to handle it. He had ordered Patton to apologize to the man he had slapped in the presence of the witnesses who had been present when the slapping occurred. He had also ordered Patton to visit his various staff headquarters and apologize to his officers so that they could communicate his apology to their men. Patton, Ike told us, had already carried out these orders and made the apologies in the right spirit.

There were sixty American and British correspondents in Algiers and Sicily at this time, and despite the fact that neither Eisenhower nor General McClure, in charge of press relations, exerted even indirect pressure, no one broke the story. It was not until four months later that the incident became known in the States, and by then thousands of Seventh Army men had written home about it. And by then, as Eisenhower had predicted, Georgie had quite redeemed himself.

The whole incident was impressive enough as an example of voluntary self-censorship—responsibility making itself felt at a critical moment—but I was also deeply impressed by Eisenhower's qualities when the heat was on. He might have asked for our silence, but he did not. He might have defended his temperamental general, but he did not. Instead, and quite sincerely, he told us he felt that both the GI and Patton were his direct responsibilities.

For a correspondent in search of a place to sleep, Algiers had little to offer at this time, being about as crowded with Americans as a New York subway at rush hour. The correspondents' headquarters, the Hotel Aletti, was jammed. I moved in anyway, since there was nothing available elsewhere, and claimed sleeping-bag space in a room occupied by five AP and UP men. For a time I was able to improve on this accommodation when I ran into an old acquaintance, Al Schacht, as he was registering at the desk. Al had once been a major league baseball player. Now he was one of the most popular of the GI entertainers, billed as the "Clown Prince of Baseball." His act consisted mostly of corny baseball stories, and once I had tried kidding him about the poor quality of his jokes. He had replied complacently that they sounded all right to him.

"You can't hear them," I had reminded him. "You're deaf as a stone."

"That's right, Quent. I'm a lucky guy, huh?"

In the hotel, after I had greeted Al warmly in his better ear, I asked if he had a room to himself.

"Of course I have!" Al bellowed.

"I suppose your aide is with you?" I said.

"I need an aide?" He was puzzled.

"All the big shots who come here to entertain need aides," I said. "Jack Benny had an aide. Bob Hope had an aide. But if you speak the languages . . ." I shrugged.

"I don't speak no French and I don't speak no Arabic, if that's what you mean." Al was concerned.

"That's bad. Suppose General De Gaulle phones you and wants you to do a benefit for the French troops. You won't know what he's talking about. Or suppose General Eisenhower calls. You're so deaf you wouldn't hear the phone ring."

"Maybe you could dig up an aide for me, Quent."

I had him on the ropes now. "Well, I can speak French myself, Al, but I'm pretty busy."

"Be a pal," he pleaded. "There's two beds in my room. How's about moving in with me?"

As we went up to his room, he said suddenly, "Why in hell should Eisenhower call *me?*"

"Because he's always asking visiting USO performers over to his place for Sunday breakfasts," I told him. "He serves bagels and lox and cream cheese."

"Gee, I'd sure hate to miss his call," Al said.

"A *swillitch* you'd really be," I assured him.

"What's that, Quent?"

"Arabic for *schlemiel.*"

"Boy, you do know these languages!" Al said happily.

In Al's room, one with a balcony and a nice view of the harbor, I asked if he had been issued a PX card. He picked it out of his wallet. It had not been used. I felt shaken. The man had three weeks' rations of cigarettes, candy, and liquor due him. I somehow managed not to pick the stuff up till he had left Algiers.

The very day I became Al's aide, it happened that four weary correspondents flew in from Sicily—my old friend Knickerbocker, now writing for the Chicago *Sun,* John Steinbeck, corresponding for the New York *Herald Tribune,* Clark Lee of INS, and Jack Belden of

298

Time and *Life*. When Al returned from doing his show that night, he found his room awash in men, bedrolls, typewriters, and trophies picked up on various Sicilian battlefields. Warm-hearted Al didn't mind a bit as long as they didn't toss him out of his bed.

About 3 A.M. an air raid began. The Germans were determined to sink two British battlewagons that happened to be in the harbor, and sleep became impossible. The bombs began falling closer to us than was strictly necessary for a harbor operation. We scurried into the hall to avoid the flying glass. When the all clear sounded, we trooped back into the room.

"My God, look at Schacht!" Steinbeck exclaimed.

The Clown Prince was blissfully asleep in his bed. "There's just the bravest man I've met yet," Knick said. "Anyone who could sleep through that doesn't know what fear is."

"Don't give him too much credit," I told the boys. "His hearing aid's turned off."

Early in September we heard that General Montgomery and his Eighth Army had crossed from Sicily and established a toehold on the Italian boot. Obviously it was now about time for the United States Fifth Army to move. Studying maps of the Italian coastline became a favorite indoor sport at the Aletti. Would we go ashore on Monty's heels, we wondered, and work up through the mountain valleys, or would we land further north, independently? And if the latter, how close to Rome could we land and still have air cover from our land-based planes? Everyone had his hunch, but we were not to know the answer until we were well on our way with the invasion force.

Through the good offices of a former INS reporter, Navy Commander Charles Duffy, I was placed aboard the *Ancon*, General Mark Clark's command ship, as the representative to cover the naval part of the operation for both the American and British press. With me were two more correspondents, Reynolds Packard of the UP and Lionel Shapiro of the Montreal *Gazette*, and photographer Sammy Schulman. The rest of the correspondents were on other vessels of the three-hundred-craft fleet. When we were twelve hours out of Algiers, the four of us were summoned to the *Ancon*'s command room. Here, General Clark and Naval Commander Richard English revealed that our destination was Salerno, forty-five miles south of Naples. They also told us that negotiations for Italy's surrender had been going on, and that she would probably be out of the war by the time we landed.

"I expected that," Reynolds Packard said happily. He had once been the UP representative in Rome. "I have complete faith in the Italians. They've double-crossed every ally they ever had. Now it's Hitler's turn."

Clark went on to say that the Italian surrender would have little practical effect on the forthcoming operation, inasmuch as the Germans were determined to hold onto Italy. It was known that the garrisons in the Salerno area had already been replaced by Germans and strengthened.

Following our briefing, at the invitation of the *Ancon*'s commander, Admiral Hewitt, I keyed open the ship's microphone, introduced myself, and made the announcement of our destination. He asked me to emphasize the fact that our air cover would be excellent. I hoped he wasn't kidding.

The *Ancon* had once plied the Caribbean as a cruise ship. The only remnant of her elegant past was a lounge containing a few comfortable leather chairs. I went there after my broadcast to see what might be interesting in the ship's large collection of paperbacks. Not much was new, but I was happy to spot an old favorite, Vincent Sheean's *Personal History*. I was beginning his chapter on Palestine, checking my own recent experiences there against it, when a voice at my shoulder said, "I admire your taste in reading, Quent."

I looked up to find Air Force Lieutenant Colonel Vincent Sheean laughing at me. It was one of those meetings that just couldn't happen, and yet during the war seemed to happen with great frequency. Sheean, whom I had last seen in London, had been through the North African and Sicilian landings, and now had been borrowed for the Salerno operation by Mark Clark because, among other things, he knew Italian.

An hour before dawn on the morning of September 9, Sheean and I stood together on the forward deck of the *Ancon* and watched the spectacle of nearly a thousand men of the 36th Division tumbling into landing craft. Still untried in combat, they were boys rather than men. Those who survived a week of what was to come would be veterans, but just now the nervous laughter, the clearing of throats, the hands wiping on shirts as if they had just held snowballs, all proclaimed that these boys were trying to beat fear.

300

"All wars are childish and are fought by boys," the novelist Herman Melville once wrote. To me, the GIs in the barges looked pathetically young, and the carbines they carried, the grenades hanging at their belts, even their heavier automatic rifles, looked like toys. What would such children be able to do against the battle-hardened veterans of the *Afrika Korps* who were awaiting them? As the barges shoved off, I could not help feeling a bitter anger against all the illustrious statesmen who had, by their failure to act effectively in the years following World War I, allowed this senseless war to come about.

But anger was a futile emotion now, and it was quickly banished by the intensifying fire of the cruisers *Savannah, Boise,* and *Philadelphia,* as well as several American and British destroyers. Their bombardment was calibrated to points well beyond the beaches, giving protection to the first wave of our forces. Bright golden flashes in the still-shadowed hills showed where the Germans' dreaded 88s were returning the fire.

As if he were trying to shut out the horror that was in the making, Sheean, standing at my elbow, said suddenly, "Paestum's over there." He pointed to the distant hills. "Ever been there, Quent?"

I told him I hadn't.

"It has some magnificent ruins, including a temple built in 420 B.C. Beyond, to the north, is a lovely little place called Cava di Tirreni. You can get there by bus from Naples in an hour."

I was about to ask him how he knew all this when he added wistfully, "Eight years ago I spent my honeymoon there."

Thinking back on the six days I spent at what was eventually to be called Bloody Salerno, I find that the spectacle of our dying men and our wounded ships is balanced by some fairly trivial incidents. Nature, it seems, has her way of smoothing the jagged edges, so that the terrors of close calls and the nightmares that replace sleep eventually fade to reasonable size.

One of the lighter moments came when I began commuting ashore from the *Ancon.* Beginning on D-Day plus 2, I went in early every morning on the fast launch that carried ashore written verifications of General Clark's radio messages. The beach, of course, was in our hands. One hot morning, when the German planes and 88s were paying no attention to the beach area, the ensign in command of our launch suggested a swim. While our message-bearing lieutenant was off delivering Clark's dispatches, the ensign and I stripped and swam with seventy or eighty GIs who were also taking a quick one. When the lieutenant returned, we dried ourselves with our shirts and clambered aboard the launch for the return trip. Halfway out, the ensign asked me what time it was. I looked—and discovered that a watch I had borrowed from Harry Butcher wasn't working. I'd forgotten to remove it from my wrist before swimming.

"That's all you can expect of those PX jobs," the ensign commented. I did not bother to tell him that the watch, which Butch had lent me just before I left Algiers, was one of Switzerland's best. However, I thought to impress him by mentioning who had lent it to me. "I bet," he said.

Little Sammy Schulman's personal way of dealing with the enemy is another of my Salerno memories. A *Luftwaffe* pilot was plucked out of the sea near the *Ancon,* and after the surgeons patched him up they asked Sammy to come in and interpret for them. I went along, interested in seeing one of Hitler's supermen at close range. We were told that his chances were poor. Sammy's job was to get his answers to the questions prescribed by the international rules of war.

Ignoring the look on the lean, hard German face, Sammy began by lighting a cigarette and putting it between the man's lips. Then he placed a chocolate bar on his chest. He came to the question "What is your religion?"—asked so that the prisoner may receive the burial service of his church if he dies.

"I am a National Socialist, *Heil Hitler!*" rasped the pilot. "You God damn Jew!"

"Take it easy," Sammy said soothingly, restoring the fallen cigarette. "You'll be all right. Just relax. I'll be back later to see if you need anything."

"You're one lousy Jew, Sammy boy," I said as we left the sick bay.

"What the hell, the guy is hurt, isn't he?" Sammy replied.

Since there were no radio facilities for the correspondents at Salerno, the sending of our dispatches became a problem. Some of the men hopefully sent them to the air fields that were captured after the first few days, even though we all knew that these fields were tied up with planes flying in supplies. Sicily was the nearest place where cabling was assured.

By September 15, in addition to the dozen stories I had written as the Anglo-American press representative on the *Ancon,* I had ready two long stories for *Collier's.* Carrying this material and that of Rey-

302

nolds Packard and Lionel Shapiro, plus a case of Sammy Schulman's films, I said good-by to Salerno without any real reluctance and hopped a night ride south on a British motor launch that was carrying dispatches from Mark Clark to General Montgomery. Another correspondent, Cy Peterman of the Philadelphia *Inquirer,* made the trip with me. Montgomery and his Eighth Army were then in the Italian hills back of Pizzo, but Peterman and I hoped that other transportation would be available there to take us on to Sicily.

At dawn we entered a picture-postcard harbor and found a command car waiting for Monty's dispatches. When I told the staff officer that I would like to meet Montgomery, he saw no reason why we should not go along with him to headquarters.

Some four miles back from the harbor we drove into an ancient olive grove and pulled up near two large trailers and a dozen tents. The officer disappeared into one of the trailers with the dispatches. A few moments later Montgomery came out and greeted us warmly.

He was the Monty of his photographs—though a smaller man than I had expected—wearing his familiar desert costume of shorts, shirt open at the neck, and black beret set at a jaunty angle. He looked very much like a well-bred expensive cat. Prepared to meet an arrogant man, I was disappointed. Monty led us to comfortable chairs beneath one of the olive trees, and for an hour we talked there and had a delightful time of it.

When an orderly brought three tall glasses of lemonade, Montgomery, looking closely at us, said unexpectedly, "How about a drop of gin in yours? I feel it would do you both good." Being invited by a notorious abstainer to have a drink was a pleasant shock.

In the tree above our heads, four parakeets were flitting about in a cage. "I bought those in Tunis," Monty told us. "They're bright little things and they chirp charmingly. They cost me a pound apiece, but it was money well spent."

Talk turned to the recent campaigning in Sicily. Monty expressed admiration for the American generals, especially Omar Bradley, who had been on his flank. Eisenhower he called "magnificent."

"I made a little bet with General Eisenhower," Monty told us, chuckling. "I bet him I'd be in Catania within ten days of our landing in Sicily."

Peterman and I knew the reason for this bet. It was common knowledge. The year before, in Africa, Monty's cautiousness had been much

303

criticized. The story of how he had defied Churchill's wishes at El Alamein was a case in point. Monty had spent the whole summer of 1942 planning his strategy, training his men, bringing up supplies. In August Churchill had practically ordered him to attack. The reply had been that an attack in September would surely fail, while the delay of one more month would guarantee the destruction of Rommel's army. There was little Churchill could do with such a commander. Meanwhile, of course, Monty lured the Germans off guard with a faked build-up in the southern sector, preparing for the stunning attack of October 23 that ended Hitler's dream of conquering Egypt.

But neither in Sicily nor in Africa could Monty's critics claim that his supposed timidity had resulted in either a defeat or a lost opportunity.

"Of course I won my bet," Monty continued gaily. "Ike had to give me a Flying Fortress. I was told that a Fortress could land on the downhill strip at Palermo, so we tried it. My American pilot almost killed us. I told Ike I'd have to have something that landed a trifle slower. He gave me a C-47 and I'm tickled to death with it. I drive my jeep aboard her, and off we go."

We asked Monty how soon he expected to move north to meet the operation at Salerno. He told us that since the Italian terrain was utterly unlike anything his men had experienced in Africa, he was giving them a few days' additional training. The spectacle of Salerno fresh in my mind, I felt like telling the Briton not to waste any time. Instead, I held myself in, drank a second spiked lemonade, and listened while the Englishman expounded on the difficulties of getting through mountain passes.

Our visit ended with Monty taking us through his trailers. One, which he had captured from Field Marshal Messe in Tripoli, was paneled in cedar. It contained a large bed, a desk, and a bathroom with shower. The other, which Monty called his guest room, had belonged to Italy's General Borgonzella—"old Electric Whiskers" Monty called him. Among its appointments was a bathtub. Showing off these trophies, Monty was as happy as a youngster with a new electric train.

As he walked us to the car that would take us to Reggio, where we would cross to Messina, Monty asked shyly if it was true that girls in New York were wearing Montgomery berets. He had read this in an American magazine. When we assured him it was undoubtedly true, he laughed with pleasure.

304

Then he told us to notice that we were no longer shouting at him, as we had been doing when we arrived. The guns at Salerno had made us deaf without our realizing it. "Possibly that gin helped you," Monty said. "That's why I served it to you."

We left him standing among the olive trees, a slight figure who should have looked comic in his shorts, but who somehow carried it off.

Two days later, after filing my stories in Sicily, I was in Algiers. I found a twelve-day-old cable from Colebaugh telling me to come home. With two Salerno stories on the wire and material for three or four more I felt I could go with a clear conscience. Furthermore, Frank Gervasi was now with the Fifth Army for *Collier's,* and he spoke Italian.

I telephoned Butcher to see if he could arrange transportation for me—and to let him know that I would soon be sending him a new watch—and the next day I was on my way.

At Casablanca we had an overnight stop, and I caught Al Jolson entertaining the troops. After the show, Jolie went wearily off to bed, while I and his long-time accompanist and song-writer, Harry Akst, repaired to the officers' club for a nightcap and the recent gossip of New York. What should have been twenty minutes there stretched out to three hours after Harry was persuaded to sit at the piano. No matter what the request was, he played it, and there were some really sentimental moments before we closed the place. As we walked to our quarters, I complimented him on his phenomenal memory for the oldies.

"The only one they didn't ask for," Harry said gloomily, "was 'Dinah.' "

"And that makes you feel bad?" I quipped.

"Kind of," said Harry. "I wrote 'Dinah.' "

17

You, too, can capture a Jap

Not since I had been in Moscow, months before, had I been asked to produce my passport, but the October afternoon I arrived at The Marine Base at LaGuardia Field I was not only asked to produce it but to turn out my luggage which was nothing but a musette bag and a typewriter. My only unusual item was a magnificent red and gold dinner plate that had, a century before, graced the dinner table of Czar Nicholas I. The customs inspector picked it up.

"Russian?" he said, noting the crest. "What's this worth?"

When I told him I had no idea, he asked me how much I had paid for it.

The story of its acquisition was so unimpressive that I hated to repeat it. When I had asked British Ambassador Sir Archibald Clarke-Kerr, an art connoisseur, to suggest an unusual present for me to take home to Ginny, he had assured me that there was nothing in the Moscow stores worth carrying out of the country. But there were other sources for acceptable souvenirs, he had indicated, and one day he had offered me this plate for his investment in it: thirty-five dollars, give or take a ruble. To this day I think he gave five times that much for it, but I took him at his word, wrapped the piece in a sweater, and carried it with me all through North Africa, Sicily, and Salerno.

306

Certainly this was a flat story to tell a bored customs inspector, so I denied paying anything for it, adding that I had liberated it during a banquet at the Kremlin. The man complimented me on my taste and passed me on through.

In the airport waiting room I found myself rich in rubles, piasters, and Sicilian occupation money, but not in anything that would be looked upon with favor by a New York cab driver. Then, as I wondered how even to pay for a telephone call, I saw Ginny hurrying toward me. I had asked the plane's radio operator to send her our arrival time via the field, but knowing that we were under radio silence till almost the end of the flight, had doubted that the message would reach her. Now, here she was, looking more beautiful than ever. While Ginny, welcoming home the husband she had lived with all of a month, quite some time before, fretted about my loss of weight and look of fatigue, I congratulated her on her being able to pay for our ride into town.

I need not have worried. *Only the Stars Are Neutral* had sold very well, and the royalties had enabled Ginny to rent and furnish a large apartment for us in the River House. Looking and smelling like something from a prisoner-of-war camp in my battered desert boots and dirty khakis, I almost hated to go into the place. An hour later, cleaned up and wearing civilian clothes again, I handed Ginny her souvenir from Moscow. I could not resist repeating the falsehood I had previewed at the airport—and once again, when the story took off, could not bear to call it back. Some years later, when Archie Clarke-Kerr was in New York, he came to have dinner with us. Ginny proudly showed him her conversation piece—and I heard for the hundredth time the story of how I had swiped it from the Kremlin. Archie's eyes widened, but he only smiled and told Ginny that he remembered the incident quite well.

I had too good a time being home again, and Charley Colebaugh's mild complaint, "You know too many people," soon seemed only too true. Not only was I falling behind on my *Collier's* articles, Bennett Cerf was badgering me to deliver the manuscript of another book. The solution seemed to be for me to underground for a while—in a comfortable way, of course—and packing my typewriter and notes, Ginny and I went to the Greenbrier at White Sulphur Springs, West Virginia.

While that spa doubtless continues to be a place that any writer

307

would be humbly grateful to work his typewriter in, I cannot doubt but that the quality of many of the guests has improved over what it was in the war winter of 1943. During our sojourn there, the Greenbrier was occupied by a conspicuously large number of elderly rich men who loathed President Roosevelt and seemingly had few other interests.

Ginny and I were able to avoid most of these characters, but one trapped us in the cocktail lounge one evening with a gambit against which no writer has a firm defense. "I've read everything you've ever written," he said, beaming at me, "and I would consider it a signal honor if you and your lovely wife would join me in a drink."

Reluctantly, I asked him to sit down. After a few minutes of listening to him tell Ginny how lucky she was to be married to me, I sensed that he was making a dreadful mistake. Sure enough, he soon announced that of all my books the one that had most impressed him was *Inside Europe*.

Before I could think how best to break the disappointing news, he had learned that we made our home in New York. "Don't you find that pretty depressing?" he asked. "I mean, living there with all those Jews?"

"You'd have loved it in Sicily," I said. "For a while I was with the First Division. There were a lot of Jewish kids from New York in that outfit. That is when they landed in North Africa, but after Kasserine Pass and Gela most of the Jewish kids were dead. You would have loved that, you son-of-a-bitch."

The man's face fell. I suppose my sickening rage showed on my face. He shrank away.

"Your hands!" Ginny pleaded.

"What about my hands?"

"You have to typewrite tomorrow," she said sweetly. "If you hit him you may hurt one of those four fingers you use."

I'm sure the man never read another book by John Gunther.

When my articles and the book were done we returned to New York. I now spent some time getting re-acquainted with my eleven-year-old daughter. Happily, I was never a step-father to Joanie—from the moment Ginny and I were married she was like a real daughter to me.

A day came during our weeks together at the River House when I

308

was to feel frightened concern for Joanie. It happened because she owned a poodle.

Every morning at seven-thirty she took him out for a walk, a routine Ginny told me she had followed faithfully ever since acquiring the dog. It rather puzzled me that Joanie and her poodle seldom returned to the apartment before Ginny and I were having breakfast around nine-thirty. One morning I mentioned that two hours of walking seemed like a lot.

"Oh, I don't *walk* him all that time," Joanie said. "There's this nice old man I meet downstairs who also has a poodle, and we usually go to his apartment and sometimes he gives me a glass of milk and—"

I glanced at Ginny. Her face was turning pale.

"And then what happens?" I asked.

"Well, some mornings he plays the violin and I play the piano for him. I guess he's pretty good, even if he doesn't know the songs I like."

Taking the anguished Ginny's silent cue, I said no more, but as I left the apartment a little later, I promised I would check around downstairs and find out who the hell was doing the fiddling.

As it happened, the elevator stopped halfway down to admit an elderly couple. The woman immediately said, "You're Mr. Reynolds. We're so glad to meet you. My husband and your daughter have been great friends ever since their dogs introduced them."

I shook hands with the husband. "You mean you actually listen to my child's piano-playing?" I asked.

He laughed. "We often play duets," he said. "My only difficulty is that I don't know her favorite tunes."

Stopping in the lobby, I telephoned Ginny to put her out of her suspense. "The nice old man and his wife just now welcomed me home," I said. "He happens to be Fritz Kreisler."

That evening when I told Joanie that her poodle-walking friend was one of the world's greatest violinists, she replied with that peculiar innocence of the young, "Really?" I was to hear the same reaction when I introduced her to Joe DiMaggio and called him the greatest living baseball player. When President Roosevelt sent me an inscribed photograph of himself, Joanie thought at first that I was playing an elaborate joke on her. She thought I was kidding again when I showed her a signed picture of General Eisenhower.

But I finally did impress her. Frank Sinatra stopped in one evening, threw his arms around me, and said, "I've missed you, Dads. And is this your Joanie?"

My daughter looked at me in awe. Until now I had been a man who spent most of his time away from home, and much of the rest of it operating a typewriter. Now, suddenly, I was somebody: I *knew* Frankie.

One day early in 1944, Robert Hannegan, the National Chairman of the Democratic Party, telephoned to say that the President hoped I would be willing to address the national Democratic Convention in July. When I pleaded innocence of any knowledge of party politics, Hannegan told me I was wanted for another reason. Clare Booth Luce was going to speak at the Republican Convention, and it was expected that she would criticize the war effort. "The President feels that she can best be countered by someone like you who has a first-hand knowledge of the problems we're up against on the fighting fronts," Hannegan said. I asked for a couple of days to think it over.

Two considerations made me hesitate. While I was still not very happy with my contribution to the war effort of a few dozen magazine articles, a few BBC broadcasts, and the attempt to see that life was made a bit pleasanter for a handful of RAF and Eagle Squadron pilots during their leaves in London, I had some standing as a reporter, and it occurred to me it might be jeopardized by my taking sides in the political arena. And then above all else I wanted to be in on what was going to be the greatest story of the war—the cross-Channel invasion. I went to Washington to see what Harriman and Hopkins could tell me about the time schedule for that event, even in guarded terms. While there I also talked with the man my brother Jim was now serving as aide, Secretary of the Navy James Forrestal. He, like Harriman and Hopkins, told me that the D-Day decision would not be made in Washington. It would be made in London by Eisenhower. Not one of these men suggested that I ought to hustle over to London.

At *Collier's* neither Colebaugh nor Chenery thought it likely that I would miss the invasion by agreeing to speak, and Tom Beck, proud that a *Collier's* representative had been so honored, told me flatly that the invasion would not take place before the end of July. He had been talking to a logistics general in Washington whose job it was to make recommendations about the Channel weather, and according to this expert there was general agreement that August would be the most

310

favorable time. Beck clinched it by reminding me that the Dieppe raid had taken place in August. While many other things had gone wrong at Dieppe, the weather had been perfect.

Ultimately, it was not my hunch about the invasion that led me to accept Hannegan's invitation. It was the consideration of our whole war effort. In baseball terms, FDR was pitching a winning game, and you don't take a pitcher out when he's way ahead. I decided that if my small voice could help in his re-election, I had a duty to raise it.

When the news came on June 6 that the invasion had been launched, I felt sick. My cup of regret overflowed when I learned that my friends John McClain, now a naval Lieutenant-Commander, and Bob Low and Ken Downs, both majors, were all on the Normandy beaches while I sat in New York.

I concentrated on the writing of my speech.

When Ginny and I went out to Chicago in July, any number of professional Democrats were eager to give me advice on what to say and how to say it. However, I let only the three top men, Robert Hannegan, his assistant Paul Porter, and Sam Rayburn, the convention chairman, see my script. They made no suggestions.

The moment arrived when the nineteen thousand noisy delegates and spectators in the Chicago Coliseum had to quiet down and listen to a war correspondent named Reynolds. It was the third day of the convention. Everyone was weary of speeches. The delegates were eager to get on with the task of selecting their candidates. When Mr. Sam introduced me, the applause was perfunctory. The noise continued. I felt angry. I had missed the invasion for this?

"Don't say a word till they're quiet," Mr. Sam warned me.

After waiting through what seemed an eternity, I began to speak. In 1944 there was no teleprompter; you openly read your speech or you had it in your head. I had recited mine many times, working it over with Ginny as my coach.

The crowd began listening, I think, because I was not the usual sort of speaker at a political convention, but I hadn't gotten far before I realized that these characters with their paper hats and banners and buttons were with me. It may have been because my voice wasn't mangled in that huge barn the way lighter voices were. Or they may have sensed my sincerity. Some may even have realized my speech was homemade—not something a ghost writer had handed me as I entered the Coliseum. I described the determination and dedication of the troops overseas:

"They are confident in their strength, these sons of yours," I said, "but here at home, criticism seems to have become our national hobby. The paragraph-troopers hurl the dumdum bullets of their phrases against our national war effort. The saboteurs of our national unity do their best to tell us that the war is not being conducted properly. The Ship of State has been torpedoed, depth-bombed, dive-bombed, and sabotaged by the armchair commandos."

But the boys overseas, I pointed out, were not criticizing. They and the enemy, too, knew that America was producing and delivering an increasing number of guns, aircraft, ships, and tanks. "Your sons know it is the American people of all parties who have worked this miracle," I said. "It is industry, it is labor, it is the farmer, it is the banker buying a million dollars' worth of bonds, it is the school kid buying his twenty-five-cent war stamp, it is the man in the mine, in the factory, in the street."

At the end I returned to the biggest fact known to the boys overseas: "Your sons know that all of the American people of both parties have contributed to making this victory possible. They also know that this achievement, which dwarfs any other in the history of our country, has been accomplished under the leadership of their Commander in Chief and ours—Franklin Delano Roosevelt."

The perspiring delegates blew their horns and flourished their banners and seemed moved by it. Mr. Sam brought me back twice to the rostrum to acknowledge the applause. When I finally sat down beside Ginny, I was shaking. Some men get nervous before they make a speech; my time comes when it's over and I can do nothing more to make it better.

"It was *good!*" Ginny said, pressing my arm, and her verdict went a long way toward making me feel better.

Next day, sifting through the press comments on my performance, I received a shock. I had not expected the Chicago *Tribune* to do other than blast me for my temerity, but a man I had long considered my friend was now lashing out at me as one who had no right to speak for Roosevelt. At a time when Westbrook Pegler was himself charging the Administration with every evil except that of stepping on little birds, his contemptuous description of me as an amateur politician was especially painful.

312

Following the convention, in an effort to keep my continuing relationship with the Bureau of Internal Revenue friendly, I began a national radio program in which I interviewed figures in the news. The fact that the series was sponsored by the Goodrich Rubber Company raised an issue with the advertising side of *Collier's* that could only be solved by the removal of my name from the magazine's masthead. My retainer was canceled at the same time, but to make up for it the magazine paid me higher prices for my articles. This technical readjustment was to figure importantly in the court action that a few years later was to cloud my life.

I was well into the radio series when a New York group billed as the Independent Voters Association urged me to run for Congress. It took me all of five minutes to make up my mind about that one. Heywood Broun had once run for Congress from my part of town, referred to as the Silk Stocking District, which traditionally elects only Republicans. Heywood had thoroughly enjoyed the street-corner speaking, the hand-shaking, the verbal sparring with his opponent. One day I had asked him if he had given any real thought to his future, warning him that he might find himself in with some choice bores and bigots who operated at the taxpayers' expense.

"That would be awful, wouldn't it?" Heywood had agreed. "Thank God, I don't stand a chance of being elected."

Nor did Quentin Reynolds, as I well knew. I based my rejection of the Independent Voters' invitation on a regrettable fact of life along the Potomac—the baseball picture. "What has Washington got?" said my letter of rejection. "A colorless, perennial last-place team called the Senators. Really, gentlemen, I could not live in a city that is not represented by a National League team."

When my radio series ended, I went back to the war. This time it was to the Pacific theater. The *Collier's* man there, Frank Morris, had been wounded, and Colebaugh asked me to fill in till he recovered. Accredited to the Navy, I flew to Pearl Harbor with high hope that I would be able to make up for my failure to report the big story in Europe. Weeks later I returned to New York as the only correspondent in the Pacific theater who never heard a shot fired in anger. Captain Harold "Min" Miller, Forrestal's public relations officer, did all he could for me, but the plain truth was, my tour occurred when things were quiet. At Pearl Harbor I had dinner with Admiral Nimitz. Admiral William Halsey attended, complaining about the paper work that he was involved in as a result. "All day long I've been writing requisitions and more requisitions," he told me as we sat together on the veranda of Nimitz' house. "And all these reports I keep sending you, Chester"—here, Halsey scowled at our host. "When you send 'em on to Washington, who in hell do you suppose finds time to read 'em?" Halsey then slipped his shoes off, saying his feet hurt. He had been dictating for eight hours, and he could not dictate sitting down.

This was an amusing sidelight, certainly, but hardly anything worth the long trip to Pearl Harbor. Things looked up a little when Min Miller sent me on a cruise with the carrier *Saratoga*. The veteran ship observed her twenty-fifth anniversary at sea, giving me the opportunity for an article entitled "Sarah Has a Birthday." Then Miller sent me on to Guam, to see an island that had recently been taken back from the enemy.

The Third Marine Division had the place in hand, and the commander, General Graves Erskine, welcomed me with a supper in his tent. Afterward, he provided me with some entertainment I could have done without. There had been talk during the meal of the many Japanese who were still hiding out on the island. When I commented that Erskine's tent seemed to have been pitched in a rather isolated spot, he told me that three Marines and three Doberman pinschers were at that moment guarding us. A few nights before, he added with relish, a Jap with homicide in his heart had crept to within a grenade-throw of the tent, only to have his throat ripped open.

"Perhaps you'd like to write a story about the dog that did it," Erskine suggested. "We'll have him in."

Though the prospect hardly charmed me, as Erskine's guest, I felt unable to say no. I learned later that a good many of his guests were subjected to this test.

Placing me in a comfortable chair and instructing me on no account to move, the general snapped an order. An evil-looking Doberman promptly appeared, attached to a Marine sergeant by a taut leash.

"Don't move," the general said again. He could have saved his breath: I had neither the capacity nor inclination to do anything but sit frozen.

"A great dog for obeying orders," Erskine said happily. "If the sergeant gave the word, he'd tear you apart."

"Very funny," I managed.

"Let the dog approach Mr. Reynolds," the general ordered.

314

Growling, the brute quivered its way toward me. Even as I felt myself aging another ten years, something prompted me to quaver, "Nice doggie!" It sounded pitifully insincere, but before any of us knew what was happening, the damn thing was in my lap licking my face. Watching the sergeant drag it out of the tent, I wouldn't have given ten cents for its chances of promotion.

Next day I went out to observe the best sport that the island had to offer: hunting wild Japs. My guide was Marine Lieutenant William Jones. Twenty miles from headquarters, in a clearing near the shore we went to work on them with a soundtruck. Ray Takahashi, late of the Imperial Japanese Army, now a very contented war prisoner, opened the microphone and began his pitch. Jones translated for me: "You Nipponese in your caves, listen to me. It is no disgrace to surrender. Do as I have done. You will die where you are. Come into this truck and you will live to serve Japan in the new era following the war."

After half an hour of it in the hot sun with no result, I was ready to quit, but Jones told me the day's work had hardly started. "It's like fishing," he said. "You go along for hours without a nibble and then a dozen of the bastards will surrender."

Another prisoner, grinning happily, took over the microphone. Shrilly, he described the amenities of the Marine stockade, the fine food to be had, the clean clothing. Takahashi, meantime, shinned up a palm and knocked down several coconuts. Their cool sweet juice was a great improvement over the warm water in our canteens.

The hours passed. The stockade salesmen grew hoarse. Still no sign that anyone was listening to us. I'd had it. With Jones' permission, I started back to headquarters by myself in one of our jeeps.

Two hundred yards from the clearing I saw a human figure on the road ahead of me. Its hair was long, its clothes ragged. It grinned at me uncertainly. Though its hands were up, I remembered Jones' warning that these die-hards often tried to toss grenades at the last minute. I climbed out of the jeep and motioned for the little beauty to come closer. At the same time I yelled for help.

Jones and a couple of his boys came on the double, carbines ready. The prisoner was frisked. Nothing on him except a little money and a pass to a movie theater in Tokyo. Speaking Japanese, Jones asked him if he had been alone or if more men were hiding nearby. Alone, said the prisoner.

Jones waved him into my jeep and assigned a corporal to drive us.

I sat in back. The corporal handed me his carbine. "If the son of a bitch changes his mind and tries to bolt," he said, "plug him." Then he lit a cigarette and offered it to the Jap. "Smoke up, greaseball." The prisoner saw the corporal's grin, took the cigarette, and inhaled gratefully.

We started off. "Been out here long, Reynolds?" the corporal asked.

I told him I had been mostly in the ETO. He made a slighting remark about the ETO, so I asked him if he had been on Guam long.

"I landed here in the first wave," he told me a bit too proudly.

"Maybe it's different out here," I admitted. "The Germans only throw small stuff at the first waves. They save their heavy stuff for the second and third. They know those are the ones that go in with the mortars and bazookas and machine guns. Was going in with the first wave really tough here?"

"Murder," said the corporal. "The first wave carried the lumber to build the officers' club."

I laughed, "OK, Marine. You win."

We delivered my Jap to the stockade where, following custom, I gave him a name. The stockade's recent arrivals had been dubbed Donald Duck, Mickey Mouse, Cue Ball, Dugout Doug. I named mine Meat Head, my pet name for Toots Shor.

That transaction completed, I handed back the corporal's carbine. If I'd kept my mouth shut, it would have been all right. "It's a good thing Meat Head didn't try to run," I said. "I couldn't have worked that thing."

The corporal saw that I wasn't kidding. "War correspondents!" he said witheringly. "ETO correspondents—God almighty!"

During the winter and spring of 1945 I made a number of speeches for the United Jewish Appeal. It was George Backer, whom I had first known in London as a representative of the Office of War Information, who got me stirred up about the plight of the stateless Jews of Europe. Their terrible ordeal was little known in the United States even at the beginning of 1945, and the ultimate horror would not be revealed, of course, until the Allies liberated the death camps. However, Backer had many of the tragic details as the result of his work in Switzerland, where he had been spiriting Jews out of Germany and the occupied countries and smuggled them to Palestine. As I listened

316

to Backer's stories, I wondered why Roosevelt and Churchill were not warning Hitler that the Allies would eventually exact retribution for his atrocities. George told me that neither of the Allied leaders really believed, yet, the extent of the Nazi bestiality.

A United Jewish Appeal dinner was to be held in the Grand Ballroom of the Waldorf-Astoria Hotel in New York on April 12. During the program, Luther Adler, Ralph Bellamy, Frederic March, and Paul Muni were to enact the roles of Jewish refugees, delivering lines written by Ben Hecht. I was to be the master of ceremonies. An hour or so before the dinner began we were rehearsing in a private room off the ballroom. It was going well until I rang for coffee. When the waiter appeared and began pouring it, he looked pale and his hands shook.

Bellamy twitted him: "What are you so nervous about? We're the ones who have to know our parts."

"Haven't you heard?" The waiter choked back a sob. "Roosevelt's dead."

We looked at one another in the awful silence. The waiter poured our coffee, told us the few details that were known, and left. We sat there, our scripts pushed aside, numb.

"Why did it have to be him?" I heard Muni whisper. "Why not one of us?"

I was thinking of the last times I had seen the President—of a recent evening when I had had cocktails with him in his study and his voice had filled with laughter as he asked, "You know why Fala loves Steve Early? Because Steve always has an old-fashioned and gives Fala the cherry." And of the time when FDR had suddenly invited Ginny and me to have dinner with him and spend the night at the White House. I had been puzzled about this hospitality until at dinner the President had said, "Young Franklin wrote that he'd seen you in Sicily. How did he look?" When I told him his son looked fine and was in the best of spirits, the President had peered at me over his rimless glasses and asked, "Do you happen to know where he is now? I mean confidentially, just here in the family?" I had to tell him I had no idea. He could have found out by picking up the phone and calling Admiral King or Jim Forrestal, but he didn't operate that way.

Remembering the FDR I admired, I thought of what I'd heard him called—the most ruthless politician who ever entered the White House and the betrayer of his class. This did not describe my Roosevelt. I knew him as a warm, human, affectionate, and great man, and my feeling of loss was shattering.

"There will be two thousand people out there in less than an hour. . . ." It was the voice of Paul Muni, calling us back to an awareness of the immediate future. "Now, Luther, let's start from the top. This time without scripts."

These four were professionals. They did not falter, as I did, on our last run-through. Their example was what I needed when we faced the audience. Ben Hecht almost seemed to have written his script in anticipation of the tragic news, since one of its points was that the Angel of Death sometimes comes so suddenly that nothing can be done against his visit. Sometimes, though, the Angel gives a warning, and prayers can be offered and practical acts performed.

When we were through, the audience pledged a stunning sum of money. It was designated for the UJA but it was given, I still think, as a tribute to the man who lay dead at Warm Springs.

18

Libel comes on horseback

To me it has always seemed that there are two kinds of prose writers. The first is the serious author who feels a compulsion to communicate a message to mankind. He usually does this in the form of the novel.

The second is the professional craftsman (no less serious) who tries to find a good story and then tells it as well as he can. I belong to this latter category. The agonies of advanced literary creativity I have known only by hearsay. On the few occasions when I have had a message I felt worth communicating (i.e., the danger of Hitler during the 1930s or my conviction that England would hold out during the early years of the war), I've used the journalistic medium either in the form of magazine articles or books.

In the postwar years I continued at my craft, only rarely feeling that I had a message. I found a message, certainly, when I returned to Europe in 1947 and toured West Germany, France, Norway, Italy, Greece, and Israel. In a series of articles in *Collier's* and afterward a book, *Leave It to the People,* my thesis was that the war-experienced peoples of these countries would reject communism by means of the ballot. The pressure was on from Moscow at the time, especially in Italy and Greece, and there was fear in the United States that the Reds would take over.

319

I worked hard at documenting my case for optimism about the democratic process, and of all my books, *Leave It to the People* seemed to me the most deserving of attention. Most reviewers agreed with me, but the book stayed in the stores in large numbers. My next effort, *Courtroom,* was a rather hurriedly written account of New York's Judge Samuel Leibowitz. I concentrated on his days as a defense lawyer and offered no message that I can recall. This time the reviewers were only lukewarm. The book stayed at the top of the best-seller lists for weeks.

The lesson, if any, is that writing books people want to read is like playing roulette. I'm still looking for the system that works.

A minor part of my trade, after the war, was reviewing other writers' books in the *Sunday Times Book Section* and in the Sunday *Herald-Tribune.* A review I chanced to write in 1949 precipitated me into five of the most difficult years of my life. The book was Dale Kramer's biography of Heywood Broun, and I liked it. However, I made the mistake of quoting some passages in which Kramer discussed Westbrook Pegler's dim views of Heywood's liberalism, in particular his part in the founding of the Newspaper Guild. While it was Kramer, not I, who was taking Pegler to task for his unfairness to Heywood, it was I, for some inexplicable reason, who became the fresh object of Pegler's wrath. I still don't understand why he didn't pick on Dale Kramer.

The eighteen inches of column this man turned out for the twelve million readers of the Hearst papers simply sought to destroy me. I was an "absentee" war correspondent, a coward, a war profiteer. I had been discharged by *Collier's.* I had been a member of the "parasitic, licentious lot" that had surrounded Broun, a member of an interracial nudist group that had consisted of Broun and his friends, in which "a conspicuous Negro Communist of the present day seduced a susceptible young white girl." Crowning these sickening charges was Pegler's assertion that I had proposed marriage to Connie Broun, Heywood's widow, while accompanying her to Heywood's funeral.

Bewildered by the publication of this incredible filth, I stayed in seclusion for two days trying to figure out a sensible course of action. There were moments when I felt like hunting the man out and killing him with my bare hands, but an inner voice warned me that this solution was no longer acceptable practice.

320

I felt that unknowingly I had lived all my life on the slope of an inactive volcano. Now, suddenly and senselessly, the volcano had erupted. The eruption didn't kill anyone but the hot lava and fragments of metal unloosed by Pegler's column seared my family, my friends, and myself. To Ginny and me these were not wounds that could be cauterized and cured in one day. The pain wasn't physical— it wasn't that easy. It was something that had crept into our hearts and remained there. Instead I sought advice from some lawyer friends and they were unanimous in telling me to see Louis Nizer.

Sitting behind his large desk, Nizer listened to my story politely but without, it seemed to me, genuine interest. Ginny and I had been told that Nizer was one of the most feared cross-examiners in the business. We found it hard to believe, that day we met. Nizer's manner seemed too mild, his voice too soft. At length he picked up the column and asked me to show him precisely where I thought it libeled me. We prepared a list of fifteen separate libels. Nizer then asked me how I could prove that the statements were false.

To me, it seemed an easy matter. A phone call to Washington would verify the unhappy fact that I still owed tax payments. Certainly that would take care of the charge that I had been a war profiteer. Possibly some of the charges would call for getting affidavits from my friends in London, but others clearly involved historical fact. Pegler's ridiculous assertion that I had covered the Dieppe raid from the relative security of a battleship would fall as soon as a jury heard that there had been no ships larger than a destroyer at the scene.

Nizer listened impassively while I explained how easy his work would be. Then he tried to discourage me from suing. "Like sickness," he said, "libel comes on horseback but leaves by foot." What this meant, I learned, was that years might pass before the suit came to trial. Gathering the evidence would take months, court calendars were crowded, the other side might resort to delays. My present determination was all very well, Nizer said, but what would count was my staying power.

There were other matters to ponder. The defendants would ransack my personal life, and we would have little or no warning of what might be brought up in court. Further, we would be opposed by the Hearst Corporation's libel lawyer. "You can be sure of one thing with Charles

321

Henry," Nizer said. "If you succeed in bringing Pegler down from his perch, it will not be before you have turned yourself inside out, factually and emotionally."

And there was the matter of expenses. Aside from the routine costs, there would be those connected with the trips abroad to take depositions. But beyond the outlay of money loomed the possibility that Pegler and the Hearst organization would find ways to exert other pressure against me. "You will have to prepare yourselves for financial hard times," Nizer warned. He saved his biggest dose of cold water for the end. "Even if we win," he said, "the jury's award may be nominal."

That had an ominous sound. I asked him to spell it out.

"They could give you six cents."

It had all seemed so much simpler before I consulted Nizer: a quick little trial, a contrite Pegler, a retraction by the Hearst papers, and an award sufficient to cover my expenses and loss of productive working time. The future that Louis Nizer was charting for me was frightening.

Perhaps I was overlooking something. I asked him what the legal alternative to suing would be. There was none, he told me.

"You have been maliciously libeled by a character assassin and by a powerful publishing corporation," Nizer summed up. "I feel you have a good case. I have warned you of the pitfalls. The decision is up to you. If you wish me to represent you, I shall be happy to do so."

I looked at Ginny, sitting beside me. There was no doubt about how she felt. "We'll be in this to the finish," I told Nizer.

As predicted, economic hardship soon developed. Mark Hanna, my agent, had been dickering with two advertising agencies, both of which wanted me to host television shows. Pegler's column took care of that. Hanna tried to soften the bad news: "It's not that anybody really *believes* Pegler's charges, Quent, but they've made you controversial. You know what that means in radio and television. You're dead."

This was bad enough, but nothing compared to the blow that *Collier's* handed me. Charley Colebaugh, the man for whom I'd worked some seventeen years, had died. Bill Chenery was retired as editor emeritus, and Tom Beck could not help me. When the magazine advertisers let it be known that they were not eager to publicize their floor finishes and sandwich spreads in a periodical that

322

carried my by-line, that was that. Things began to get rough around the Reynolds' place.

Many of our friends offered their help. Toots Shor called up to growl, "You can have half of anything I got." Sidney Bernstein, my London friend, borrowed in the United States so that he could help me with my immediate legal expenses. Furthermore, when Nizer went to see Sidney in London, he declined to give a deposition, saying he would prefer to testify in person.

When a deposition is taken in a foreign country, the opposing side is entitled to cross-examine the witness and file a counter-affidavit. After Nizer had done his work in London, the Hearst lawyers were faced with the question of whether to cross-examine such men as Lord Mountbatten, Lord Beaverbrook, General Sir Frank Messervy, Brigadier Desmond Young, and Sir Walter Monckton. It was at this point that the defendants probably began to worry about the soundness of their case.

One day a friend of many years' standing came to me with a proposition. If I would drop the action, he said, Pegler would never again mention my name in his column. I could see that Bill Corum was unhappy about the role he had been asked to play. Pointing out that he had known both Peg and me for a long time, Bill commented that it was a tough thing to be in the middle.

I reminded him that it was Pegler, not I, who had written the libel column, and that it was a hell of a lot tougher to be on the receiving end. Bill agreed and said that the "front office" had urged him to make the try.

Richard Berlin, the president of the Hearst Corporation, made the next attempt. During a conference with Nizer he said that Pegler and I, as men of temperament, had indulged in a quarrel that could certainly be resolved with a handshake. Nizer rejected Berlin's "quarrel" as not descriptive of the facts and declined his offer to provide us with Pegler's hand.

Undaunted by the case that was building against him, Pegler continued to blast away at me—and the Hearst Corporation went right on printing it. Learning that I was to address a New York businessmen's group, Pegler warned all organizations not to hire me. His message contained the ludicrous statement that I had joined the Harriman-Beaverbrook mission to Moscow in order to "thrust on the

Soviet dictator the riches of the United States." Further, my attitude toward Congressional investigations of Soviet propaganda was "exactly what the communist traitors in the United States have been arguing for years."

His new charges had their effect—my speaking engagement was canceled. I took this hard, but Nizer was delighted. It was a further proof of malice.

The evening of Pegler's second column, Ginny and I went to a cocktail party Earl Wilson of the New York *Post* gave for Ernest Hemingway. Though I would have preferred not to show myself, Ginny persuaded me that I couldn't hide from my friends. Toward the end of the evening, Ernest asked me where Pegler was living. I named the hotel. "Let's go over there and knock his brains out," Ernest said. "On second thought," he said, "you better stay out of it. I'll go alone and work on him."

We had quite a time talking Ernest out of it. After Earl Wilson's party, it took me a long while to go to sleep. When I awakened late the next morning, I found that Ginny had gone out. It struck me as strange that she had left no note. When she returned, she told me that she had gone to have a talk with Pegler.

Listening to Ginny's account of their conversation, I could feel only awe for her courage. She had begged him to let up on me. Pegler had replied that it was I who was suing him, just as it was I who had done the first attacking in my book review. Nevertheless, he had said, he would be willing not to write another line about me if I would drop the suit.

"I told him that you hadn't sent me and that I couldn't speak for you, but that I didn't think you would withdraw the suit," Ginny concluded.

Almost as soon as it occurred to me, I think Ginny realized that her impulsive action might have harmed our cause. Trying not to alarm her needlessly, I telephoned Nizer and told him what had happened—prefacing it with a plea for him not to be angry at Ginny.

His first question was "Did she sign anything?," his next, "Did she promise him anything?"

I relieved his mind on both points.

"Pegler and Henry will believe that you sent Ginny," Nizer said. "They undoubtedly think you're ready to surrender."

He was right of course. Henry soon got in touch with Nizer to tell

324

him that the case was being settled. He was informed that Ginny's plea had been her own idea—brought on by the almost unbearable strain.

Now began the ordeal of the pre-trial examinations. Mine took place in Henry's office. Nizer had warned me that anything I would say while under oath could be introduced at the trial. "I want you to do just one thing with Henry," he said. "No matter what questions he asks, tell him the absolute truth. We may lose a few battles that way, but I think we'll win the war."

I got on fairly well with Henry from the beginning. He was a Giant fan, which didn't hurt. A tall, white-haired man, he said courteously, "You're not going to like some of my questions, but believe me, there's nothing personal in this. I am merely your legal opponent. Mr. Nizer and I have often crossed swords, but we remain good friends."

With Lou at my side to object to any legally unfair line, with a court stenographer taking it all down, we went to work. As the sessions went on, I felt easier in my mind. No matter what phase of my life Henry wished to explore, I found I had nothing to hide. When the examination was finished, the transcript was given me to review. Because of the tension under which one replies, and because one's memory of apparently unimportant events may be hazy, the law allows the witness to make corrections in the record. Lou was delighted to find that I could swear to the transcript's truth without making a single correction.

It was now Pegler's turn to be examined. But Pegler proved to be elusive. Before Nizer could get him into his office he had to petition the court to punish Pegler for contempt. Then, week after week, Nizer questioned him, eliciting more than five thousand pages of testimony. Before swearing to it, Pegler made over a hundred corrections. But for all his care, Nizer had lured him into making a terrible self-denunciation, and it was still in the record when he signed it. It waited there to make a mockery of Pegler's judgment, of his grasp of world affairs, even of his view of his own work. Nizer referred to it as our delayed-action bomb.

While these preparations for the trial went slowly ahead, I did my best to concentrate on other matters. One of the magazines that came to my rescue after my virtual rejection by *Collier's* was *The Reader's*

Digest. One day in 1952 the publisher, DeWitt Wallace, proposed that I do an article for him on a remarkable Canadian who, as a British secret agent during the war, had lived a fantastic life in France and Germany. The man's name was George DuPre. With kindling interest I listened to what Wallace knew about him. After arriving in England as a member of the Canadian Air Force, he had been transferred, given a year of special training, then dropped into France near St. Lo. Assuming the identity of a halfwit garage mechanic in a nearby village, he had become the leader of the local underground and a vital link in the chain of agents that rescued downed British airmen and conveyed them to points on the coast where they could be taken back to England. Twice he had been picked up by the Gestapo, but even after boiling water had been poured down his throat and his right hand had been crushed in a vise, he had not given himself or his associates away. The answer to how the man had survived was that he possessed a secret weapon—a profound faith in God.

But this dramatic story was only the beginning. After helping to blow up troop trains and bridges in France, DuPre had gone into Germany and worked in a submarine yard near Hamburg. Here, until suspicion of him had forced him to flee, he had sabotaged Hitler's U-boats. Later, British Intelligence had placed him in a prisoner-of-war camp to ferret out Germans who were attempting to masquerade as Canadians. When the war was over, I learned, DuPre had spent months in English hospitals undergoing surgery for the injuries resulting from his torture. In recent years he had been lecturing about these experiences to Canadian audiences, stressing the religious message. "You can't have guts without God," was DuPre's summary of what he had been through.

I felt, as did Wallace and his senior editors, that this sounded like one of the best spy stories to come out of the war. My only question was whether the man didn't have too much of a story to cram into an eight-thousand-word article.

When I telephoned DuPre in Calgary, he was delighted to learn that his experiences and message might see print in a large international magazine. He startled me only when I mentioned that the *Digest* planned to pay him a good sum.

"I wouldn't want to make a financial profit," he said. "Please see if you can make the payment direct to the Canadian Boy Scouts."

326

Impressed by his humility, I urged him to get a leave from his work
—he was a government employee, the confidential assistant to a
cabinet minister—and come to New York for a week of work with
me. The magazine wired him travel money, and a few days later I
met George DuPre at LaGuardia field. He proved to be a pleasant-
looking man of forty-eight.

"Has anybody ever told you that you look like a small edition of
General Eisenhower?" I asked as we shook hands.

He smiled engagingly. "Yes, they have. And a good man to look
like."

George had never been to New York before. I suggested showing
him the city before we drove out to Bedford Village, where Ginny
and I were then living. He was delighted at the thought and wondered if we could possibly begin by going to the top of the Empire
State Building. Acrophobe that I am, I did not go for the view.
George, happy as a child, bought some post cards and statuettes of
the building in the souvenir shop. "My wife and boys will love these,"
he said. He seemed to me one of the nicest, most sincere men I had
ever met.

For lunch we went to Toots Shor's. Toots was duly respectful when
I told him who my guest was, though shaken to learn that his favorite
drink was Coca-Cola.

After a look at Times Square, George wanted to see the Museum
of Natural History. By then my feet were balking. As we headed for
Bedford Village, he was embarrassingly grateful for the wonderful
day I had given him.

During dinner, I saw again something I had noticed at lunch.
"Some of those British customs brushed off on you," I remarked.
"I never saw a Canadian use a fork with his left hand."

"It isn't that, Quent." He held up his right hand, showing us the
crippled index finger. "This is weak. It's been so ever since they
smashed it for me. That was the first time. The second time they gave
me this." He touched the scar on his chin. "And smashed my nose,
too. The surgeons did a fine job of fixing it, don't you think?"

They had indeed. Except for a faint scar across the bridge, his nose
looked normal.

Next day we began our work. My part was to ask questions. I asked
hundreds. With unfailing patience, George went over and over his
experiences, pinning down every detail for me. He had a remarkable

327

knack for describing people. I soon felt I knew them all—the priest, Père Gauraud; Girard Benois, the café owner; Henri Rennet, the doctor; Albert Baudoin, the blacksmith—and the brave young girls who had carried messages in the handlebars of their bicycles and paid for their hatred of the Germans with their lives. In the whole account, George told me, there was only one falsification, and that was the name of the village. For reasons best known to British Intelligence, he had been asked not to reveal its real name.

George flew back to Canada and I put his material in final shape. Sometimes the raw data for a magazine piece has to be shaken a bit and have life breathed into it. Not so with George's saga. My typewriter could hardly keep up with it. For the better part of a week I worked with time off only for meals and sleep. When I handed *The Man Who Wouldn't Talk* to DeWitt Wallace it was about ten times longer than it should have been. I told him I saw no way to boil it down.

Wallace had met George and had been as captivated by him as Ginny and I were. He read the script overnight, then telephoned me. "You're right about the length, Quent. This has to be a book. I've already talked to Bennett Cerf about it. He'll publish it and we'll condense the book."

The next step was checking the facts. Besides wanting to be sure that they were accurate, the *Digest* wanted assurance that DuPre had not inadvertently violated any security secrets. The simplest way to prove this, it seemed to me, would be to airmail a carbon of the manuscript to British Intelligence. When I got in touch with a man at the Embassy in New York about it, he suggested that he cable before sending the manuscript.

Next morning he telephoned me the answer to his inquiry:

IT IS THE POLICY OF BRITISH INTELLIGENCE NEVER TO REVIEW, AFFIRM, OR DENY BOOKS WRITTEN BY FORMER AGENTS. TELL REYNOLDS WE WISH HIM WELL WITH HIS BOOK.

The cable was signed by a man I had known well in London.

To Hobart Lewis, the senior editor working with me and to myself, this amounted to at least partial confirmation. Still cautious, Lewis was not entirely satisfied. DuPre himself had not checked over my manuscript. He suggested that I fly up with a copy.

Two days later I was in Calgary. George met me at the airport with several of the people who had been sponsoring his talks. That evening they gave a dinner for me and I heard a good deal of praise for their distinguished neighbor George DuPre.

While DuPre checked the manuscript, I checked on DuPre. The man he worked for, Nathan Tanner, the Alberta Minister of Mines, Forests and Lands, was delighted that George was at last going to get the recognition he deserved. Tanner, who was also a Provincial Commissioner of Boy Scouts, told me of George's inspirational appeal as a lecturer, and added that he regularly turned his fees over to the Scouts, keeping only his travel expenses.

Next I called on Allan Bill, the editor of the Calgary *Herald*. Bill, whom I had known in London when he was a war correspondent, vouched for DuPre and said he hoped to serialize my book in his paper.

Finally, I went to see the Commander of the Royal Canadian Air Force Fighter Squadron at the Calgary base. He knew DuPre well. I asked him if he thought there might be anything in the story that should be screened by censors. "DuPre has been telling this story all over Canada since 1947," the Commander said, "so obviously nobody over here or in Britain has any objections."

When George handed back my typescript, it bore on the last page his signature and this statement: "The story you have written is a true factual story of my war experiences as I told them to you."

My book and the magazine's condensation of it appeared in October, 1953. The reviews were excellent and the sales of the book were so good that Bennett Cerf had to rush through a second printing. The reception was also good in the magazine, with the newsstand sale in Canada way above normal.

Then the blow fell.

It came in a phone call from Calgary. DuPre's story, Allan Bill informed me, was a fabrication from start to finish. A former RCAF member had just walked into Bill's office and told him the real story. In 1943 this man and DuPre had been intelligence officers at an airbase in the north of England. Here, their job had been to interview airmen who had gone down in France and then escaped with the help of the underground. DuPre had learned all that he knew about life under the Nazis from such men. When Bill had sent a reporter, armed with this story, to confront DuPre, he had immediately confessed.

I could hardly believe it. George's crippled finger, the scar on his

329

chin, his voice that sometimes failed him . . . Bill told me that DuPre had admitted receiving these injuries as a boy, and having had a throat disorder for years. "Sorry I have to let you down so hard," Bill said. "Just remember he fooled us all."

DeWitt Wallace soon phoned me. The AP had picked up Allan Bill's story and called him for a statement. He had told them the exact truth, he said, emphasizing that it was the *Digest* who had discovered DuPre and then called me in to do the writing.

The next man on the phone was Bennett Cerf. Like Wallace, he tried to buck me up. "I've always wanted you to write a novel for us," he said. "Now you've done it, and it's a good one."

Though I dreaded to pick up a newspaper, I found that most of them let me off lightly, accepting Wallace's explanation in full. Several of them used imperturbable Bennett Cerf's line about my writing a work of fiction for him.

A few days later, while I was still feeling pretty low about it all, a pitiful letter arrived from George DuPre. He gave me what explanation he could. The deception had begun in 1946 when he had started speaking to church and Scout audiences on religion as a force against tyranny. He had soon discovered how to make his own ordinary war experiences into something that would grip a listener. "Now that the truth has come out," he wrote, "I feel that a huge burden has been lifted from me."

With his letter was one from his wife, whom I had not met when I went to Calgary. At the time, I had been told she was on a vacation with her children. Actually, I now learned, she had been hiding, unable to face me. Until the moment when her husband's story was to be published, she wrote, it had not occurred to her that his falsehoods could actually hurt anyone.

There was a pathetic postscript to her letter. When DuPre had visited us, Ginny had bought some clothing for him to take home to his sons. Every time she saw them wearing the clothes, Mrs. DuPre wrote, she cried. Her last words were, "I pray to God that he will forgive us for all the suffering that George and I have brought upon you."

I found myself reliving my several days with DuPre, trying to recall anything he had said or done that should have made me suspect. My reluctant conclusion was that he was an almost perfect fraud.

330

In all the time we had spent together, only one incident might have exposed him.

Once, as we knocked off work, I casually said something to him in German. His reaction to my few words was startling. He went pale, clutched his heart, and nearly fainted.

As he rested on a couch, recovering, he whispered, "I'm sorry, Quent, but whenever I hear German, I can only think of the men who questioned me. Even when they were torturing me, they cursed at me in those frightful voices."

That seemed reasonable enough at the moment. The truth was, of course, that he didn't know a word of German.

After a while, when I could look back on the whole thing without feeling a sick wave of humiliation, I realized that none of us—Wallace, Cerf, Ginny, or I—felt much except pity for DuPre. His lack of interest in financial gain didn't hurt his case. We could at least appreciate that his motives had been lofty.

While the literary hoax of the decade (as the newspapers called it) was still in the news, DeWitt Wallace gave me another assignment for the *Digest*—a kindness that did more to restore my sense of proportion than even he may have realized.

Bennett Cerf, too, showed his confidence in me. He had just introduced the Landmark Books, a series of books aimed specifically at juvenile readers. He selected writers who had never before written for youngsters. His conviction was that most writers of juveniles wrote down to their young readers. He chose such writers as John Gunther, Bob Considine, Samuel Hopkins Adams, and Laura Hobson, and now he asked me to try my hand. I did a book on the Wright Brothers, one on General Custer, and then Cerf asked me to do one on St. Patrick. This was an interesting and rewarding task. Patrick left a last will and testament but nothing else to posterity. I read everything written about the good saint and found to my surprise that he had been born in Wales, had been educated in France, and had then been sent to Ireland to convert the savage tribes. He did not banish the snakes from Ireland; snakes were not native to Ireland. They were brought to Irish ports by ships that came from India at least a century after Patrick's death. Separating the fact from the legend was fascinating work. When I gave Bennett the completed manuscript he was so delighted with it that he sent it to Cardinal Spellman, who, after reading it, put his Imprimatur upon it. This meant that it was satisfactory to Catholic ecclesiastical authority.

After that I did *The Story of the F.B.I.* with the cooperation of John Edgar Hoover, who even wrote a preface for the book. It was nice to know that the director of the F.B.I. (he had read Pegler's column) had enough confidence in me to open the files of the Bureau to me.

But I was still unable to get even with the Bureau of Internal Revenue. I just couldn't write fast enough to do that. About this time Ginny's grandfather died, leaving her $25,000. Without a word she sent the check to Mark Hanna, who forwarded it to Washington. No man deserved the loyalty Ginny gave me during those dark years. Lou Nizer had warned us to prepare for a long war. In May, 1954, nearly five years after the case began, we began our day in court— the United States District Court in Foley Square. Lou had brought the action in the federal court rather than the state court because the federal procedure permitted us a more searching pre-trial examination of the man we were suing. To be measured against this advantage was the fact that a favorable verdict would require the agreement of all the jurors, rather than the ten out of twelve that would have sufficed in the state court.

We had our first serious setback in the composition of the jury. There were three defendants—the Hearst Corporation and Hearst Consolidated Publications in addition to Pegler—and Judge Edward Weinfeld permitted them more challenges than we were allowed. The result was that Lou was unable to prevent acceptance of two members who admitted that they were steady readers of Pegler's column. It seemed to me this might mean we were licked before we started. Lou, conceding the doubtfulness of their impartiality as they entered the box, told me that we would eventually win their minds with all the rest. Was this Lou's confidence showing, or was it what any lawyer would tell his apprehensive client? I could not be sure.

I sat at the plaintiff's table with Lou and two of his associates, Walter Beck and Seymour Shainswit. Behind us, at the defendant's table, sat Charles Henry, his assistant, James Bowden, and the tall, now somewhat flabby man who had been my ideal of a sports writer when I was learning the trade. Fleetingly, I thought of the days when Peg, as a slim, sandy-haired, good-looking Irishman, had been a member in good standing of Heywood Broun's poker circle. I thought

332

of my mother's high opinion of Peg—how she had admired him for being a good Catholic, for the sweetness of his nature, and for the graciousness of his wife, Julie. In the old days it had seemed to me that Peg and Heywood had a trait in common. Both, in their way, were puritans. Within my hearing, neither had ever told an off-color story or enjoyed listening to anyone else tell one.

The old days seemed very distant now, as Peg and I sat, one in front of the other, in the stark setting of the courtroom, neither speaking to the other, avoiding even the chance to meet one another's eyes.

I listened closely to Lou as he made his opening statement. He spoke without notes and in a conversational tone, explaining the issue and what it was we wanted to prove. I studied the jury. It seemed to me that Lou had their respect from the beginning. Toward the end of his statement, his tone became solemn. "We don't mind putting Mr. Reynolds under a microscope," he told the court, "but we are going to take the same privilege and put Mr. Pegler under a microscope and find out what his reputation and character are.

Then Lou called me to the stand. From our table it was only twenty feet, but it seemed to me one of the longest walks I had ever taken. Seated, I glanced around the courtroom. Judge Weinfeld, looking moderately like Abraham Lincoln without the whiskers, waited impassively. The jurors' eyes were upon me. Sitting beside his glowering client, Charles Henry seemed expectant. Beyond him, sitting with Ginny, were my sisters Con and Marge, my brothers Don and Jim (now Vice President of the American Locomotive Company) and our good friend Marie Fauth.

Quietly, Lou began. His tone and manner gave me confidence. There came a moment when I could almost forget the importance to our case of each question, each answer. Lou sounded almost as if he were interviewing me over a luncheon table. He asked about my early life, my education, the first jobs I had held. He was interested in why I had been fired from my job at the Dreamland Pool in Newark. I mentioned my allergy to sunlight. "They didn't like the fact that one of their guards was spending most of his time in the shade," I said.

Lou paused to let that make its effect. I saw Henry half rise as though to object, then think better and sit down. Lou had gotten my difficulty with the sun into the record to help in refuting Pegler's charge that I had been seen "nuding along the public road with a wench, absolutely raw," at Broun's place.

I was now led through my years with INS and then with *Collier's*. Lou put into evidence every article I had written during the war, reading excerpts that described my experiences at Montmédy and Beauvais, during the London Blitz, on my convoy trips between England and the United States, in the Libyan Desert, on the Dieppe raid, in Sicily, and at Salerno. My answers to all his questions were spontaneous. Lou had purposely not rehearsed me, saying that my testimony would be more effective that way.

After I had told my story of the Dieppe raid, even to the loss of my gold inlay and the loosening of the rest of my teeth, Nizer put questions that covered Pegler's specific charges.

"Did you witness the raid from a battleship?"

"There were no battleships on the Dieppe raid. I was on a destroyer, the *Calpe*—the headquarters ship. The *Calpe* was never out of range of the German six-inch guns, and was subject to constant bombing. Our casualties were very high. About fifty per cent of the crew—killed or wounded. When the raid was almost over, the *Calpe* went as close to shore as the depth of the water would allow to pick up survivors of other boats or men who had swum or waded out from the shore."

In his formal answer to our complaint, which had enlarged on the libels of his column, Pegler had charged that I had remained safely on the alleged battleship while other correspondents went ashore. Nizer spiked that one with two questions:

"Did any American correspondents go ashore at Dieppe?"

"No."

"Did any officer or crew member from the *Calpe* land?"

"No."

Lou turned to another topic. "During all the time you were ever in any combat zone, were any of your stories subject to military censorship?"

"Of course. In Russia we had Russians censoring our stories. In England and in the desert and when we traveled on a British ship, our stories had to be censored by British authorities before they could be cabled to New York. When we were in North Africa, Sicily, Salerno, or the Pacific, our stories were censored by American military authorities."

"In effect, then, when a military censor stamped an article as approved, he was saying 'This is a truthful story?'"

334

"Yes."

"Would it be possible for a war correspondent to fake a story, saying he had been on some operation without, in fact, having been there?"

As I explained why this would be absolutely impossible—correspondents were under semimilitary discipline on operational trips, and were usually accompanied by press relations officers—I knew that Nizer was undermining Pegler's accusation that I had been an absentee correspondent. One of the exhibits that the jury examined was a British army photograph of me in the desert. Besides helping to establish me as a correspondent in a combat zone, this evidence would also play its part in refuting Pegler's charge of nudism, since it showed me wearing scarf and gloves.

Nizer now went into the charge that I had been dropped by *Collier's* because my "medicine grew too strong" for the magazine. Two points emerged: that I had consented to the removal of my name from the mast-head in order that I might do a sponsored radio program, and that *Collier's* had continued to print my articles. Later, Bill Chenery and Albert Winger, the president of the Crowell-Collier Corporation, took the stand as witnesses to these facts.

Still another of Pegler's charges—that I had been a profiteer— looked pretty silly when Lou had me reveal that, when the war ended, I was forty thousand dollars in debt to the Government. Mark Hanna, and Fred Rohlfs, the lawyer who handled my tax returns, verified this later on.

At last we came to Pegler's ghoulish claim that I had proposed marriage to Connie Broun while riding with her to the cemetery. After denying the charge, I testified that Connie had been under sedation and had dozed most of the trip. I testified further that the other occupants of the car had been Heywood's twenty-year-old son and Monsignor Fulton Sheen.

Putting all this information before the court required me to be on the stand for five days. Between sessions, Lou assured me that the jury was listening with sympathetic interest, even the two *Journal-American* readers. But I knew that Lou's friendly direct examination would be the easiest part of the trial for me.

When Lou announced, "The plaintiff is ready for cross-examination," I felt that I was indeed ready. More than a year before this, Lou had assigned one of his assistants to be the devil's advocate.

Putting himself in Henry's place, the assistant had probed for every imaginable weakness in our defense. Then Lou himself had put me through the cross-examination that we foresaw.

When Henry asked if I didn't hate everyone connected with the Hearst organization, I suggested he pick up my book *Convoy* from among the exhibits and read its dedication. He discovered that I had dedicated it to my old boss at INS, Barry Faris. Pursuing the subject, he asked me who my friends were in the Hearst organization. I rattled off names of executives, editors, reporters, and columnists. I told him I had known practically the whole staff of the *Journal* at one time or another. Then I found out what Henry was driving at.

"Is not the malice in this case, if any, entertained by Mr. Pegler and you?" he asked.

Here, as I knew from my preparation with Lou, we were touching the heart of the suit. It would be comparatively easy to prove that Pegler had published untruths about me. It would be harder to prove that he had been motivated by malice, and that this malice extended to the Hearst organization whose representatives had signed the answer to our complaint. A moderate award might be given for my loss of income as a result of Pegler's charges. Only if malice was proved could we hope to collect punitive damages.

Hoping I was saying the right thing, I replied, "All I know is that Pegler made the bullets and the Hearst papers shot them. I don't know the complete meaning of malice in its legal sense."

Lou told me afterward that this reply staggered Henry. Although he should have broken off his line of inquiry right there, he persisted. "It is not true in the ordinary sense, then, that the malice is between Pegler and you?"

I referred to the answer that had been made to our complaint. Until I had read that, I said, I hadn't been able to conceive of the Hearst executives even implying their approval of Pegler's attack. "I was horrified," I continued, "to find that in effect this was signed by these top executives whom I knew, and who knew me and who knew better." I said that Richard Berlin, for one, knew better than to think I was the grotesque moral degenerate that Pegler had portrayed, and yet Berlin and the organization had backed him up.

Some of Henry's other questions backfired because of his humorless approach. A case in point was the silly cable I had addressed to Presi-

336

dent Roosevelt in an attempt to get accredited to the French Army.

"Did you intend for this French official to whom you showed the cable to believe that President Roosevelt was your uncle and Mrs. Roosevelt was your aunt?" Henry demanded.

"I have to confess that I did intend that," I replied, "and it hurried my accreditation considerably."

Henry couldn't leave well enough alone. "Did you intend to deceive him?"

"I exercised whatever journalistic enterprise I was capable of, and that I had learned from my friend Barry Faris at INS," I said.

"Did you intend for him to believe that you were the nephew of President Roosevelt?" Henry persisted.

"Well, I didn't really think he would be idiot enough for that," I said. "I hoped he would, though."

For the first time laughter swept through the courtroom. It seemed to me that even Judge Weinfeld, gaveling for order, was suppressing a smile. In that moment I lost most of my tenseness.

Henry was not to be denied his right to pursue all such trivialities with deadpan seriousness. It happened again when he questioned me about my departure from Tours with Ken Downs and the INS staff. I had written that as a group we had decided "the better part of valor was to run like hell." Henry tried mightily but unavailingly to turn this into evidence of cowardice. Likewise, he tried to turn our taking of a few gallons of gasoline from the Embassy cars at Candé into an act of stealing. The fact that France itself was falling to pieces and that half the people in France were in flight seemed to Henry insufficient excuse for our grave crime of pilfering.

All this I could take with some equanimity. Then we came to something more serious. In my book *Dress Rehearsal* I had told the story of a British scientist who had gone ashore at Dieppe with the Commandos, hoping to examine a new German radar device. The Commandos assigned to guard the scientist had been instructed to kill him rather than let him fall into German hands. That I had written that it was the scientist himself who had requested that he be executed if need be was too much for poor Henry.

"The whole incident of this scientist is fiction, isn't it?" he demanded, overlooking the fact that my story had passed through Lord Mountbatten's office as well as that of the censor.

337

I assured Henry that the story was true, even though in my book I had given the scientist a fictitious name for security reasons.*

When Henry asserted again that I had invented the incident, I blew up and told him to stop calling me a liar.

At the next recess, Lou encouraged me. "Since we have to prove that these libels have hurt you emotionally as well as financially," he said, "the more Henry batters away at you, the better."

Lou's repeated admonition, "Tell the truth," served me well. Once Henry asked me if I hadn't been afraid during the bombing of Sidi Omar. Perhaps he hoped that I would claim to have been calmly objective during that episode. Instead I blurted out, "Afraid? I was scared stiff."

As the cross-examination continued, Henry addressed himself to the problem of proving me to be pro-Russian and by implication pro-Communist. He asked me if I had not beaten the drums for the second front, suggesting that this indicated an affiliation with the Communists. This was offset when we went into my article "Second Thoughts on a Second Front," which had angered left-wingers on both sides of the Atlantic and which apparently neither Pegler nor Henry had ever read. Then Henry stalked me to a statement I had made about the difficulty of getting my visa to Russia. To get it, I had written, I would have joined the Party, sold my two brothers into slavery, and even learned to speak Russian. Henry obviously hoped I would not dismiss all these as figures of speech, but I disappointed him. I likened them to another exaggeration:

"I said last night, 'I would give my right arm to see the Giants win the pennant,' but if they do, I don't think Leo Durocher would expect me to send him my right arm in a flower box."

Next, I had to defend my endorsement of opening the subways of London's East End as bomb shelters for the poor. This was a proposition that had been vociferously pushed by the English Communists, *ergo* I must be one of them. All I had to do on this one was call Henry's attention to a later passage in the book he was citing, where I noted that Buckingham Palace had also favored the move.

* Just as this book was going to press I received a letter from Jack Nissenthall of 33 Bureau Lane, Pretoria, South Africa, stating that he was the scientist involved. He wrote: "All of your statements regarding my taking part in the raid were correct. They would never have gotten me in one piece. Had I known of your trial I would have been there 'boots 'n all' just to put that lawyer in his rightful place."

338

Henry returned again and again to the matter of my courage. He thought he had something in a wish I had expressed while being dive-bombed at Sidi Omar. The passage was read to the court:

> I felt a little sick because these magnificent men of Britain . . . were not men of New York's 69th. They would, I felt, have been just as good and as truculent and as disdainful of both death and the Hun as these farmers and sons of farmers of the First Royal Sussex. Life would be so much happier if we could only pick those with whom we want to die. As it is we are only granted the lesser boon of being allowed to pick those with whom we want to live.

I explained what had been in my mind that night at Sidi Omar: "I never made any secret of my love for the British and my admiration for the way the British had fought and suffered, but if you are born in the Bronx and brought up in Brooklyn and worked in New York most of your life, you have but one loyalty, one allegiance. I was saying, when you think you are going to die, as we literally thought during this dive-bombing attack, one regret I had was that as long as I had to go I wasn't going with an American outfit."

Mr. Henry did not appear exactly happy about this statement, and we left Sidi Omar for other matters. At last he took up the intent of my review of the Kramer biography—doing his client more damage.

The book itself became admissible evidence only when the defense introduced it. Though expecting that Henry would be wise enough to avoid the issue of whether I had attacked Pegler first, Lou had nonetheless prepared me, and when Henry challenged, I was ready. I told him that I had wanted my review to be a balanced one, and had therefore not used many of Kramer's unfavorable references to Pegler.

Henry wanted the jury to hear some of the unfavorable references I had not included. I obliged, citing the pages. Perhaps the most devastating passage was Kramer's account of Pegler's notorious column in 1933 in which he had come out for lynching. I read Kramer's words. "A mob in San Jose, California, had lynched and mutilated two men accused of kidnapping and murdering a Santa Clara University student, an action which Governor James Rolph, Jr., described as a 'fine lesson for the whole nation.' In his third column for the *World-Telegram,* Pegler, in the rowdy brutal style of his sportswriting days, raked over the affair, finding himself in agreement with Rolph. The storm of protest from the liberal readers of the Scripps-Howard papers almost blew him out of his new home."

339

It seemed to me Henry was doing his client quite a bit of damage in his attempt to prove that I had attacked him. The judge raised the point: "The only reason I am letting this in is because you put the direct inquiry."

"I am quite content with that," Henry returned, and instead of dropping the matter, he asked if I had ever read the lynching column.

I told him I had read it when it appeared, and that it had shocked me just as it had shocked everyone who knew Pegler.

At Henry's request, I read another of Kramer's passages that I had not quoted in my review: "Broun stated a belief that an income tax had bitten Pegler severely at an early age. Once Pegler, after a particularly cutting attack on Broun, came up to him in a night club and suggested they forget what they wrote during the day and be pals at night. 'What I write by day,' Broun said, 'I live by night.' "

Lou told me later that Henry had talked himself into a trap and didn't know how to get out of it. He also said that my reading of Kramer's paragraphs had brought a furious flush to Pegler's face. On this note, after eight days of cross-examination, Henry turned me back to Lou for the redirect examination. This consisted largely of reviewing the many quotations from my books, and showing how Henry had tried to discredit me by taking passages out of context.

Then, to put the final nail in the coffin of the implied (but never stated) Communist issue, Lou read passages from my 1947 book *Leave It to the People,* giving my conviction that communism was a threat to world order and peace.

Following this, Henry attempted, on re-cross-examination, to make me admit that as a slacker, I had taken a vow never to fire a shot in defense of the United States. His basis for this absurd claim was my response to the BB-gun shooting of my brother Jim when I was a boy. A wrangle developed when the judge pointed out that Henry's line of inquiry was out of order, and before it was over Henry was shouting at me, and I was shouting back.

On this note I was dismissed from the stand.

Now began our parade of witnesses. The first was Edward R. Murrow, who told of a night during the Blitz when he and Vincent Sheean and I had been driving through Trafalgar Square when the flames were so bright I bet fifty dollars I could read a newspaper by their light. While the bombs had fallen around us, Sheean had stopped the car, and I had proved my point and won the bet. Lou suggested to the court that this may have been a reckless way of showing defiance of the German attack, but that it hardly helped Pegler's charge of cowardice.

Another of our witnesses, John Gunther, in a casual answer to one of Lou's questions about my standing as a correspondent, said, "All I know is that he was about the only one who never had to make an appointment with General Eisenhower. The general's door was always open to him." Henry sprang up in protest. The judge allowed his objection. While the statement was stricken from the record, we wondered how much the jury would ignore it.

Sidney Bernstein, who had flown over from London to testify, told of how I had refused compensation for the film work I had done under his supervision, and about my open house at the Savoy for the RAF and Eagle Squadron boys. Then, quietly, he told the court of something I myself had long ago forgotten: that in 1940, at the height of the Blitz, I had tried to enlist in the RAF, only to be turned down as over-age for anything except a press officer.

George Halvorsen, another witness, as an American, had been a member of the Eagle Squadron. He recalled that he and his fellow pilots had often stayed at the Savoy at my expense while on leave. An emotional man, Halvorsen lashed out against Pegler's charges before Henry could silence him with an objection.

One of our key witnesses was Connie Broun. Henry had avoided asking me about my alleged marriage proposal to Connie as well as my alleged nudism at the Broun home in Connecticut, but Lou was determined not to let these issues go by default. With indignation and horror, Connie denied Pegler's claim that I had proposed marriage to her in the funeral car. The charges of nudism and miscegenational seduction she denied as malicious and untrue. To demonstrate the real atmosphere of her home, she testified that Heywood had been so fond of my parents that he had invited them out for week ends at times when I was not even present. Then Connie offered a representative list of Heywood's friends, to counter Pegler's charge that he had been surrounded by licentious parasites. The list included Herbert Bayard Swope and his wife, Paul de Kruif and his wife, Averell Harriman and his wife, Harry Guggenheim and his wife, President Roosevelt and his wife, Joseph Patterson, two or three priests, Gene Tunney, and Harry Hopkins. "To speak of these people," Connie said, "as a licentious and parasitic lot is as low a use of language as I have ever encountered."

Connie went on to say that at the end of the period in question the Brouns and the Peglers and I had been "one little group of friends, joined frequently by other intimates whom we all knew in the same way." When she finished her testimony, Henry announced, not unexpectedly, "No cross-examination." Nor had he wished to cross-examine our other witnesses.

Now, the defendant was called to the stand. There was utter silence in the room as Pegler rose and stalked past us to take the oath. White-faced, grim, he glared at us from the chair. This was the beginning of his big moment.

He told a story of my visiting his home in Pound Ridge one Sunday in 1933. I had brought with me a young woman. After taking a shower together, the young woman and I had displayed ourselves naked on the balcony above the living room, before Pegler, his wife, and several of their relatives and guests.

Listening helplessly to Pegler telling this preposterous fabrication, I found it impossible to conceive the reason for his malice. Then I remembered reading something an anthropologist had written to the effect that man is the only known animal to deliberately torture his fellow men.

In a somewhat different version, Pegler had told this story during his pre-trial examination. Under a statute permitting the introduction of hearsay evidence for the limited purpose of showing what he relied on when he published his libel, he offered an entirely new instance of my lascivious conduct that he had not personally witnessed. Connie Broun had told him, he said, that I had been standing waist deep in her lake at North Stamford and had asked her to take me for a ride in her rowboat. "She said she rowed over to where he was," Pegler testified, "and believing that he had on his swimming trunks, invited him to get into the boat. She said he then got into the boat and she was shocked to discover that he was absolutely naked, and in her phrase, he didn't have on even a hairnet." Pegler's voice betrayed his nervousness as he gave the clincher: "She said she looked around at the trees and the sky, trying to avoid this spectacle."

I began to feel that I was not the only one who should be suing Pegler for libel.

Henry knew by now that our witnesses had completely shown the

342

factual accusations of Pegler's columns for what they were. It was apparent that he was attempting to minimize our claim of malice by establishing that Pegler had innocently published untruths that had been given him by others.

After three days of it, Henry was finished. Almost casually he said the words we had been waiting five years to hear: "You may cross-examine, Mr. Nizer."

Lou rose from the table. Standing well away so that the jury might concentrate its attention on Pegler, he asked a few preparatory questions in a friendly manner. Then the tempo picked up. Pegler was soon floundering in contradictions, disavowals, evasions, memory lapses, and deviations from the pre-trial record. He lost control and shouted at Lou. He mimicked Lou's manner. Several times the judge reprimanded him.

Taxed with his conflicting versions of my alleged nude display in his home, Pegler was forced to admit that much of the story could not possibly be true.

Lou took up the charge that I had been "nuding along in the raw" with a nude girl near the Brouns' property. After reluctantly admitting that he himself had swum in the nude when people were nearby and had not considered himself immoral for having done so, Pegler testified that his sole authority for the charge was a hearsay statement by Heywood Broun. At this point Lou obliged Pegler to admit that he had written about Broun that he was a notorious liar who could not be trusted to be truthful about even ordinary matters.

In his pre-trial examination Pegler had said that he believed Connie Broun to be an honest person who could be trusted under oath. It was not difficult to understand why Pegler had since changed his mind. Lou asked him if he thought Connie's honesty was such that he would believe her if she were not under oath. Pegler replied sweepingly, "I think everybody is subject to doubt not under oath."

This faced him with a difficult problem. He had believed Connie when she was not under oath and allegedly had told him of my climbing nude into her boat; he had not believed her when under oath she had denied that there had been any nudism at her place. Under Lou's pummelling, Pegler admitted the discrepancy, but could not account for it. Then Lou returned to his original statement about the credibility of anyone not under oath.

"Including yourself?" Lou demanded.

"Certain people make inexact statements that draw on their imaginations, to be amusing," Pegler said.

"That has been true about you, has it not?" I could sense Lou's excitement as Pegler wilted.

"Yes."

"You have actually written, haven't you, sir," Lou went on, "that it is perfectly all right to create fiction about a real person, because if you do it several years after it happens nobody will know the difference anyhow?"

"Yes, I wrote that," Pegler admitted.

Abruptly, Lou took up the matter of my alleged marriage proposal. Pegler said that if he had known that Monsignor Sheen and Heywood's son were in the funeral car, this would have cast doubt on his charge that I had proposed to Connie. Lou then made him admit that he had known ten years before writing the libel column that Woody Broun and Monsignor Sheen had been in the car with us. Pegler also admitted that he had failed to check the accuracy of his charge with Sheen, Woody, or Connie Broun, either before publishing it or before filing the repetition of the charge in the answer to our complaint.

Pegler had answered my libel suit by filing a suit of his own, asserting that my book review had besmirched his reputation and character. How unwise a move this was now became clear, since it allowed Lou to put Pegler's personal history before the court.

In World War I, as a war correspondent of twenty-three, six feet tall, unmarried, and healthy, Pegler had made no move to enlist in any branch of the military service. After writing an offensive statement about Secretary of War Newton D. Baker, he had been recalled as a correspondent. He had then enlisted in the Navy, serving as an office clerk, never requesting to be transferred to a fighting ship, never holding a gun in his hand.

In World War II, Pegler had received national publicity for his campaign to have Americans remove the bumpers from their cars and give them to the Government as strategic material—a campaign that he admitted on the stand was unnecessary, of no help, and soon discontinued. At the same time Pegler had applied to the War Priorities Board for permission to use strategic materials in a costly rebuilding of his Connecticut home on the grounds that he was going to engage in farming. Even though Pegler admitted that he had been in full charge of his farm, he could not or would not tell the court how many

344

bushels of potatoes he had raised. "More than one bushel and less than ten thousand," was all he would say.

Lou elicited Pegler's admission that his farm operation had resulted in an income-tax-deductible loss.

Pegler had charged in his libel column that while I was "a giant and a bachelor," I had let several million young men do the fighting I should have been doing. Lou insisted on hearing if Pegler had meant this to brand me as a slacker. No, he had not.

Lou then referred to Pegler's statement that I had a "mangy hide with a yellow streak glaring for the world to see." Had he intended to be hateful with that charge?

"I don't hate anybody," Pegler protested angrily. "Not even you!"

The courtroom rocked with laughter at this, bringing the judge's familiar reprimand. Despite numerous objections from Henry, Lou investigated Pegler's credo of hatred, as exemplified in his columns. "It is odd that honesty and friendship both are held in such tender sentimental regard," Pegler had written, "considering that both are so little patronized and that their opposites have by far the greater appeal. For myself, I will say that my hates always occupied my mind much more actively and have given me greater spiritual satisfaction than my friendships."

It was another awful moment of self-condemnation, and Pegler's admission, soon afterward, that he had not intended to portray me as a coward with his use of the word "yellow" seemed an anticlimax.

As part of establishing Pegler's shaky understanding of communism, Lou drew from the witness the admission that he had called Eisenhower's Republican Party "Socialistic," and that he had written that "all the crooks and Communists wanted to give us Ike."

We were drawing near the moment of exploding our delayed-action bomb. When Lou, during the pre-trial examination, had found Pegler reluctant to say whether certain statements in my book *Leave It to the People* were pro-Communist or anti-Communist, it had occurred to him to test Pegler on some of his own statements about communism—without letting him know that he was the author of them. Pegler had blindly stumbled into Lou's snare. That section of the examination was now read to the court.

"Communism," as Pegler had once written, "is the reaction to poverty, oppression, and the exploitation of the masses by the few, and represents the demands of the masses for a strong central authority to curb their enemy."

Believing that I had written this, Pegler had called it "utter non-sense" and "certainly part of the Communist line."

Lou had then presented Pegler with another of his own statements: "Communism will never get to first base in the United States because it is strictly a foreign article and identified with atheism. On the other hand there is a good deal of native Fascism in the American make-up."

Again assuming that I was the author, Pegler had called this non-sense. Daringly, Lou had asked him what he would have considered the statement if he had written it himself. "I couldn't imagine myself making that statement," Pegler had replied.

Lou had then presented Pegler with a third excerpt from his columns: "But Communism, if it should ever make a break, would be slapped down in a few days."

Pegler had not only called the statement false; in his view it was part of the Communist line.

After Pegler had confirmed on the stand that he had answered these questions as read, Lou handed him his columns containing the para-graphs he had denounced. "Do you happen to know, Mr. Pegler, that the statements which you said were the Communist line were written by you?"

A gasp and then a hush—everyone in the courtroom waited for Pegler's answer. It seemed to me he shrank in the chair like a man who had been struck physically. His answer finally, was nearly in-audible. "Yes."

Lou repeated his question: "When you said 'it is pro-Communist propaganda, it is very familiar in the Communist line, and it is false,' were you referring to what you yourself wrote in 1937?"

"Yes," Pegler admitted. "I was mistaken."

Lou set about the task of proving that Pegler's libels had been malicious. As close a student of Pegler's columns as he was of my writings, he had discovered that long before I had published my al-legedly defamatory book review, Pegler had called me an artful check dodger and also the Ferdinand the Bull of war correspondents. Pegler admitted that this was so. He also admitted that subsequent to the date of the libel column, he had communicated with several prominent and influential men in order to discourage my prospective employment as a lecturer and writer.

346

"Wasn't it your intention in making these calls and in writing your column to pursue Mr. Reynolds and cut off his economic income right up to the date of the trial?" Lou asked.

Pegler did everything he could to avoid a forthright answer. For a time he insisted that he expected the men he so advised to use their own judgment after he gave them the facts. Judge Weinfeld finally directed him to answer Lou's question. Lamely Pegler told the jury, "I don't know whether fair presentation of the facts would be for or against Mr. Reynolds."

The beating continued for seventeen days. Then Pegler stepped down and his witnesses marched to the stand. Their evidence was hearsay, and Lou made short work of them until Julie Pegler was called. Loyally, she backed up everything her husband had said, even to the episode of my climbing into Connie Broun's rowboat. Some of my sympathy for Julie evaporated as I heard her repeat this fabrication. It is a horrible feeling to sit in a courtroom and listen to a witness whom you have known well make such statements about you.

Lou was gentle in his cross-examination, but deadly nonetheless. Julie said that she had often visited the Brouns' lake, but had never seen Connie Broun in a rowboat. She had never even seen her swim. Julie said she believed that Connie Broun was "a fine, decent, religious woman," and she confirmed the fact that we had all been friends for years after the alleged rowboat incident.

The defense now produced two noted war heroes in its final effort to brand me as a coward. The first was Admiral Richard Connolly, a man I had never met. He had commanded the amphibious task force at Salerno, and a very imposing witness he made, describing the hazards of landing troops on the enemy's beaches. It was the defense's claim that when I had left Salerno with my articles I had in reality been fleeing from the German counterattack. In cross-examining Connolly, Lou established the fact that the counterattack had not begun until several days after I had left the area. He also drew from the admiral some other information not exactly helpful to the defense; Connolly acknowledging that the *Ancon* was not an armored ship, and that, as the flagship, she had been singled out for attack.

The next witness, General Albert Wedemeyer, was, like Connolly, sprung on us without warning. Again, he was a man I had never met. At some length he described the invasion and occupation of Sicily as he himself had experienced it, but this recital led only to the thin point

347

that when I had visited General Terry Allen's division at Enna, the men had been resting rather than fighting.

Lou told me later that he had been on the point of letting the general go without cross-examination, expecting to minimize his testimony in his summation, when he sensed the possibility of wringing a helpful admission from him. It came after considerable testimony about the relative dangers of being in the combat zone or back near headquarters. General Wedemeyer admitted that the place of assignment of a soldier, officer, or correspondent had nothing to do with his courage, and stated that nothing in his testimony was to imply that I had not been doing my duty faithfully as a war correspondent.

As Lou saw it, the appearances of Connolly and Wedemeyer had helped us rather than Pegler.

After nearly eight weeks before the jury, we rested our case, as did the defendants. It was time for the summations. Henry spoke first.

For five hours he belittled my character, my record during the war, and my suit. "Let's have it assumed," he told the jury, "that every place Reynolds went was absolutely teeming with mines. The fact was, they never exploded, never hurt anyone, and they probably were not even there. Plaintiff says he got wounded in the knee while lying in a trench, something I leave to you to figure out." If sarcasm was the method with which to convince a jury of Pegler's innocence, it seemed to me that the defense would win.

Henry wound up by declaring that there had been no damage and no libel, and that the only malice—he could not resist one more belittling crack—appeared to be between his client, who resented my counsel's behavior in cross-examination, and my counsel, who complained of his client's insolence.

Lou had worked through the intervening night to perfect his summation and his reply to Henry. When he took the floor, it was to remind the jury of all the false issues the defense had raised and then abandoned, and in this way send the members to their deliberations with the facts of the case fresh in their minds. Noting that the defense's claim of my cowardice narrowed in the end to my having run away from Salerno, Lou denied that this made any sense in the light of my long periods in combat areas. As for my thieving, nothing more had been heard of that charge after it came out that Ken Downs, the INS man, had helped me put the gasoline into Hearst cars. The charges of nudism had evaporated when Henry declined to cross-examine

348

Connie Broun. Henry's jeering at my knee wound at Sidi Omar gave Lou a chance to refresh the jury's memories of the depositions by General Messervy, Desmond Young, and Clive Burt—witnesses whom the defense had declined to cross-examine when they made their depositions.

To me, the striking feature of Lou's summation—almost more telling than anything Lou said—was that Pegler was not present in court to hear it. His absence from the defendants' table gave Lou a magnificent opportunity. Addressing the empty chair as if it were Pegler himself, Lou took him and his counsel to task for having suggested that we could dish out the punishment but not take it. Before Lou finished, that empty chair seemed the personification of a guilty and frightened man.

Lou made much of the fact that not a single witness had appeared to testify to Pegler's good character. Nor had a single Hearst executive appeared to defend the organization's publication of the libels.

Reviewing Pegler's attempts to dry up my income, Lou labeled his actions "economic murder." Calling my suit one of the historic cases of the generation, and asking for punitive damages, Lou equated slander with assassination. "An assassin uses a gun and a slanderer uses his pen. When he destroys the most precious thing a man has, his reputation, it is time that one of our juries made a lesson of that man."

The jury retired to reach its verdict. We settled down for an afternoon of waiting, but after only fifteen minutes we were notified that the jury was returning. Lou was jubilant. To him, the brief deliberation meant that we had won. From the jury's smiling faces as they entered the box, he deduced that there had been no argument among them.

But then came the let-down. The jury had not reached a verdict; it had only wanted to have the exhibits sent to the jury room. Judge Weinfeld gave instructions that any further communications should be sent to him in writing. As the afternoon wore on, five requests came out for reviews of portions of the record and of the judge's instructions. With each request, our hopes sank a little deeper. Obviously, there was disagreement in the jury room.

At seven o'clock we heard that the jury had gone out for dinner. We went out and tried to enjoy a meal. The situation was too tense. A few attempts at encouraging banter fell flat. When we returned to the anteroom, Mildred Nizer, Lou's wife, played two-handed canasta with Ginny. Neither one had her mind on the game. For a time, Lou paced the marble corridor outside the courtroom. Then he and I discussed again the risk we had taken in suing in federal court, where the verdict had to be unanimous. One juror, Lou said, could bring all the weeks of the trial, all the years of preparation, to nothing. And even if the jurors gave us a favorable verdict, they might well chop the awards down to nothing. The longer they deliberated, he said gloomily, the less likely we were to be recompensed.

After midnight word came that the jury was returning. Court was hastily reconvened. Again, Pegler was not present. Judge Weinfeld came from his chambers. As soon as he was on the bench, the jury filed into the box. Since Lou had told me that jurors usually smile at the attorney they have favored, I was alarmed by the sight of their angry faces. The only consolation I could derive from that picture was that no juror was smiling at Charles Henry either.

The clerk asked the formal question: "Ladies and gentlemen of the jury, have you agreed upon a verdict?"

"We have," replied the foreman. Had he possessed a stronger voice, the next few seconds would have been easier on us. As it was, we could hardly hear either his first or second announcement. "We find for the plaintiff in the sum of one dollar," he began.

This, I knew, was the jury's estimate of my actual loss of income resulting from Pegler's attack. My thoughts flew back five years to Nizer's warning that a jury could award me even less than a dollar. But horrid though the sensation was, we had won our case. I shook Lou's hand and tried to appear happy.

The foreman continued with the rest of his reply: "We also find for the plaintiff in the sum of one hundred and seventy-five dollars punitive damages."

Somebody grabbed my arm and said "Wait! He's correcting himself!"

In the tension of the moment the foreman had made a slip of the tongue, and now he was announcing punitive damages in the amount of one hundred and seventy-five thousand dollars.

By this time my nerves were so shot that I could hardly believe what I was hearing: twenty-five thousand dollars against Hearst Consolidated Publications, fifty thousand dollars against the Hearst Corpora-

350

tion, one hundred thousand dollars against Westbrook Pegler. The formalities of dismissing the jury went by without my being aware of them. I tried to comfort Ginny, who was crying as brokenly as if we had lost.

We moved into the corridor, and there we were surrounded by the jurors. Several of them apologized for not having awarded us half a million dollars. We learned that eight of them had wanted to award this amount. For hours the only point at issue had been the amount of the award, and the bitterness of the dispute had accounted for the stern faces of the jury when it returned to the box.

But even as a number of the jurors were expressing their disappointment over their compromise decision, Lou was pointing out to me that never in the history of libel actions had so large a verdict in punitive damages been associated with so small a compensatory award. Our victory was not only a personal triumph but a history-maker.

It was now long after midnight. One elevator was still running in the courthouse building. We stepped into it. Charles Henry followed. He congratulated Lou on his victory and then offered me his hand.

"If only the Giants can win the pennant, I figure this will be a good year," I said to him. Probably it was the most anticlimatic remark ever made by the winner in a lawsuit, but I was trying hard to forget the ugliness that was now behind us.

Henry seemed grateful for my opener. He was still our opponent, and would continue to be through the appeals to the higher courts that would affirm the verdict, but aside from that he was an honorable man who had ably defended his clients. His tired face let up at my mention of baseball. "I think we have a chance," he said cheerily. "I'll see you one day at the Polo Grounds." And with that he stepped out of the elevator and out of our lives.

The Nizers, Ginny, Marie Fauth and I stood at the curb waiting for a taxi. Lou gallantly suggested that we go to a night club and celebrate with champagne.

"Dear Lou," Ginny said, half laughing, half crying, "it's sweet of you to suggest it, but all I want now is sleep."

Lou understood; he, too, was exhausted. When Lou and Mildred dropped us at our door, Ginny kissed them both good night. I grasped Lou's hand. "You gave me back my life," I told him.

Next day, it seemed to Ginny and me that people no longer looked at us with questions in their eyes. Magazines and television producers soon let me know that they were again interested in having me work for them. Life became something greater than a trial, in its double sense. It became what it had been in years past—a privilege.

19

Epilogue

Well, that's about it—the story of a life that Dottie Parker encouraged me to write two years ago. This chapter, of course, is not the ending—it is merely a convenient stopping place. Too many words, like too many sweets, are apt to make you sick, and right now I'm sick of words. Or perhaps I'm a little sick of the many painful episodes I forced myself to dredge from the dim recesses of memory.

Reliving the agony of my mother's death, reliving the frightening experiences during the bombing of London, Dieppe and Sidi Omar, was not pleasant. Nor was it pleasant to relive the years preparing for the Pegler trial and the eight weeks of the trial itself. Nature provides us with the soothing anesthetic of time to lessen the pain of such experiences, but if we insist upon dragging them up from our subconscious minds where they have been lying dormant there isn't much that nature can do about it. Putting a book such as this on paper is, I imagine, much like going to a psychiatrist regularly over a long period. Those who have undergone such mental therapy tell me that it can become extremely painful. Now I can believe them.

Dante selected the wondrous wise Virgil to be his guide through purgatory. As they climbed the steep hill toward their goal Virgil said, "Turn your eyes downward. It will be good for you to tranquilize your way to see the imprint of your own footprints." (Parenthetically, I've often wondered why Dante didn't select his good friend Boccaccio as the guide instead of Virgil. He might have been a gayer, more sophisticated guide than the sober-minded, humorless poet.)

When you write a book such as this you are looking down the hill you have climbed and sometimes you are horrified at the imprint of the footsteps you see which are your own. You wish you could recall those footprints or rub them out. In any case, a sight of them does not at all "tranquilize your way."

Often during the course of writing this I was tempted to abandon the whole thing. Such a project as this is filled with pitfalls. The most obvious danger is that in exhibiting yourself you are apt to repel the reader. What you think to be frankness might well be considered by others to be arrogance. The unavoidable repetition of the personal pronoun might also be distasteful to the reader; it has always been distasteful to me.

The words "Know Thyself" were inscribed on the Delphic Oracle but the oracle never explained how this was to be done. One way to know yourself is to write an autobiography. Reading the previous pages over I have discovered things about myself I wasn't conscious of before. I never before realized how dependent I was on reading. This was especially true during the war when I so often used books I'd read as a sort of shield. When I traveled from Moscow to Vyazma I saw the horrors of war through the eyes of Tolstoy. When a hurricane threatened to destroy a wallowing, groaning freighter on which I was a passenger, quite unconsciously I found myself looking at the hurricane through the eyes of Joseph Conrad. One of the most fearsome experiences we had in London was the Blitz, which almost destroyed the city by fire. At the height of the fire Ed Beattie, of the United Press, and I went to the roof of the Savoy Hotel, to see the extent of the fire. Across the Thames there was a mile of solid flame. The greedy fingers of the flames stretched high into the night and we felt sure that they would reach the Houses of Parliament on our side of the narrow river. Looking down the Strand we could see the dome of St. Paul's lighted by the fires of hundreds of burning buildings. It seemed as though the Savoy was ringed by the fierce crackling flames. None of what I was watching seemed real to me. That afternoon I had been reading James Stephens' *The Crock of Gold,* and the characters in that story filled my thoughts. The Grey Woman of Dun Gortin; the Thin Woman of Inis Magrath; the Shepherd Girl, Caitilin Ni Murrachu; the God Angus Og who sang in his cave so sweetly that the shepherd girl never even heard the doubled reed pipes of Pan who was also trying to woo her—they all seemed so much more real to me than did the sight of London on fire or the angry hum of German bombers above or the thousands of anti-aircraft shells bursting gold and white against the dark canopy of the sky. Sometimes you can believe fiction when your mind rejects reality.

During noisy nights like this one it was quite impossible to sleep. More than once I consoled myself with the thought expressed by the Philosopher in *The Crock of Gold*. He said: "In certain ways sleep is useful. It is an excellent way of listening to the opera. As a medium for daydreams I know of nothing to equal it. As an accomplishment, it is graceful, but as a means of spending the entire night it is intolerably ridiculous." Remembering those words I would give up trying to sleep, instead I'd find a book and read until the unreal cacophony outside my bedroom faded away before the truth of what I was reading—even if it was the truth as contained in something as fantastic as Arthur Machen's *Hill of Dreams*.

Perhaps reading was nothing but a crutch in those days but it was a good crutch for which I have to thank my father and Ben Clough who taught me that reading was just about the ultimate in civilized pleasure.

I have no delusions about this imperfect document. It is neither important nor is it significant. "In the long run," Heywood Broun once wrote, "history is compounded of small things which may seem trivial at the time." I have recorded hundreds of small, trivial things in the preceding pages and I doubt if any of them will ever be part of history.

I have made no judgments in this book except to condemn Adolf Hitler for making a shambles out of part of the Twentieth Century. I don't think that history will contradict me on that score. But one never knows. When I was an undergraduate I was taught that Machiavelli was an evil and cynical prophet who believed that reform could only be achieved by violence, and order only imposed by fear of the superman who ran the state. His thinking, of course, later became personified by Hitler, and *Mein Kampf* is little more than a modern and badly written version of *The Prince*. Yet in recent years many philosophers have defended Machiavelli as the supreme realist, the prophet of Realpolitik and the champion of the unitarian state. The extreme views of ultra right wing organizations in our country to the effect that democratic liberalism must always prove a weakness in the state might have stemmed from Machiavelli. And his tomb is honored by the Florentines of today.

In some parts of the world neo-fascist movements are attracting some support. Will the philosophers eventually try to persuade us there was something to say for Hitler after all?

It has happened before, notably in the case of Alexander the Great, who, after subduing the Greek States (and destroying Thebes in the process) conquered Asia by acts of extreme violence and cruelty on a scale never seen before. Yet even Aristotle, the most clear-thinking of all the philosophers, made excuses for the inhuman warrior king by saying that Alexander's complete dictatorship was the form of government best suited to the backward Macedonian people. Plutarch too expressed his admiration for the reckless courage of Alexander, and attributed to him an almost mystic quality of greatness. Perhaps one day Hitler too will find his Aristotle or his Plutarch. It is a depressing thought. But to return to the present.

Perhaps the visitor who sat on my windowsill one night and who virtually commissioned this book will not be too displeased. If I rambled on any further he might suspect that I was trying to outsmart him by stalling for time and pay me a final angry visit.

And when at last he does visit me, you can be sure there is one question I'm going to ask him—"What is the name of Paul Revere's horse?" I still don't know.

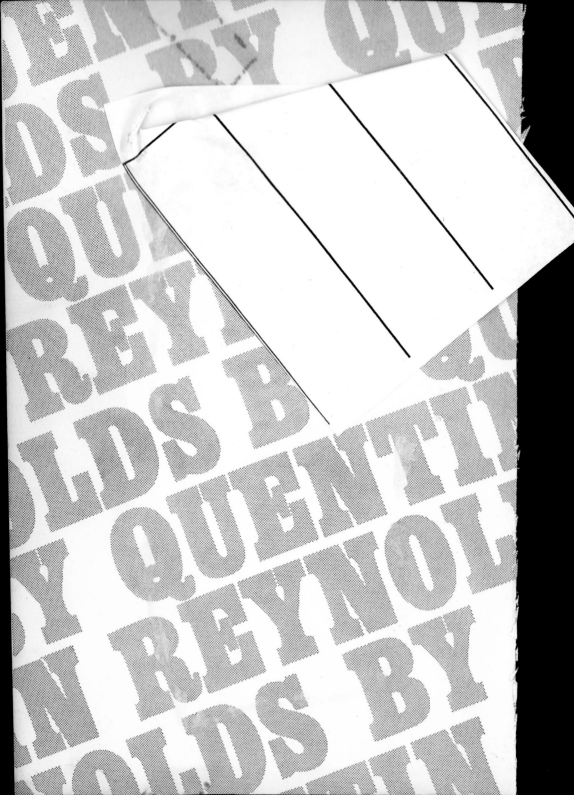